THE COHESION OF OPPRESSION

THE COHESION OF OPPRESSION

CLIENTSHIP AND ETHNICITY IN RWANDA 1860–1960

CATHARINE NEWBURY

COLUMBIA UNIVERSITY PRESS • NEW YORK

*Unless otherwise noted, photos are from the collection of the Musée
Royal de l'Afrique Centrale, Tervuren, Belgium,
and reproduced by permission.*

COLUMBIA UNIVERSITY PRESS
New York   Guildford, Surrey
Copyright © 1988 Columbia University Press

LIBRARY OF CONGRESS

LIBRARY OF CONGRESS CATALOGING-IN-PUBLICATION DATA

Newbury, Catharine.
The cohesion of oppression : clientship and ethnicity in Rwanda,
1860–1960 / Catharine Newbury.
p. cm.
Bibliography: p.
Includes index.
ISBN 0–231–06256–7 (alk. paper) : $35.00 (est.)
1. Rwanda—Politics and government. 2. Social structure—Rwanda—History.
3. Patronage, Political—Rwanda—History. 4. Patron and client—Rwanda—
History. 5. Political anthropology—Rwanda—History.
6. Rwanda—Ethnic relations. I. Title.
JQ3567.A2N48 1988
306'.2'0967571—dc19   88–7349
                                                              CIP

Book design by Jennifer Dossin
Printed in the United States of America
*Casebound editions of Columbia University Press books are Smyth-sewn
and are printed on permanent and durable acid-free paper.*

TO DAVID AND ELIZABETH

CONTENTS

              Photographs appear as a group following page 174

LIST OF MAPS

LIST OF TABLES

LIST OF FIGURES

PREFACE

THE DATA on which this study is based are concentrated on a period of about 100 years, from the mid-nineteenth century, just before Kigeri Rwabugiri's accession to the throne, to 1960, when the first communal elections in Rwanda resulted in an overwhelming victory for candidates of the majority ethnic group. For much of this period, Rwanda experienced colonial rule under two European powers. Germany ruled Rwanda for eighteen years, after which Belgium took control of the kingdom in 1916. Belgian colonial overlordship was recognized by the League of Nations in the 1920s; then after World War II Belgium administered Rwanda as a Trust Territory under the United Nations. Having experienced almost half a century of Belgian rule, Rwanda regained its independence on July 1, 1962.

During the three years before independence, the country was in the throes of violent conflict that resulted in the abolition of the monarchy, the expulsion of the ruling Tuutsi ethnic group from power, and the installation of Hutu authorities to take control of a presidential regime with an elected Assembly. The "événements" of 1959–1961, however, were more than a coup d'état and more than a rebellion of localized nature and limited aims. They were brought about by popular participation oriented to changing the ideological basis of power, and resulted in long-term, if not permanent, changes in the political system.

During and after the revolution basic Rwandan cultural norms persisted. Nonetheless real and significant alterations had taken place in the locus of political power and the social categories that had access to high office. Moreover, the political upheaval was a symptom and result of transformations in the basic fabric of Rwandan society. This book attempts to identify and examine some of these transformations, which encapsulated and molded the daily lives of the population, and in some ways served as preconditions to the political changes at the national level.

The alterations in the Rwandan power nexus were influenced significantly by non-Rwandan individuals and institutions. In particular, the Catholic Church, the United Nations, and the Belgian Administration played major roles in the political evolution that occurred during the colonial period, especially during the "événements" themselves. But the political changes that took place in Rwanda in 1959–1961 were not simple alterations of the power structure introduced from outside. Although "outside influences" were not unimportant, the sociological mutations that had occurred previously within the local-level political framework were also significant. The present analysis attempts to take account of the interaction of both internal and external influences; nevertheless, it concentrates on the internal processes of social and political transformation, not because these are in themselves more important, but because such an approach has in general been more neglected.

It could be argued that the real "revolution" took place slowly, almost imperceptibly, before the political transformations at the national level did or could occur. The alterations in political structure and personnel characterizing the terminal colonial period could not have been effected without radical changes in social organization, the emergence of new political identity patterns, and the cohesion of the vast majority of the population rallying to the ideals of "Demokrasi." While in part the result of foreign presence, these social transformations were significantly influenced by the local Tuutsi colonial context along lines determined by Rwandans and Rwandan cultural patterns. They were not determined by any single group of individuals or social class. Rather, they resulted from the interaction of many different factors and of many groups and individuals acting within a common social context, and in turn affected all classes.

The following chapters, therefore, do not consider the political activities of the central court or the small Rwandan political elite except where these help to illustrate the nature of basic social transformations in the local context. Without negating the important role of individuals, cliques or parties in effecting political changes at the center, this book attempts to account for the wider social framework within which the elite activities took place. It is the local experience—the lives of Rwandans living in the hills and the sociopolitical changes that served as preconditions to effective revolutionary action—that constitutes the focus of this study.

A study of this type could not have been undertaken without the help and encouragement of many people. I would like first to thank the Rwandans who so willingly shared with me their knowledge of the past. This book is intended to record some of the tumultuous transitions through which they have lived—I hope that it expresses their concerns, and that they will recognize in it their voices. Several talented assistants guided me through the intricacies of Rwandan etiquette, sharing in the rigors and joys of fieldwork. Joseph Rwabukumba made invaluable contributions as interpreter, colleague, and friend; Bernadette Mukarurangwa, Emmanuel Nsanzabaganwa, and Guillaume Ntasangirwa also helped in various phases of the research.

During my stay in Rwanda the personnel of the Institut National de Recherche Scientifique furnished generous hospitality and logistic support. Particular thanks go to Marcel d'Hertefelt for his exacting standards and unflagging faith in this project; Simon Bizimaana for initiating me to the study of Ikinyarwanda; and André Coupez for advice on linguistic matters. In Kinyaga the research was facilitated by the Prefect of Cyangugu, Esdras Mpamo, and his eleven burgomasters. I am indebted to these government officials as well as many other local residents—missionaries, Rwandan clergy, medical personnel, traders, clerks and cultivators—who proffered hospitality, help, and, at some critical moments, humor.

In Belgium, I wish to acknowledge help from the staff of the Musée Royal de l'Afrique Centrale, the Archives Africaines, and the Bibliothèque Africaine. In Rome, Father René Lamy, Archivist for the Société des Missionnaires d'Afrique, provided generous assistance locating missionary documentation. For advice on archives and sources I am particularly indebted to Alison Des Forges and René Lemarchand.

The archival research and fieldwork were funded by grants from the Foreign Area Fellowship Program and the Institut National de Recherche Scientifique du Rwanda. Later, assistance for writing and additional library research was provided by the Institut pour la Recherche Scientifique en Afrique Centrale (Lwiro, Zaïre), a postdoctoral fellowship from the Izaak Walton Killam Fund at Dalhousie University, and a semester of sabbatical leave from Wesleyan University. I am grateful to all of these institutions for their support; responsibility for the views expressed here, of course, remains my own.

Jan Vansina, who originally conceived the program of local/regional studies in Rwanda, has offered much inspiration and encouragement over the years. I thank him particularly for nurturing my interest in historical inquiry, for his enthusiastic support during the fieldwork, and for astute comments on early drafts of the manuscript, when his probing questions helped me to make sense of seemingly contradictory data. Crawford Young has been a most patient mentor. He inspired my interest in Belgian colonial policy and encouraged me to explore the politics of ethnicity in a novel way; his generous advice and support have been important through all phases of this project. Others who read and made helpful comments on an earlier version of the manuscript include John Flint, Fred Hayward, Marcel d'Hertefelt, and René Lemarchand.

For their suggestions and comments on later versions of the manuscript I am grateful to Jean-Pierre Chrétien, Nelson Kasfir, Donald Moon, David Titus, Jean-Luc Vellut, and two anonymous referees for Columbia University Press. James Scott, Stephen White, and Elisabeth Young-Bruehl read all or parts of the book and offered particularly valuable advice. I also wish to thank Bogumil Jewsiewicki, David Konstan, Timothy Shaw, and Nancy Schwartz for their friendship and support.

Kate Wittenberg, Executive Editor at Columbia University Press, has given excellent editorial guidance, bringing the book to publication with patience and skill. Expert typing of the manuscript was done by Valborg Proudman, Mary Jane Arico, and Janet Hendrix, while the maps and figures were drawn by the Cartography Laboratory of IRSAC and by Bonnie Morris of the Department of Geography, University of North Carolina at Chapel Hill.

Especially important has been the help of my family. I thank my parents for encouraging me to undertake this study and gracefully tolerating the long absences it required. I especially thank my husband, David; not only did he give generous and loving support in all phases of the project, but as counsellor, colleague, and intellectual companion he has profoundly influenced my thinking and writing on the issues discussed here. Our daughter, Elizabeth, has helped in her own way by luring us away from work whenever she could. It is to David and Elizabeth that I affectionately dedicate this book.

Chapel Hill, North Carolina
September 1987

THE COHESION OF OPPRESSION

I

THE SOCIAL PRECONDITIONS
OF REVOLUTION

EVOLUTIONS ARE often seen in terms of a spontaneous burst
of political activity of great intensity. Less attention is generally given to the social preconditions of revolution—the
structures, processes, and perceptions that make such activity possible. This book reflects on such long-term transformations as
they relate to the Rwandan Revolution, focusing on changes in clientship institutions, the expansion of labor control systems, and the development of ethnic cleavages. While these are processes important to
the history of Rwanda, they are also found in colonial and neocolonial
contexts elsewhere in Africa; the significance of the analysis presented
in subsequent chapters, therefore, transcends the boundaries of a single
local area. The conceptual approach developed here attempts to explain
how in southwestern Rwanda these processes were molded by the
growth of state power, and how the interactive impact of these changes
affected rural political consciousness, creating the preconditions for
revolution.

While the Rwandan Revolution proper lasted less than two years,
from 1959 to 1961, its effects were far-reaching. The monarchy was
abolished, replaced by a republican government with a popularly
elected assembly. The ethnic composition of the ruling group was drastically altered, as Hutu leaders, members of the majority (but formerly
subordinate) group, replaced the earlier Tuutsi rulers. And relations
between rulers and others also changed in important ways. The primary
focus of this study, however, is not on the revolution itself and its
outcome, but on the span of some one hundred years that preceded the
revolution. This period began with the reign of Rwabugiri, a king who
greatly increased the power of the Rwandan central court over both
internal and external affairs. His reign, which extended over the last

third of the nineteenth century, was followed closely by the imposition of German colonial rule (in 1898). During World War I Belgium supplanted Germany as the colonial power in Rwanda.

The kingdom of Rwanda held a remarkable fascination for a succession of early travelers, missionaries, and colonial officials who came to know it. But the highly developed state system, the relatively clearly defined forms of social stratification, and the apparently rigid divisions between the three major ethnic groups—Hutu, Tuutsi, and Twa—in this supposedly "remote" kingdom also attracted the attention of scholars after World War II. Historians, anthropologists, political scientists, and others (supplementing the substantial ethnographic and historical work on Rwanda by missionaries and administrators) studied the nature of the Rwandan state, the impact of European colonialism on it, and the polarization of ethnic relations in the 1950s. Such theoreticians applied primarily functionalist models to their study of Rwanda. This has provided much provocative theorizing. But on the basis of both the earlier missionary accounts and recent studies at the local level in Rwanda, it has become clear that a rethinking of these models is required. The time has now come to combine theoretical approaches and new empirical research.

When I first undertook work on this project in 1970, my initial research design was influenced by this earlier literature and by the concepts of "political development" that so preoccupied American political scientists of the 1960s. I had intended to examine the role of patron–client ties in promoting political and social integration in Rwanda. In the course of my field work, however, this focus shifted in important ways. While it builds on earlier work—much of it of great value—the perspective on Rwandan political development presented here differs from such earlier interpretations in two major respects. Much of the earlier work tended to concentrate on the study of the Rwandan royal court; this book adopts a local-level perspective and tries to account for the activities and perceptions of both those not related to the central court network and those who were. Most of the earlier studies assumed that social stratification, ethnic cleavage, and clientship institutions were rigid, unchanging "givens" of precolonial Rwandan society which were little changed by colonialism; the analysis here questions those assumptions. To explain this shift in perspective it is necessary to look briefly at the prevailing model of the precolonial Rwandan sociopolitical system portrayed in earlier studies and to discuss how it has been used in explanations of the Rwandan Revolution.

THE FUNCTIONALIST MODEL OF RWANDA

BEFORE EXPLAINING the significance of my focus on ethnicity, patron–client relations, and labor-control practices as dynamic elements related to the growth of state power, I want to show why the prevailing models of the 1950s and 1960s distorted or neglected these elements and how new empirical research can bring them to the fore. I have focused on these in part because of their importance to Rwandan political development, in part because their processual aspects have been so neglected.

The prevailing model of Rwandan political organization arose from an attempt by social scientists to explain how integration in the society was possible despite the political domination of the population at large (mostly of Hutu identity) by a minority ethnic group. According to the most reliable colonial census available, that of 1956, Hutu constituted about 83 percent of Rwanda's population in that year; Tuutsi, 16 percent; and a third group, the Twa, about 1 percent.[1] Yet virtually all positions of power and prestige were held by Tuutsi, and cattle (one of the major forms of wealth, whose transfer served as an important representation of social relations), were predominantly owned by, or their transfer controlled by, Tuutsi. Social scientists who studied Rwanda during the 1940s and 1950s assumed that the ethnic and class stratification between Tuutsi and Hutu, as it existed at that time, had been unchanging features of "traditional" Rwanda.

The work of Jacques-Jean Maquet has been perhaps the most influential in this regard, for many of the later studies accepted the general lines of his view of precolonial Rwanda. In his 1954 study, *Le système des relations sociales dans le Rwanda ancien*,[2] Maquet relied on the concept of "caste" to characterize what he saw as the rigid separation between the three principal groups and the hierarchical unchanging character of relations between them.[3] In this presentation, Tuutsi pastoralists, although a minority, held all political power, controlled most sources of wealth, and exploited their agriculturalist Hutu subjects. Despite the imbalance in numbers and the evident inequality in the society, social and political cohesion was assured, Maquet argued, through three mechanisms: value consensus, expressed in a communally-accepted "premise of inequality"; *ubuhake* cattle clientship; and a complex system of administrative arrangements. As conceptualized by Maquet, the premise of inequality involved a consensus that all

Rwandans are by birth fundamentally unequal. Such value consensus implied an acceptance on the part of the dominated that some (in this case Tuutsi) are born to rule and to exploit, while others (Hutu and Twa) are born to obey and to serve.[4]

In Maquet's view, integration in such a society resulted from the *ubuhake* clientship institution, whereby Tuutsi pastoralist patrons granted the use of cattle to particular Hutu who were their clients. Although Tuutsi ultimately controlled the use and distribution of cattle, cattle clientship (represented in the loan of cattle) provided Hutu cultivators with both access to cattle and juridical protection, as a patron was expected to protect his client. According to Maquet, this institution incorporated all Rwandans within a dense network of reciprocal, if unequal, ties. Therefore, he argued, clientship moderated the exploitative aspects of the system: it provided a place, a status, within the hierarchical system. Even Tuutsi patrons of Hutu were clients of yet other Tuutsi; in theory the only person ultimately not a client in this system was the king himself.

Moreover, Maquet argued, the Rwandan state was organized administratively so that there existed built-in competition between local authorities who competed for royal favor. A provincial chief did not exercise the full scope of political powers within a given geographical region; the centralized character of the Rwandan polity provided for competing jurisdictions among political appointees, and this situation gave Hutu opportunities to utilize alternative channels of appeal in cases of grievance. The establishment of the premise of inequality, *ubuhake* dependency relationships, and the Tuutsi-dominated state, Maquet believed, had occurred too far in the past to be empirically studied.

Maquet expected that only external influences could disturb the Rwandan "equilibrium." But, if precolonial Rwanda was both highly stratified and yet also well integrated, despite (or because of) the inequality, then what accounts for the explosion of hatred against Tuutsi chiefs and the widespread manifestations of protest that occurred among Hutu in Rwanda during 1959–1961? Attempts to explain this violence have varied in the emphasis they place on class or ethnicity. However, most interpretations, following (with some modifications) Maquet's portrayal of precolonial Rwanda, have assumed that ethnic groups in Rwanda were primordial and the stratification between them was static and unchanging. They also assume that ethnic stratification was changed but little during colonial rule.[5]

In accounting for the radical political transformations of the terminal colonial period, such analyses then place great stress on externally derived social, economic, and ideological changes introduced by Europeans. Particularly important in this regard was the introduction of Christian ideas and especially the rationalist concepts of *liberté* and *egalité* (if not also *fraternité*): The spread of new ideologies through the system of mission education and the printed media was seen to undermine the previous assumed value consensus—the premise of inequality—and the introduction of elections in preparation for independence from Belgium provided for the expression of ethnic (or class) solidarity which had previously been inhibited by the crosscutting ties of clientship. The impact of these changes was to destabilize an earlier "equilibrium" and ultimately to erode the legitimacy of the ruling elite. Internal social change, and especially political struggle, were almost entirely neglected for most areas of Rwanda.[6]

This version of why revolutionary protest occurred in Rwanda is only partially correct. While it is true that changes during the colonial period eroded the legitimacy of Tuutsi rulers and that the spread of new ideologies was important in the revolution, this is inadequate as an explanation: it is based on a view of precolonial Rwandan society that is seriously flawed, and it ignores certain crucial aspects of changes in Rwandan political structures during the colonial period—changes that indicate just how legitimacy was eroded and in what way ideologies were important. Maquet's conceptualization of precolonial Rwanda reflects elements of an ahistorical functionalist view of social systems. Selected features drawn from diverse time periods are combined into a synchronic model said to represent a particular society that endured over a span of many years. The model assumes a social system in equilibrium, and focuses on those features that function to maintain such equilibrium.

THE MODEL REASSESSED

As it was used for Rwanda, the functionalist model portrayed a single static "traditional" Rwandan political organization, unchanging over time and (for the most part) undifferentiated over space. Maquet's reconstruction is partially correct, for in some areas of nineteenth-century Rwanda there did exist administrative structures that provided for competition among local authorities, and in some contexts *ubuhake* clientship could serve an integrative role. But the ahistorical character of the model led to distortions. It fostered a belief that centralized authority in the precolonial period was politically effective throughout the entire area that later came to be defined by the colonial state. The model implied that Hutu had been dominated by state structures[7] from long before the nineteenth century and, consequently, that political participation by Hutu was minimal in the precolonial period. This model was also based on, and frequently was used to justify or promote, a view of ethnic groups as static and unchanging.

In fact, the functionalist model of "traditional" Rwanda reflects features of both precolonial and colonial Rwanda, but it is a valid portrait of neither. Political relations were more complex, and identities less rigid. The structures of Tuutsi domination were more recent and less extensive than the model assumed, and they were transformed in important ways during the European colonial period. It is these transformations that need to be studied if we are to construct an adequate explanation of the impact of colonialism and the role of social changes in creating the preconditions for revolution in Rwanda.

The questions raised here about the functionalist model of recent Rwandan history emerged only very slowly in the course of my fieldwork. I approached the work with a firm implicit acceptance of the conventional model. As the research progressed, however, and especially with my increasing acquaintance with the Rwandan people and growing familiarity with their conceptualization of Rwandan history, the accepted explanations seemed less compelling, less satisfactory; ultimately they were at variance with the empirical record, and this prompted me to reassess the conceptual bases and explanatory framework of the prevailing paradigm through which Rwandan social phenomena have been perceived.[8]

My first reservations related to Maquet's synchronic perception of social institutions and his methods of collecting the data on which his 1954 book was based. The questions posed in the standardized questionnaire used in his study generated normative responses about how the Rwandan political system was "supposed" to have functioned in the eyes of the elite and beneficiaries of the system. Moreover, Maquet based his analysis on the responses of 300 Tuutsi informants—in fact the sample had included members of other social groups, but these responses were discarded.[9] It is clear that the primary norms represented were those of central Rwanda, and particularly those of the central court.[10]

In part to avoid the concentration on royal perspectives so evident in earlier accounts, I chose to conduct my research in Kinyaga (Cyangugu Prefecture) (see map 1), a region in southwestern Rwanda far from the

MAP 1: Prefectures of Rwanda

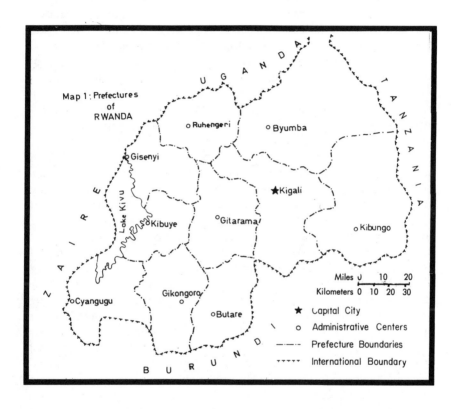

Map 1: Prefectures of RWANDA

UGANDA

o Ruhengeri   o Byumba

o Gisenyi

Z A I R E

Lake Kivu

o Kibuye   o Gitarama   ★ Kigali

o Kibungo

T A N Z A N I A

o Cyangugu   Gikongoro
o

o Butare

B U R U N D I

Miles ∪   10   20
Kilometers 0   10   20   30

★   Capital City
o   Administrative Centers
—·—·—   Prefecture Boundaries
⊤⊤⊤⊤⊤   International Boundary

central court.* The project was to focus on processes of political centralization, to discover how *ubuhake* clientship served as a key mechanism of political integration and "nation-building." In some ways, Kinyaga may seem unrepresentative, because it is only one region of many and because it is located outside the central regions of the kingdom. Yet Rwanda is a country of strong regional variations, as pointed out in many recent works;[11] distance from the center in political as well as geographic terms is not so idiosyncratic as geographical location might indicate. Local historical conditions vary, of course, but in one crucial respect similar patterns carry over from one region to another: regions incorporated during a given period of Rwandan state development tend to exhibit strong similarities in the types of mechanisms used by the state for social control, military conquest, and administrative hierarchy. Thus, insofar as the relations between center and periphery are crucial to this study, the findings may be applicable to other areas of Rwanda as well.

My field work in Rwanda spanned 22 months during 1970–1971, with brief return visits during 1972 and 1974. I consulted archival materials where available, including colonial government reports and missionary records. But most of the data analyzed for this study consist of oral accounts by Kinyagans in the local language (Ikinyarwanda).[12] Included among those interviewed were Tuutsi as well as Hutu, former chiefs and political activists as well as cultivators with no formalized political roles. These people, living in rural areas, offered concrete examples of their experiences with the evolving structures of colonial rule. Their perspectives—independently provided—were instrumental in altering my perceptions, although this is not to say that I was willing to accept uncritically the interpretations offered. As the research advanced, my confidence in the accepted functionalist model, and its assumptions, was profoundly shattered, for the data from these interviews contradicted a portrayal of the Rwandan state that, it became clear, reflected the ideal norms held by political elites associated with the central court, but did not correspond to the reality of Rwandan life as related by rural non-elites. The model itself lost much of its compelling force. To accommodate these empirical findings, I reoriented the substance

---

* Separated from the central regions of Rwanda by a mountain range covered with dense forest, Kinyaga is located along the southern tip of Lake Kivu. The region is bordered on the west by Zaïre and in the south by Burundi. At the time of the research in 1970, Kinyaga's population of about 250,000 amounted to almost 15 percent of the total population of Rwanda (3.7 million). Referred to for administrative purposes as Cyangugu Prefecture, the region forms one of ten such administrative units in contemporary Rwanda. For a description of major ecological and sociopolitical features of contemporary Kinyaga, see Appendix I.

of my work, its temporal focus, and the methods used to interpret the data, and ended up, as so often happens, researching an entirely new subject whose fullest dimensions emerged only very slowly and tentatively.

Understanding Rwandan political processes requires a study of the development of state power and its impact on local power relationships over a long period of time, spanning both the precolonial and colonial periods. Thus this study came to include a period of about a century, c. 1860 to 1960. Also important is examination and reassessment of the conceptual assumptions that had guided and limited earlier analyses. In interviews with Kinyagans I strove to probe behind the many assertions about what Rwandan political authorities could (theoretically, or "legally") do, and to reconstruct political processes from an empirical viewpoint. Questions about who held power and of what kinds; about how the actors gained, maintained, and used political resources, and to what ends; and about who derived advantages or disadvantages became important factors in my understanding of the system. I examined changes in the access to and use of power, the role of the Rwandan central court in these changes, and the effect of European economic policies on local political realities. Finally, I explored the impact of these changes on the development of identity groups in the society, and in particular their effect on ethnic and class distinctions. The primary focus was on the diverse political interactions at the local level and how these changed over time.

Kinyaga's location outside the central core of the state proved an excellent vantage point from which to construct a new perspective on Rwandan political development. Here, political penetration of the royal court was recent, imposed only late in the nineteenth century (that is, within the memory of very old Kinyagans consulted for the work), and ideological penetration, involving the imposition of Tuutsi political norms developed in central Rwanda, was as yet imperfect. Therefore, it was possible to examine how central institutions were in fact introduced and developed. Once the conceptual paradigms that had informed earlier studies for Rwanda as a whole had been brought into question for Kinyaga, it became clear that processes similar to those observed in Kinyaga had occurred elsewhere in the country as well.

The following chapters will examine the complex relationships that mediated between ethnic identity, clientship, and statebuilding. Data from Kinyaga suggest that while the terms Hutu and Tuutsi existed in Rwanda in precolonial times, the meaning of the terms and their political significance varied over time and differed from one region of the country to another. More particularly, the groups identified with these terms and the nature of the relations between them were substantially altered within the evolving context of the colonial state. It is proposed here that many features conventionally assumed to be "facts" of Rwandan social structures and therefore unchanging elements, are more properly analyzed as changing elements—socially produced and shaped by the dynamic processes and interactions of statebuilding in general.

CONCEPTS AND PARADIGMS

As noted, my experience in the field shifted the focus of my inquiry, and brought four concepts into the foreground of my concern: ethnicity, clientship, labor control practices, and state formation. To illustrate the significance of these four elements in contrast to their underemphasis in the existing theoretical literature, I shall review the concepts one by one, indicating why they were neglected or distorted. In general this survey will suggest that the major flaws in the existing conceptual frameworks can be attributed to their ahistorical character, their failure to view ethnicity, clientship, labor control practices, and statebuilding in terms of historical transformations. Associated with this has been a tendency to privilege the perspective of Rwandan elites. As I have indicated, the empirical research for this study spans almost a century, from approximately 1860 to 1960. Thus it takes into account developments within major Rwandan historical epochs that have been consistently overlooked. The analysis here suggests that the way to correct flaws in the existing models is to take a detailed historical look at how institutions and relationships evolved in the context of a changing state.

Ethnicity

ALTHOUGH THE terms "Hutu" and "Tuutsi" are probably very old in Rwandan social discourse, there is evidence that the meanings attached to these categories and the political significance of membership in them changed significantly over time. In Kinyaga, before the introduction of central Rwandan rule toward the end of the nineteenth century, identification as "Hutu" appears to have had little political importance.[13] Since Hutu/Tuutsi categorizations are today such essential components to ideology and conceptualization of Rwandan social relations, relevant data from within Rwanda are scarce on this point. But indications from neighboring areas not controlled by the Rwandan state are suggestive. Just to the west of Kinyaga, on Ijwi Island (now part of Zaïre), an area with which Kinyagans maintained intensive but informal contacts and with which there had once been considerable population mobility from Rwanda, "Hutu" and "Tuutsi" are not relevant social categories (except as they relate to immigrants who came to the island after 1960). Despite these longstanding contacts, however, and despite their intimate knowledge of other aspects of Rwandan society, most people on Ijwi do not know of or do not clearly understand the term Hutu. On Ijwi all Rwandans are referred to collectively as "Badusi" (derived from the Ikinyarwanda term Abatuutsi), but individually a Rwandan is identified by his clan—"Mudaha," "Musinga," etc. This is often more significant in terms of identity than are current ethnic terms "Hutu" and "Tuutsi."[14]

Moreover, in the accounts of Kinyagan informants, the status of "Tuutsi" is often viewed not merely as a function of descent, but as dependent on the control of wealth (particularly in cattle) and power. The data in this study strongly imply that before political factors made the labels of "Hutu" and "Tuutsi" meaningful and necessary in Kinyaga, social identification belonged principally to the unit that performed corporate political functions—in this case, the lineage or neighborhood residential group. The introduction to Kinyaga of central Rwandan administrative structures during the reign of Rwabugiri (c. 1860–1895) brought contact with political institutions and social distinctions at a new level, and it was under these conditions that current ethnic identifications became salient.

With the arrival of Rwabugiri and his chiefs, classification into the category of Hutu or Tuutsi tended to become rigidified. Lineages that were wealthy in cattle and had links to powerful chiefs were regarded as Tuutsi; lineages lacking these characteristics were relegated to non-Tuutsi status. During the period of Tuutsi rule, later overlaid by European rule, the advantages of being Tuutsi and the disadvantages of being Hutu increased enormously. In this context there occurred a gradual enlargement to scale of "ethnic" awareness among Hutu through realization of common oppression.

For three reasons, the term caste—which in any event bears the connotations of rigid hierarchy and immutability—will not be used in this study. First, there existed no religious ideology sanctioning separation between ethnic groups in Rwanda.[15] Second, economic specialization between the groups was not so clear-cut as has sometimes been thought. For example, both Hutu and Tuutsi engaged in activities associated with the care of cattle (since Tuutsi cattleowners often put their cattle in the charge of Hutu herders), and cattle were esteemed by both groups. The major differences between Hutu and Tuutsi in control over cattle could be reduced to control over political power—this then becomes a criterion of political and legal, but not economic, differentiation.[16] Third, the categories Hutu and Tuutsi were in the past relatively flexible; social mobility and "passing" from one category to another did occur (though opportunities for mobility out of the Hutu category apparently diminished in the later colonial period). Such flexibility is attested by the Kinyaga data; it is indicated for Rwanda in general by written sources from the interwar period. In 1922, for example, Father Léon Classe (a missionary with many years of experience in Rwanda) wrote:

> It should be noted that the term "Tuutsi" often refers not to origin (descent) but to social condition, or wealth, especially as regards cattle: whoever is a chief, or who is rich will often be referred to as Tuutsi. Frequently also, because of their manner or their language, . . . the inhabitants of the provinces of Central Rwanda, Nduga and Marangara, as well as those of Buganza are referred to as Tuutsi.[17]

As Classe suggests, there was a tendency to associate the appellation "Tuutsi" with possession of wealth and power, and particularly with wealthy powerful persons coming from central Rwanda. Those who were wealthy and powerful were likely to be regarded as Tuutsi, so that the category came to be in some respects self-defined as an elite. Moreover, a person's "ethnic" status was not immutable; it could change. As Louis de Lacger pointed out in his history of Rwanda (published in 1939):

> Tuutsi and Hutu are words which tend to lose their specially racial meanings and become no more than qualifiers, accepted discourse, within which are included capitalists and workers, rulers and ruled, without bringing seriously into play the question of birth. . . . A "petit mututsi" lacking the means of satisfying the monetary demands of providing wives for his offspring is obliged to fall back on the peasant world. He obtains wives from families of peasant status and if the condition of his family is prolonged, if his sons and grandsons are forced to resign themselves to the same type of indigence, his family will see itself gradually eliminated from the society of "the right kind" of people; it will descend to the level

of the rural mass. The inverse is no less frequent. A muhutu capable of providing his father-in-law with a cow will be able to obtain a wife from a median level Tuutsi family; with time and a growing prosperity his offspring would come to be considered as descendants of a "good" family.[18]

The conviction that Hutu and Tuutsi groups constituted "castes" resulted in the neglect of significant variations over time in both the degree of stratification between Hutu and Tuutsi and the factors conditioning such variation. Considering the development of the terms Hutu and Tuutsi historically and empirically provides a foundation for criticizing the conceptualization of these terms found in much of the theoretical literature. Such an analysis also prompts a reassessment of two major theories about ethnic politics that have oriented much of the writing about ethnicity in the third world. These include the primordialist perspective, associated with modernization and political development approaches of the 1950s and 1960s, and the instrumentalist perspective, which modified primordialist concepts in important ways. These theories are inadequate, however, because they do not take into account the complexity of ethnic interaction that the above sketch of the terms Hutu and Tuutsi indicates.

The modernization and political development analytic frameworks (on which the primordialist perspective was based) clearly distinguished between what were seen as "traditional" features of society and "modern" features. "Traditional" societies were conceived of as relatively static and undifferentiated, consisting of groups defined by ascriptive, parochial identities; "traditional" features of society were therefore associated with "internal" factors, and stasis. "Modern" features, on the other hand, tended to be equated with change and with external factors such as colonialism or other forms of contact (willing or unwilling) with the "modern" West.

Traditional cultural elements were thus seen as opposed to modern elements. In particular, traditional identities, it was believed, posed a threat to the development of modern politics (especially the development of loyalties to a modern nation-state) because of their "primordial" character and parochial concerns.[19] According to the political development literature of the 1950s and 1960s, over the long term modernization would result in the dissolution, and eventual transcendence, of such primordial identities. However, in the short run (a vague, unspecified period describing a category within which would be included most of the third world today), changes associated with modernization were expected to exacerbate conflicts between groups whose basis had been defined by primordial, ascriptive, loyalties.[20]

If one adopts a view that stresses the "primordial" ethnic or "tribal" basis of political activity, then solidarity based on cultural affinities tends to be assumed, rather than seen as a phenomenon to be explained. From such a perspective ethnic groupings are generally portrayed as having existed before the political interaction between the groups so defined. In analyses of conflicts between ethnic groups, this often led to a focus on ancient cultural differences, rather than specific issues that divide and define groups, as the primary source of conflict.

This book takes a different perspective. It argues that to understand the politics of ethnicity one must study the changing context within which ethnic interaction occurs. The following chapters concentrate not on ethnicity per se, but rather on changes in state power that transformed relations between groups, created new forms of cleavages, and fostered new forms of solidarity. Such analysis indicates that far from being "primordial," ethnic solidarities in Rwanda were engendered in large part by transformations within the political system itself. Of course, cultural affinities can serve as an important basis for building cohesion and collaboration. And there do (and did) exist cultural differences between Tuutsi, Hutu, and Twa in Rwanda. Yet the definition of group boundaries and the recognition of cultural affinities as a basis for solidarity could, and did, change over time, as did the mobilization of ethnic identity (to be differentiated from regional solidarities) to further political purposes. Like all relative categories they were conditioned by the larger context of political activity. To capture this processual aspect of political identity, a diachronic approach to studying ethnicity is adopted here. This approach examines the changing socioeconomic and political environment in which group interaction occurred. It focuses on how individuals and groups (elites as well as non-elites) attempted to shape change. And it shows how these interrelated processes have molded patterns of social cleavage and conflict in the state.

The processual approach to ethnicity to be articulated later in this book shares certain elements with the "instrumentalist" perspective on ethnicity. Over the past two decades many studies of ethnicity in Africa and elsewhere have demonstrated the often subjective, relative nature of ethnic identities and their potentially elastic and situational qualities.[21] In building on these findings, a number of scholars have recognized that it is essential to understand the dynamic aspects of ethnicity in order to explain how and why ethnic identities become mobilized into politics—and to account for their potential and their limitations in this process. Such studies, labeled "instrumentalist," view ethnic groups "less as 'primordial groups' emerging into consciousness than as cultural categories transformed into self-conscious communities by leaders, elite groups, or the state and seeking to provide social, economic, and political advantages for the groups in question."[22] Instrumentalist studies retain from earlier theories of political development and modernization a primary focus on the impact of "modernization," but provide more specific insights than did the earlier theories as to how social, political, and economic changes may alter relations between groups.[23]

In particular, instrumentalist studies emphasize that modernization creates new forms of competition over scarce resources. It is precisely this competition that is instrumental in the crystallization of ethnic identities, giving rise to new or transformed "ethnic" groupings. Within this fluid political context, so the major thrust of this form of analysis goes, such groups gain self-awareness (become "self-conscious communities") largely as the result of the activities of leaders who mobilize ethnic followings in order to compete more effectively. Improved communications and the spread of writing are important in this process; so is "ethnic learning," where groups develop ethnic awareness as a result of seeing others using ethnic solidarities to compete. The state is important, instrumentalists suggest, as an arena in which competition between these groups occurs (the state controls many of the scarce resources over which elites are competing), and also because government policies can significantly affect the strategies chosen by ethnic leaders.

Instrumentalist studies that focus primarily on leaders and their role within the state arena usually fail to explain the role of followers in this process of crystallizing ethnic identities: Why do the followers follow? Do they, in fact, follow? Despite their advances on modernization theories in certain respects, some of these instrumentalist studies still portray rural people as essentially quiescent until mobilized by elites. The elites, then, are seen as the major forces in the creation of ethnic consciousness—or at least in the political mobilization of ethnic identities. In this respect such studies appear to retain and expand the basic concepts of modernization theories even while accepting the fluidity of ethnic identities. They do not examine, empirically and at the local level, the role that rural populations have played in these dynamic, essentially dialectic processes of ethnic identity formation and political activity.

Like instrumentalist analyses, this book emphasizes the importance of structural changes—changes in the political, economic, and social context within which group interaction occurs—as an essential means to understanding ethnicity as a political factor. But unlike many of the instrumentalist studies, the approach adopted here attempts to provide a "view from below." Looking beyond the more narrow focus of many instrumentalist studies on competition among elites for resources at the level of the formal state political arena, this study highlights the wider ramifications of changes that affected non-elites. It focuses particularly on shifts in the powers of chiefs, and on exploitation: The growing powers of chiefs transformed patron–client relationships and led to more exploitative forms of control over land and labor. In general, modernization theories tend to ignore exploitation because they view social change as a more or less neutral process. Similarly, instrumentalist analyses, in their concentration on leaders and competition, often fail to account for perceived exploitation as a factor in the mobilization of ethnic identities.

Statebuilding, Patron–Client Politics, and Labor Control

IF ETHNIC solidarity is to be seen as a variable, a social phenomenon to be explained rather than a pre-existing immutable given, then to understand the preconditions of the Rwandan Revolution we need to shift the focus away from a concentration on ethnic factors to examine the processes of class formation that underlay perceived ethnic stratification. For such study it is necessary to "unpack" the concept of the state[24] and examine at close hand the changing character of relationships between state power, subjects/citizens, and ideology.

The growth of state power in Rwanda translated into increasing control by Tuutsi authorities over resources that could permit individuals and groups to improve their material condition (or prevent their material condition from deteriorating).[25] Particularly in the colonial period, politics very clearly involved a process of attempting to "gain control over public resources for private ends."[26] And the state served not just as an arena for competition, but also as an active agent creating, maintaining, and attempting to justify patterns of ethnic inequality.[27] Political centralization and changes in land tenure arrangements under colonial rule thus altered class relations and created new forms of social cleavage. Patron–client ties were a key element in these changes. A study of how such clientship relations were transformed in the context of the evolving colonial state is essential to understanding the extent and impact of Tuutsi power.

Patron–client ties are often seen as inhibiting the development of horizontal solidarities among lower-class groups; they provide vertical linkages between powerful political actors and individual, less powerful individual clients.[28] In studies of Rwanda, *ubuhake* cattle clientship was often described as performing such an integrative role. The analysis here will propose, on the basis of empirical data from Kinyaga, that clientship does not necessarily promote social integration; it can—and in Kinyaga it did—promote social cleavage. It is essential that the political significance of clientship be assessed in terms of the larger historical and political context. Clientship in Rwanda was not a static social "given"; it was a dynamic phenomenon. Forms of clientship changed over time.

Patron–client ties can best be assessed in terms of the power relations holding between the parties involved. A concept of clientship is needed that will reflect the potentially dynamic character of such relationships. I view clientship as a form of "instrumental friendship" between two persons of relatively unequal socioeconomic status. The relationship usually involves the exchange of protection and/or benefits from the person of higher status (the patron) for general loyalty and service from the lower-status person (the client). But the degree of reciprocity in the relationship may increase or decrease over time, and the exchanges between the partners may vary from rather fixed and defined duties to diffuse and ad hoc demands.[29] In Rwanda, patron–client ties sometimes linked a client who represented a group such as a kinship or local residential unit to a patron.

The direction of change in clientship forms in Rwanda tended to be unidirectional, toward less reciprocity and more exploitation. These transformations were related especially to the growth of state power and changes in the social relations of production. Growth in the power of the state (expressed particularly through political centralization and growing government penetration at the local level) placed increased prerogatives in the hands of Tuutsi authorities, who used these powers to enhance their control over key resources: land, cattle, and people. In the context of the colonial economy, control over people became particularly important in the mobilization of labor—for private accumulation (as in the growing enrichment of chiefs) and "public" projects, such as roadbuilding. The development of labor control mechanisms was thus intimately linked both to transformations in clientship and to expansion of state power. These interactive processes reflected the economic underpinnings to state policies; they also indicated the key role of state power in processes of accumulation.[30]

Thus, in colonial Rwanda, patron–client ties tended to become highly coercive. Reciprocity declined as exploitation intensified. In precolonial Rwanda, patron–client ties did not link all of Rwandan society together and contribute to some static "equilibrium." Instead, far from being static, they were changing in the precolonial period, and they expanded rapidly within the power context of colonial rule. Political relations between patrons who were Tuutsi and those of their clients, who were Hutu, were exclusionist, so that over time clientship tended to sharpen lines of social differentiation. These and other transformations associated with the growth of state power and the expansion of capitalism were critical in the development of political consciousness among rural dwellers and in the configuration and political salience of ethnicity in Rwanda.

The structure of the argument advanced in this book reflects the conceptual concerns discussed above. The three chapters in part I describe the development of state power in Rwanda and its imposition in Kinyaga, providing a dynamic view of the political context which influenced changes in clientship and rural class relations. Thus, chapter 2 outlines conditions in Kinyaga during the eighteenth and nineteenth centuries, when political penetration by the central court was quite limited and the local population enjoyed considerable autonomy. Chapter 3 explains how this autonomy was eroded and Tuutsi/Hutu distinctions deepened with the expansion of state power under Rwabugiri. These expanding structures of state power were then further transformed during the period of European colonial rule. As Europeans dictated changes in state structures and attempted to bureaucratize the roles of chiefs, Tuutsi factions at the central court and regional elites in Kinyaga each jockeyed to gain benefits from the evolving statebuilding process (chapter 4).

Chiefs who were willing to collaborate with the Europeans saw their power and wealth enhanced; in return, they were expected to impose heavy demands on their people, to supply porters and food to Europeans in the early period, or carry out forced cultivation and roadbuilding later on. To these exactions the chiefs added many of their own (which they claimed were "traditional"). The three chapters in part II examine how such changes in administrative structures and the powers of chiefs shaped rural class relations, as reflected in changing patterns of clientship. In the context of an expanding, Tuutsi-dominated colonial state, patron–client ties intensified cleavages and generated sharp distinctions between Tuutsi and Hutu. Meanwhile, discrimination in education and employment further deepened these differences.

Part III analyzes the development of political consciousness and the growth of solidarity among rural Hutu. Colonial economic policies, described in chapter 8, shaped this process in important ways by increasing the burdens on Hutu cultivators. To escape such oppressive conditions some rural dwellers fled their home areas and sought wage work at European enterprises—either in Rwanda or in neighboring areas. Labor migration as well as other forms of economic change (and, for some, Western education through mission schools), gave some individuals a measure of autonomy from local structures and acquaintance with new ideas. Hutu leaders emerged who used ideas and views from outside as tools to articulate a nascent Hutu political consciousness, itself a product of the discriminatory statebuilding process.

Throughout these three parts to the book, it will be apparent that the critique of existing theoretical frameworks sketched here depends, again and again, on careful historical analysis and on archival and oral materials collected through fieldwork. It is my hope that the blend of empirical research and conceptual rethinking that my years in Africa have provoked me to develop will bring to the study of Rwandan political institutions and to the larger issues of third world politics a synthetic perspective—one that will be of importance to the ways in which political scientists as well as other scholars in the social sciences approach these issues.

PART I

STATEBUILDING IN PRECOLONIAL AND COLONIAL RWANDA

2

KINYAGA AND CENTRAL RWANDA: EARLY CONTACTS

STUDIES OF Rwanda often assume that before the arrival of Europeans, Rwandan state power extended uniformly to most (or all) regions of the kingdom. Such studies also tend to imply that the features of Rwandan society observable in the 1950s—monopolization of power by Tuutsi, highly unequal political and social relationships, and control over land and cattle by Tuutsi political authorities—were primordial characteristics of the Rwandan polity. In such studies, Tuutsi dominance and Hutu subordination are often presented as unchanging features of the Rwandan past. But family histories of Kinyagans from diverse social and economic backgrounds portray a very different view of precolonial social and political relationships. These data cast new light on the dynamics of central court penetration in one region; they also raise issues fundamental to understanding the growth of Tuutsi power in other areas of the country as well.

As a basis for reconstructing such processes in Kinyaga, this chapter explores the character of the early Kinyagan populations and discusses the nature of their relations to the central Rwandan state. People coming from areas that are now part of Rwanda moved into the hills and onto the peninsulas of Kinyaga from at least the eighteenth century. They lived alongside, traded with, and intermingled with local groups whose culture resembled that of peoples living to the west of Lake Kivu. Some Kinyagan families claimed ties to the Rwandan royal court and built up followings on a few hills which they thus claimed to "govern." But there was no political authority encompassing the entire region, and the population of Kinyaga enjoyed substantial autonomy vis-à-vis the royal court of Rwanda. The power of the central state and its delegates was as yet quite limited in this frontier region.

Toward the last quarter of the nineteenth century this situation

changed significantly. The next two chapters delineate some of the
alterations in administrative structures (aspects of statebuilding and
expansion of central power) which marked the passage of Kinyaga from
a position of relative autonomy to one of intrusive central government
control. It is only in the context of these broader political transformations that the growth of Tuutsi power and its impact on rural class
relations, analyzed in part II, can be understood.

THE EARLY POPULATION AND
IMMIGRANTS TO KINYAGA

FROM ABOUT the middle of the eighteenth century, the indigenous
population of Kinyaga was gradually augmented by immigrants
from areas that were, or later became, part of Rwanda. They came seeking greener pastures and freedom from difficulties or domination (famine, wars of conquest, family conflicts). One element attracting these
new immigrants was Kinyaga's location far from the central Rwandan
court, which permitted the region to preserve a high degree of local
autonomy. Other factors included the rich soil, abundant rainfall, and
available land in the region. Immigrants came from areas to the north
and east of central Rwanda (Ndorwa and Gisaka) and from central
Rwanda itself.[1] Kinyaga was also settled by people from the south
(Burundi) and the west, from among the Shi, Fulero, and Havu peoples
found in present-day Zaïre. From the intermixture of these groups
emerged a heterogeneous population, a relatively open social structure,
and political forms exhibiting a high degree of diversity; these characteristics of Kinyagan society in the mid-nineteenth century were important influences in the developments to follow. As we shall see, for
example, several of the key local activists during the revolution were
drawn from families that had enjoyed status and autonomy in the past,
but had seen this autonomy transformed into dependence by changes
during the colonial period.

Little is known about the population encountered by immigrants to
Kinyaga during the eighteenth and nineteenth centuries. The commonly accepted view about the earlier inhabitants is that they were
agriculturalists living in family groups.

> At the beginning of the reign of Kigeri III [Ndabarasa] the kings of
> Ruanda held only a nominal sovereignty over Kinyaga, and the
> population, composed uniquely of Bahutu, depended in fact on fam-

MAP 2 : **Kinyaga—Central Rwanda**

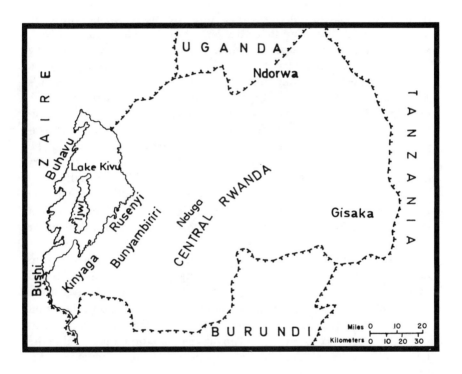

ily heads. This period was characterized by the extension of cultivated land at the expense of the forest, which disappeared rapidly.
The king Kigeri decided to have the region occupied by Tuutsi.[2]

Aside from such generalities, we lack reliable data about the early Kinyagan population, its nature and clan composition.

The family traditions collected for this study do not provide much
help in this regard. The accounts of those who claim a Kinyagan origin
for their lineage characteristically report only a very short genealogy
(two or three generations) or a very long one (up to ten generations).
Short genealogies indicate that little family history has been preserved,
and it is difficult to determine whether the Kinyagan origin is being
claimed on an empirical basis or for lack of knowledge of actual origins.
Where a genealogy is long, but there is no memory of an ancestor's
having immigrated to Kinyaga, a very long residence in the region is
plausible. But it is rare that such accounts provide extensive information on the distant past. Family traditions which record the immigration of an ancestor to Kinyaga are also of little help regarding the
indigenous population. When asked what other people their ancestors
encountered upon arrival in the region, those interviewed usually cited
lineages on their hill which possessed significant land-holdings during
the nineteenth century or (on a regional level), large lineages which
enjoyed political prominence at the end of the nineteenth century or
after.

It is interesting, however, that many of those who claimed a Kinyagan
origin for their lineage and cited very long genealogies, also claimed
membership in the Abasinga clan. Most of these informants live in the
mountains of northeastern Kinyaga, not far from Bunyambiriri (a region
known to have been an early center of the Abasinga). In 1960 the Abasinga comprised 20.60 percent of Kinyaga's population, making this the
largest clan in the region (see table 1); moreover the percentage of Kinyagans who were Abasinga was significantly higher than the percentage of Abasinga among the Rwandan population as a whole in 1960
(14.60%).[3] These factors suggest that the Abasinga were among the earliest and perhaps the largest group of early inhabitants in the region.

The size of a clan, however, does not in itself indicate length of
residence in Kinyaga. The clan names of many authochtones could have
disappeared, being assimilated into the identity group patterns that
evolved later.[4] This appears to have occurred for the Abahande, who
some Kinyagans claim were among the earliest inhabitants of the region.[5] Today where the name Abahande is found in Rwanda it is used

to refer to a "lineage" of the Abanyiginya clan. In non-Rwandan areas to the west, the Abahande are known as a royal clan from which the present ruling dynasty in Buhavu is said to descend.

We know more about immigrants to Kinyaga from regions that were or later became Rwandan than those from the west or south, because the fact of moving was more likely to have been preserved in family traditions which retain a Rwandan tie. Significant immigration of people from regions that are today part of Rwanda began during the reigns of Rujugira and his son Ndabarasa in the eighteenth century, and then increased steadily during the first half of the nineteenth century. Immigrants during that period were of four major types: refugees from war or political disturbances, colonizers sent directly by the Rwandan court, refugees from famine, and immigrants seeking better land or who could not recall the reasons for their move.

i. Refugees from War or Political Disturbances

MANY IMMIGRANTS fleeing war or domination came to Kinyaga from Ndorwa and Gisaka, located to the north and east of central Rwanda. These two regions, subject to invasions from Rwanda and efforts at incorporation during the eighteenth and nineteenth centuries, were devastated by the wars.[6] Some of the refugees seeking asylum in places distant from control of the Rwandan court eventually found their way to Kinyaga. There is a general belief among Kinyagans that "most of the population came from Ndorwa and Gisaka." Though exaggerated, this claim does have some basis in fact. Statistics on clan distribution in Kinyaga (see table 1) show that the Abagesera clan, which was the former ruling clan in Gisaka, constituted 11.36 percent of the Kinyagan population in 1960, ranking third behind the Abasinga and the Abanyiginya. This figure approximates the percentage of Abagesera in the population of Rwanda as a whole (11.04%). The Abashambo figure is more revealing. In 1960, more than one of every ten Kinyagans (11.2%) claimed membership in the Abashambo clan, making the Abashambo the fourth largest clan in Kinyaga. But the percentage of Abashambo in Rwanda as a whole was much smaller (3.94%). Moreover, the percentage of Abashambo closely approximated the percentage of that clan in Kibungo Prefecture (11.41%); Kibungo includes Gisaka and part of Ndorwa, the regions from which the Abashambo are said to have come.

Examples of refugees from war in Gisaka or Ndorwa immigrating to Kinyaga are illustrated in the following summaries distilled from Kinyagan family histories:

The ancestor of the Abarari, Abahima lineage (Abashambo clan) was driven from Ndorwa by *Umwami* [the Ikinyarwanda term for king] Kigeri Ndabarasa. Murari came to Kinyaga bringing many cattle, his wives and children, and many relatives. His descendant, who was born before 1892, asserted that Murari was his great-grandfather. This is possible, but probably the genealogy has been telescoped.[7]

The Abarindi lineage (Abashambo clan) at Rukunguri hill was founded by Mirindi, first member of the lineage to come to Kinyaga. Mirindi's father, Gahuliro, left Ndorwa as a small child, at the time when the Rwandan king defeated Ndorwa. Mirindi himself immigrated to Kinyaga and settled at Gashonga hill, the major center of the lineage until this century, when members moved to Rukunguri. Mirindi was the fourth-generation ancestor of a Kinyagan who was born after the establishment of German rule in Rwanda; he was old enough to herd cattle at the time of World War I.[8]

TABLE 1: Distribution of Kinyagan population by clan, 1970

Clan	Kinyaga	Rwanda
1. Abasinga	20.60%	14.60%
2. Abanyiginya	15.92	10.90
3. Abagesera	11.86	11.04
4. Abashambo	11.20	3.94
5. Abazigaaba	5.06	11.46
6. Abatsoobe	4.71	0.86
7. Abasindi	4.53	13.33
8. Abeega	4.17	8.00
9. Abacyaba	4.14	6.46
10. Ababanda	1.07	6.69
11. Abongera	0.89	0.11
12. Abanyakarama	0.84	0.28
13. Abaha	0.54	0.55
14. Abashingo	0.28	0.43
15. Abasiita	0.16	0.14
16. Abungura	0.11	5.84
17. Abakono	0.11	0.68
18. Abeenengwe	0.01	0.004
19. Others	13.80	4.686

SOURCE: d'Hertefelt, *Clans*, Annexes, Tableau 2.

Rwambika, a member of the Abazirankende lineage (Abagesera clan) living at Ibanda hill, said that his ancestor, Kibuzi, left Gisaka during the time of *Umwami* Rujugira. Kibuzi left Gisaka because of "conflict with neighbors"; there was a war in Gisaka. Kibuzi, Mweko, and Kigogo came at the same time. They cleared the forest (*ishyamba*) first at Mubumbano; then members of the lineage later moved to Ibanda. Rwambika was a small child able to fetch water when Rwabugiri died (1895); he said that Kibuzi was his great-great-grandfather.[9]

Rurangwa, a man at Mugera hill who is a member of the Abaganda lineage (Abagesera clan) recounted that his ancestor Bijeli left Gisaka "to escape the king there at the time, Kimenyi." Bijeli, a hunter, came to Mugera accompanied only by his wife. Rurangwa, who was born in 1914, traces his genealogy back six generations to Bijeli.[10]

Kagamba, ancestor of the Abagamba lineage (Abagesera-Abazigaaba clan) left Gisaka after a fight with Tuutsi who "were pasturing their cattle in his sorghum fields." He came to Kinyaga and settled at Muganza hill, in Busoozo. According to the lineage genealogy, Kagamba was the fourth generation ancestor of a man who was a small boy able to herd goats when Rwabugiri died in 1895.[11]

A man at Ruganda hill (born just after the death of Rwabugiri), recounted that his fourth-generation ancestor, Mukajanga, left Gisaka because of war; there was an attack by the "Abanyoro and Abanyambo."[12]

ii. Colonizers Sent by the Rwandan Court

SOME IMMIGRANTS to Kinyaga from Rwandan areas came to settle either as clients of the royal court or as followers of such clients. In lineage traditions about immigrants of this type, their immigration to Kinyaga is often linked to efforts by the central court to "subdue" Kinyaga, or to install Rwandan settlers in order to guard the border against "incursions" from the peoples to the west. They were frequently of Tuutsi status and usually had (or claimed) close links to the central court.

Rwanteri, son of Biragara (Abeega clan) is the most famous of the early immigrants who came as clients of the court. According to central court traditions, this warrior was sent to Kinyaga during the reign of

Sentabyo (at the end of the eighteenth century). Rwanteri was given command of a newly created army called the Impara with which he was to occupy Kinyaga. He was to expel from the region a certain Bijeli, "a warrior from Ijwi Island who had settled there not long before." Another newly formed army, the Abiiru, under the command of Rukoro, son of Ngaruyinka (Abakoobwa clan), was sent to aid Rwanteri. The two armies conquered Kinyaga, then settled there, each army giving its name to the region it had conquered. Such was the origin of the provinces of Impara and Abiiru.[13]

Kinyagan versions of Rwanteri's arrival differ in some details from the central court account described above. For example, Nyarugabo, a man born in 1916, who is a sixth generation descendant of Rwanteri, traced his ancestor's conquest of Kinyaga not to the time of Sentabyo, but to the reign of Sentabyo's father, Ndabarasa.[14] Like the central court traditions, Nyarugabo's account also noted that Rwanteri had to face the opposition of Bijeli and his lineage, a large and powerful kin group. The lineage traditions preserved by Bijeli's descendants in Kinyaga make no mention of an Ijwi origin. They recount that their ancestor, a hunter of the Abagesera clan who originally lived in Gisaka, left his homeland to escape the king of Gisaka at the time. He came to Kinyaga and settled at Mugera hill on the northern slope of Nyamirundi peninsula, opposite Ijwi Island. Bijeli's descendants, called the Abaganda, distributed land on Mugera to immigrants who came after them. Members of this family remained important in subsequent times, gaining fame during the reign of Rwabugiri (c. 1860–1895) for their vigorous resistance to rule by Tuutsi chiefs.[15]

Other local versions of these events link Rwanteri's arrival in Kinyaga to the rivalry between lineages of the Abanyiginya and Abeega clans— a jockeying for power between these two powerful court factions that, as we shall see, was a prominent feature of nineteenth and twentieth century Rwandan politics. It seems that Rwanteri was a flamboyant, aggressive fellow who competed in feats of bravery with a certain Nyarwaya (of the Abanyiginya clan).[16] Nyarwaya, feeling overshadowed by Rwanteri, plotted to have his rival killed. But the queen-mother tried to protect Rwanteri, who was her son-in-law.[17]

Initially, efforts were made to placate Nyarwaya with other compensations. Later, it was decided that Rwanteri should be sent to Kinyaga, considered a "rebellious" region. If he were not killed there, he would conquer the region for the court (and, in any case, he would be far removed from the power centers of the kingdom). Thus, "Rwanteri came [to Kinyaga] as an exile, for Kinyaga had become invincible."[18]

When it became clear that Rwanteri was succeeding in his mission, leaders at court started to have second thoughts. Should Rwanteri control all of Kinyaga, he would then be capable of asserting his independence vis-à-vis the central court. They decided that Rukoro and the Abiiru army should be sent to "help" Rwanteri, and thus to reassert royal influence by diffusing power in the region, assuring the court a role of arbiter among competing factions. After the conquest of Kinyaga, Rwanteri wished to give Rukoro a reward and dismiss him. Rukoro, however, refused, insisting that he should retain control over the region he had conquered—the hills near to and bordering the Rusizi River, in the southern part of Kinyaga. When the matter was taken to the central court for settlement, the court decided that Rukoro should retain his portion of the conquered territory, and Rwanteri could keep only his part. Rukoro, whose lineage held a position among the Abiiru ritual specialists (guardians of the Esoteric Code of the kingdom), and who was a known partisan of the royal court, was to watch over and serve as a check on Rwanteri.[19]

Some accounts deny that Rwanteri came on a special mission, maintaining that he arrived in Kinyaga just like any other immigrant, seeking land where he could settle.[20] These accounts may be based on the fact that Rwanteri and Rukoro did not establish political control over the whole region. They did establish the predominance of their lineages in two relatively small areas of Kinyaga (Rwanteri's descendants, around Mubumbano, and later, Shangi; Rukoro's descendants at Nyamagana and Mushaka). They then distributed land to followers who accompanied them to Kinyaga and others they recruited once there.

Perhaps the most important aspect of the installation of Rwanteri and Rukoro in Kinyaga was that they were the first to arrive as official envoys of the Rwandan court, and their arrival marked the beginning of a period of colonization in the region by the court. This colonization did not, however, bring close political incorporation until almost a century later. Additional evidence that the central court made a conscious effort to colonize Kinyaga, particularly during the reigns of Gahindiro and Rwogera (early and mid-nineteenth century) is found in the claims of certain Kinyagan lineages that an ancestor had direct ties to the king of Rwanda. While there is undoubtedly an element of ideology in such claims (direct clientship to the king was prestigious, infinitely preferable to being subject to a chief or other intermediary), some of the claims are substantiated with details as illustrated in the following accounts.

A man of the Abakuriyingoma lineage (Abashambo clan) recounted that his sixth-generation ancestor, Ntindo, left Bunyambiriri to come to Kinyaga with Rukoro; Ntindo settled in the Abiiru region of Kinyaga.[21]

Rugarama, fifth-generation ancestor of a Kinyagan member of the Abakaganyi lineage (Abanyiginya clan), lived at Gaseke in Nduga; he belonged to the Abiiru social army and came to Kinyaga as a client of Rukoro.[22]

A member of the Abakoobwa-Abanyiginya clan recounted that his fifth-generation ancestor, Ruhuugo, came to Kinyaga from Buganza in the time of *Umwami* Sentabyo. He received land in Kinyaga from the king, and the lineage was given charge of the royal herd Imisugi.[23]

Muhinda, a client of Rugondana (daughter of *Umwami* Cyirima Rugwe [sic] and wife of Rwanteri), lived at Mutiwingoma, Bufundu before he came to Kinyaga with Rwanteri and Rugondana. Muhinda was the third-generation ancestor of an informant who is a member of the Abaroha lineage (Abazigaaba clan).[24]

Bahufite, a very old man (of the Abeega clan) said that his second-generation ancestor, Nyawita, was a client (*umugaragu*) of Rwanteri. Nyawita lived in Bwanamukari before coming to Kinyaga with Rwanteri. The informant was a grown man when Rwabugiri died in 1895; he had participated in Rwabugiri's military expedition to Gacucu (west of Kinyaga, in present-day Zaïre).[25]

Mwerekande, founder of the Abeerekande lineage (Abasinga clan), came to Kinyaga from Gisaka. He was sent by *Umwami* Gahindiro to settle in Kinyaga and help to annex the region. One of his descendants, who was born in 1921, traces four generations to his ancestor Mwerekande.[26]

Nyantwa, the fourth-generation ancestor of a Kinyagan who identifies himself as a member of the Abasinga clan (descendants of Burora), came to Kinyaga with Mwerekende; they cleared the forest (*ishyamba*) at Nyarushiishi.[27]

Nsheenyi, founder of the Abasheenyi lineage (Abiitira clan), left Rwesero, Kabagari, to come to Kinyaga. A client of the king (Gahindiro), he asked permission from the court to settle in Kinyaga. Nsheenyi was the fifth-generation ancestor of Ngendahiimaana, who was a child when Rwabugiri died. This Kinyagan explained that his ancestors were Abiiru (ritual specialists) of the court whose function was to play the drums.[28]

Mugondo, fifth-generation ancestor of a man of the Abanenge lineage (Abashambo clan) was sent to settle in Kinyaga by *Umwami* Gahindiro. Mugondo came from Gakoma in Buhanga (southeastern Rwanda, near Burundi).[29]

Teganya, sixth-generation ancestor of a Kinyagan who was born around 1916, was sent by *Umwami* Rwogera to guard the frontier in Kinyaga. Teganya settled on a hill bordering the Rusizi River; his descendants form the Abateganya lineage (Abakoobwa clan).[30]

Ntango, a poet of the royal court, was a client of the king. Ntango or his father, Kababa, left Gaseke (Nduga) to settle in Kinyaga, sent by Nyiramavugo, mother of Rwabugiri. Ntango was the great-grandfather of an informant belonging to the Abatango Abeene-mugunga lineage (Abanyiginya-Abashambo clan).[31]

Ndikumwami came to clear the forest and settle in Kinyaga during the reign of Rwogera. The king had entrusted Ndikumwami with ritual items (*ibishegu*) to be thrown into the Rusizi River. Ndiku-mwami lived at Misumba, in Kabagari, before coming to Kinyaga; he was the fifth-generation ancestor of an informant of the Abanyi-ginya-Abashambo clan.[32]

iii. Refugees from Famine

KINYAGA'S RICH soil and abundant rainfall attracted immigrants seeking relief from famine. Famines occurred from natural causes in precolonial Rwanda, as central court traditions attest. Famines were also caused at times by the disturbances of war; in such cases, immigrants fleeing famine could also be considered as refugees from war. The following accounts provide examples of immigrants to Kinyaga whose descendants claim they came seeking relief from famine.

Gahiri, a hunter who lived in Suti (Bunyambiriri)[33] left his home because of famine; he came through the forest, hunting, and settled at Bitare hill in Kinyaga. Gahiri was the fourth-generation ancestor of an informant of the Abahiri lineage (Abasinga clan).[34]

Kanyamakara, grandfather of an informant of the Abango lineage (Abashambo clan) came to Kinyaga from Nduga. Previously Kanya-makara's ancestor had left Ndorwa because of famine. There was a war in Ndorwa, and the Tuutsi were attacking local lineage heads; people did not cultivate their fields.[35]

Gahanya, founder of the Abahanya lineage (Abeega clan), came from Gisaka looking for pasture land in Kinyaga. He was fleeing a famine called Rwamukanirwa. Gahanya, a client of the king, received land in Kinyaga at Shangi from Seekadegede, son of Rwanteri. Gahanya was the sixth-generation ancestor of a Kinyagan who was born just before the death of Rwabugiri (1895).[36]

Bireke lived at Kivumu in Nduga; he left there because of famine, and went to live in Irhambi (north of Bukavu, in the present Zone of Kabare, Zaïre). Gasigwa, son of Bireke, was a fourth-generation ancestor of an informant of the Abasigwa lineage (Abanyiginya clan) who lives in Kinyaga.[37]

Bajyujyu, founder of the Abajyujyu lineage, came to Kinyaga during the reign of Rwogera. He had left Gisaka because of a famine; there was insufficient pasture land for his cattle. Bajyujyu was the great grandfather of a Kinyagan who was born three years before the death (in 1908) of Mugenzi son of Nkombe.[38]

iv. Immigrants Seeking Fertile Land, or No Reasons Remembered

THIS CATEGORY overlaps to some extent those already listed—the search for land could ultimately be linked to population increase, political pressure, wartime conditions, or famine; but accounts in this category do not specify the presence of such conditions. The numbers of immigrants seeking land (both for agricultural purposes and for pasturage) and their ability to obtain it locally seems to support the contention in many of the traditions that the region had once been relatively sparsely populated. Family traditions in Kinyaga claim that on their arrival the earliest immigrants in all four of the categories cited here found abundant *ishyamba* (unoccupied forest or bush country) on which to settle.

v. Immigrants from Non-Rwandan Areas

IN ADDITION to the immigrants from north and east of Kinyaga, others came to Kinyaga from Havu, Shi, and Fulero regions in the west, and from Burundi in the south. These immigrants came for reasons similar to those enumerated above: family quarrels, war or political pressure, famine, search for fertile land.

Shi immigrants often settled on the hills along the Rusizi River and on a few of the southernmost peninsulas of Lake Kivu's eastern shore.[39] Farther inland, the small kingdom of Bukunzi in Kinyaga was a pole of attraction for immigrants from Bushi. The royal family of Bukunzi traced its origins to Rwindi (the origin claimed also by the royal families of Bushi and Buhavu) and maintained marriage ties with the ruling groups of the Shi kingdoms.[40]

Immigrants from Havu regions (Ijwi Island in Lake Kivu and the Ir-hambi area on the western shore of the lake) settled on the peninsulas from the Rusizi River north as far as the Kilimbi River and beyond. This location permitted the Havu immigrants to continue their fishing and facilitated communication with relatives to the west. The prox-imity of some of the Kinyagan peninsulas to Ijwi Island and Irhambi is striking. The extreme northern tip of Nyamirundi is only a 15-minute canoe ride from the southern tip of Ijwi Island. From the shoreline just south of Nyamirundi (the region around Mwito hill) to the Havu-in-habited peninsula of Ishungu on the western side of the lake takes about one hour by canoe. From Nkombo Island (Rwanda) to Ibinja Island and Bujombo (formerly Havu territory in Zaïre) is less than a half hour by canoe. In the past, communication with the west was relatively easy and frequent, and it still is today.

Fulero immigrants to Kinyaga usually settled on the hills in the southern part of Kinyaga opposite the Rusizi River (facing the Fulero regions to the west). Immigrants from Burundi tended to settle in the southern part of Kinyaga, particularly in Busoozo[41] and Bugarama, but also in Bukunzi. A small kingdom located in the mountains of south-eastern Kinyaga, Busoozo was easily accessible to immigrants from Bu-rundi. Ancestors of Busoozo's royal family, although tracing their origins to Gisaka, passed through Burundi before settling in Busoozo.[42]

KINYAGANS AND CULTURAL IDENTITY

As THE previous survey indicates, Kinyagan society in the mid-nine-teenth century was heterogeneous, composed of both non-Rwan-dan and Rwandan elements. It is not clear to what extent this heterogeneity was reflected in the cultural identity of early immigrants. For example, before the nineteenth century there are no data indicating whether early pioneers coming from regions outside central Rwanda considered themselves "Rwandan" or wished to have close ties to the Rwandan court. Nor do we know to what extent these immigrants from the east and north distinguished themselves from the indigenous Kinyagan population or from immigrants coming from the west.

It is clear that stereotypes about people from the west (usually referred to indiscriminately as "Abashi") are accepted now (and used in reference to the past) by Kinyagans who consider themselves as being of "Rwandan" background. Such stereotypes include ideas about food habits (Shi are despised for eating mutton, a meat which is thoroughly distasteful to most Rwandans),[43] general social conduct (Shi are regarded as rude and uncultured, particularly in their public eating habits), ornamentation (Shi are said to have walked in public like "naked savages"; they filed their teeth), and language (Shi are thought to speak a tongue thoroughly laughable compared to the beauty of Ikinyarwanda). Many of these stereotypes are still vigorously applied today, especially by educated Rwandans, but we do not know to what extent they were important in Kinyaga before the introduction of central Rwandan control.[44]

For the nineteenth century, toward the end of Gahindiro's reign (died c. 1830) and during the reign of his son Rwogera (died c. 1860), there are indications that identification with the central Rwandan court was growing. During this period the court made efforts to extend its influence into the region; early clientship to the royal court and membership in Rwandan social armies (umuheto groups) is often associated by informants with the time of Gahindiro and Rwogera. Understandably, such information on early linkages to the Rwandan court appears more often in the accounts of those who trace an origin for their ancestors to areas that are now Rwandan, and who consider their lineage to be of Tuutsi status.

Yet at least some immigrants from the west also began seeking ties to the Rwandan court in the nineteenth century, directly or through a Kinyagan intermediary of Rwandan culture. Even so, such action used as an assertion of cultural identity remained ambiguous, for many Kinyagans with origins in the west maintained commercial and social links with their home regions. Inhabitants of the peninsulas of Lake Kivu and the hills bordering the Rusizi River carried food, goats, and sometimes cattle to the west, exchanging these for fiber bracelets (amatega) and hoes.[45] Commercial ties were facilitated and reinforced by such social ties as blood brotherhood, friendship exchanges of cattle, and affinal kin relationships.

Some residents of Kinyaga began to assert identity with the Rwandan central court during the nineteenth century; others apparently did not. But later, under Rwabugiri, the assertion of Rwandan identity became common among those who could trace links to areas that had been incorporated into the Rwandan state. People with close ties to the west felt divergent loyalties under Rwabugiri, and probably later as well. Some saw opportunities for status and security by asserting Rwandan identity; others cherished their links to the west, and although perhaps willing to acknowledge the political sovereignty of Rwanda, were reluctant to abandon their own culture. These divergent identities existed among different groups and sometimes within the same individual. Over and above these sometimes conflicting loyalties, inhabitants of Kinyaga shared a common love of the autonomy they enjoyed before the reign of Rwabugiri.

Thus by the mid-nineteenth century at least some Kinyagans had links to the royal court or to central chiefs, and these links probably reflected sentiments of identification with Rwandan culture and the Rwandan king. It is not known how strong or widespread such identification was, but it seemed to be closely linked to a tradition of minimal interference by central authorities in local affairs. Loyalty to "Rwanda" initially involved few obligations but served as a source of local status.

3

STATE AND SOCIETY
UNDER RWABUGIRI

B
Y THE time of the European arrival at the end of the nineteenth century, Rwanda had grown, over a period of three centuries, from a small polity into a sizable state. In the past, the territory controlled by the kingdom had fluctuated as a result of succession struggles, conquest by enemy powers and, at times, successful annexation of new areas. But from the eighteenth century Rwanda experienced a steady expansion in both territorial scope and royal power. Some key elements that served to enhance the king's status and reinforce his power included the development of centralized military organization, the elaboration of a royal ideology glorifying the king and attributing strong ritual powers to him, and the growth of a complex hierarchy of political authorities with overlapping and competing jurisdictions.[1]

The growth of royal power did not, however, occur simultaneously in all regions. During the nineteenth century, transformations generated by increased central government penetration were concentrated in the Rwandan heartland (Nduga and nearby areas); in many areas of what is today Rwanda, local forms of political organization retained their vitality. Kinyaga was one such region, where geographical separation from the central court inhibited extensive central government involvement until the reign of *Umwami* Kigeri Rwabugiri (c. 1860–1895). Subsequently, two key developments altered the political landscape of Kinyaga: the growth of intensified linkages with the royal court, and the imposition of European colonial rule. These forces brought important changes to the region, but the changes were, of course, conditioned by what had come before.

Until Rwabugiri took the throne the central Rwandan government placed few demands on people in Kinyaga, and Kinyagan participation in central affairs was correspondingly limited. Some Rwandan immigrants to Kinyaga preserved previous links to a central Rwandan *umuheto* chief. And during the reigns of Rwabugiri's two predecessors *umuheto* chiefs living in central Rwanda established ties with certain prominent lineages in Kinyaga. But the majority of Kinyagans experienced little or no contact with representives of central government.

At that time Kinyaga was a geographical area, not a political entity; diversity of origins and topographical divisions contributed to heterogeneity in a population lacking any overall unity. With the exception of Bukunzi and Busoozo political authority within the region rarely encompassed units larger than the individual lineage or localized neighborhood group. Where such broader authority existed, it involved mainly the predominance of one older lineage over individuals or groups on the same or neighboring hills.[2] A good example of this in Impara was the Abadegede lineage, composed of the descendants of Rwanteri. But there was no hierarchical political authority incorporating all or a substantial portion of the region. The administrative structures introduced under Rwabugiri therefore represented a substantial break with the past.

The separate status of Bukunzi and Busoozo reflected Kinyagan autonomy in extreme form. Relative to the rest of Kinyaga the political organization of these small kingdoms was distinct: Organized along hierarchical lines, each was headed by a king *(umwami)* who presided over a small group of political and ritual officials. He was viewed as the ultimate owner of land in each kingdom, and inhabitants gave him tribute (collected from lineages) in the form of food products, beer, hoes, or cattle. The populations of these kingdoms were agriculturalists, living in family groups, but in both Bukunzi and Busoozo the *umwami* possessed cattle, and so did many of their subjects.[3]

The political autonomy of Bukunzi is well illustrated by the ritual role of this kingdom within the Rwandan dynastic code. Included in two key ceremonies is a ritual war in which the Rwandan royal court symbolically raids Bukunzi of cattle, goats, sheep, household utensils, and luxury basketware.[4] Busoozo, though not formally recognized in the same way, held much the same status. The *umwami* of each kingdom gave nominal recognition to the king of Rwanda, but local administrative structures in these two areas were not penetrated by central Rwandan officials until well into the European colonial period.

POLITICAL INCORPORATION UNDER RWABUGIRI

T HE REIGN of Rwabugiri marks an important watershed in the history of the Rwandan kingdom.[5] An energetic organizer and ambitious politician, Rwabugiri strove to break through traditional restraints and augment the prerogatives of the throne. His internal policies reflected two complementary goals—centralization of power and extension of central political structures to peripheral areas of the kingdom. In foreign policy, Rwabugiri led a series of military campaigns against the countries bordering Rwanda.[6] He created new army regiments to fight these wars, mobilizing the population and gaining additional offices to distribute. Foreign campaigns also served as a means of rewarding followers through the distribution of booty.

To undermine the hereditary power held by old families of the kingdom, Rwabugiri dismissed incumbent officials and appointed men dependent directly on him. He created new administrative positions and used frequent transfers or dismissals to ensure that no one chief could become powerful enough to oppose the king. The stakes were high; official positions were well rewarded but risky, since the penalty for losing royal favor was often death.

Chiefs dependent on the royal court assumed power in regions that previously had been relatively autonomous. Since a major role of these chiefs was to collect prestations (a portion of which they sent to the court), the material resources available to the monarchy increased significantly. Efforts to extend central Rwandan administrative structures to peripheral areas of the kingdom thus advanced Rwabugiri's goals of centralization while enhancing his prestige.

Historically in Rwanda, the growth of central administration was marked by the appropriation of control over people, cattle, and land by political authorities. A brief survey of these lines of control will illustrate the overlapping character of different jurisdictions in precolonial Kinyaga, and will serve as a basis for gauging the extent of later changes.

LAND (UBUTAKA)

W HEN PROVINCIAL organization was first introduced to Kinyaga (under Rwabugiri) the region was divided into two main provinces, Impara and Abiiru, and one semi-province, Bugarama, nominally subordinate to Impara (see map 3). (Bukunzi and Busoozo retained their

MAP 3: Provinces of Kinyaga

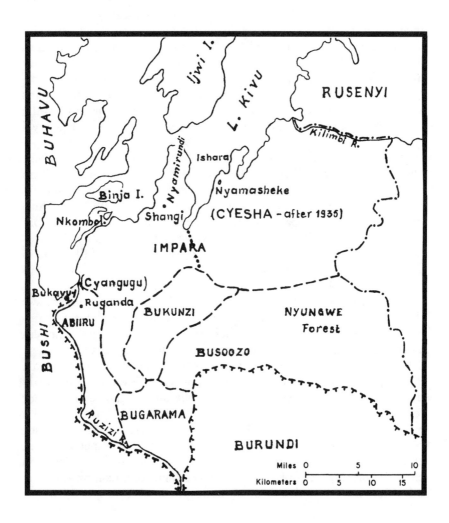

separate status, sending tribute directly to the royal court.) For each province Rwabugiri appointed a provincial chief *(umutware w'ubutaka or umutware w'intebe)* with authority over most of the hills concentrated in the province's geographically defined area. But a provincial chief did not hold exclusive authority since some lineages in each province had crosscutting political links with other central chiefs. The provincial chief appointed hill chiefs *(abatware b'umusoozi)* to represent him on the hills under his control. Each hill chief exercised authority over people on one or two hills, and his major role was to collect prestations for land *(amakoro y'ubutaka)* in food products or other items such as hoes, fiber bracelets, or banana beer. He sent a portion of the prestations to his superior, who then forwarded some to the royal court.[7]

The provincial chief of Abiiru normally dealt directly with lineage heads, or with the hill chiefs he appointed, who were usually from locally prominent lineages. In Impara, by contrast, the provincial chief often used an intermediary between himself and the hill chiefs. Thus, one delegate of the Impara provincial chief assembled prestations from the hill chiefs located north of the Mwaga River (the region that was later called Cyesha), another assembled prestations from hill chiefs in the central part of Impara, and a third collected prestations from hill chiefs in the Bugarama region of Impara.[8]

One obvious reason for the additional level of officials in Impara was the sheer size of this province. But other factors were at least as important. The regional delegates under the Impara provincial chief enjoyed high status and usually claimed direct clientship ties to the king. These regional divisions within Impara may thus have been embryonic forms of the district organization found in central Rwanda. From early in the nineteenth century, the royal court began to organize the interior regions of the state into districts, each headed by a land chief and a pasture chief appointed directly by the king. Several districts constituted a province, governed by a provincial chief who appointed hill chiefs (at a level below the district chiefs) in each district. The land chief and pasture chief of a district collected prestations from the local hill chiefs and forwarded these to the royal court.[9]

UMUHETO GROUPS

WHILE LAND prestations in Kinyaga were collected on the basis of territorial units, another form of payment referred to as *ama-*

koro y'umuheto was collected on the basis of membership in named groups responsible to an *umuheto* (social army) chief. These prestations, collected annually or every second year, consisted of locally available products (often luxury items) and therefore varied from one region to another. A lineage with many cattle would normally give a cow; others would be called upon to give fiber bracelets, fine mats, hoes, perfumed woods, honey, or, in some cases, food products.[10]

When the *umuheto* organization first emerged in Rwanda the groups incorporated mainly Tuutsi and involved some form of military service (as the term *umuheto,* meaning bow, implies). But by the end of the nineteenth century *umuheto* had become primarily an institution for collecting prestations, from Tuutsi as well as wealthy Hutu lineages. The *umuheto* chief selected lineages to be members of his *umuheto* group and then sent a client to collect prestations from those lineages. As one Kinyagan put it:

> When a chief such as Rwidegembya held authority for *umuheto,* a man could go and ask him, "Rwidegembya, I want authorization to collect beans as *umuheto* [as prestations] for you from a certain Hutu man." And another person would come and ask, "I want to collect a cow from this person and that other person. . . ." Alternatively, a chief appointed by the king, such as Rwidegembya, would tell a subordinate, "Go and collect prestations for me from the following Hutu families. . . ."[11]

Both the delegate and his *umuheto* chief stood to gain from recruitment of new lineages for *umuheto;* the former, because he kept a portion of the goods collected; the latter, because he commanded the loyalty and support of the delegate in addition to the material rewards. Normally a single representative of the *umuheto* chief supervised all the Kinyagan lineages belonging to a given *umuheto* group, regardless of their place of residence. In theory, at least, *umuheto* (unlike *ubutaka*) authority was not defined on the basis of territorial units. For example, if there were six lineages on one hill, two might belong to one *umuheto* group, one to a different group, and one to yet another, while two of the lineages might belong to no *umuheto* group at all. (see fig. 1).

The provincial chiefs, *umuheto* chiefs, and their delegates interacted in complex ways that varied from one region to another. In Kinyaga, one person often held the roles of provincial *(ubutaka)* chief and *umuheto* chief simultaneously. Where there were separate provincial chiefs

FIG. I: Schematic representation of *ubutaka* and *umuheto* structures for one province of Kinyaga during the time of Rwabugiri

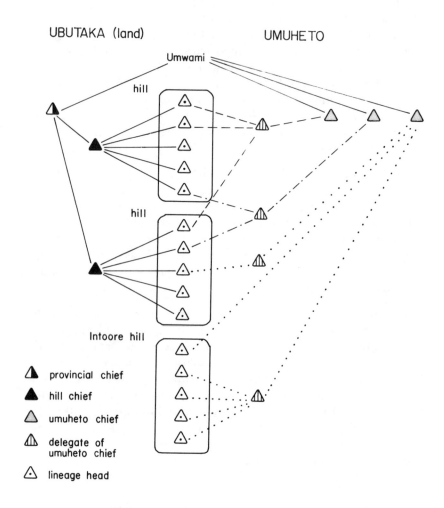

and *umuheto* chiefs in a single province, these authorities were often in competition for royal favor as well as for access to local clients.

In Abiiru province, the provincial chief during most of Rwabugiri's reign was Rubuga, son of Seenyamisange. Rubuga, as provincial chief, was responsible for collecting land prestations. But he was also *umuheto* chief of the Abiiru social army, with authority over those lineages that were considered members of the Abiiru social army. These lineages gave prestations to Rubuga only once, satisfying both land and *umuheto* obligations at the same time.[12] But certain of the lineages under Rubuga's control for land had been "chosen" by other *umuheto* chiefs in central Rwanda; these lineages then had to provide land prestations to Rubuga, and also send, separately, *umuheto* prestations to their *umuheto* chief.[13] One obvious effect of these diverse ties was to place constraints on the territorially based power of the provincial chief.

In Impara the administrative structures introduced by Rwabugiri were more complex than in Abiiru. The first well-known provincial chief appointed by Rwabugiri was Ntiizimira, son of Musuhuuke.[14] Ntiizimira himself appointed hill chiefs to represent him, and also, as we have noted, used three regional deputies as intermediaries to these hill chiefs. At the same time, Ntiizimira was also the *umuheto* chief of Impara social army. Like Rubuga in Abiiru, he thus combined the functions of provincial chief and *umuheto* chief. But other central chiefs had *umuheto* ties with certain lineages living in Impara; these lineages therefore belonged to social armies other than Impara, such as the Abashakamba or the Abazimya. Such lineages were expected to give land prestations to Ntiizimira, and *umuheto* prestations to their central Rwandan *umuheto* chief.

An additional division of authority was introduced to Impara after the dismissal and death of Ntiizimira. Rwabirinda, son of *Umwami* Mutara Rwogera and thus brother of Rwabugiri, assumed the post of provincial chief in Impara. But the position of *umuheto* chief of Impara went to Cyigenza son of Rwakagara, of the Abakagara lineage (Abeega clan). Cyigenza died shortly afterward and the position was taken over by his son, Rwidegembya. This meant that Rwabirinda's territorially based authority was circumscribed by the *umuheto* ties of Rwidegembya as Impara *umuheto* chief, and also by the earlier links between some lineages in Impara and other central *umuheto* chiefs.

The division of authority between Rwabirinda and Rwidegembya resembled in some respects the division in central Rwandan districts between a land chief *(umunyabutaka)* and a pasture chief *(umunya-*

mukenke) who exercised authority over the same geographical area. However, in Kinyaga the *umuheto* chief collected cows from cattle-owning lineages, and luxury items or food products from other lineages—his role, unlike that of a pasture chief in central Rwanda was not limited to affairs affecting cattle and pasturage. Moreover, while in central Rwanda all cattle-owning lineages were (theoretically at least) subject to a pasture chief, not all Kinyagan lineages were part of an *umuheto* group; the reach of *umuheto* was not universal, although it was substantially extended under Rwabugiri and in the period after his death.[15]

Just as the structural opposition between land chief and pasture chief in central Rwanda spawned conflicts, so did this divided authority in Impara give rise to competition and tension. Each chief tried to increase the size of his following at the expense of the other. Rwidegembya eventually succeeded in eliminating Rwabirinda, who was deposed in 1905. From that time, Rwidegembya combined the functions of provincial chief and *umuheto* chief of Impara, as Ntiizimira had done before him.[16]

INTOORE HILLS

CENTRAL CHIEFS who sojourned with Rwabugiri during his residence in Kinyaga became aware of the wealth and fertility of hills in the region. It became a sign of special favor to receive the command of an *intoore*, or "chosen" hill there. Rango hill in the Abiiru province provides a good example of this type of enclave. The chief Kanyonyomba, representing Rwabugiri's son Rutarindwa in Kinyaga, received permission from the king to select lineages for the prince's *umuheto* group. One of the lineages chosen lived at Rango hill in the Abiiru province. "I choose Murari and his sons," Kanyonyomba said, "as well as the hill where he lives, Rango."[17] Subsequently, the lineage no longer depended on Rubuga for *umuheto* nor, in this case, for land. Rango had become an *intoore* hill, and Rubuga, provincial chief of Abiiru who had formerly held both land and *umuheto* authority over the lineage, apparently had little to say in the matter.

These hills thus held an ambiguous position in the regional administrative structures. In theory, the population of an *intoore* hill owed allegiance and prestations not to the chief of Impara or Abiiru, but to the central chief who received the hill as an *intoore*. But in practice, tension often arose over the obligations of *intoore* hill residents toward the local provincial chief. The policy of granting *intoore* hills was thus a means of rewarding loyalty and bravery, while (like *umuheto*) it also served to prevent any one provincial chief from holding total sway within his administrative district. (See fig. 1 for a schematic presentation of these administrative structures).

MILITARY ORGANIZATION

WHEN RWABUGIRI began his external military campaigns, Kinyaga assumed great importance as a base for military operations against the Havu and Shi peoples on Rwanda's western border. The court turned its attention directly to this frontier region, and Kinyagans witnessed the establishment of the king and his retinue in their midst. Of course, geography and military strategy were not the sole determinants of Rwabugiri's interest in the region. Historically in Rwanda, a major means of imposing central rule in new areas had been the construction of a royal residence *(ibwami)*, particularly in regions regarded as rebellious. Such was the case when the eighteenth-century king, Kigeri Ndabarasa, set up virtually permanent residence in Ndorwa, a northern region that he had recently conquered.[18]

For Rwabugiri, Kinyaga held a similar attraction—the region he visited most often,[19] and where he established at least six residences. His principal residence was at Nyamasheke, constructed in preparation for attacks against Ijwi Island. Next in importance was his residence at Ruganda, near the Rusizi River (see map 3). The others, including a residence on Nyamirundi peninsula, served as temporary camps for specific expeditions.[20] Thus in addition to the *umuheto* and land prestations exacted by provincial chiefs, during the reign of Rwabugiri Kinyagans supplied materials and manpower for construction and maintenance of the royal capitals. And once Rwabugiri was installed in one or another of his local residences the people of nearby hills were enlisted to furnish food, firewood, banana beer, and other supplies to the king and his retinue.

Many Kinyagans were also called up for military service. Every lineage was expected to contribute one or two men for active combat or auxiliary duty in Rwabugiri's campaigns. It is interesting that recruitment for such duty normally occurred under the leadership of the provincial *(ubutaka)* chief of Impara or of Abiiru, or through delegates of these chiefs. Even men from lineages that depended on an *umuheto* chief other than the provincial chief fulfilled military duty under supervision of the provincial chief.[21] Thus Kinyagans were mobilized for war on the basis of the region in which they lived—residents of the Impara province under the Impara provincial chief, residents of the Abiiru province, under the Abiiru provincial chief. Residents of the *intoore* enclaves served under their *intoore* chief. But even here they fulfilled military service under the chief with authority for land, since the chief of an *intoore* hill cumulated authority over *umuheto* and land for all lineages on the hill except those that had previous ties to *umuheto* chiefs living outside Kinyaga.

This trend toward regionally based armies was an innovation of Rwabugiri's reign; he reorganized the Rwandan military so that each administrative region furnished troops, and the chief of the region became at the same time army commander of the men from his area.[22] Here is further evidence that during Rwabugiri's reign the major function of *umuheto* was not mobilization of people for military service (which increasingly became the responsibility of provincial chiefs), but rather collection of prestations.

AUTONOMY VS. STATUS

THE ADMINISTRATIVE innovations introduced in the time of Rwabugiri heralded profound changes in social relations. Kinyagans of Impara and Abiiru provinces basically had to choose between maintaining their autonomy and elevating their local status. Earlier, these two were mutually reinforcing; with the arrival of central power in the region, they became mutually incompatible. If Kinyagans cooperated with the new demands placed upon them by the chiefs appointed by the king they sacrificed their former autonomy. But the costs of noncompliance were high—loss of position and wealth (cattle/land), and hence of status.

The rewards of compliance included the chance to participate in substantial opportunities for power, honor, and enrichment brought in by the royal court and the central chiefs. Yet compliance meant submerging oneself in the system and in the larger arena of court politics—the escape from which had been a major reason for the arrival of many families to Kinyaga. So some Kinyagans directly resisted the exactions of Rwabugiri's chiefs, and others fled to the west. Descendants of pastoralist lineages that left Kinyaga during that period are still to be found living in the mountains west of Uvira in Zaïre, where they have preserved their Rwandan language and culture.[23]

But many Kinyagans saw benefit and opportunity in collaborating with the royal court. Some of those who collaborated were members of wealthy cattle-owning lineages of Tuutsi status, with long traditions of Kinyagan residence, and sometimes with early ties to the central court. A few came from important Hutu lineages that in some way or another had attracted the attention of the king and his court and obtained favors. The very "dazzle" of the king's physical presence, the proximity of the court to the local region, encouraged the acceptance of royal power. It is significant, however, that the acceptance was directed more toward the king himself than toward his representatives, the chiefs.

The opposition that arose against Ntiizimira provides a fascinating example of this phenomenon. Local people, conspiring to dislodge Ntiizimira from command of Impara Province, charged that he attempted to impose a tax on water, a practice totally unknown to local custom (or Rwandan custom in general), and highly resented.[24] In Abiiru Province, where Ntiizimira governed for a short time, prominent local lineages exerted pressure to have the chief removed and replaced by Rubuga, a son of the chief who had formerly commanded the province. Later, having lost favor at court, Ntiizimira was also dismissed from command of Impara, and eventually was executed on Rwabugiri's orders.[25]

There is no attempt to argue that local grievances (especially from Kinyaga) had a direct influence on political decisions in Rwabugiri's state. Ultimately grievance was only a lever to be used by one party or another to a particular power struggle within the confines of the central court. The presence of Rwabugiri and his court in Kinyaga may have furnished an occasion for the local elite to air grievances, thus providing one excuse for eliminating Ntiizimira, who had become so powerful as to constitute a "threat." But the "faults" attributed to Ntiizimira as an explanation for his loss of favor were less a cause of his downfall than a reflection of attacks on him by his rivals.

Among the faults of which Ntiizimira was accused was the allegation that he had led an expedition against Ijwi Island without prior authorization of the royal court. The foray ended in a humiliating defeat for the Rwandans, and many of Ntiizimira's men were killed.[26] Later, Ntiizimira allegedly lagged behind during an important battle against the Shi (at Kanywiriri). The Rwandans suffered a disastrous defeat and some of their greatest military leaders were killed. Ntiizimira, whose warriors emerged virtually unscathed this time, was blamed for the loss of Rwanda's heroes.[27] Finally, Ntiizimira was accused of having mistreated the population:

> Ntiizimira put people into chains. When the Court heard of this, that's when Rwidegembya asked for Ntiizimira's property. He received the cattle herd called Ingaaju; Ingaaju which had belonged to Ntiizimira and Rugaaju. He received them from the court, and the others [Ntiizimira and Rugaaju] fled.[28]

As this account suggests, the most important reason for Ntiizimira's demise was the maneuvering of powerful rivals who wished to get rid of him.

NDUGAN ATTITUDES TOWARD KINYAGANS

As central chiefs and the royal court moved into Kinyaga the local population became sharply aware of differences between themselves and the haughty courtiers from Nduga, the Rwandan heartland. Attitudes of Ndugans toward Kinyagans ranged from mere disdain to complete mistrust. They noticed different manners among local people and linguistic variations from the Ikinyarwanda spoken in central Rwanda. They considered Kinyagans not only less sophisticated than themselves but dirty, crude, and uncouth as well. Ndugans also feared to eat locally prepared food, not wanting to risk being poisoned.[29] Even Kinyagans who considered themselves solidly Rwandan and Tuutsi were viewed with scorn by the Ndugans.

While needing local support for the successful execution of Rwabugiri's expeditions in the west, Ndugans had little confidence in the Kinyagan population.[30] Nevertheless, Kinyagans played an important part in the Rwandan campaigns against Ijwi and Bushi. People living along the peninsulas of Lake Kivu were (and still are) superb boatmen, and their navigational skill proved critical in transporting and supplying Rwabugiri's troops. Perhaps most important were the contributions made by Kinyagan spies and guides who were acquainted with the terrain and social and political conditions in the west.

Two residents of Mururu hill, for example, played a key role during an attack against the Shi at Kanywiriri. Before setting out to guide the troops, the two Kinyagan guides were compelled to drink a truth potion (*igihango*), taking an oath not to betray the Rwandan cause. The guides successfully led Rwabugiri's troops to the Shi forces, but to no avail. Rwanda suffered a catastrophic defeat, during which several renowned heroes were killed.[31]

Later, some years after Rwanda's defeat at Kanywiriri, Rwabugiri again took up the campaign against the strongholds of the Shi to the west of the Rusizi River; he was determined to subdue this tenacious people. Rubago son of Nyamunonoka, a Hutu said to be originally from Bukunzi, with kin ties in Bushi but at that time a resident of Mururu in Kinyaga, came forward offering his services to Rwabugiri. Guided by Rubago, Rwabugiri's forces launched a surprise attack on the Shi camp and managed to capture the (widowed) queen mother and her son.[32]

The frontier position of Kinyaga gave rise to ambiguity of attitudes, both in how Kinyagans viewed central Rwanda, and in the views of Ndugans toward Kinyagans. Ndugan distrust of Kinyagans arose from the region's distance from central Rwanda (which made close supervision difficult) and the proximity of the region to different cultures in the west (which made the population "different," and therefore suspect). These differences earned Kinyagans the epithet of "Abashi," a term applied by Ndugans indiscriminately to people from southwestern Rwanda, implying "barbaric" or "uncultured":

> The Banyakinyaga, more than anyone else, were looked down upon and no more needed to be said when the word "bashi" was uttered: the "foreigners from beyond the frontiers."[33]

ETHNIC DIFFERENTIATION

THE STATEBUILDING efforts of Rwabugiri heightened awareness of ethnic differences in Kinyaga. With the arrival of Ndugan authorities, lines of distinction were altered and sharpened, as the categories of Hutu and Tuutsi assumed new hierarchical overtones associated with proximity to the central court—proximity to power. Later, when the political arena widened and the intensity of political activity increased, these classifications became increasingly stratified and rigidified. More than simply conveying the connotation of cultural difference from Tuutsi, Hutu identity came to be associated with and eventually defined by inferior status. It should be noted that there existed many criteria for ethnic identification, among them birth, wealth (especially in cattle), culture, place of origin, physical attributes, and social and marriage ties. It is impossible to single out any one element

as the basis for ethnic identity in all situations. But the political salience of membership in one ethnic category or another came to depend
on power.[34]

It is probably with this in mind that many Kinyagans trace the first
arrival of Tuutsi in the region to the time of Rwabugiri. In fact, Rwandans who owned cattle and would, in central Rwanda, have been considered culturally and socially Tuutsi arrived in Kinyaga in the
eighteenth century. But to many Kinyagans, "Tuutsi" is associated
with central government power and institutions, and particularly with
the exactions of chiefs backed by central government.

Under Rwabugiri, Tuutsi and Hutu became political labels; "ethnicity," such as it was, came to assume a political importance, determining a person's life chances and relations with the authorities. With the
establishment of European colonial rule in the country, ethnic categories came to be even more rigidly defined, while the disadvantages
of being Hutu and the advantages of being Tuutsi increased significantly. Passing from one ethnic category to the other was not impossible, but over time it became exceedingly difficult and, consequently,
very rare.

4

DUAL COLONIALISM

RWANDA'S MOUNTAINOUS terrain and renowned military might shielded this small state from European occupation until late in the nineteenth century. But in a startling intrusion on the kingdom's previous impregnability, the German Count von Götzen traversed Rwanda in 1894, the first European to reach the royal court.[1] Then in mid-1896, a small contingent of Belgian officers with African soldiers arrived to set up a camp in Kinyaga, the first region of Rwanda to experience European occupation. Initially, Rwanda's rulers attempted to resist by force of arms. When this failed, they later collaborated with the German authorities who established colonial rule in the country from 1898.

There was, however, no single Rwandan "response" to the colonial invasion. Some Rwandans resisted, some collaborated, and many maneuvered to create opportunities from the presence of these foreigners who had clearly come to stay.[2] The colonial apparatus which emerged involved the interaction of two complementary systems of power. Through superior force, prestige, and wealth, the colonial authorities persuaded and often coerced the incumbent (Tuutsi) elite to serve as intermediaries for colonial administration, thus establishing a form of indirect rule. But these intermediaries were not mere puppets. While sacrificing much of their former autonomy, Tuutsi chiefs gained new and more effective forms of power. These were weapons, to be used in the statebuilding objectives of the royal court, in political infighting among the powerful, and in the efforts by chiefs to consolidate a position of superiority vis-à-vis the populations over whom they ruled.

Dual colonial rule in Rwanda accommodated efforts of Europeans to build an economically solvent colonial state. It also accommodated the internal goals of various factions among the Tuutsi ruling groups in Rwanda. Efforts of these different groups to mold colonial policies to their interests intersected with a series of internal Rwandan conflicts:

between central (Tuutsi-led) factions seeking to control the royal court (Abanyiginya vs. Abeega); between regional elites and central authorities, each seeking to establish new bases of power (central-local disputes); and between different strata of the population (nascent class conflict). This chapter focuses mainly on the first two types of conflict, dramatized in the history of relations between Kinyaga and central Rwanda during the period from 1895 to 1950.

EUROPEAN COMPETITION OVER SOUTHWESTERN RWANDA

THE DEATH of Rwabugiri in 1895 plunged the kingdom into mourning for four months, and his chosen heir, Rutarindwa, assumed power. Meanwhile the royal court moved out of Kinyaga, not to return. The period of mourning was scarcely ended when the first Europeans to occupy Kinyaga arrived, an event remembered vividly by local people as the beginning of a period of anarchy and destruction. The "Abapari," as these Europeans are called, crossed the Rusizi River in the south, and then moved north through the Bugarama Valley. They were accompanied by African soldiers armed with guns, dressed in black clothes with red hats and belts. The Kinyagan descriptions of the uniforms leave no doubt that these were soldiers of the Force Publique of the Congo Free State. The European officers leading them were attempting to establish Belgian claims on the area—Kinyaga's location as undetermined territory falling between Belgian spheres of activity (in the west) and German interests (in the east) attracted early European attention.[3]

The chiefs in Kinyaga put up a brave resistance, but found their spears and bows and arrows sadly inadequate before the Abapari guns. After several unsuccessful attacks on the invading force,[4] all the central Rwandan chiefs as well as several Kinyagan chiefs fled with their cattle. Included among the chiefs were Rwabirinda (chief of Impara Province); Rubuga (chief of Abiiru); Nyankiiko and others of the Abeerekande lineage; and Mugenzi, son of Nkombe (chief of Bugarama).[5] The refugees reported to the royal court that it would not be easy to oust these European intruders. But military leaders at court called Rwabirinda and the Kinyagans cowards, unable to put up a decent fight. The top military units of the kingdom were then mobilized, including some ten companies with more than 8000 men.[6]

The Rwandan forces proceeded to Nyamugari, a hill adjoining Shangi.

There they waited until dawn to launch the attack. They caught the Abapari unawares, while several members of the group were away looking for food. But even with this in their favor, the Rwandans found that their weapons were no match for the Abapari rifles,[7] and retreat soon turned into a rout. Many Rwandans were killed in the battle.[8] Others fled, but those who sought refuge in the direction of Nyamugari were shot down as they tried to climb the hill. Some who fled into a nearby swamp were killed by Abapari returning from the Nyamirundi peninsula. At Gafunzo hill near Lake Kivu, many Ndugan soldiers escaped in canoes, crossed the bay to Nyamasheke, and from there returned to central Rwanda.[9] The Tuutsi chiefs of Kinyaga also fled with their cattle to Bunyambiriri and Itabire.[10]

Not long after this battle, the Abapari left Shangi, apparently on the intervention of German authorities in Bujumbura, and returned to Luvungi (near the Rusizi River, on the Congo Free State side). A few months later, another small group of Belgians again entered the region. These Abapari built a post at Nyamasheke, on the land where Rwabugiri's former residence had been located. There they remained for about a year, cutting down the trees and thus desecrating this *ikigabiro* (royal grove).[11] The Abapari occupation lasted less than two years, but during most of this time the central chiefs and the prominent Kinyagan chiefs were absent. This was to be a fact of some importance in the later shifts in power constellations which occurred in the region.

Several Kinyagans stepped in to fill the power vacuum after the central chiefs had left. These were often Hutu from strong lineages, who had enjoyed autonomy and status in the pre-Rwabugiri period. A few were poor Tuutsi who saw in clientship to the Europeans a chance to gain status and wealth. Serving as intermediaries for the Europeans, these Kinyagans requisitioned (some say extorted) livestock and other products that the Abapari demanded for food; the Europeans rewarded these collaborators with cattle obtained in raids.[12]

Perhaps the most infamous of the early European clients was an outsider. Seevumba, the Rundi guide of the Abapari, imposed a harsh control in the south of Kinyaga, backed by the indiscriminate use of force. Said to be the son of Rurenzwa, Seevumba was a close relative of Rwabishuugi (also a son of Rurenzwa), the chief of Bugarama during Rwabugiri's reign. Seevumba's interest in Kinyaga arose in part from his desire to repossess cattle that Rwabishuugi had taken when he left Burundi to become chief of Bugarama. To achieve his goal, Seevumba sought European aid.[13]

Seevumba's conduct was thus an early example of what later became a common practice in Rwanda (or in any colonial situation). Through cooperating with and aiding the possessors of superior force (the Europeans in this case), Seevumba was able to manipulate the situation to his personal advantage. Forwarding his own ambitions, he gained power that he then used in a way that his European patrons would have condemned, in principle at least. But the Europeans were Seevumba's accomplices. They left him a wide degree of latitude so long as he continued to serve their goals.

Oral traditions from Kinyaga leave no doubt that Seevumba was a tyrant. Reinforced by European backing, he seized cattle and other livestock and burned huts; he also apparently appropriated women and children.[14] Local lineage heads were coerced into cooperating with him, but often they submitted only after one of the lineage members had been killed. One man, who had been a young child during Seevumba's occupation, conveyed some of the terror of the time:

> When they killed people I witnessed that; meanwhile the rest of us were crouched down in the grass. When they came from the direction of Cyato we were lying in the high grasses where we had spent the night; they came upon us. The guide was a native of here and knew the local people. He saw my mother and her daughter-in-law and us two children. Then he said, "look out, there are some men here who've been dead for a long time; turn back to avoid smelling their bad odor." They climbed back up the hill and there they killed two men at Nyakanyinya. They continued past Murangi while some other *ingabo* went to Winteeko, where they killed three men and pillaged cattle. We were small children at the time, though capable of understanding things; but I was still young enough to cry when I was hungry. The others told me to be quiet so that the attackers wouldn't hear. I stopped crying only when my mother gave me something to eat.[15]

The Abapari occupation ended abruptly with the arrival in Kinyaga of a group of Africans armed with guns, coming from the north. These men, whom Kinyagans call the Abagufi, were mutineers of the Dhanis column fleeing from the Congo Independent state.[16] They attacked the Abapari at Gataka (Nyamasheke), then pursued them along the path toward Bukunzi. During a battle in the Nyamyazi forest (Bukunzi) the Abagufi killed several Abapari. Then both groups and Seevumba, the Abapari guide, left Kinyaga in the direction of Bujumbura. Their departure was followed quickly by the return of the chiefs from Nduga.[17]

The next year, in 1898, German authorities established a military post at Shangi. This was, along with Gisenyi at the northern end of Lake Kivu, the first German installation in Rwanda.[18] The boundary dispute that drew on Kinyaga such early intense interest from Germany and Belgium continued for several years. It was only settled in 1910 when Kinyaga was declared to be German territory, as part of a larger agreement on colonial boundaries negotiated by Belgium, Germany, and Britain.[19]

Some of Rwanda's proudest warriors had suffered a humiliating defeat in the battle against the Abapari. Ndugan chiefs blamed Kinyagans for this catastrophe. They heaped scorn and derision on local people, accusing them of having betrayed the country by cooperating with the Abapari. Muhigirwa, a prominent military leader, swore vengeance: "If I ever manage to vanquish these Shi [Abapari], I'm going to kill all of you, residents of Kinyaga."[20] The central court withdrew its cadre from the area, leaving the local population to endure the ravages of Seevumba and others.

These events demonstrated the inability of the Rwandan court to defend outlying regions of the expanding state from new types of military power. The Abapari episode also provided local people opportunities to build up clientele networks, to show the court that they were their equals. This alacrity to take up positions of command under the Abapari was important for the later imposition of European rule in Rwanda. It indicated the frailty of central authority in the frontier region and served as a warning to the royal court that it would have to come to some kind of agreement with the European intruders to preserve its power. But the court, preoccupied with its own power struggles, initially failed to develop a coordinated response.

CENTRAL COURT CONFLICTS

IN BROADER Rwandan politics, the sequel to Rwabugiri's death was the emergence of an intense and bitter power struggle at the central court. This conflict, which culminated in late 1896 with a bloody coup d'état, affected not only the personnel of power, but also the whole nature of the political process in Rwanda. For a time, at least, the balance of power shifted strongly into the hands of the Abeega clan, particularly the Abakagara lineage of this clan. The factions involved later continued their struggle throughout the period of European rule.

Only a few months after the Abapari arrival in Kinyaga, two brothers at the central court, Kabaare and Ruhinankiiko, and their nephew Rwi-

degembya plotted to overthrow the legitimate king, Mibambwe Rutarindwa. They planned to replace Rutarindwa with a young boy,
Musinga. Like Rutarindwa, Musinga was a son of Rwabugiri. But while
Rutarindwa's mother belonged to the Abakono clan, Musinga's mother,
Kanjogera, was a member of the Abakagara lineage of the Abeega clan,
and she was the sister of Kabaare and Ruhinankiiko. Here, as in many
other cases, the political ties of the mother's family proved critical in
the succession dispute which ensued, even superseding the former
king's explicit instructions. Rwabugiri had gone so far as to enthrone
Rutarindwa as co-ruler before his death.

Three of the five previous queen mothers had come from the Abakagara lineage, and in the years before 1895, aided by the purges Rwabugiri
staged against his own (paternal) Abahindiro royal lineage (Abanyiginya
clan), leaders of the Abakagara lineage had moved into many of the
most influential political posts of the kingdom, including first political
counsellor to the king and principal military commander of royal armies, as well as queen mother. Only the kingship itself remained to be
seized.[21]

Abakagara control over the position of queen mother resulted directly
from policies pursued by Rwabugiri. Several years before his death Rwabugiri had executed Rutarindwa's mother after she had been implicated
in a court intrigue. He then appointed his favorite wife, Kanjogera, as
the adoptive mother for Rutarindwa, who was at that time heir-appar-
ent. The Esoteric Code of Rwanda specifically proscribed appointing an
adoptive queen mother who had given birth to her own royal son; in
appointing Kanjogera, Rwabugiri went directly against the Code, as he
seemed to have done on so many other occasions during his reign.[22] As
queen mother (umugabekazi) Kanjogera assumed not only ritual obligations but important political prerogatives. She actively encouraged
her brothers' plan to win the throne for her son Musinga, and remained
as the power behind the throne for many years thereafter.

With his paternal lineage split over the succession and his maternal
kinsmen weak, cut off from institutional access to him by the appointment of Kanjogera as queen mother, Rutarindwa found himself in a
precarious position. Army corps loyal to his side were seriously weakened in the battle against the Abapari at Shangi; the Abeega may well
have planned to put those soldiers at risk. Rutarindwa's most prominent supporters were the ritual specialists (Abiiru) of the kingdom, especially the three principal Abiiru (Bisangwa, Sehene, and Mugugu),
executors of Rwabugiri's last testament. But shortly after Rutarindwa's
accession to power, Bisangwa son of Rugombituuri perished at Shangi

in the battle against the Abapari. Bisangwa's brother, Sehene, and Mugugu son of Shumbusho were assassinated through the machinations of Kabaare. Several of the powerful army companies which these three had commanded were placed under chiefs loyal to Kabaare and Kanjogera; the other companies were left weakened by the loss of their leaders.[23] In early December 1896 the Abakagara forces made their move, attacking the royal court at Rucunshu, near Kabgayi in central Rwanda. Though Rutarindwa's men put up a valiant defense, the Abakagara emerged victorious. Rutarindwa and his closest advisors committed suicide and the triumphant Abeega proclaimed Musinga king.[24]

In the aftermath of the Rucunshu coup, Kanjogera undertook a purge of Rutarindwa's brothers, uncles, and more distant cousins, thinning the ranks of the royal Abahindiro lineage. Some were assassinated on orders from the court, others fled into exile. The purge not only eliminated potential pockets of resistance; it also vacated positions which could then be filled by members of the Abakagara lineage and their supporters. The struggle between the Abakagara and Abahindiro lineages (often described as Abeega vs. Abanyiginya, using the clan categories), was to form an ongoing theme of political competition over the next five decades.

This shift in power at the center generated significant changes in local patron–client ties, since those with links to a central patron who was on the losing side at Rucunshu found it necessary to switch allegiance. Consequently the role and importance of Abeega (in Kinyaga and elsewhere in Rwanda) increased substantially, as did the status of those who were linked to Abeega patrons (particularly members of the Abakagara lineage). And the Abeega seized on European occupation as an opportunity to augment their power.

ADMINISTRATIVE UNIFICATION IN KINYAGA

WHEN GERMAN authorities established themselves in Rwanda they embarked upon a policy of indirect rule, using existing "traditional" authorities to govern the country for them, supposedly without altering existing patterns of authority. In fact, the very presence of the Europeans and the new resources they brought with them had a profound impact on power relations, both among elites and between ruling groups and the governed. Yet it was Rwandans who largely determined the ways in which colonialism influenced the transformation of clientship ties (discussed in chapter 7). European rule also introduced new policies on recruitment to political office and the organization of administrative structures. The discussion below examines how Rwandan groups and individuals participated in and influenced this process.

After the departure of the Abapari, and in the wake of the Rucunshu coup, a fierce struggle occurred between two central chiefs with claims on overlapping political commands in Kinyaga. Rwidegembya, a member of the Abakagara lineage, attempted to enlarge his role as *umuheto* chief of the Impara Province. He engaged in a protracted struggle to dislodge Rwabirinda, the provincial chief of Impara. The conflict was more than a simple attempt by Rwidegembya to augment his area of command; it was part of the larger Abakagara–Abahindiro conflict: Rwabirinda, a member of the Abahindiro lineage, was a son of Rwabugiri, and thus a half-brother of the deceased King Rutarindwa.

The Abakagara won this duel, for in 1905 Rwidegembya secured Rwabirinda's dismissal from his *umuheto* command in Impara.[25] Rwidegembya then combined two official roles in Kinyaga—provincial chief and *umuheto* chief of Impara. But, like other influential chiefs involved in central politics, Rwidegembya spent most of his time at the court (at Nyanza, now called Nyabisindu, in the present Gitarama Prefecture). Also, like other central chiefs of the time, Rwidegembya held commands in several different regions, and so he left local day-to-day administration to his delegates. In Kinyaga, he chose delegates from among the leaders of prominent local lineages. They were left relatively free rein to consolidate their power—and, with aid from the Germans installed in the Impara region, this was what they proceeded to do.

In Abiiru, the royal court appointed a central chief, Nyamuhenda, son of Kajeje, to govern after Rucunshu. Altering the policies of his predecessor, Rubuga, this new chief introduced hill chiefs from outside Kinyaga, using his own trusted followers from his home region of Bufundu. But Nyamuhenda met with recurrent resistance from the people of Abiiru, and in 1910 he "resigned."[26] Abiiru Province then returned to Kinyagan stewardship, when Rubago, a hill chief at Mururu hill, was appointed to replace Nyamuhenda. Later, Rubago was deposed, this time by Belgian authorities, ostensibly for abuses committed by his son Toreero. Although the abuses were real, Rubago's demise resulted primarily from the plottings of Rwidegembya's son, Rwagataraka.

During the period after Rucunshu to 1920, *Umwami* Musinga also granted selected hills in Kinyaga to several trusted followers. These delegates were instructed to keep watch on the Europeans there (as well as the chiefs) and to ensure defense of the frontier through magic.[27] Thus, in a modified form, the diversity of administrative arrangements in Kinyaga which had characterized the time of Rwabugiri survived during the first two decades of colonial rule. This diversity was expressed in extreme form by the special, autonomous status of Bukunzi and Busoozo, and by a lack of consistency in lines of control and responsibility in the collection of prestations for Impara and Abiiru provinces.

But from 1917, after the defeat of the German forces in World War I and the introduction of Belgian administration, changes in administrative structures were introduced in Kinyaga and other areas of Rwanda, designed to create larger, more unified regional units. The political structures came to resemble more closely a "feudal" type of government whereby a king holds power over relatively autonomous local lords, each of whom exercises the full range of administrative powers within his own domain.

In Kinyaga the unification of the region was inextricably linked with the career and policies of Rwagataraka, son of Rwidegembya (and hence a member of the famous Abakagara lineage). Rwagataraka arrived in Kinyaga in 1911 to represent his father, but it was not until after World War I and the establishment of Belgian administration that the dynamic qualities of this ambitious "modernizer" cum "collaborator" came to the fore. Skillfully accommodating to European policies, he gradually eliminated from office any whom he regarded as rivals to his monopoly of power. He filled the vacated positions with his own clients. He recruited some from Kinyaga and others from outside. These efforts to build a local empire pitted Rwagataraka directly against the interests of the royal court, as in his ongoing feud with Birasinyeri.

Birasinyeri came from a family (Abareganshuro lineage, Abanyiginya clan) with longstanding connections in Kinyaga. His father, Seerutabuura, a client of the court, had established *umuheto* ties with several Kinyagan lineages from early in the nineteenth century, and Birasinyeri himself served as delegate of Rwabirinda for collection of prestations in Impara. Later, when Rwagataraka came to Kinyaga, Birasinyeri was hill chief at Kirambo hill (in northern Impara, an area later established as the province of Cyesha). He was also regional representative of Rwidegembya for collection of prestations in Impara. He enjoyed a semi-autonomous position by virtue of his ties of direct clientship to the king.[28]

Rwagataraka first managed to dislodge Birasinyeri from his hill in northern Impara and from his regional command. When the king then appointed Birasinyeri chief of Abiiru Province (in 1917), Rwagataraka subjected both the chief and his son Ndabikunze to harassment. Some thirteen years later, Rwagataraka had a hand in the Belgian administration's decision to remove Birasinyeri. He also used his influence to have Biniga, one of his own protégés, named as successor.[29]

The conflict with Birasinyeri illustrates Rwagataraka's ambivalent relations with the central court. He depended on the court, yet was jealous of any autonomous power it might preserve in what he came to regard as his "domain." The powerful position he held in central politics served as a useful resource in the implementation of his goals at the local level, while the remoteness of the royal court at Nyanza inhibited frequent interference by other central chiefs in local affairs. This was another aspect of the continuing theme of autonomy versus status—the attempt by a succession of chiefs to use a regional power base for status at the central court. On another level, it was later the quest for these, autonomy and status, that led to the ethnic split in Rwanda.

Rwagataraka's efforts to expand his domain dovetailed with policy goals of the Belgian authorities. Beginning in 1926, the colonial authorities implemented a program to regroup and consolidate administrative units throughout Rwanda. This plan organized the state into subchiefdoms of roughly equal size, with at least 100 taxpayers in each, and grouped these subchiefdoms into chiefdoms, following roughly the boundaries of the precolonial provinces. Chiefdoms were then grouped into Territories, each headed by a European territorial administrator ("Administrateur de Territoire," or A. T.). The king appointed chiefs with the consent of the administration; chiefs usually selected their own subchiefs subject to approval by the territorial administrator.

Particularly in line for reconsideration under these policies were the diverse enclaves and *intoore* hills, which to territorial administrators represented merely a source of extra work. From their point of view, it would be much simpler to appoint a single provincial chief with hierarchical control over all the subchiefs in one area. As a 1929 report complained:

> The Territory of Shangugu contains many subchiefs who depend directly on the Mwami. . . . They are currently independent of the native provincial chiefs for prestations in taxes, labor, and cattle, provided that they have received no cattle from a native provincial chief in Shangugu. . . . Until now, these subchiefs, called "abaragu b'u Mwami," [clients of the king] have been under the direct authority of the [European] Territorial head. This situation leads the Territorial head to enter into constant relations with certain sub-

chiefs who have no great importance, [but need supervision] because of their meddling and impolitic administration, arising from
the fact that they are [nothing but] former boys or auxiliary soldiers
for the Germans.[30]

The same report recommended the elimination of such "irregular" lines
of command, and this was in fact the policy that was adopted. The
reforms also envisaged the appointment of European-educated "clerks"
(abakaraani). As sons of chiefs they were to attend an official school
for a few years to learn basic skills (reading, writing, elementary arith-
metic). In later years, such study would be extended to a post-primary
program of administrative training.[31]

This reorganization was meant to serve the interests of order and
efficiency, making it easier for the Belgian administration to convey
and enforce execution of orders along hierarchical channels. The policy
was also justified in part (in the European view) by presumed benefits
it would have for the general population. Administrative regroupment
was supposed to deliver local inhabitants "from the abusive demands
of numerous and useless petty chiefs. . . . Since the chiefs are now provided with an income sufficient to satisfy their material needs, exactions [on the population] have become rare."[32]

The regroupment policy had important implications for the role of
central (royal) power at the local level. The intoore hills and other
enclaves, formerly used by the king to ensure that men loyal to him
kept an eye on political activities in the frontier region, existed no
longer. The umuheto ties, which had held in check the power of the
provincial chiefs, were now abolished. The result was a diminution of
central control in the region and an augmentation of power for the
provincial chiefs, for each now governed a single geographically contig-
uous region. In Kinyaga, Rwagataraka was the major beneficiary. During
the 1920s and early 1930s, he dismissed or brought under his patronage
chiefs who, as direct clients of the king, held individual hills granted
them by the royal court. He also exchanged his own hills in other parts
of Rwanda with intoore hills in Kinyaga held by other central chiefs.[33]

The convergence of Rwagataraka's political ambitions with the administrative aims of Belgian authorities is illustrated in their joint action against the small independent kingdom of Bukunzi. From the point
of view of the Abakunzi, the Tuutsi chiefs of Kinyaga coveted their
cattle. These chiefs complained to the German authorities that the
people of Bukunzi and Busoozo should contribute to the food and labor
requisitions of the colonial authorities. But until the 1920s neither Ger-

man administrators nor the Belgians who followed them succeeded in collecting taxes in Bukunzi, imposing corvée, or even meeting Ndagano, the *umwami*. In 1907 German authorities had unsuccessfully attempted to capture Ndagano, but later abandoned the undertaking on Musinga's intervention. In 1909, and again in 1914, German-led forces made forays into Bukunzi but again did not manage to capture Ndagano. In February 1918, a Belgian force raided Bukunzi in retribution for the alleged killing of three men by the local inhabitants.[34] Later that year, Major Declerck (who became Belgian Resident of Rwanda in May 1917) reported that he had decided on a policy of persuasion to gain Ndagano's surrender. Noting that German military operations against Bukunzi had been unsuccessful, he opted for a policy of persuasion rather than force. But it was not until 1923, when the death of Ndagano triggered conflicts in the small kingdom, that Belgian authorities, aided by Rwagataraka, found the opportunity to subdue this "difficult" region.[35]

Ndagano's chief wife, Nyirandakunze, planned to place the youngest of her sons, Ngoga, on the throne. To forestall her husband's expected opposition, she and her brothers arranged to have him poisoned.[36] Nyirandakunze then ordered the execution of two men whose corpses, she maintained, were needed (allegedly as prescribed by tradition) to form the "pillow" of the dead *umwami*. Conveniently, those she chose to be executed were men who posed a threat to her ambitions. The two had been great favorites of Ndagano, and Nyirandakunze had reason to fear they might thwart her plans to install Ngoga as *umwami*. She also wanted to prevent one of the men, Shyirakeera, a long-time emissary to the Rwandan royal court, from bearing news of her misdeeds to Musinga. Further killings were planned—supposedly of a ritual nature but whose effect would have been to eliminate potential opposition.[37]

Several people from families that were thus threatened, hoping to defend themselves by appealing for outside aid, sought help from the European Catholic missionaries at Mibirizi Mission (adjacent to Bukunzi) and the European governmental administrator at Cyangugu. Their plea received prompt attention. In April 1923 the Belgian administration organized a military foray into the kingdom, credited with having prevented the murder of several people. In the wake of this action, the chief administrator of the region (Administrateur de Territoire, A.T.) assumed direct control over several hills near Mibirizi Mission which had formed part of Bukunzi; he forbade the inhabitants of these hills to work in Bukunzi or to take gifts to the royal family of the small kingdom. And Rwagataraka announced that he had received authorization from Musinga himself to take over Gashashi hill in Bukunzi.[38]

Toward the end of 1923, a new A.T. arrived in Cyangugu, who made it his first and urgent priority to conquer the Abakunzi. Shortly afterward, Rwagataraka told the missionaries at Mibirizi that Musinga had granted him control over all the hills of Bukunzi. In the face of these pressures, and hoping to save his kingdom from complete dissolution, Ndagano's son Bigirumwera (who had assumed interim command of Bukunzi) initiated negotiations with the A.T. at Cyangugu. Using the Mibirizi Mission as intermediary, the A.T. informed Bigirumwera that to demonstrate submission he must produce 50 cows as payment for taxes, 25 cows as a penalty, and 30 men every day to cut wood in the forest. Further, he was to surrender the guns possessed by the Abakunzi.

When Bigirumwera proved unable to meet all of the demands within the time specified, the A.T. resolved (in April 1924) to invade Bukunzi and arrest Bigirumwera. The invading force lost its way, even though it was accompanied by Rwagataraka and other Kinyagan chiefs, as well as a Kinyagan guide, who knew the proper paths perfectly well. Bigirumwera managed to escape, while Nyirandakunze and her sons remained hidden. The A.T., empty-handed and chagrined, blamed Rwagataraka and reproached him publicly for having misled the expedition. Bigirumwera, who fled across the border to Murenga (in Bupfureero, Zaïre), never was captured.[39]

Bukunzi was then subjected to a regime of military occupation, an extremely harsh form of rule, which lasted for more than two years (until September 1926). Meanwhile, a few months later the *umwami* of neighboring Busoozo, recognizing the futility of continued resistance, decided to surrender.[40] But it was not until March 1925 that Nyirandakunze and her sons were found. Having managed to wrench information on her whereabouts from a man they had arrested, the Belgians sent a joint European-Kinyagan expedition to attack Nyirandakunze in her cave hideout. She resisted to the last, hurling a spear at the commanding officer of the patrol. The spear missed, and he immediately shot her. Two of her sons were also shot in the fighting, but her son Ngoga surrendered and was sent to prison in Kigali. Several of the Rwandans involved in the expedition suffered injuries, including Rwagataraka, who was wounded on the hand.[41]

Whatever Rwagataraka's intentions in these events,[42] the outcome was indisputably to his benefit. After the "pacification" of Bukunzi, it fell to Rwagataraka to distribute the booty, in the form of cattle and political offices. Both Bukunzi and Busoozo were attached to Impara Province, greatly expanding the geographical limits of Rwagataraka's domain.[43] And as the Belgian regroupment program proceeded and sub-chiefdoms were created from the former smaller administrative units, Rwagataraka exercised a predominant influence in the appointment of subchiefs. Impara Chiefdom, like the former provinces in other areas of Rwanda, came to be organized along clear, hierarchical lines of control. Rwagataraka, as chief of Impara, presided over subchiefs who had been appointed by him, or who had recognized his authority by becoming his clients—and their tenure in office depended on his continued favor. As one Belgian administrator commented of Rwagataraka, "in fact, all the hill subchiefs in Impara are his *abagaragu* (followers) and hold cattle distributed directly by him."[44]

By 1933, most of the land area and population of southwest Rwanda was united administratively under a single authority, the chief of Impara. Only Abiiru chiefdom preserved its own chief, responsible to the king; and even there Rwagataraka was attempting to impose control, by contracting client ties and arranging the appointment of a man chosen by him to be chief of Abiiru.

European support was important in Rwagataraka's ascendance. He was a model chief who fulfilled requests on demand (for tax collection, supplies of food to European ports, recruitment of workers). He cultivated amicable relations with the Catholic missionaries—as, for example, when he facilitated the efforts of Father Delmas to establish a Catholic Mission at Nyamasheke (site of Rwabugiri's residence and later of an Abapari post). He aided European settlers *(colons)* who became an important presence in Kinyaga during the 1920s, and he attempted to maintain cordial relations with Belgian administrators. In return the Europeans reinforced and extended his power.[45] Rwagataraka's charm and helpfulness impressed many of the Europeans with whom he dealt. Alexander Barns, a British zoologist whom Rwagataraka helped with porters and food during his visit to Kinyaga's Nyungwe forest in the early 1920s, described the chief in glowing terms:

When I met this gentleman and got to know him a bit, I at once became his friend as well as his great admirer. He was a prince amongst black peoples. Tall—he is six foot seven—broad-shouldered, yet slim and graceful with the pride of race stamped indelibly upon him, albeit, a touch of wildness and savagery were written there—no guile. When the man smiled he was captivating, for his teeth were white and even and the whole face seemed to shine and the eyes to sparkle—an effect of his brown-black satiny skin. He wore a slight beard and his hair combed up high on his head. He would certainly make a sensation if he came to London with his appearance alone.[46]

In a 1929 report, the Belgian A.T. Cyangugu lavished praise for Rwagataraka's collaboration and competence:

Has the exterior bearing of a great Tuutsi chief. Has uncontested authority over his subjects, all the while preserving an imperturbable calm. Like all Tuutsi chiefs is supple and diplomatic. Has a proven devotion, it would seem, to the European authority. . . . The replacement of Rwagataraka would present a serious social disorder, in the case where his replacement were not as rich as he.[47]

Rwagataraka's policies and European efforts at regroupment had a significant impact on local political configurations in Kinyaga. Administrative consolidation brought together diverse parts of what had been merely a geographical entity with no particular regional identity, and there emerged a conception of "Kinyaga" over and against other regions of Rwanda. Rwagataraka as a dynamic and effective leader became a symbol of Kinyagan pride, however much he may have been resented for particular local policies.

One source of strength for Rwagataraka was the support he could count on in central Rwanda against rivals. There was an inherent interdependence between his hold on a local power base, which aided politicking in the central arena, and his powerful position in central politics which he used to augment his power in Kinyaga. But he, like chiefs before him, was also vulnerable to shifts in power at the center.

THE REASSERTION OF CENTRAL CONTROL

TOWARD THE end of 1931, the Belgian administration made plans to replace *Umwami* Musinga. The Europeans had found their efforts to "modernize" the Rwandan polity hampered by Musinga's steadfast loyalty to ritual obligations and practices. The king was unwilling to adopt the Christian religion, he lacked formal education, and he was suspicious of the Belgian authority. European missionaries, particularly Mgr. Léon Classe, wished to install a younger man who would be more amenable to Catholicism; Classe put pressure on Belgian administrators, some of whom were receptive to the idea that a younger king sympathetic to Western beliefs would more actively cooperate in the colonial enterprise. So it was that on November 12, 1931 the Governor of Ruanda-Urundi decreed that Musinga's reign had come to an end. Two days later, Musinga and a large caravan set out from Nyanza toward Kamembe, in Kinyaga, where the deposed king was to live out his exile; on November 16 Musinga's son Rudahigwa was enthroned as *Umwami* Mutara Rudahigwa. During the ceremonies at Nyanza, one of the chiefs with a major role was Rwagataraka, who delivered an Ikinyarwanda translation of the Governor's speech.[48]

The choice of Kinyaga for the residence-in-exile was significant. Musinga was informed that should he cause any difficulties, he would be sent west of Lake Kivu, outside Rwanda entirely. Moreover it was thought that Rwagataraka, a known rival of the deposed king, would keep a watchful eye on his enemy.[49] Rwagataraka's career had reached its apogee. So influential was he that Kinyagans thought he wished to be king, and some even believed he would be the successor to Musinga.[50]

But during the next ten years Rwagataraka witnessed a gradual decline in his power. After a conflict with the A.T. at Cyangugu in 1934, Rwagataraka was "punished" by the reduction of his domain. The area north of the Mwaga River was removed from Impara to become Cyesha Chiefdom, and Munyakayanza (Abagereka lineage, Abeega clan) became its chief, responsible to the king.[51] This change in chiefdom boundaries in fact restored an earlier administrative division from Rwidegembya's era, and corresponded with cultural differences between the two areas. The partition of Rwagataraka's domain was also a logical extension of the Belgian program to standardize administrative units.

Whatever the logic of the policy, it did nothing to soften the impact for Rwagataraka. Aside from losing territory and revenue, Rwagataraka lost control over appointments of subchiefs in Cyesha—an important form of patronage. The measure forced him to vacate his principal residence at Ishara Peninsula and move south to Shangi, the new center of the Impara chiefdom. Yet the creation of Cyesha was more a symbolic action than a systematic reordering of power relationships. Even without the area north of the Mwaga, Rwagataraka still controlled more land and population than all the other chiefs in Kinyaga. The number of subchiefs under him in 1938 was more than double the total number of his subchiefs in Cyesha and Abiiru chiefdoms, and the number of taxpayers was at least half again as large as the number of taxpayers elsewhere in the region (see table 2). Rwagataraka's power was diminished, but it was by no means destroyed.

Despite the erosion of his influence, the local empire constructed by Rwagataraka was dismantled only after his death (1941) when *Umwami* Rudahigwa moved to install his own men in Kinyaga. In 1942, Impara chiefdom was subdivided again by the creation of Bukunzi-Busoozo-Bugarama Chiefdom, with Etiènne Gitefano, an Ndugan of the Abaya lineage (Abanyiginya clan) as chief. Joseph Bideri—a member of the Abahindiro lineage (Abanyiginya clan) and one of Rudahigwa's favorites—took charge of the remaining portion of Impara chiefdom. Scarcely a year later, Rwagataraka's son, who had commanded briefly in Cyesha, was deposed in favor of a Kinyagan, Ambroise Gakooko, of the Abanama lineage (Abanyiginya clan). Thus, by the end of 1943, three of the four chiefdoms in Kinyaga were led by men of the Abanyiginya clan, and all of these were members of lineages claiming descent from a former king. The only chief not from a royal line was Biniga, chief of Abiiru, who had been appointed during Rwagataraka's time; he was a member of the Abahanya lineage (Abeega clan).[52]

This imposition of Ndugan chiefs was part of a general program pursued by Rudahigwa to restore members of the Abanyiginya clan to power. It was, so to speak, his "revenge" against the Abeega for their

TABLE 2: Distribution of subchiefs, adult men and cattle in Kinyaga by chiefdom, 1938

Chiefdom	Chief	Subchiefs	Adult Men[a]	Cattle[a]
Impara	Rwagataraka	29	10,873	5,198
Bukunzi[b]	Rwagataraka	8	2,795	366
Busoozo[b]	Rwagataraka	5	1,475	219
Total under Rwagataraka		42	15,143	5,783
Cyesha	Munyakayanza	11	5,576	1,373
Abiiru (Sud)	Ntumwa	2	1,035	701
Abiiru (Nord)	Biniga	6	2,935	3,036

[a]Figures refer to number of adult men and cattle that had been counted by 1938.
[b]Bukunzi and Busoozo, although not autonomous chiefdoms, were separate from Impara; in each of these areas, Rwagataraka appointed his own representative, who acted as intermediary to the subchiefs.
SOURCE: Territoire de Shangugu, "Rapport sur le nombre des H.A.V. et gros bétail pour chaque souschefferie," 25 May 1938.

murder of Rutarindwa and their treatment of his father Musinga. The unification of Kinyaga achieved earlier under Rwagataraka facilitated these efforts by Rudahigwa. Rwagataraka had used central Rwandan techniques of imposing and consolidating his control; once the administrative structures of hierarchical command and clientship had been established, it was easier for other central chiefs to take over their operation.

The chiefs appointed by Rudahigwa, perpetuating patterns of rule forged by their predecessors, weeded out incumbent lower officials to make room for their personal followers. One important result at the local level, particularly in the two Kinyagan chiefdoms commanded by Ndugans (Impara and Bukunzi-Busoozo-Bugarama), was an increased percentage of outsiders (non-Kinyagans) as subchiefs. Even where Kinyagans were appointed as subchiefs, they were rarely assigned to their natal hills. The trend was reinforced by the Belgian program (which began in the late 1920s) of replacing uneducated subchiefs with literate *abakaraani*. In the 1930s, after the Ecole des Batutsi at Cyangugu was closed, few Kinyagans obtained access to training in administration (and therefore could not qualify for chiefly posts), while the relative proportions of Ndugans who studied increased.[53]

The imposition of Ndugan chiefs and subchiefs in greater numbers during the reign of Rudahigwa often provoked severe conflicts, contributing to rural discontent. Ndugans attempted to impose clientship and customs from the center; the local population, unaccustomed to such practices, resented these efforts. These changes generated particularly strong reactions in the former kingdoms of Bukunzi and Busoozo, where people had preserved their autonomy well into the colonial period.

Noncooperation on the part of the population was not simply a manifestation of cultural values posing an obstacle to modernization, as some of the political modernization theories of the 1960s might lead us to believe. Colonial statebuilding in Rwanda reinforced and consolidated a process of peasantization, which for many areas of the country had not begun until the reign of Rwabugiri at the end of the nineteenth century or, for regions such as Bukunzi and Busoozo, even later than that. From the perspective of individual rural dwellers, increased government penetration under colonial rule implied a profound rearrangement of opportunities for political and social mobility and changes in security of access to basic economic goods such as land. Understandably, non-ruling groups in Rwanda evaluated (and responded to) dual colonial rule in terms of how these changes affected their lives.

PART II

PATRON–CLIENT POLITICS

5

EARLY CLIENTSHIP

T HE NATURE of clientship in Rwanda has been the focus of a long-standing debate on the characteristics of Rwanda's pre-colonial political system. Most analysts agree that patron–client ties were politically important in the Rwandan state. These analysts disagree, however, on just how clientship was important and on what role patron–client ties played. Some observers have emphasized the integrative functions of patron–client ties in Rwanda; for them, clientship linking persons of different social status served to mitigate the harshness of Tuutsi rule, affording protection and succor to the less powerful in a highly stratified society. Others, stressing the role of power in the Rwandan state, have viewed clientship as a coercive institution, simply one more means by which the powerful could control subordinates and extract services.[1]

Each of these positions contains valid elements but neither is adequate in itself. Until recently the analysis of clientship in Rwanda has been dominated by an intense focus on *ubuhake* clientship to the exclusion of other forms of cattle ties and, most important, of land clientship. These studies often neglected consideration of the significance that these forms of clientship held for human relations—some accounts merely described the mechanisms of creating clientship rather than analyzing its social repercussions. The earlier writings also failed to examine changes in patron–client ties, in the relationships of different types of clientship to each other, and in the wider political context as this affected clientship. Finally, the debate on *ubuhake* tended to portray cattle clientship as a homogeneous institution[2] found in the same form in all regions of Rwanda, and incorporating virtually all men in the society.[3]

To understand the extent and impact of Tuutsi power in Rwanda, we need to explore how clientship relations were transformed in the context of an evolving colonial state. This requires a move away from the exclusive concentration on cattle clientship. We need to account for more diverse types of patron–client ties as well as changes in clientship patterns over time. And we need to see this diversity and these alterations in their relation to state power. As the Rwandan state expanded, clientship patterns in peripheral areas such as Kinyaga were altered in important ways by the growing penetration of political norms and the projection of political power from the center, even as these norms and the exercise of power were themselves being transformed throughout the kingdom. A study of such processes shows how state power, particularly during the European colonial period, served as an active agent creating and maintaining patterns of ethnic and class inequality.

A processual concept of clientship helps account for the diversity of clientship forms over both place and time. As noted previously, I view clientship as an "instrumental friendship" formally established between two persons of relatively unequal socioeconomic status. While in theory both rights and duties of different kinds are incumbent on the two roles, in practice these claims and obligations may vary according to the individual status of the partners and the political context in which the relationship occurs.[4] Conventionally, clientship is said to involve the exchange of protection from the superior partner (the patron) for services of the inferior (the client). It will become evident that during the later period in Kinyaga protection was often not forthcoming, and during the earlier period it was often not so much services that were expected from the client as political support in the context of "alliance."

CLIENTSHIP IN
MID-NINETEENTH-CENTURY KINYAGA

UNTIL THE last part of the nineteenth century, only a small proportion of the population in Kinyaga engaged in patron–client relationships. At the local level, protection and economic security were usually provided by kinship or neighborhood groups and other social institutions such as friendship transfers of cattle and the blood pact. Land for pasturage and cultivation was relatively abundant, and there was little administrative supervision by central authority. The conditions favored a relatively open social framework, making the need for a patron minimal.

Of those patron–client ties that did exist during this period, three major types can be distinguished: direct clientship to the king, *umu-*

heto clientship, and land clientship. In subsequent periods, *umuheto* was abolished, land clientship was substantially altered, and direct clientship to the king was replaced by ties to administrative officials; in fact, royal client ties served as a wedge facilitating the later proliferation of client linkages with other officials.

Clientship to the king linked the local lineage directly with the royal court. Normally the client lineage sent an annual or biennial gift to the king (usually cattle), and one or two of its members would pay court at the king's residence for part of each year. Among Kinyagans interviewed for this study, those who knew of any client ties in their lineage before the reign of Rwabugiri often described these as direct clientship to the king, sometimes claiming that their ancestors immigrated to Kinyaga as emissaries of the royal court. While perhaps influenced by considerations of prestige, many such claims are well-founded; it was in fact the policy of the royal court to send colonizers to peripheral areas, both to establish a political foothold and to reward the king's men with grants of land.[5] Where accounts do not cite evidence of an ancestor's having been sent to Kinyaga by the king, they sometimes claim that the royal court had given cattle to the lineage.[6] Some Kinyagans described in detail the type of linkages their ancestors had with the kings Rwogera or Gahindiro (father and grandfather of Rwabugiri), including gifts and services provided by the lineage as client.

However, to claim direct clientship to the king is sometimes to view this form of client tie as a residual category, one that must have existed in the absence of any other known client ties. Such claims may also reflect identitive commitment to the royal court by pioneers of the frontier region. Most important, since clientship to the king precluded the need for subordination to any intermediary authority, claims of this type imply an assertion of autonomy from local officials.

Umuheto was another form of clientship in which lineages participated as corporate groups. The role of *umuheto* groups in Kinyagan administrative structures has already been discussed, and we shall now consider the client characteristics of the institution. A major function of the *umuheto* tie in mid-nineteenth-century Kinyaga was to link client lineages to *umuheto* patrons living in central Rwanda. The patrons acted as "protectors" for the lineage's cattle while they received certain prestations or services from their client lineages. *Umuheto* was thus in some ways a precursor of *ubuhake* cattle clientship, but there were important differences between the two client forms.

First, in Kinyaga *ubuhake* clientship most commonly linked an individual to his patron,[7] while *umuheto* clientship normally linked a lineage as a group, not as individuals, to an *umuheto* chief or his delegate. Second, *ubuhake* clientship as it was introduced to Kinyaga in the late nineteenth century involved the cession of a cow in usufruct from a patron to his client; *umuheto* clientship, on the other hand, involved the gift of a cow at regular intervals from a client lineage to its *umuheto* patron.

This latter distinction was important. It means that *umuheto* clientship in Kinyaga was initially limited to lineages possessing cattle, since during the early years it was the client lineage which was the cattle donor. Moreover, in *ubuhake* the transfer of the cow from patron to client symbolized the dependency of the client and ultimately (at a later period) exposed his personal cattle to potential confiscation at the pleasure of the patron. In the early *umuheto* relationship, by contrast, a client's personal cattle were rarely taken as long as the transfer of the cow was effected. In short, while originally they resembled each other the different forms of cattle transfer influenced the later evolution of the two institutions. While both became exploitative, *ubuhake* was adapted to broader and more arbitrary forms of exploitation.

Kagame's study of social army organization indicates that new social armies were formed at the beginning of each new royal reign, but previous social armies normally retained their corporate status. The king appointed *umuheto* chiefs, who were then authorized to select lineages or portions of lineages to be included in the new armies.[8] The commonly accepted model of Rwandan administrative structures implies that all Rwandans were incorporated into social armies (*umuheto* groups).[9] Clearly this situation had not been realized in pre-Rwabugiri Kinyaga. Many Kinyagans insist that *umuheto* did not become widespread in the region until the reign of Rwabugiri and after; even then, it affected only those lineages specifically selected for *umuheto*, not the entire population.[10]

Data on the recruitment process before the reign of Rwabugiri are scanty, but generally informants attribute early *umuheto* clientship of a lineage to its wealth in cattle, or to the preservation by earlier immigrants to Kinyaga of *umuheto* ties that had been formed in their home regions. Their wealth in cattle as well as the higher status implied by their *umuheto* ties qualified such lineages as Tuutsi. As one Kinyagan put it, the chiefs of central Rwanda "sought to find a Tuutsi and his cattle; . . . each pursued the section of which he had received command and they looked for the cattle-owners."[11]

The data available afford no examples of attempts to refuse *umuheto* clientship in the early- and mid-nineteenth century, though examples of such resistance are clearly remembered for later periods. There is a similar absence of data concerning potential conflict between different chiefs who might have tried to select the same lineage.

For the reigns of Rwabugiri and Musinga information on the recruitment process and patterns of competition and conflict between patrons reveals tensions between *umuheto* patrons and other powerful officials—land chiefs and *ubuhake* patrons. During this later period, it was difficult for Kinyagans to refuse overtures from an *umuheto* patron or to avoid *umuheto* altogether.[12] In these cases, success in recruitment of clients rested to an important extent on the relative political power of the potential patrons who sought to incorporate Kinyaga into the wider political arena of the Rwandan central court during and after the time of Rwabugiri.

The limited extent of early *umuheto* ties, as well as the informants' direct accounts, suggest that such clientship initially symbolized prestige and status. *Umuheto* ties to a central chief enhanced the status of a lineage and brought opportunities for political prominence through linkages to the center. Surely the threat of sanctions was not entirely absent. But central government administration in Kinyaga was as yet in embryo form in the early nineteenth century. The sanctions which could be effectively brought to bear against entrenched lineages in remote areas were limited or nonexistent; at this period voluntary association with *umuheto* clientship seems to have been more frequent than coerced participation. On the other hand, if *umuheto* clientship implied status and prestige, it also implied an acceptance of central authority on a broader basis and hence seems also to have signaled an erosion of political autonomy. These considerations are evident in the experience of the Abazirimo lineage as recounted by a very old Kinyagan named Yoboka. He explained that his fourth-generation ancestor, Nzirimo, had no *umuheto* patron:

> It was his children who had *umuheto* chiefs. They received as their chief Rugagi, who had been given command over Nzirimo's lineage. It was during Rwogera's reign that chiefs were distributed. For *ingabo* [*umuheto*] the Abazirimo were called Abazimya. Formerly they had depended on no one. They became subjects of Rwogera, whereas in the past they had been independent and no one had held command over anyone else.[13]

Umuheto obligations were limited in scope. Most commonly, a client lineage was expected to send a cow to the *umuheto* patron at intervals of one or two years. The *umuheto* cow *(inka y'umuheto)*

symbolized the lineage's submission to its patron and ensured the protection of the lineage's cattle *(imbaata)*.[14] In addition to the *umuheto*
cow, some client lineages performed annual courtship *(gufat'igihe)* during which a representative of the lineage would spend some months of
each year at the residence of the *umuheto* patron. Duties included
accompanying the patron in his daily travels, repairing the fence of the
patron's residence, or serving him in other ways. The *umuheto* client
lineage could also be called upon to send a member to fight in wars,
should the social army be mobilized for active military service.[15]

The ideal conduct of an *umuheto* chief consisted of a complex of
obligations toward members of the social army, including intervention
to aid a client accused of theft. Generosity in distribution of cattle was
also a desirable quality. But the primary role of the *umuheto* patron
was to protect the client lineage's cattle. According to central court
tradition, all cattle which would normally be considered personal property *(imbaata* or *ingwate* cattle, obtained through marriage payment,
gift, purchase, or reward for bravery in battle) were known as the "king's
cattle" *(inka z'umwami)*, and hence could be confiscated by delegates
of the king. From the perspective of the central court again, cattle belonging to members of a social army *(umuheto* client lineages) were
supposed to be grouped in named "cattle armies," also under the jurisdiction of the social army *(umuheto)* chief.[16]

Kinyagan lineages associated with *umuheto* clientship tended not to
be concerned with such distinctions. To them, the *umuheto* tie represented a type of insurance for the continued possession of their personal cattle. The "protection" afforded by the *umuheto* patron was
usually indirect; so long as a lineage preserved good relations with its
patron, no other chief would be likely to threaten the lineage's cattle.
But in cases where a member of a client lineage became involved in
litigation over cattle, the *umuheto* patron was expected to intervene
on his client's behalf.[17]

Once established, the *umuheto* tie usually endured over several generations; the relationship which developed between an *umuheto* patron
and members of his client lineage was one of mutual respect, often
characterized by strong affective ties.[18] Although Kinyagan client lineages were not prominent in the national political arena, their wealth,
local status, and kin connections nevertheless gave them a favorable
bargaining position in the client–patron relationship. The payments or
services required of *umuheto* clients were moderate, and these responsibilities were shared by the lineage as a group. Because *umuheto* pa-

trons of Kinyagan lineages in the mid-nineteenth century normally lived outside the local region, they found it difficult to impose overly burdensome exactions in any consistent fashion.

LAND CLIENTSHIP

CONTROL OVER land in pre-Rwabugiri Kinyaga was normally vested in lineages. Although land clientship was practiced in some forms these were of only minor significance in determining access to land. Nevertheless, land clientship will be considered here because the early role of land patrons appears as a prototype of the role assumed by political authorities in subsequent periods. The growth of central administrative penetration in Kinyaga was reflected to a large degree in political control over land; as authorities appointed from above extended and consolidated their power, certain of the obligations which had earlier been associated with land clientship (to private land patrons) came to be imposed in a regular fashion on the general population (subject to "political" patrons).

The two principal types of land tenure in mid-nineteenth century Kinyaga were *ubukonde* (land which had been cleared and settled by the lineage occupying it or their ancestors) and *igikingi* (land held by a cattle-owning lineage, granted by the king or another political official).[19] As used in Kinyaga, the term *ubukonde* generally referred to land which had not been received from a political authority, and which had been occupied for many years by the same lineage.[20] Immigrants to the region who received land from lineages holding *ubukonde* land would become land clients *(abagereerwa)* and they would be expected to contribute certain food products to the donor lineage as a form of rent.[21] Land clients sometimes worked for one or two days per five-day week for their land patron, but it appears that this was only casually enforced, and was shared among the client lineage as a group.

Social relations between land patrons and their clients were characterized by strong affective ties; outsiders who received land on the *ubukonde* domain enjoyed the position of a "relative of inferior rank."[22] Even this subordinate status could disappear over time, as land clients often forged close ties to the donor lineage through neighborhood friendships, or marriage alliance.[23] The descendants of those who married into the lineage would sometimes come to be recognized members of the donor kin group. A practice of imposing an excessive demand for marriage payment encouraged such adoption of children into the donor lineage. The *ubukonde* patron would demand a cow as marriage payment for his daughter; the suitor would pay several hoes, promising to produce the cow later. As the young man could rarely come up with the promised cow, his children would remain legal members of their mother's lineage, since the bridewealth had not been paid in full.[24]

During the 1930s, it was reported that the obligations of land clients consisted of giving a portion of the harvest to land patrons, and gifts of beer from time to time. However, these obligations were carried out only erratically, and boundaries of agricultural land other than banana plantations were neither carefully demarcated nor rigidly enforced.[25] While this situation may have resulted from changes during the colonial period, evidence about early land clientship in Kinyaga suggests that the casual nature of land clientship obligations represented a continuation of precolonial practices.[26]

Another form of land clientship was associated with *igikingi* holdings, containing land suitable for pasturage of cattle. Such domains were held by cattle-owning lineages and by political officials (who generally had cattle). In addition to pasturage, an *igikingi* (pl. *ibikingi*) normally included agricultural land cultivated by the proprietor lineage and any land clients attached to that lineage. The king granted rights over an *igikingi* to his army chiefs and other favorites; they in turn could grant portions to subordinates.[27] The recipient of an *igikingi* exercised total jurisdiction within the boundaries of his "domain," so that groups or individuals who came to settle within the *igikingi* became the "clients" of the proprietor, and, presumably, no administrative official was authorized to interfere with the proprietor's jurisdiction over these clients. *Ingobyi* was a smaller portion of land held by a cattle-owner, normally sufficient only for the single lineage to which it was granted.[28]

The proprietor of an *igikingi* could permit others, Tuutsi as well as Hutu, to live within the domain; they furnished, in return, certain obligatory prestations. Cattle-owning Tuutsi who lived within the *igikingi* and grazed their cattle on *igikingi* land were expected to aid in the construction and maintenance of the proprietor's enclosure, and to perform other duties relating to care of the proprietor's cattle. Hutu contributed agricultural labor or other services to their land "patron." Need for protection was sometimes important in seeking *igikingi* land clientship. Such was the putative motivation for Hutu to take up residence on one *igikingi* near the Rusizi River; by grouping themselves around the land "patron," they obtained protection from raids by Shi coming from the western bank of the river.[29]

The appearance of *ibikingi* marked an important development in Rwandan political organization. This institution was of relatively recent origin; it did not become common in the central regions of the kingdom until early in the nineteenth century (during the reign of Rwabugiri's grandfather Yuhi Gahindiro)[30] and was introduced to peripheral areas such as Kinyaga only much later. Although Kinyagans are familiar with the meaning of *igikingi*, traditions are vague about such grants for the nineteenth century; it is probable that *igikingi* and *ingobyi* land holdings were rare in the region until the time of Rwabugiri. Indeed, many Kinyagans assert that until late in the nineteenth century control over land depended on the right of occupation. Specified rights over pasture were allocated only to a few hills in Impara and Abiiru that were settled by cattle-owning lineages with links to central Rwanda.

In pre-Rwabugiri Kinyaga, land clientship, whether on *ubukonde* or *igikingi* domains, was less important than other forms of land tenure. Lineages holding *ubukonde* land or *igikingi* land did not necessarily have clients.[31] Moreover, although immigration to Kinyaga by people from central Rwanda dated from at least the eighteenth century, informants maintain that until the reign of Rwabugiri there was still unoccupied land available. Thus, immigrants coming to Kinyaga often could mark out their own domains, not being constrained to enter into land clientship. Land could also be obtained through purchase in some parts of the region.[32] Early land clientship was practiced mainly by those having limited resources, needing protection, and lacking kin to assist them. Thus the control over land later obtained by political authorities from central Rwanda and the exactions imposed on Kinyagans as the price for continued occupation of their land must be seen as innovations, representing a major departure from past practices.

CLIENTSHIP DURING THE REIGN OF RWABUGIRI

IN PRE-RWABUGIRI Kinyaga economic and political security could usually be obtained by means other than clientship. Alternatives included ownership of land, protected by membership in a kin group exercising jurisdiction over the land, and personal ownership of cattle, obtained by marriage transfer payment, gift of friends, or purchase. Friendship exchanges of cattle between persons of relatively equal status were also common.[33] The local kin group could normally deal with threats to security of ownership, although for some cattle-owning lineages, clientship to an *umuheto* patron assured additional protection of herds.

Thus, clientship in Kinyaga during most of the nineteenth century was restricted in both its geographical extent and the proportion of the population affected. Most people remained autonomous from any of the forms of clientship described above. Many Kinyagans maintain that their ancestors arrived in Kinyaga without any clientship ties, either as patrons or clients. Some Hutu acquired land clients, others did not. Although some cattleowners acquired clients, many others tended to their own cattle and fields without seeking clients to work for them. In fact, the more status-conscious Tuutsi from the central regions of the country were frequently astonished by the relatively simple lifestyles of Tuutsi in southwestern Rwanda, and their willingness to attend to their own needs without servants.[34] Under these circumstances, the negotiating position of clients was relatively favorable. This situation was to change significantly under Rwabugiri and his successors.

We have seen that during Rwabugiri's reign, central Rwandan administrative structures were established in Kinyaga and new chiefs were introduced from outside the region.[35] Associated with these changes came alterations in clientship. *Umuheto* links were extended and altered, while two new forms of clientship were introduced: *ubuhake* clientship, and *ubureetwa*. These appeared in Kinyaga only with central administration; they thus came to be identified with rule by Nduga, and to symbolize loss of the autonomy formerly enjoyed by many lineages of the region.

These new developments, heralding significant alterations in the political arena, were initiated in Kinyaga by Ntiizimira, who, as we have seen, rose from relative obscurity to a position of power and fame under Rwabugiri's patronage. It was he who extended *umuheto* in Kinyaga, who introduced *ubureetwa*, and who laid the groundwork for the extension of *ubuhake*. The king first appointed Ntiizimira chief of a region north of Kinyaga, including Rubengera, site of the first and most important royal capital in the west (in present-day Kibuye Prefecture). Later, Ntiizimira extended his domain southward, gaining command over the Impara social army, as *umuheto* chief, and of the Impara province, as *ubutaka* (land) chief. He thus controlled a continuous area stretching along Lake Kivu from the Koko River in the north (now the boundary between Kibuye and Gisenyi Prefectures) to the Rusizi River in the south.[36]

Ntiizimira has been described as "like a brother" to the king, and "so favored that he was lauded in proverbs."[37] The origin of his special relationship with Rwabugiri is unclear. One explanation suggests that Rwabugiri was indebted to Ntiizimira for having cured him of leprosy, and that the king gave him Kinyaga as a reward.[38] Another account views the grant as a recognition of heroism in war.[39] Most probably, however, Ntiizimira was elevated by Rwabugiri to counteract the power of established chiefs, leaders of the traditionally influential lineages of the kingdom. Owing his wealth and status to the favor of the king, Ntiizimira was initially more dependent on the royal court than were those chiefs whose prestige derived at least in part from their family connections. Rwabugiri's appointment of Ntiizimira to govern such a vast territory is understandable in the context of a policy of centralization. Attempting to limit the autonomy of traditionally powerful groups, the king recruited and rewarded persons who were closely dependent on him. Yet if such chiefs began to acquire an independent power base, they were expendable.[40]

A native of Budaha (Kibuye Prefecture), Ntiizimira came to Kinyaga as a stranger with virtually no local ties. Accompanying him were several relatives and other followers who were members of the social army company *(umutwe)* Imbanzamihigo, the group Ntiizimira recruited when he received command of Rubengera district.[41] Ntiizimira used these followers, many of whom were his relatives, to establish control in the northern part of Impara region, later known as Cyesha.[42]

Other, non-Kinyagan representatives of Ntiizimira accompanied the chief into the region or arrived on their own. One of these, Rukeezamuheto, a native of Bukonya, represented Ntiizimira at Kagano. Muragizi, from Gisaka (on Rwanda's eastern border) also commanded several hills for Ntiizimira.[43] Strong backing from the central court, as well as control over substantial material resources (principally herds of cattle and political offices), permitted Ntiizimira to enlarge progressively this early core of supporters.[44]

Ntiizimira used the *umuheto* institution to attract collaborators among Kinyagans and to augment prestations for the court. Particularly in central and southern Impara, he appointed representatives from wealthy Kinyagan families, instructing them to collect *umuheto* prestations from designated lineages. These representatives often delegated the actual collection to others, and so a hierarchy of authority emerged. It was customary for officials at each level to take out a "taste" *(umusogongero)*, or portion of the prestations, which constituted their reward. This provided an incentive for individuals to seek appointment and, once appointed, to augment the number of lineages paying prestations.

Under Ntiizimira, many cattle-owning lineages previously without any *umuheto* patron thus had to begin giving an annual *umuheto* cow. More important, Ntiizimira, through his delegates, recruited non-cattle-owning lineages into *umuheto* companies. Unable to give cows, these lineages (referred to as "Hutu") contributed hoes or luxury items such as sleeping mats, *ubutega* fiber bracelets, *ikirungu* snake bones, animal pelts.[45]

A Kinyagan will often date the introduction of *umuheto* clientship in the region to the time of the chief who commanded when his own lineage was incorporated into an *umuheto* company. For some this occurred under Ntiizimira; for others it was under Ntiizimira's successors, Rwabirinda and Rwidegembya. Those whose lineages were incorporated into *umuheto* companies for the first time during this period portray such membership as an extra burden imposed on them which served to enrich the chiefs, but was of little advantage to those recruited.

It was difficult to reject the authority of an *umuheto* patron, but escape was sometimes possible through forging client ties with another powerful person—sometimes the direct superior of the local *umuheto* representative. The following account, referring to a period shortly after Ntiizimira's demise, suggests the kind of maneuvering that occurred.

> When my grandfather went to Rwidigembya—this was in the time of Rwabirinda—they had just put us in the Akamarashavu [*umuheto* group]. Then my father gave them a cow of the color *urwirungu*. They refused it, because it was a heifer; they wanted him to give a milk cow—the mother of this heifer. It was then that my grandfather fled and took refuge with Rwidegembya who was on a [military] expedition at the place called Gacucu. When he returned from Gacucu, Rwidegembya said to Nyankiiko, 'Don't bother my Hutu any more, he's a client like the rest of you, he's one of mine as well.' This was how we separated ourselves from the *umuheto* [demands]. That's what it was like, when you didn't go to [pay court to] Rwidigembya you became a slave of *umuheto*.[46]

For this Kinyagan, the way to escape *umuheto* was to bypass Nyankiiko, the local representative exercising authority over the Akamarashavu group, and seek the direct patronage of Nyankiiko's superior, Rwidegembya.[47]

Perhaps the greatest source of fame (or infamy) for Ntiizimira in Kinyaga was his imposition of control over land. When Ntiizimira came to the region, most Kinyagans held land through the right of occupation; they or their ancestors had cleared their fields or obtained them through purchase or friendly agreement from those who had arrived earlier. By what right then, Kinyagans asked, could a chief such as Ntiizimira claim authority over their land?

Oral accounts from Kinyaga generally concur that prestations for land *(amakoro y'ubutaka)* and *ubureetwa,* a form of clientship involving manual labor for a hill chief, were introduced to the region during the time of Ntiizimira.[48] Although land prestations and *ubureetwa* did resemble in some respects the earlier forms of land clientship to an *ubukonde* proprietor or agricultural work for an *igikingi* holder,[49] Kinyagans see these demands as innovations, significantly different from what came before. Most accounts are less clear on how such authority over the land was acquired, but Yoboka provided insights on the process as it occurred at Muramba hill in the northern part of Impara.[50]

Yoboka explained that members of his lineage had occupied their land at Muramba for at least two generations before Ntiizimira arrived in Kinyaga. Nzirimo, Yoboka's fourth-generation ancestor and founder of the Abazirimo lineage, had left Butumbi in Ndorwa (northern Rwanda) seeking grazing land for his cattle. He made his way to Buremo in present-day Kibuye Prefecture, while some of his sons moved on south to Kinyaga, one of them settling at Muramba.

As noted above, the lineage was incorporated into the Abazimya social army during the reign of Rwogera; at that time, Rugagi commanded the Abazimya, so the Abazirimo became Rugagi's *umuheto* clients. The lineage began sending Rugagi a cow for *umuheto* at regular intervals; these animals were contributed by the lineage as a corporate group (regardless of where members of the lineage lived) through the intermediary of Ryingoma, their lineage head at the time. The *umuheto* ties linking the Abazirimo to Rugagi and later to Rugagi's son Nyandekwe continued to operate through to the end of Rwabugiri's reign.

But when Ntiizimira arrived he imposed an additional form of prestations on lineage members. At Muramba, Ntiizimira prevented the Abazirimo from pasturing their cattle on the lineage land. In order to graze their cattle, they were compelled to offer Ntiizimira an *"ubutaka* cow"* (cow for the land). Ntiizimira then "granted" the lineage an *igikingi* domain—consisting of the land they already occupied and used.

Yoboka explained that Ntiizimira not only required a cow for *ubutaka,* but also demanded the cow from local residential units (regardless of lineage ties). Thus, Abazirimo living at Muramba had to give one cow for their land; other Abazirimo living farther south at Rwahi also had to give a cow, and so on. This represented an important change from the *umuheto* form of prestations which had required only one cow from the lineage as a corporate group. Other lineages at Muramba, poorer and unable to give a cow for *ubutaka,* had to contribute food prestations, and to work for Ntiizimira's local representative for two days out of each five-day week.[51]

According to Yoboka, Kinyagans were reluctant to recognize Ntiizimira's authority, for he made them give prestations for the land and work for the chiefs, practices to which they were not accustomed. At Bitare, a hill several kilometers south of Muramba, Ntiizimira met with stiff resistance. People there, preferring to retain their autonomy, resented having an outsider impose such demands on them. A certain Rutamu son of Rukiza led his lineage in open revolt. Ntiizimira sent his men to attack the recalcitrants, overcoming them and "forcing them to work" *(kuganduura).* Ntiizimira met with similar resistance at Muraza hill, and dealt with it in similar fashion. After these incidents, people in other areas submitted, giving Ntiizimira the prestations demanded.[52] Thus, although overt resistance was not widespread, it is clear that prestations for the land were imposed by force, or at least the threat of force. Rebellion did resurface later, however, in events associated with Seevumba.

As provincial chief, Ntiizimira and his delegates posed as distributors of the land (a kind of legal fiction) and required of their "beneficiaries" the payment in cattle or food and services that had traditionally been the perquisites of a land patron. In Kinyaga, however, land clientship had been neither very common nor, where it occurred, very rigid. The idea that chiefs should control the land was new; so also was the insistence that regular prestations and services be delivered to these chiefs. It was also at this time that *ubureetwa* was introduced in Kinyaga—the gifts of beer and manual labor for chiefs which later became a hated symbol of Tuutsi rule.

Ntiizimira used coercion to implement his goals, but he relied on persuasion as well. He recruited allies among wealthy local families, incorporating one or more of their members into his elite corps, the Imbanzamihigo. Those who cooperated received substantial material benefits. Participating in military expeditions under Ntiizimira's leadership, they might achieve fame and gain booty as war heroes. As favored supporters, they received official authorization to collect land prestations on one or more hills, or authority over a group of lineages for *umuheto;* sometimes a single delegate combined both roles. In addition to providing opportunities for the client to increase his wealth, these positions also permitted him to expand his own following. Some of the families coopted by Ntiizimira achieved prominence in this manner for several of their members, not only for the lineage head. And some clients acquired their own elite corps of supporters, thus replicating the pattern by which their patron increased his power.[53]

All whom Ntiizimira appointed to positions in the administrative hierarchy were regarded as his clients (*abagaragu*). The nature of the ties linking patron and client is not entirely clear, but there are indications that elements of both *umuheto* and embryonic *ubuhake* forms were present. One Kinyagan described Imbanzamihigo, Ntiizimira's corps of followers, as a section of *intoore* (the close followers of a chief recruited as youths for social and military training), pointing out that each member of the group gave a cow to Ntiizimira every year.[54] According to this account, the linkage resembled an *umuheto* tie.

For some Kinyagan lineages membership in Imbanzamihigo clearly did have the character of *umuheto* clientship. The Abadegede lineage, for example, had been *umuheto* clients of Seerutabura until Ntiizimira's arrival in Kinyaga. When Seerutabura was deposed and Ntiizimira inherited his position as chief of the Impara social army, he became *umuheto* patron of the Abadegede.[55] Since this lineage had been *umuheto* clients of Ntiizimira's predecessor their *umuheto* patron changed with changes in command of the social army.

The situation was more complicated, however, when a Kinyagan lineage possessed previous *umuheto* ties to a patron who commanded not the Impara, but some other social army. Under Rwabugiri, lineages normally preserved their earlier *umuheto* ties, assuring protection of their cattle by the former *umuheto* patron. But a lineage needed pasturage for its cattle, and perhaps individual members had ambitions to gain political power as land chiefs. Ntiizimira controlled the land, and it was he who appointed land chiefs. Thus, such lineages often found it advantageous to establish some kind of alliance with Ntiizimira, probably by having one or more of their members recruited into the Imbanzamihigo. In such a case, if the tie linking a lineage member to Ntiizimira is characterized as *umuheto*, then the lineage had two *umuheto* patrons, which served perhaps as one means of splitting a lineage. Alternatively, it was an embryonic form of *ubuhake* clientship.

Ntiizimira's Imbanzamihigo company thus resembled an *umuheto* group, but it also showed similarities to *ubuhake*. This was reflected particularly in the role of hill chief positions sometimes associated with membership in the Imbanzamihigo. Even for those lineages linked to Ntiizimira through *umuheto* ties, there were advantages in gaining hill chief positions. But in later periods these positions were invariably contingent on *ubuhake* links; their association with the early Imbanzamihigo company therefore can be taken to indicate the presence of certain *ubuhake* elements.

In fact, early *umuheto* links represented by Imbanzamihigo can be seen to have facilitated the later emergence of *ubuhake* ties. It is not clear whether a cow was always transferred from patron to client in such a relationship in the time of Ntiizimira. However, later (under Ntiizimira's successors, Rwabirinda and Rwidegembya) favored *ubuhake* clients did receive a cow, or a herd of cattle. A number of Kinyagans today believe that all members of a chief's elite company, such as the Imbanzamihigo of Ntiizimira, had received cows directly from the patron. This view may reflect subsequent practices rather than the original character of the chief's elite company, but it suggests that the patron–client tie involved was an embryonic form of *ubuhake*. In this context, the introduction of *ubuhake* in Kinyaga was associated with the acquisition of control over land by political authorities, in a process parallel to the one which occurred earlier in central and southern Rwanda.[56]

Clientship under Ntiizimira may indeed have been less institutionalized than portrayed in this *post facto* formal analysis. It is, however, less important to know the precise label attached to clientship under Ntiizimira than to understand the nature of the relationship involved. Evidence on this latter question is clear. The early ties between patron and client under Ntiizimira were bonds of alliance, characterized by mutual respect. Clientship was of relatively limited extent, still involving only a minority of the population. Clients enjoyed high status and a favorable bargaining position vis-à-vis their patron, Ntiizimira. These conditions favored a situation where clients derived significant benefits from the relationship, and in which the demands a patron made were limited.

The Abeerekande lineage, living at Nyarushiishi hill and neighboring areas in the Impara region of Kinyaga, provides a good illustration of the advantages to be gained through early clientship. They were one of the older Rwandan families in the region, enjoying wealth and status even before the arrival of Ntiizimira. The Abeerekande later extended their power through skillful use of alliance ties to superiors, originally to the king, and later to Ntiizimira and his successors. By about 1911, when Rwagataraka entered the region, the Abeerekande had become one of the most powerful lineages in Kinyaga.

The founder of the Abeerekande lineage, Mwerekande, came from Gisaka to settle at Nyarushiishi hill in Kinyaga during the reign of Yuhi Gahindiro. He is said to have been a client of the king, charged with helping the court to annex Kinyaga.[57] Mwerekande's grandson, Rwanya-mugabo, was head of the lineage when Ntiizimira came to Kinyaga. Entering into client ties with Ntiizimira, and preserving earlier client-ship links to the royal court, Rwanyamugabo assured his lineage a prominent position in the later politics of Kinyaga. The client ties and political offices of some members of the lineage are indicated in figure 2, below.

Even though the data on the Abeerekande are incomplete, certain patterns can be discerned. Until Rwabugiri's reign, clientship to the royal court was the dominant form for this lineage. Both Mwerekande's son, Kanywabahizi, and his grandson, Rwanyamugabo, received a herd of cattle from the king. But from the time of Rwanyamugabo the focus began to shift, and client ties to central chiefs appointed to govern the region began first to supplement, and later to replace, the links to the royal court. The descendants of Rwanyamugabo, for example, claim that he had client ties to the king and to Ntiizimira, as well as to the two chiefs who took power after Ntiizimira's demise (Rwabirinda and Rwidegembya). During the time of Rwanyamugabo's son, Nyankiiko (roughly the period of German rule and early Belgian rule) the family developed a dense network of ties to Rwidegembya, and later to his son Rwagataraka. Nyankiiko took over authority for his father's *ubuhake* and *umuheto* clients after the death of Rwanyamugabo in the war against the Abapari. He and his brothers and cousins commanded a total of at least eleven hills in Kinyaga for Rwidegembya. It is interest-ing, however, that although not all Nyankiiko's brothers held command of specific hills, at least six of them each received a herd of cattle from Rwidegembya, whom they recognized as their patron.

The nature of ties between the Abeerekande and another prominent Kinyagan lineage, the Abadegede, is revealing. The head of the Abade-gede, Seekabaraga, was also a favored client of Rwidegembya. Like Nyankiiko, he and other members of his lineage gained status and wealth through client ties to chiefs such as Rwidegembya and, as we shall see, to Europeans. Patron–client ties between the Abeerekande and the Abadegede were relatively rare. But the families were closely allied through marriage ties. Nyankiiko's cousins Ndaayi and Nyirin-

gango each married a sister of Seekabaraga. Nyankiiko's brother Karama
married a sister of Seekabaraga's paternal uncle, and Karama's son Nzogera married Seekabaraga's only daughter. As our data on marriage ties
of the Abeerekande are incomplete, these examples probably underrepresent the number of marriage links between the two families.

For Ntiizimira, continued tenure in office depended upon his ability
to collect prestations and produce manpower for military service and
the construction and maintenance of royal capitals. To aid in imple-
menting his policies, he recruited supporters among wealthy Kinyagan
lineages. For such lineages, alliance with Ntiizimira offered the chance
to broaden their political network; they could expect not only enhanced
prestige but also greater access to resources with which to enlarge their
personal followings—increased power in the local context.

Early *ubuhake* contracts thus provided both parties considerable benefits; they can properly be viewed as a form of alliance. While not a
contract among equals, *ubuhake* surely represented in the eyes of both
parties a bond of elites, and it was based more upon a positive attempt
by a client to maximize his power position than upon fear of refraining.
It is not clear whether central chiefs sought out clients who already
enjoyed local status, or whether local status resulted from client ties.
What is important is that the two aspects were closely related: early
ubuhake clientship linked elites; it was not a simple exploitation of
subordinates.

In terms of the debate mentioned at the beginning of this chapter,
early clientship in Kinyaga conformed more to an integrationist interpretation than a coercive interpretation. However, this occurred in a
specific political context, where the power of patrons was limited,
where local corporate groups (lineages) were still important political
units enjoying substantial autonomy, and where central government
penetration was still embryonic. When extended to the less powerful,
institutions which initially displayed integrative elements evolved into
forms (such as *ubureetwa*) which were essentially exploitative. These
changes in clientship were an integral part of the transformations associated with statebuilding in Rwanda, especially during the European
colonial period. Increasing government penetration effected important
changes in the status of local corporate groups while it enhanced the
power of chiefs, and altered the balance of exchange between partners
in the patron–client relationship. Ironically, the institution which
served as a major instrument in this statebuilding process, *ubuhake*,
was itself molded and transformed in the changed political context. It
is to these concerns that we now turn.

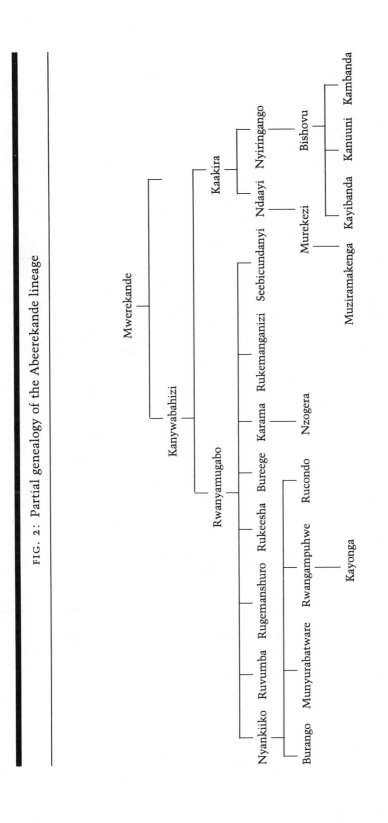

FIG. 2: Partial genealogy of the Abeerekande lineage

NOTES TO FIGURE 2

Mwerekande—came to Kinyaga as emissary of *Umwami* Gahindiro, to help annex the region to Rwanda. Settled at Nyarushiishi.[58]

Kanywabahizi—client of *Umwami* Gahindiro, from whom he received a herd of cattle. Lived at Nyarushiishi.[59]

Rwanyamugabo—client of *Umwami* Rwabugiri, from whom he received the cattle herd Izirunyinya. Also a client and favorite of Ntiizimira, with whom he participated in military expeditions. Played an important role in the conquest of Ijwi Island, achieving fame as a military hero.

Became favorite client of Rwidegembya after fall of Ntiizimira. Commanded several hills, as *ubutaka* (land) chief, representative first of Ntiizimira, later of Rwabirinda. Included among the hills he is said to have commanded were Nyamugari, Nyarushiishi, Gabiro, Gihinga, Nyamuhunga, Rubayi.

The favorite clients of Rwanyamugabo were organized into a section called Abahuurambuga. His *umuheto* group, which included companies of Hutu, was called Abakemba or Abahuurambuga. Such *ubuhake* and *umuheto* clients of Rwanyamugabo resided in different parts of Kinyaga, in Abiiru as well as Impara.

Married his daughter, Nyiragore, to Seekabaraga (Abadegede, Abeega). Famous in Kinyaga for his heroic resistance and death during the Abapari invasion.[60]

Kaakira—married his daughter to Seekabaraga, son of Bihutu (Abadegede, Abeega). No information on client ties.[61]

Nyankiiko—lineage head and most prominent of Rwanyamugabo's sons. Succeeded to his father's position as client of the royal court, under Rwabugiri and Musinga; is said to have participated also in the attacks against Ijwi. Also a favorite client of Rwidegembya; later became client of Rwagataraka. Took over from his father the Abahuurambuga and Abakemba *ubuhake* and *umuheto* clients.

Commanded several hills as *ubutaka* representative first of Rwabirinda, later of Rwidegembya. Among these hills were Nyamugari (where Nyankiiko lived), Bigutu, Rubaayi, Gabiro, Bitare, Nyarushiishi, Mutimasi, Biguzi, Munyove. In addition Rwidegembya appointed him chief of part of Rusenyi region (north of the Kilimbi River, present Kibuye Prefecture), where Nyankiiko constructed a residence at Karora.[62]

Ruvumba—client of Rwidegembya from whom he received the herd Umuhoozi; later, a favorite client of Rwagataraka. Received command of Nyamavugo as *ubutaka* representative of Seekabaraga.[63]

Rugemanshuro—client of Rwidegembya, from whom he received a herd of cattle.[64]

Rukeesha—client of Rwidegembya, from whom he received a herd of cattle. Represented his brother Nyankiiko at Gihanga, where he collected prestations.[65]

Bureege—client of Rwidegembya, who gave him a herd of cattle. Later, a favorite of Rwagataraka. He succeeded his brother Ruvumba as representative of Seekabaraga at Nyamavugo hill. He was later deposed, to be replaced by Ntaabukiraniro, younger brother of Seekabaraga.[66]

Karama—client of Rwidegembya, from whom he received a herd of cattle; lived at Rubaayi; married daughter of Gashuuhe, son of Bigaruranshuro (Abadegede, Abeega).[67]

Rukemanganizi—client of Rwagataraka, who gave him a herd of cattle. Lived at Nyamugari.[68]

Seebicundanyi—client of Rwubusisi (Abakagara lineage, Abeega clan), who gave him a herd of cattle. When Kayondo (first cousin, father's brother's son of Rwubusisi) received Nyamugari and Shagasha hills, he appointed Seebucundanyi as his representative on them.[69]

Nyiringango—client of Rwidegembya, member of Imbanzamihigo. Rwidegembya appointed him representative for *ubutaka* at Mubumbano hill; later he was a client and diviner *(umupfumu)* of Rwagataraka. It is said that Nyiringango was one of the most favored clients of Rwagataraka. Both Nyiringango and his brother, Ndaayi, married daughters of Bihutu, who were thus sisters of Seekabaraga (Abadegede, Abeega). Nyiringango gave one of his daughters in marriage to Rukoro, son of Gisazi (Abajonge, Abashambo), a chief in Bugarama region.[70]

Buranga—inherited position of lineage head from his father Nyankiiko, and of clientship to the king, Musinga. Was also client of Rwidegembya; participated in the expedition against the rebel Basebya in northern Rwanda, as member of Rwidegembya's *intoore* section, Inkuubiri. Later became client of Rwagataraka; he remained loyal to Rwagataraka during the Ibaba conflict and thus did not lose his position when his father Nyankiiko was deposed. After the raid and conquest of Bukunzi, Rwagataraka gave Buranga fifty of the cows which were captured.

Among the hills Buranga commanded at different times were Gabiro (as representative of Nyankiiko), Gahinga, Mutimasi, Bigutu and Nyarushiishi (two hills which Buranga passed to his nephew, Kayonga), Nyamuhunga. He received the latter hill as representative of Kayondo (Abakagara, Abeega). Buranga was married to a daughter of Kizima (Abasinga clan) and was thus brother-in-law of Gakwavu and Ngegera, sons of Kizima who represented Rwagataraka on hills in the northern part of Kinyaga.[71]

Munyurabatware—subchief in Bukunzi for a short time, as representative of Gitefano. Represented Rwagataraka at Nyamugari.[72]

Rwangampuhwe—client of Rwagataraka; Rwagataraka gave him forty cows, from the booty captured in Bukunzi.[73]

Rucondo—client of Rwidegembya; fought against Basebya as member of the Inkuubiri *intoore* group. Represented his father Nyankiiko at Gabiro, but was deposed after Ibaba. It is said that Rwagataraka pierced Rucondo's nose, to punish him for participating in the Ibaba revolt.[74]

Nzogera—married to the only daughter of Seekabaraga (Abadegede, Abeega). No data on client ties; no known official position.[75]

Murekezi—attended school and became a teacher at the Ecole des Tuutsi in Cyangugu. Was first a subchief at Gashonga, representative of Biniga (the chief of Abiiru). Later, commanded Bumazi (Impara) as representative of Rwagataraka; he was then transferred to become subchief of Kigurwe subchiefdom, in Bukunzi.[76]

Bishovu—client of Rwagataraka, chosen by his patron to be member of the Indugaruga (auxiliary troops recruited and trained by the Germans). Died during the conflicts of World War I.[77]

Kayonga—client of Rwagataraka; subchief representing Rwagataraka in Bigutu subchiefdom, including Bigutu, Nyarushiishi, Nkurubuye, and Rwamiko hills.[78]

Muziramakenga—appointed by the Territorial Administrator as interim subchief in 1958 to command Rusunyu subchiefdom (including hills Rusunyu, Muhari, Kamembe, Gihundwe, Nkombo, all in Impara). No data on client ties.[79]

Kayibanda—client of Munyakayanza (chief of Cyesha Chiefdom); subchief at Butambara subchiefdom as representative of Munyakayanza (who was then chief of the newly created province of Cyesha). Butambara subchiefdom included Butambara, Mutusa, Bitare, Mushekeri, Mpumba, Ruvumbi, and Rwumba hills.[80]

Kanuuni—client of Bideri (chief of Impara from 1942); subchief of Munyove subchiefdom including the hills Munyove, Isha, Shagasha.[81]

6

THE CHANGING STATUS OF CORPORATE KIN GROUPS

WHEN REFLECTING on the political changes they (or their parents) had observed during the last 100 years, elderly Kinyagans consulted for this research would often stress the autonomy, status, and material well-being enjoyed by their lineages in the past. But from the time of Rwabugiri, they say, important changes occurred in the status of kin groups and their relations with political authorities. What these people witnessed was a growth in the power and scope of the Rwandan state, a process manifesting itself at the local level in efforts by chiefs to divide and weaken pre-existing corporate groups—in this case, lineages. Erosion of the autonomy, unity, and size of local lineages facilitated the acquisition of greater control and prerogatives by the chiefs. This augmentation of chiefly power, a form of increased state penetration at the local level, interacted with the transformations in clientship (noted above) and fostered new forms of social identity among those affected.

Two major types of kinship groups, the lineage and the clan, are important in Kinyaga today, as in the past. A lineage *(umuryango)* in the broadest sense constitutes the group of all those who can trace agnatic ties to a common ancestor, usually three to six generations in the past, and who often bear a common name, normally derived from the name of the ancestor recognized as founder of the group. Thus, the descendants of Seekadegede are referred to as the Abadegede; the descendants of Seemutega, the Abatega, and so on. In Kinyaga, lineages of today are frequently named after the first person of the lineage to have come to the region.

Over time, the size of different lineages could vary considerably, depending on the social context and the time depth by which lineage members count back to their corporate eponym. Where memories have been preserved of ancestors several generations back, the group could be, theoretically, quite large. Even where direct agnatic ties cannot be traced today, people bearing a common lineage name and postulating descent from a common ancestor will recognize a common identity. In the past, however, new lineages were continually being formed through scission.[1] Moreover, the effective (functional) size of lineages tended to diminish over time as a result of increased central government penetration. Despite this change, in Kinyaga the term *umuryango* is still used to designate the smaller functional unit, as well as the larger grouping defined in terms of descent and exogamy.[2]

Lineages in Rwanda are grouped into clans *(ubwoko)* on the basis of putative agnatic descent from an eponymous ancestor. However, unlike lineages, clans are more a social category than a corporate descent group.[3] Members of a clan cannot normally trace their descent links to each other and clans as such have no leader, no political roles, and no functions apart from social identity.[4] Each clan includes members from all three ethnic groups represented in Rwanda, a fact that has proved problematic for those who view social distinctions in Rwanda as rigid and unchanging, resembling castes.[5]

In addition to *umuryango* and *ubwoko*, a further classification of individuals based on kinship is the *ikinege*, described by Kinyagans as a person "without any family" (an undesirable status under most circumstances). Such a person is often a recent immigrant to the area where he lives, or someone whose kin have disappeared through death or emigration.[6]

LINEAGES IN NINETEENTH-CENTURY KINYAGA

DURING THE nineteenth century the lineage *(umuryango)* formed the most important political unit in Kinyaga. Local affairs were normally handled by lineages acting as corporate groups,[7] represented by their lineage head, and there was no hierarchical political authority encompassing the entire region. For internal matters concerning the lineage, the lineage head *(umukuru w'umuryango* or *umutware w'umuryango)* was the ultimate authority. In cases of dispute between different members, he held responsibility for making final judgment. If land belonging to some member of the lineage fell into disuse without heirs (through death or emigration), the lineage head controlled distribution of that land; he was also consulted before land could be granted to non-members, and any payments made as rental for the land were paid to him. The position was hereditary; normally the incumbent himself designated his successor from among his sons and, although the eldest son was often chosen, there was no rigid rule of primogeniture.[8]

Lineages held rights over land and cattle in common, although an individual adult man controlled the distribution of his household's land among his own sons. A lineage large in numerical size was considered highly desirable, both for the defense of group interests, and for the opportunities it offered to give and receive mutual assistance within the descent group. As one Kinyagan explained, when a lineage was more powerful (numerically) than another, it could decide to appropriate land from smaller lineages; in land disputes, "might" was crucial.[9]

We have seen that immigrants coming to Kinyaga with few or no kin sometimes attached themselves to large established local lineages, obtaining protection as well as land. They often married into the donor lineage, and their children might come to be considered full lineage members. Alternatively, the immigrant and his descendants would remain a separate lineage, while adopting the clan identity of the land donor. In such cases, lineage or clan membership was not determined solely by birth and patrilineal descent.

The lineage acted as a unit most often in cases of blood feud to avenge homicide, and to protect members from encroachments on their land and property. Where *umuheto* ties existed between a Kinyagan lineage and an *umuheto* chief living in central Rwanda, the kin group acted as a corporate unit in fulfilling jointly the obligations of the relationship; lineage members benefited jointly from the *umuheto* chief's protection.[10]

In such relations with external political authorities, the lineage head acted as intermediary, representative of his lineage. He decided which members would perform services ("pay court") in the name of the group, and he collected from his kinsmen any prestations delivered to the political authority. His power was based on support from his lineage; it was not delegated to him from outside the group. Though he possessed significant moral authority, he disposed of only minimal material sanctions.[11] His actual power in lineage affairs was thus limited, for lineage members who did not wish to comply with his decisions could simply leave and settle elsewhere. Availability of land in Kinyaga and to the west in Zaïre made this a realistic possibility, so that scission of lineages sometimes occurred.

The statebuilding efforts of Rwabugiri at the end of the nineteenth century initiated important changes in the status of corporate kin groups. Under Rwabugiri, the extension of central administration and clientship tended to reduce lineage autonomy, which favored the growth of central power and clientship. At first, *ubuhake* cattle clientship and land prestations (*ubutaka, ubureetwa*) were particularly important instruments used by chiefs to divide lineages. Later, taxes, corvée (*akazi*), and other exactions introduced under European rule served similar ends.

LINEAGES AND UBUHAKE CLIENTSHIP

W E H A V E seen that during Rwabugiri's reign chiefs from central Rwanda introduced *ubuhake* clientship to Kinyaga. Unlike early *umuheto* clientship, which usually involved the gift of a cow at regular intervals from a client lineage to its patron, *ubuhake* involved the transfer of one or several cows from patron to client. The client was entitled to usufruct (but not ownership) of the cow. Another important distinction lay in the different characteristics of clients in the two institutions: In *umuheto* the "client" was normally a kin group, and thus *umuheto* clientship could reinforce small-scale horizontal ties; in *ubuhake* the client was usually an individual, so that where several members of a single lineage had different patrons this could weaken local solidarities.

But the differences were not always so great—before this century *ubuhake* clientship in Kinyaga resembled *umuheto* in important ways. At the time of Rwabugiri's death in 1895, *ubuhake* was still rare in Kinyaga, and the full implications of individual clientship for corporate groups were not yet clear. Although lineage members who had *ubuhake* patrons were regarded as the individual client of their patron, the client ties could protect other members of the lineage as well. In the early years often only one or two members of a lineage became clients, and local corporate identity remained strong. Over time, however, *ubuhake* came to be preeminently an individual bond. *Ubuhake* ties reached farther down into the descent lines of single lineages, so that the sons of one man would often attach themselves to different patrons. To illustrate this process, we will examine the client ties for several Kinyagan lineages, three from Impara (figures 3–5), and three from Abiiru (figures 7–9).

The Abasigwa lineage at Gafuba first experienced *ubuhake* clientship at the end of the nineteenth century or early in the present century. Gasigwa, founder of the lineage, had no *ubuhake* ties, nor did his descendants in the next two generations. But this changed in the generation of Gasigwa's great-grandsons. Among the eight sons of one grandson (referred to as A in figure 3), five were *ubuhake* clients, with a total of four different patrons. In the same generation, of A's three nephews one (G) was an *ubuhake* client. In subsequent generations,

FIG. 3:   *Ubuhake* client ties for some members of the Abasigwa lineage (Abanyiginya clan) at Gafuba hill (Impara)

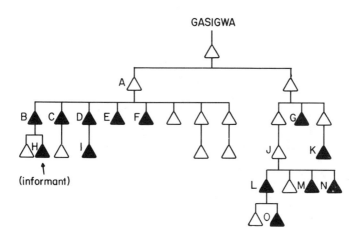

B: client of Kabano (umudegede)
    client of Ntaabukiraniro (umudegede)
C: client of Seekabaraga (umudegede)
D: client of Ndongozi (umudegede)
E: client of Seekabaraga (umudegede)
F: client of Mukara (umudegede)
G: client of Tabaaro (umudegede)
H: client of Nyarugabo (umudegede)
 I: client of Sengimwami (umudegede)
K: client of Busiine (umukagara)
L: client of Kabano (umudegede)
M: client of Kabano (umudegede)
N: client of Ntaabukiraniro (umudegede)
O: client of Ntibenda (umuduru)

SOURCE: Mutarambirwa 3/6/71.

G's nephew (K) was an *ubuhake* client, and three of K's four nephews became *ubuhake* clients.

A similar pattern of gradual growth in *ubuhake* appears in client ties for the Abafanga lineage, also at Gafuba hill (fig. 4). Again, the earliest *ubuhake* clientship for the lineage occurred shortly before the death of

FIG. 4: *Ubuhake* client ties for some members of the Abafanga lineage (Abongera clan) at Gafuba hill (Impara)

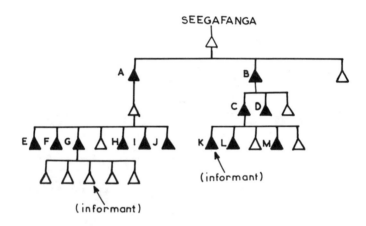

A: client of Rwidegembya (umukagara)
   client of Kajonge (umudegede)
B: client of Rwidegembya
C: client of Rwagataraka (umukagara)
D: client of Ruvugabigwi (umudegede)
E: client of Seekabaraga (umudegede)
F: client of Gashuuhe (umudegede)
G: client of Seekabaraga
   client of Seruvumba
H: client of Rwamaserabo
I: client of Rwamaserabo
J: client of Rwamfiizi (umuhanya)
K: client of Rucondo (umwerekande)
L: client of Nkeramihigo (umwerekande)
M: client of Kabeera (umuhwege)

SOURCE: Marekabiri and Mbonyiyeeze 17/6/71.

Rwabugiri (1895) or not long afterward, when two of the three grandsons of Seegafanga, founder of the lineage, became *ubuhake* cattle clients of Rwidegembya.[12] Among the three sons of one of these clients (B), two (C and D) were clients, each with a different patron. In the next generation, three of C's five sons were clients, again each to a different patron. In another branch of the lineage, all but one of the seven sons of the one son of A on whom data are available became *ubuhake* clients, with a total of five different patrons among them. (The reasons why people sometimes abandoned clientship in the following generation—cf. the sons of G—are discussed in chapter 8.)

The Abanyamagana lineage (figure 5) at Bunyangurube hill provides

---

FIG. 5: *Ubuhake* client ties for some members of the Abanyamagana lineage (Abazigaaba clan) at Bunyangurube hill (Impara)

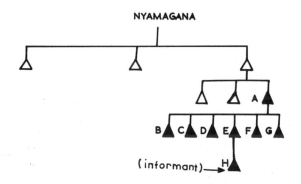

A: client of Gashuuhe (umudegede)
   client of Seemutwa (umutobo)
B: client of Kanyantaama (umudegede)
C: client of Mutsinzi (umutobo)
D: client of Nyampeta (umuhima, umushingo)
E: client of Rwambibi (umukoobwa)
F: client of Nyampeta
G: client of Nyampeta
H: client of Munyurangabo (umufata)

SOURCE: Nkundiye 28/9/70, 29/10/70, and 11/6/71.

another example of how individual client ties reached into kin groups. For one of the branches descended from Nyamagana, founder of the lineage, only one of three grandsons (A) sought *ubuhake* clientship. As in the case of the Abasigwa and Abafanga lineages, this initial *ubuhake* clientship occurred late in the reign of Rwabugiri, or a short time after his death. In the next generation, all six of A's sons became *ubuhake* clients, to four different patrons.

Frequently, in cases where several members of a lineage were clients of different patrons, these patrons were themselves linked by kin ties. This was particularly noticeable during the early growth of *ubuhake* clientship, after the death of Rwabugiri in 1895. It is illustrated clearly by the Abasigwa lineage, where eight patrons of lineage members shown in figure 4 were from the Abadegede lineage; only two patrons of the Abasigwa were from lineages other than the Abadegede (figure 3; figure 6). Therefore, although loyalties of the Abasigwa lineage members were cross-cut by individual *ubuhake* ties, control over the lineage from above was concentrated in a single local lineage.

We have seen in earlier chapters that the Abadegede were a Tuutsi lineage long established in Kinyaga and wealthy in cattle. Gafuba, like Shangi hill nearby, was a center of settlement for the Abadegede and several members of the lineage controlled pasturage near to where Abasigwa lineage members lived. Moreover, during the period 1900–1916 support for a leading member of the Abadegede from German authorities and from the central chief Rwidegembya had bolstered the power and prestige of this lineage. It was thus understandable that the Abasigwa cultivated a dense network of clientship ties to members of the Abadegede.

Ubuhake ties for the Abafanga lineage were more diverse than those of the Abasigwa. Among twelve patrons of Seekafanga's descendants shown in figure 4, four were Abadegede, two were Abakagara (Rwidegembya and his son, Rwagataraka—both chiefs of Impara and hence "patrons" for several Abadegede), and two were members of another prominent lineage, the Abeerekande, linked to the Abadegede by marriage ties. The remaining four patrons each belonged to a different lineage. One of these, Seruvumba, was a half-brother of Rwagataraka through the maternal line[13] and was therefore closely tied to the Abakagara lineage.

Patrons of the Abanyamagana lineage were also from a limited number of lineages. Two patrons of lineage members shown in figure 5 were Abadegede, while one was a member of the Abafata, a lineage closely

FIG. 6: Affinal ties between Abadegede patrons of clients belonging to the Abasigwa, Abafanga, and Abanyamagana lineages

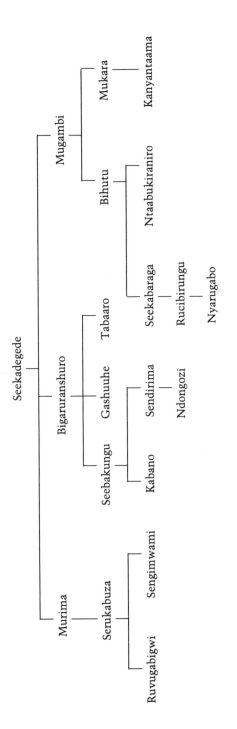

SOURCE: Mutarambirwa 3/6/71; Nyarugabo 10/8/70 and 11/9/70.

related to the Abadegede.[14] Three other patrons of lineage members came from two different lineages.

People in Abiiru region, like Impara, experienced growth in *ubuhake* cattle clientship from the end of the nineteenth century. But in Abiiru fewer lineages became involved in this form of clientship and the number of patrons for members of one lineage was often quite small. For example, among the Abakaragata at Nyakarenzo (figure 7) the first *ubuhake* client ties appeared only during the early years of European rule; in the generation of Bukaragata's great-grandsons, two of four brothers (A and B) were clients. A's older brother had no patron, and only one of his four sons (C) became an *ubuhake* client (to Biniga, chief of Abiiru region). Among C's five cousins, only two were clients.

Ubuhake ties were even more limited for the Abarari lineage at Rango and Murehe (figure 8). For the generation of Murari's great grandsons in one branch of the lineage, only three of ten brothers had *ubuhake* patrons. One of these, A, was a client of Karara, son of Rwabugiri, who gave A three cows. Later, A's younger brother, B, became client of

---

FIG. 7: *Ubuhake* client ties for some members of the Abakaragata lineage (Abacyaba clan) at Nyakarenzo hill (Abiiru)

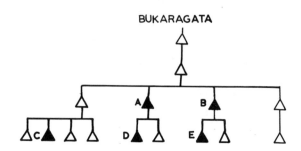

BUKARAGATA

A: client of Seerugaba
B: client of Murekezi (umwerekande)
C: client of Biniga (umuhanya)
D: client of Gasisi
E: client of Seebadiha

SOURCE: Rukubashyamba 13/5/71.

Kayondo (Abakagara lineage) for the same three cows—presumably when Kayondo appropriated the property of Karara after the Rucunshu coup. Another brother, C, was client of Mugenzi, son of Nkombe (who was chief of Bugarama region). Neither of A's sons had an *ubuhake* patron, but one of his grandsons, D, was a client of Mutiijima.

For this lineage, as for a number of other lineages in Abiiru region, *umuheto* ties remained strong through the early years of colonial rule and sometimes precluded the need for *ubuhake* patrons. Wealthy in cattle, the Abarari were considered to be of Tuutsi status. More important, the patrons of this lineage were influential in central politics. The Abarari had first been *umuheto* clients of Kanyonyomba (a delegate of Rwabugiri's son Rutarindwa), but after the Rucunshu coup, they came under Kayondo (a member of the powerful Abakagara lineage which had masterminded the Rucunshu coup). One member of the

---

FIG. 8: *Ubuhake* client ties for some members of the Abarari Abahima lineage (Abashambo clan), at Rango and Murehe hills (Abiiru).

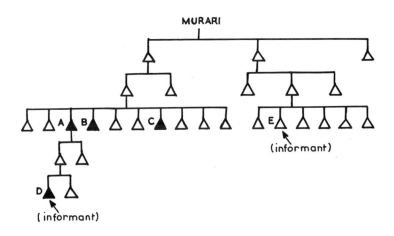

A: client of Karara (umuhindiro)
B: client of Kayondo (umukagara)
C: client of Mugenzi son of Nkombe
D: client of Mutiijima (umunyiginya from Bushi)

SOURCE: Bakomeza 12/5/71; Rukemampunzi 18/5/71.

Abarari lineage (E in figure 8) who was born before the Umuryamo cattle epidemic explained that as a youth he had paid court *(guhakwa)* at Kayondo's residence in Nduga, thus fulfilling the obligations of the lineage toward its *umuheto* patron. But neither E nor his brothers were *ubuhake* clients—they received no cow from Kayondo.[15] One of E's cousins (B) from a different branch of the lineage did become an individual *ubuhake* client of Kayondo, under the circumstances described above. The pattern of early client ties for this lineage thus confirms the tendency we have already noted, for *umuheto* and *ubuhake* to become intermingled.

The Abajyujyu lineage at Busekera and Ruhoko hills (figure 9) first acquired an *ubuhake* patron when Rwabugiri was living at his Ruganda residence near the Rusizi River. A grandson of the lineage founder (A in figure 9) cultivated ties to Rugereka, who was a powerful chief and

FIG. 9: *Ubuhake* client ties for some members of the Abajyujyu lineage (Abashambo clan) at Busekera and Ruhoko hills (Abiiru).

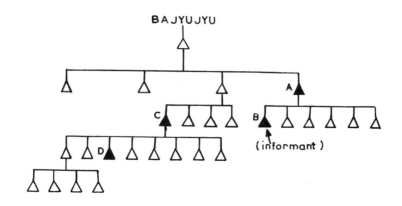

A: client of Rugereka
B: client of Ndabikunze (umureganshuro)
C: client of Rwigemera (umuhindiro)
D: client of Rwigemera
   client of Suusa (umuteganya)
   client of Bubaya (umuteganya)

SOURCE: Ndaseezeye 21/5/71; Polisi 19/5/71; Ruvuzacyuma 29/5/71.

close associate of the king. At the time, A possessed personally owned cattle, as well as an *igikingi* domain at Ruhoko. Oral histories of the lineage recount that A became Rugereka's client because the chiefs of Rwabugiri were in the region seeking clients and he needed to protect his cows. In the next generation, among A's six sons only one (B) had an *ubuhake* patron. One of A's nephews (C) sought protection for his cows from Rwigemera, son of Rwabugiri, for he feared that the local chief, Birasinyeri, would seize his cattle. Although C did not receive a cow from his patron, his son (D) underwent training in Rwigemera's *intoore* group and each time he returned home after a training session he received one cow (up to a total of four). These ties were terminated abruptly when *Umwami* Musinga allowed Birasinyeri to seize all the cattle belonging to D's father. C and his sons subsequently fled to Zaïre, where they remained for several years before returning to settle at Butambamo in Abiiru region.[16]

Two conclusions emerge from these examples. First, in Abiiru as in Impara, *ubuhake* cattle clientship expanded during the last years of the nineteenth century and the first two decades of colonial rule, as individual lineages acquired multiple patrons. Second, an important result of this process was the erosion of lineage unity and a reduction in the autonomy of these groups. *Ubuhake* cattle clientship was less important as a means of dividing lineages in Abiiru than in Impara. However, the clientship involving transfer of a cow was not the only type of *ubuhake* tie. Another form of *ubuhake* found in both Impara and Abiiru (and perhaps more important in terms of numbers of people affected), was "clientship for land," or as Kinyagans describe it, *guhakwa y'ubutaka*. This involved performance of certain services for the local hill chief by the "client" but omitted the transfer of a cow. The services often duplicated those which in other contexts were reserved for clients who had received a cow: carrying the patron's tobacco pouch and pipe, providing services to the patron's household, accompanying the patron on voyages.

The significant aspect of *ubuhake* clientship, both for cattle and land, was its individual nature. If only very few members of a given lineage (or none) acquired patrons from whom they received a cow, several might become individual "land clients" of the local chief, particularly as hill chiefs became established and their powers augmented. For some lineages, land clientship served a function similar to that of cattle clientship by granting favored status in relation to the chief. Both types, land clientship and cattle clientship, served to reduce lineage autonomy.

LINEAGES AND HILL CHIEFS

T HE HILL chiefs introduced to Kinyaga from the time of Rwabugiri resembled lineage heads in several respects. They collected prestations, settled disputes, and served as intermediaries to outside authority. But unlike the lineage heads they displaced, each hill chief *(umutware w'umusoozi)* was appointed from above, by a politically more powerful superior, the provincial chief; the hill chief relied less on support from below than on power transmitted through the administrative hierarchy. Initially the area administered by a hill chief was fairly small, ranging from a small portion of a hill *(umurenge)* to an entire hill *(umusoozi)* or, less frequently, several hills. Later during regroupment under Belgian rule, these small administrative units were consolidated into larger entities (subchiefdoms), each headed by a subchief.

Many of the early hill chiefs were appointed from Kinyagan lineages, to collect prestations from people in their own area, including their kinsmen. Particularly in Abiiru the provincial chief often selected as his delegate a member of a large and wealthy local lineage; the delegate might be the incumbent lineage head, or some other member. Later during the European period subchiefs were usually recruited from outside Kinyaga. When a Kinyagan was appointed, he was seldom posted to his natal hill. But whether the hill chief was appointed from a local lineage on the hill or imposed from outside, a significant change had occurred. Henceforth, other lineages on the hill found themselves subordinated to the authority of one person, whose position depended on his ability to please superiors in the patron–client network.

The power of hill chiefs to control resources became an important incentive for Kinyagans to seek *ubuhake* patrons, just as at a higher level *ubuhake* clientship was an important mechanism in recruiting hill chiefs. The effect of these changes on individual lineages varied, of course, depending on local circumstances. But the general impact was to diminish the political role of the legitimate lineage heads. A brief case study will help to clarify the complementary roles of *ubuhake* patron and hill chief in the erosion of lineage autonomy.

Nduruma was the founder of the Abaruruma lineage at Cyete in Abiiru region; he lived during the reign of *Umwami* Rwogera, when there were no hill chiefs as such in Kinyaga. As head of his lineage, Nduruma was the principal political authority on his hill, a position he shared with the lineage head of the Abageshi, the other numerically strong lineage at Cyete. The Abaruruma were Tuutsi; the Abageshi were Hutu.

Nduruma's designated successor, Rukubita (B in figure 10) witnessed the introduction of hill chiefs into Kinyaga. Aside from assuming the powers formerly held by his father, Rukubita became the local representative of the Abiiru provincial chief, Rubuga (who had himself been appointed by Rwabugiri). The extent of Rukubita's jurisdiction is not clear, but he apparently acquired authority over other lineages on the hill in addition to his own; he became hill chief *(umutware w'umu-*

FIG. 10: Succession to office of hill chief and lineage head among the Abaruruma lineage (Abongera clan) at Cyete hill (Abiiru).

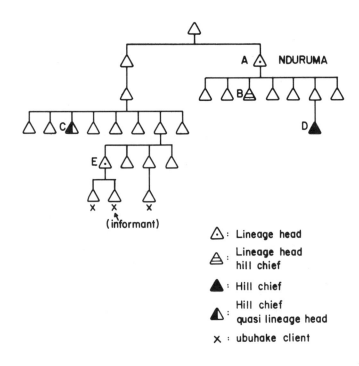

△ : Lineage head

⊜ : Lineage head hill chief

▲ : Hill chief

◭ : Hill chief quasi lineage head

x : ubuhake client

SOURCE: Gihura 15/6/71 and 22/6/71; Bakomeza 23/12/70.

soozi) representing Rubuga, and he combined this role with that of lineage head.

When Rwabugiri was preparing his final expedition against Bushi, he assigned several hills near the Rusizi River to a prominent army chief, Seemakamba. One of the hills was Cyete, home of Rukubita's lineage; Cyete was withdrawn from the jurisdiction of the Abiiru provincial chief and placed under Seemakamba's authority. Seemakamba dismissed Rukubita from his position as hill chief, and replaced him with Nduruma's grand-nephew, Seebutimbiri (C).

Seebutimbiri distinguished himself in war, and he acquired prestige and power as *ubuhake* client of Seemakamba. The new hill chief came to be regarded as "leading member" of his lineage. But Seebutimbiri was not the legitimate lineage head of the Abaruruma. His status depended not on his role within the lineage but on the favor of his patron, Seemakamba. The locus of power had thus shifted from one branch of the lineage to another, and from representative to delegated power. Moreover, though technically Seebutimbiri's role was restricted to his functions as hill chief, these tended to spill over into what had previously been the domain of the lineage head.

When the Abapari and Seevumba invaded Kinyaga, Seebutimbiri took a leading role in the attempts to repel them. He was killed in the conflicts, and the position of hill chief reverted to the Rukubita branch; a nephew of Rukubita (D) took over, representing Seevumba at Cyete, but his tenure ended with Seevumba's departure. From that time the lineage held no further administrative posts; a man from another lineage gained administrative authority over Cyete hill, and the position of lineage head of the Abaruruma returned to Seebutimbiri's line.[17]

The introduction of hill chiefs and clientship provided opportunities for social mobility to some members of the Abaruruma lineage; power gravitated toward those who were willing and able to attract favor from political superiors. But this new status was precarious. Power oscillated between different branches of the lineage, reflecting the changing political fortunes of lineage members' patrons—Rubuga, Seemakamba, Seevumba. Ultimately, authority within the lineage was divided, and the past political role of the lineage was undermined.

LINEAGES AND GOVERNMENT EXACTIONS

THE INTRODUCTION of land prestations to Kinyaga during the reign of Rwabugiri altered the hereditary rights which Kinyagan lineages had previously held over their land, as occupation became conditional upon compliance with a hill chief's demands. Subsequently, authority which formerly had resided in the corporate group (defined by kin ties) and been embodied in the lineage head, came to be vested in a hill chief appointed from above. Since the lineage member appointed by the hill chief to collect prestations was not always the legitimate lineage head, there emerged a potential for conflict between persons with competing claims to leadership within the group.

A subtle modification also occurred in the definition of the prestation-paying unit. Although in the past the group which paid *umuheto* prestations had been defined by kin ties (and corporate ownership of cattle), for land prestations the criterion of residence was introduced as well. Each localized kin group was constrained to pay prestations to the chief of its hill. Thus, if members of a single lineage lived on two different hills (A and B), each of which had its own hill chief, the lineage members on hill A would give prestations to the chief of hill A, while members of the same lineage who lived on hill B would pay prestations to the chief of hill B. This change led to a diminution in the effective size of the "lineage" which gave prestations as a corporate group (though the terms to designate that group remained the same, *umuryango*).

The experience of the Abazirimo lineage at Muramba in Impara Province provides a good example of this shift. We have seen that this lineage began to give cows for land prestations during the time of Rwabugiri. The Abazirimo did not give one cow as a corporate group, however. Instead, members of the lineage who lived at Muramba were required to give one cow to the local hill chief each year, while other Abazirimo living farther south at Rwahi also gave a cow to the local hill chief on their hill. Here was the cutting edge between the demands of the hill chief and the *umuheto* prestations which had required only one cow from the lineage as a corporate group.[18]

The Abazirimo were wealthy in cattle. Other lineages which owned few or no cattle were expected to contribute prestations in food products, normally a portion of their harvest of beans, peas, or sorghum each year. It was from among such lineages, defined as Hutu, that the hill chief would recruit victims for *ubureetwa*, a particularly servile type of clientship. *Ubureetwa* entailed services performed for the local hill chief as "payment" for occupation of the land. Initially, hill chiefs imposed *ubureetwa* on selected localized lineage groups. Later, *ubureetwa* came to be imposed on individual adult men as a result of European colonial policies.[19]

European policy also modified the basis on which land prestations *(amakoro y'ubutaka)* were paid, and eliminated *umuheto* prestations. In 1926, the position of *umuheto* chief and the prestations due to him were officially abolished.[20] Some Kinyagans, unaware of the changes, and not informed by the chiefs, continued to pay *umuheto* prestations for several years afterward. From 1931 to 1933, steps were taken to modify and eventually substitute money payments for the land prestations in kind. By 1934, a money payment had been introduced to replace all prestations in agricultural or other products. This consisted of a tax on each adult man in Rwanda, in Kinyaga amounting to 4 francs (1 franc for the king, 1 franc for the provincial chief, and 2 francs for the subchief).[21] The Belgian administration intentionally did not introduce a money payment for *ubureetwa* at the time of this change, on the grounds that to do so would undermine the chiefs' authority over the population.[22]

Thus, as Rwanda entered its fourth decade under European rule, the three major political functions performed on the basis of corporate kin groups had either been transformed into responsibilities incumbent on individual adult men *(ubutaka, ubureetwa)*, or abolished entirely *(umuheto)*. While abolishing, modifying, or attempting to limit "traditional" prestations, the administration also introduced new exactions. Chief among these were the head tax collected from 1917, and *akazi* (corvée, for public works projects and various forms of obligatory cultivation), which became generalized in the 1920s. A central feature of these levies was that they were imposed on individual adult men, not on lineages. Whereas the payment of prestations had initially reflected the corporate character of kin groups (even while leading to a reduction in their effective size), taxes and corvée (and *ubureetwa* in its modified form) bypassed the lineage to confront the individual directly. The role of kin groups as intermediary between an individual and the state was thus substantially reduced.

Supposedly every adult man was liable to pay taxes and perform corvée; *ubureetwa*, however, was imposed specifically on Hutu. But the local chief decided who actually paid and participated. Moreover, the type of work assigned to individuals for corvée often depended on their standing with the hill chief. The less irksome tasks (such as capita for work gangs, or messenger) went to those who were more favored: A poor man of low status most often would be called on to do the least desirable jobs. Many oral accounts attest to the hardships and insecurities these conditions created. Kinyagans often tried to escape the exactions by moving elsewhere in the region or by emigrating to the west:

Members of the Abatsuri lineage (Abiitira clan) at Nyamirundi left their homes and fled to another hill; the local chief had destroyed their huts because they had little land and thus had few mats or beans to give as prestations.[23]

A son of Munambari (Abaganda lineage, Abagesera clan) left his home at Mugera because of the exactions of the hill chief, and went to live on another hill.[24]

A member of the Abajyujyu lineage at Butambamo lost his cows when they were seized by Birasinyeri, chief of Abiiru region at the time. The victim and his sons fled to the Congo.[25]

Rukara, the grandfather of a man now living at Gashonga hill (Abiiru) was a client of Seekabaraga; Seekabaraga wanted to take Rukara's cows, so Rukara left his home at Rwamiko (Impara) along with two of his brothers. Rukara obtained land from Cyimbuzi, hill chief at Gashonga; his two brothers obtained land at Mushaka. This incident occurred during the period of German rule, when Kaana-yooge (Kandt) was at Shangi.[26]

Some members of the Abateganya (Abakoobwa clan) at Gashonga were attacked and deprived of their property by Mutiijima, hill chief of Gashonga. They went to a neighboring hill, Rukunguri, which was part of Impara province (whereas Gashonga was in Abiiru). In this case, however, lineage unity was only impaired, not destroyed. Although responsible to a different chief for questions of land, those at Rukunguri still recognized the lineage head at Gashonga.[27]

Mucyurabuhoro, a member of the Abarundi lineage (Abacyaba) at Gashirabwoba (Impara) left his lineage's settlement because the lineage head, Yeeze, wanted to take cows from him to give to the Belgians for food. This occurred while Rwagataraka was chief of Impara. Mucyurabuhoro left Gashirabwoba and went to Gashonga where he obtained land from the hill chief, Mutiijima; one brother of Mucyurabuhoro came to Gashonga also.[28]

Hill chiefs claimed for themselves land left vacant by such changes of residence. In distributing the land to others, the chief enhanced his power, for the recipient was then dependent upon the land donor (hill chief) as his "benefactor." The original inhabitant of the land, who had fled, was not only separated geographically from his lineage mates, but was in addition rendered dependent upon the local chief of the place where he sought to settle. Rather than being absorbed into an existing lineage on the hill, the new resident would normally remain as a separate "taxpayer" before the hill chief.[29] General population mobility within a small area therefore would ultimately benefit all chiefs.[30]

REVIVAL OF KIN-GROUP STATUS

ALTHOUGH LINEAGES gradually lost their corporate and political functions, they continued to serve as an important medium for social identification and, to judge from later events, kinship linkages retained their organizational potential. When alternatives became available through socioeconomic change, younger members of formerly powerful and prestigious lineages (often Hutu) would try to escape clientship, and the exactions of the chiefs, by seeking wage work from Europeans. Such young men chafed with memories of past glory, when their fathers or grandfathers had been leaders of wealthy and politically autonomous lineages, free from the harassment which came to be a byword of Tuutsi rule in Rwanda. In breaking out of the local authority system, they gained acquaintance with new ideas and skills which later proved useful for mounting protests against the system; but besides the new skills, these Hutu leaders manipulated ties to mobilize followings, stressing particularly the past prestige associated with their lineages.[31]

The emergence of organized protest was facilitated by three more factors. First was a broadening of kinship concepts. Changes introduced by central government policy, the spread of Christianity, and the effects of socioeconomic forces appear to have encouraged an expansion of the "kinship universe" of Kinyagans. Through clientship ties, for example, a person came into contact with others of different lineages, who were clients of the same patron. Such contacts may have served as a basis for the formation of new groupings which borrowed kinship terminology in the regulation of relations among the participants.[32] A similar process can be hypothesized for contacts among persons working for wages, or even for those who fell victim to corvée. Their collective subordination to the goals and interests of the chiefs provided them with a common structural status which cut across occupational, kin, or geographical differences. The broadening of horizons through shared experience may well have contributed to the emergence of pan-Hutu cohesion in the 1950s.

A second and related factor was the ethnic discrimination implicit in the extension of central government control at the expense of local lineage groups. Before the introduction of central administration under Rwabugiri, lineage heads in the region enjoyed status and prestige as representatives of their kin groups. This role was significant for both Hutu and Tuutsi lineages, so that there was extensive participation by Hutu in local affairs. When hill chiefs were introduced, lineage heads lost many of their former prerogatives, and saw the corporate character of their kin groups weakened.

Alternatives to the former prestige of lineage leadership existed for some Tuutsi in the form of appointment to political office or jobs in the colonial administration. But this alternative was virtually inoperative for Hutu from the 1920s, as European policies expanded and entrenched Tuutsi predominance. Where Hutu retained any participation in the administration, this was only as *ibirongozi*, the subordinates of hill chiefs, or (occasionally) as lowly clerks. *Ibirongozi* performed particularly unpopular functions for the hill chiefs, such as extracting prestations, services, and taxes from the population.

Finally, the life chances of most Hutu were further restricted by the discrimination introduced in the Catholic schools (by far the largest educational system throughout the colonial period). Beginning in 1926, Tuutsi who previously had resisted conversion began to flock to the Catholic missions seeking instruction. The bishop at the time, Mgr. Léon Classe, saw this as an opportunity to strengthen the political role of the Church in Rwanda, and to create an ethnically defined Christian "aristocracy" composed of Tuutsi. Therefore to accommodate and further encourage this trend the Church adjusted its educational policies and introduced overt discrimination, favoring Tuutsi and discriminating against Hutu. While Hutu would also receive education, this would be shaped and constrained to fit the status Mgr. Classe envisaged for them: "they will take up places in mine-working and industry."[33] By the end of 1928 the explicit guidelines issued by Mgr. Classe had resulted in clear discrimination against Hutu in most of Rwanda's Catholic mission schools, including Mibirizi Mission in Kinyaga.[34]

At Save Mission near Astrida, for example, Tuutsi and Hutu pupils studied many of the same subjects, but only Tuutsi received special additional instruction in skills useful for maintaining records in a chiefdom, and in the French language. At Kansi, another Mission in the Astrida area, Tuutsi pupils received French instruction while Hutu did not, and Hutu children often missed school because of the heavy corvées they were required to perform in the subchiefdoms.[35] Thus, as Mbonimana emphasizes, a form of segregation in the Catholic mission schools paralleled (if perhaps in milder form) the discrimination found in the Groupe Scolaire d'Astrida, the only government school in the country.

The Groupe Scolaire, which enrolled its first students in 1932, replaced the earlier Ecole des Fils des Chefs (also called the Ecole des Batutsi) located in Nyanza. It was administered and staffed by an order of Catholic brothers, Les Frères de la Charité, but funded by the colonial government. One of the goals of this school was to create a "new social class," and in accordance with this goal (and the concerns of Mgr. Classe) very few Hutu were admitted; indeed, until after World War II the school even had a minimum height requirement for admission. Graduates of the Groupe Scolaire considered themselves superior to other educated Rwandans (e.g., those, many of them Hutu, who had obtained post-primary education in the Catholic seminaries), and their diplomas were accorded greater value by the Belgian administration. Thus, in theory because of their professional qualifications but in reality because they were overwhelmingly drawn from among the families of Tuutsi chiefs, the graduates of the Groupe Scolaire enjoyed the benefits of both the "traditional" economic structures, and of the higher status jobs and better pay available in the "modern" sector.[36]

Such changes in the government structures and educational system represented a marked reduction in status for Hutu, and introduced a more marked stratification between ethnic groups than had existed in the past. And as stratification was intensified, ethnic distinctions were sharpened. In this sense, ethnic discrimination was a corollary to the reduction in kin group autonomy, while the collective subordination of this ethnically defined group contributed to the emergence of a broader identity. The state successfully weakened the perceived threat of one kind of corporate group, the property-owning lineage, while the state and the Catholic Church encouraged the creation of a new Christian "ruling class," to be composed exclusively of Tuutsi. These processes helped to foster the emergence of a new and broader identity group (Hutu) based on the resentments of the dispossessed.

7

THE TRANSFORMATION OF CLIENT INSTITUTIONS

HE COLONIAL policies of Germany and Belgium altered the powers of chiefs and accelerated the growth of social stratification in Rwanda. At the same time the progressive incorporation of this state into the world economy—an integral part of the colonial experience—provided both incentives and rationalizations for the powerful to make further exactions on the rural masses. While the goals of European administrators and their Rwandan collaborators differed, their interests were often complementary; each made use of the other. It is therefore hardly surprising that changes occurred in relations between state and people.

What we wish to explain, though, is why these transformations should have resulted in the intensification of cleavages between Tuutsi and Hutu. Part of the answer lies in European policies that openly favored Tuutsi as rulers, excluding Hutu from powerful positions. But to understand the depth of anti-Tuutsi protest which emerged in Rwanda during the 1950s, we need to explore how Tuutsi chiefs used their power—what was the character of relations between them and the less powerful? A study of transformations in patron–client ties in Kinyaga offers revealing insights on such relationships. As a dynamic process articulating and channeling relations among people, clientship was in fact many institutions: One form of clientship evolved into other forms, and patron–client ties branched into new fields of relations. A survey of changes in patron–client relationships in Kinyaga over the five decades of colonial rule will help to illuminate this dynamic role of patron–client ties, and the changing character of rural class relations reflected in them. But first, we need to look briefly at the alterations in clientship that occurred during the years just preceding colonial rule. Many of these changes resulted from ecological factors but they had strong influence on subsequent political developments, affecting the way that people viewed clientship and the way that patron–client ties and the state affected their lives.

THE FINAL YEARS OF RWABUGIRI'S REIGN AND THE PERIOD OF GERMAN COLONIAL RULE (1890–1916)

THE LAST decade of the nineteenth century was a period of great upheaval for Rwanda in general, and Kinyaga in particular. The decade opened with an epidemic of rinderpest which swept through the country killing many cattle (more than 90% in some locales). Almost simultaneously the population suffered an outbreak of smallpox. The period also saw the introduction of "jiggers," (sand fleas) a parasite new to the area. These embedded themselves in the human body (often under toenails); if left unattended, jiggers could lead to serious infection and eventually loss of limb. In the initial stages, these parasites caused great concern as the population did not know how to treat them. Then, as we have seen, Rwabugiri's death in 1895 plunged the country into mourning; not long after, the Abapari (the first Europeans to occupy Rwanda) arrived to set up a camp in Kinyaga. And about the same time the central court was riven by internal conflicts culminating in the Rucunshu coup d'état. These events were all important in the development of clientship, because of the insecurities, as well as opportunities, they created. But the rinderpest epidemic, the Abapari occupation, and the Rucunshu coup affected clientship institutions in specific ways, structuring the later development of patron–client ties.

   In its effect on the lives and fortunes of people, the Umuryamo cattle epidemic was comparable to a major depression in an industrialized country. At a stroke, a family's wealth and entire social apparatus of security, identity, and relationships were wiped out. One Kinyagan observed that "The cows would come home in the evening, and the next morning, they would all be dead."[1] Another remarked that "Some Tuutsi who saw their cows die committed suicide; others died from *ubwori*, lack of milk."[2]

   Cattle in Rwanda served as a source of wealth, a symbol of prestige, and a mechanism to record relationships and establish alliances. Thus Umuryamo destroyed not only material wealth but the very means of contracting and recording social ties as well. In Kinyaga, as elsewhere in the country, the damage to local herds was catastrophic. People who had subsisted mainly on cattle found themselves impoverished, deprived of their principal source of livelihood. Lineages which had possessed several herds of thirty to forty head each were left with only one or two cows, if any at all. Even chiefs who had possessed many herds were hard hit.[3] Rubuga, chief of Abiiru Province and reputed to have had many herds, remained with only ten or twenty *imponooke* (cows "rescued" from the epidemic). Rwanyamugabo, leader of the Abeerekande lineage and one of the largest cattle-owners in the region, had about twenty cows left. At the central court, the effects were similar and this led to even more losses of cattle in Kinyaga. For Kinyaga's location as a frontier region bordering on forest areas permitted some herders to take cattle back into the forest, and other small groups of cattle in isolated corners of the region had been spared the epidemic. But after Umuryamo Rwabugiri sought to rebuild the depleted royal herds; he ordered a general "review" *(umurundo)* throughout the kingdom, and his agents requisitioned many of the cattle which had survived the devastation of the epidemic.[4]

Kinyagans speak of the post-Umuryamo period in ecological terms: with so few cattle left, pasture was left ungrazed, and this blurred the distinctions between homestead and "bush." "The grass grew and grew, right to the interior of the houses."[5] And the hills became overgrown "like forests."[6] Economic relations were also affected. With the paucity of cattle, a primary goal was to rebuild the herds. This inflated the value of heifers and altered commercial relations between Kinyaga and the non-Rwandan neighboring areas. To obtain a single heifer in Bushi to the west, for example, Kinyagans were willing to offer a sterile cow and three bull calves.[7]

In Kinyaga control over *igikingi* pasturage temporarily declined in importance, as the ratio of pasturage to cattle available changed so dramatically. And Kinyagans found it difficult to supply the normal prestations in cattle for their *umuheto* patrons, even while the pressures increased on them to furnish cattle, as the patrons too sought to recoup their losses. These new realities altered the general approach to clientship and the parameters of client arrangements. Some Kinyagans, deprived of their cattle by the rinderpest, apparently saw in *ubuhake* clientship an opportunity to rebuild their herds through the usufruct of a cow and its offspring.[8] It is likely that Umuryamo was, then, important to the growth of *ubuhake* in the early years of this century.

Other means of obtaining cows existed, however—such as purchase (even at inflated prices) or cattle raids across the border to the west and south.[9] Seeking client ties, therefore, was not the only means available for rebuilding herds. Besides, with such a global devastation one might have thought that the entire structure of cattle clientship would be altered. And so it was, but in the direction of increasing importance of cattle ties and greater dependence of the client on the patron. Therefore the causes of the increased importance of *ubuhake* must be sought in the power politics of the time.

Rwabugiri died toward the end of 1895, about three years after the rinderpest epidemic. His death had a great impact on Kinyaga as he had launched his final military campaigns (which were in process at the time of his death) from hills in western Kinyaga.[10] Only a few months after his death the Abapari (a small group of Belgian officers and African soldiers) invaded the region. We have seen in chapter 4 that after the central chiefs had fled several Kinyagans became the clients of the Abapari intruders. In the oral accounts about these men two significant characteristics stand out: They became rich and powerful as a result of European support; and they used their power arbitrarily, terrorizing the population. The cruelty of Kabundege, one of the Abapari's Kinyagan collaborators, was captured in the dictum, "Anyone who didn't rally to the side of Kabundege, was not seen again by Seekabaraga," referring to the belief that those who opposed Kabundege had been killed; they were no longer around to welcome Seekabaraga on his return after the Abapari departure.[11] Another of the collaborators, Gato, gained fame for his audacity. He began to take on airs, acting as if he were king, and he reportedly destroyed Rwabugiri's former residence at Rubengera, north of Kinyaga.[12]

When the central court chiefs returned to Kinyaga, they quickly deposed Kinyagans who had cooperated with the Abapari: some lost their power and their cattle; at least one (Gato) was killed.[13] But often former collaborators of the Abapari tried to curry favor with the returning chiefs. The surest way to do this was to seek "protection" through *ubuhake* clientship, to show submission, and (hopefully) avoid the wrath of the powerful by becoming an *umugaragu* (client). This was the stratagem pursued by Gisaaza, a Kinyagan collaborator who had received a number of cows from the Abapari. Gisaaza offered one of these cows to Rwidegembya, the *umuheto* chief of Impara. Rwidegembya then placed one of his own cows among those of Gisaaza. This symbolized that the latter's cows were under Rwidegembya's protection, "and therefore no one could (legally) seize them."[14] The man recounting this episode thought Gisaaza very clever: He sought protection of his cattle before he could be dispossessed of them. This became a common motive for *ubuhake* clientship in the years that followed.

The power struggles associated with the Rucunshu coup also generated shifts in existing patron–client ties and an impetus to create new ones. When the central chiefs returned to Kinyaga, Musinga was on the throne, and the Abeega perpetrators of the coup were carrying out their purge of those believed to be partisans of the dead Rutarindwa. In Kinyaga, individuals and lineages linked by residence on *intoore* hills, or by clientship to powerful chiefs who had supported Rutarindwa at Rucunshu, found it necessary to shift their allegiances. These changes reflected both the growing intermingling of clientship with central administration in Kinyaga, and the increasing incorporation of the Kinyagan elite into politics of the central arena. Local oral traditions single out three central chiefs—Seemakamba,[15] Kanyonyomba,[16] and Rutiishereka,[17] whose deaths were felt directly by their clients in Kinyaga.

Kinyagans who already had client ties to the victorious Abakagara lineage found their opportunities for advancement greatly enhanced after Rucunshu. The rise to prominence of Seekabaraga and his lineage, the Abadegede, is a case in point. We have seen that the Abadegede, who lived at Shangi, were descendants of the famous Rwanteri. They had become clients of Ntiizimira when he took over command of Impara, and after his fall from favor the Abadegede became clients of Cyigenza, a member of the Abakagara lineage. Later, at the time of Rucunshu, the Abadegede were clients of Cyigenza's son, Rwidegembya, a nephew of Kabaare. In subsequent years, as representatives of Rwidegembya, the Abadegede substantially enlarged their local following.

The establishment of the Germans in the region was important to the rise to power of the Abadegede as well as several other local lineages. The center of activities for the German East Africa military administration in Ruanda-Urundi was at Bujumbura (then called Usumbura) in Burundi. But the major German outpost in Rwanda was initially in Kinyaga at Shangi (and later Kamembe). It was not until 1907, when German civil administration was established, that Kigali (in east-central Rwanda) became the capital for European activities in Rwanda. Captain von Bethe and a contingent of African soldiers set up the first German military post at Shangi in 1898. At about the same time Dr. Richard Kandt undertook geographic and ethnographic studies of Rwanda and Kivu, establishing Shangi as his western base in 1899.

By 1902 the entire German military force in western Rwanda consisted of Lieutenant von Parish with twenty-one African *askaris* at Shangi, and *Unteroffizier* (Sergeant) Ehrhardt with four *askaris* at Gisenyi, at the northern end of the lake.[18]

The small size of the German force, however, was no measure of its influence on power relations. In Kinyaga, Dr. Kandt, known locally as Kaanoyooge or Bwana Kooge, was particularly influential. Though he visited his residence near Shangi (which he called Bergfrieden) only irregularly over a period of three years, Kandt established firm ties with local notables such as Seekabaraga and Nyankiiko. Ndaruhuutse, a very old Kinyagan living at Shangi, used the traditional Rwandan form of *igiteekerezo* to recount Kinyagan perceptions of early relations between Kandt and Seekabaraga:

> A few days after [the departure of the Abapari and Abagufi], the chiefs returned with their cattle. Then we came back with our mothers and fathers who were still alive. A short time later we learned that some Europeans had arrived at Shangi. People said, "the Europeans who've arrived at Shangi, it's not known what they're like, these are not Belgians." They set up their tents at Shangi. Then they asked, "Who is the chief who commands this hill?"
>
> They were told, "Seekabaraga."
>
> "Where is Seekabaraga," they asked.
>
> "He's at home."
>
> The Europeans sent word to Seekabaraga to come and meet them at their camp. These were the Europeans Bwana Kooge and Bwana Bethe. Thus they told the messenger, "We aren't going to kill anyone; on the contrary we want to have friendly relations with the people. We will even give them positions of command and we will enrich them."
>
> So the messenger went to inform Seekabaraga. Then Seekabaraga said, "Since the Europeans want peace and not war, we must send them food." Food was given to a certain Kagoro who lived right near here. Kagoro's father was Sinayobye. He took that [food] to the Europeans, Bwana Bethe and Bwana Kooge. They accepted it, and then said, "Well, good—you who come to bring food, and this gift of welcome, go tell Seekabaraga that he should not be afraid, that we do not kill people; rather we want only understanding and good relations with the Rwandans. If he was away yesterday, let him come to see us tomorrow." They gave this man cloth and beads

for Seekabaraga. They commissioned him to give the gifts to Seekabaraga and to tell him to come and see them.

The man went and showed Seekabaraga what they had given
him. Having seen that, Seekabaraga took some more food and set
out. He went to the camp of Bwana Kooge and Bwana Bethe. When
he arrived there, Bwana Bethe grabbed him by the arm and shook
it a little, as they do by way of greeting, and said to him: "Don't
be afraid." Bwana Kooge took him by one arm, and Bwana Bethe
by the other, and they went to sit him down on a chair. They asked
him: "Yesterday you were afraid to come?"

He said: "No."

They told him, "Don't be afraid because we don't kill people and
we don't wish to kill people."

Seekabaraga said: "Yes."

Seekabaraga and his clients remained there a while. Then in bid-
ding him good-bye these Europeans told him, "Come more often,
we are going to chat and we will get along well and we will give
you a position of command." So Seekabaraga went home and came
back the next morning.

Then one day they said to Seekabaraga, "Seekabaraga?"

Seekabaraga said, "Yes?"

They said, "Find us some men."

He gave them some men, he gave them to Bwana Bethe, while
Bwana Kooge stayed [at Shangi]. Bwana Bethe went to Cyoya's
country, to Burundi, in the region of Cyoya son of Ngwije. . . . He
said to Seekabaraga, "Cyoya has scorned me, and that's the reason
I'm going to pillage cows from him to give you." So he went and
seized many cattle. (It was at this period that someone gave Bwana
Bethe the name Rukiza. You understand? He called him Rukiza,
the one who enriches—because he had just given the cow as bridewealth for the girl he had married. So Bwana Bethe married the
daughter of this man called Rutebuuka; the daughter of this man
was called Mutuurwa, and I witnessed that.) After the arrival of
these cows [from Burundi] they said to Seekabaraga, "Choose forty
with their bull." So he took them home.

Then several days later they said, "Kabaraga?" [familiar form of
address]. And he said, "Yes?"

They said, "Give us some more men to go to Ijwi."

He gave them around forty men and they went to Ijwi where they
raided innumerable cattle. The udders of these cows were as long
as a hand. Moreover, they brought back a man from there. His name

was Rwango, son of Mudanga. He was the herdsman for those cows from Mihigo's country.

So the cows arrived and once again Seekabaraga took forty of them. He placed one of these herds at his residence here and another at his residence on Mwito hill. Thus Seekabaraga kept his command and also his cattle. The Europeans gave him much power. His younger brothers, Minyago and Ntaabukiraniro went to collect prestations on the hills while he sat as chief, and he became rich. These were the men I saw come to Rwanda. The cows multiplied and the people also received lots of things—Seekabaraga distributed these cows to many people. The cows multiplied and could graze in the grass which had grown right up to the inside of houses because there had been no more cows after the epidemic.

Later Bwana Kooge and Bwana Bethe moved down and built their post closer to the lake. (At first they had been near the big tree, near Seekabaraga's residence.) So they moved down close to the lake and built there. They settled there and stayed a long time. Rugira became their client and so did Nyampeta, and [the Europeans] enriched them.[19]

Although Seekabaraga and Nyankiiko did not themselves have guns, people knew of their friendly relations with Kandt and other Germans, and the potential this gave of calling upon European coercive force. Another advantage of friendship with the German authorities was access to cattle which otherwise would not have been so readily available. As Ndaruhuutse stressed,

> It was the Europeans who helped Seekabaraga become a cattle owner, for previously he had perhaps no more than a single cow! The others had been exterminated by Umuryamo. It was those Europeans Bwana Kooge and Bwana Bethe who distributed cattle in this region. They brought some from Ijwi and others from Burundi.[20]

Raids for cattle were carried out within the region as well. Often the Germans would attack men on the express request of Seekabaraga. As one man explained,

> It's as if it were he [Seekabaraga] who commanded the Germans; it was sufficient for him to see you were rich and he would go and accuse you of rebellion, and the Germans would come to kill you, and then Seekabaraga would seize your belongings.[21]

The power of Seekabaraga and Nyankiiko was also enhanced by their position as clients and local representatives of the central chief Rwidegembya. This position, as well as the resources they acquired through clientship to Europeans, enabled them to increase their followings of *ubuhake* clients and extend *umuheto* clientship. The reduced military role of the social armies, the power struggles following the Rucunshu coup, and the uncertainties of early dealings with European administrators and missionaries diverted the attention of many *umuheto* chiefs in the center. Kinyagan clients of central chiefs thus often found it necessary to accept clientship to local *umuheto* patrons such as Seekabaraga.

The experience of the Abaruruma lineage described in chapter 6 illustrates this pattern. The lineage had belonged to the Abakwiye social army, as *umuheto* clients of a central chief, for several generations before 1900. But after Rucunshu and the arrival of Germans in the kingdom, the Abaruruma found it necessary to accept Seekabaraga as their *umuheto* patron. Gihura, a senior member of the lineage, explained that Seekabaraga had become his lineage's *umuheto* patron

> because he was powerful. Because the men from Nduga did not return any more [to collect prestations]. So this other one appropriated command over us for himself. We gave him about fifteen cows, while he hadn't given us a single cow and we also paid court to him *(guhakwa)* without his having given us any cow. I went to carry out *gufat'igihe* at his residence; I stayed for a long time, then he set me free telling me to return home. It was truly exploitation.[22]

Reluctantly, the Abaruruma paid court to Seekabaraga to protect lineage cattle. To judge from Gihura's account, in this case *umuheto* was seen as more onerous than *ubuhake*, for the Abaruruma received nothing in return for the cows and service they provided.

Continuing the practice begun under Rwabugiri, chiefs also extended *umuheto* to lineages, both Hutu and Tuutsi, which had not had such ties in the past. But, as in the earlier period, not all Hutu were constrained to pay *umuheto* prestations; those selected were often relatively wealthy or had access to prized items such as honey, *ubutega* fiber bracelets, or luxury mats coveted by the chiefs.

The extension of *ubuhake* clientship, like that of *umuheto*, was associated with the growing power of the political elite. At the same time, *ubuhake* ties served as a key instrument for Tuutsi to gain and maintain control over the population. Through *ubuhake*, the elite gained support and services and, most important, control over cattle. Consequently, though Gihura lamented the fact that Seekabaraga had never given a cow to his lineage, other Kinyagans saw the transfer of cow from patron to client as a mixed blessing. An account by Seekimondo,[23] a resident of Nyakaninya hill in the Abiiru region, dramatizes the methods by which *ubuhake* clientship was used to undermine possession of *imbaata* (personally owned) cattle.

Seekimondo's lineage had belonged to the Abashakamba social army for two generations before 1900. During Rwabugiri's reign their *umuheto* patron was Rutiishereka, who was, as we have seen, a favorite of the court and a renowned military hero. Rutiishereka transferred two cows to Maruhuuke, Seekimondo's father; these cows may have established an *ubuhake* tie, but it is not clear that they did. At least one of the cows was given for Seekimondo's sister, who became Rutiishereka's *inshoreke* ("traveling companion," or concubine).

After Rutiishereka's death in the aftermath of Rucunshu, one of his clients, Ntaabwoba, took over for him in Kinyaga. Ntaabwoba began collecting prestations from Seekimondo's lineage, demanding a cow at intervals of one or two years:

> Seekimondo ... took control over our lineage because our chief had just died. He said to himself, "These men of Kinyaga live far away [from the court] and no one else will concern himself with them."[24]

Ntaabwoba's demands went beyond the *umuheto* obligations of the past, and continued to escalate. The lineage was required to contribute as prestations not only cows, but also European cloth. Ntaabwoba held an *umurundo* (review of cattle by a chief), in the course of which he took two or three cattle from Seekimondo's lineage. Later, his son appropriated two cows belonging to widows of the lineage. When the lineage received cows as bridewealth, Ntaabwoba would sometimes take these.

Later, after being deposed from his position as hill chief of Bushenge in Impara region, Ntaabwoba came to live at Nyakanyinya and was appointed hill chief there by the chief of Abiiru at the time, Birasinyeri. This only exacerbated the situation for the Abakoobwa. Each day they sent milk to Ntaabwoba but this proved insufficient. Deprived of his previous wealth at Bushenge, Ntaabwoba sought to rebuild his herds. He seized all eighty of the lineage's cattle (of which forty had been received for bridewealth and therefore theoretically were the exclusive property of the lineage). Fearing attack, the men of Seekimondo's lineage fled the region. Ntaabwoba then expelled their mother from the lineage land.

Seekimondo attributes the loss of his cattle to the fact that he had received but a single cow from Ntaabwoba. During the reign of Musinga, Seekimondo and two others of his lineage had been called to the royal capital for training as *intoore* of the Abashakamba. The lineage had originally given three cows to Ntaabwoba, one for each recruit. Then when Seekimondo returned to Kinyaga, Ntaabwoba gave him one *ubuhake* cow, which as he sees it, was the source of many of the excesses perpetrated by Ntaabwoba.[25]

What is important about Seekimondo's experience is the drastic changes in patron–client relationships that it indicates. What had formerly been a bond of elites, a form of alliance, became a means of increasing the power of the patron to the disadvantage of the client. It is also significant that the victims of this particular patron–client relationship were from a wealthy, cattle-owning lineage that would have been viewed as Tuutsi. As clientship was extended to Kinyagans who had less wealth and status in relation to the power of the chiefs it tended to take on even more of an exploitative character. The changes were closely associated with the growth of government penetration in the area.

We have seen that during the period of German administration the imposition of hill chiefs by the central court was continued and extended. This was a process, begun under Rwabugiri, by which lineage heads who had formerly preserved direct ties to the provincial chief found themselves placed under an intermediary authority (a hill chief) who represented the provincial chief. The change was most noticeable in Abiiru Province, where the organization of administration had been less developed under Rwabugiri. During the tenure of the central chief Nyamuhenda (who held authority from after the departure of the Abapari to 1910) and Rubago (1910–1917) hill chiefs were introduced in virtually every part of Abiiru. In Impara Province, most of the hill chiefs were relatives or clients of Seekabaraga or Nyankiiko, sharing in the enhanced power these two men had gained under German rule. In both regions, the power of hill chiefs augmented as channels of appeal diminished.

One of the Abiiru hill chiefs, Mukangahe, acquired a particularly notorious reputation. A resident of Winteeko hill, he occupied a key "modern" role in the colonial context: He was an interpreter for the Germans. He was also one of Nyamuhenda's favored clients. Mukangahe and another Tuutsi named Rwabiri (Nyamuhenda's younger brother) engaged in regular cattle raids against the population; on at least one occasion, they killed the victim of their raid.[26] Later, Nyamuhenda's successor, Rubago, launched mini-wars against his subjects. At one point, he and his men attacked the Abahande lineage at Mutongo. The Abahande held off the attackers for two days, killing nine of Rubago's men, but ultimately Rubago succeeded in seizing many of the lineage's cattle.[27] In a separate incident, several of Rubago's sons and their followers attacked a lineage at Nyakarenzo, seized a bull, and burned the homesteads of several lineage members.[28] And in Impara Province, the Abadegede and their clients achieved notoriety for their treatment of Hutu.

> The Abadegede leaders would report to their superior, Rwidegembya, "This Hutu is a rebel and I'd like to teach him a lesson." Rwidegembya would answer: "I grant you this Hutu's cows." [The Abadegede] would say there was only one cow when in fact it was a whole herd.[29]

In this way, political office was seen as an opportunity for personal aggrandizement. The chiefs, their kinsmen, and their clients used power to extract surplus from the common people, or forcibly to create a surplus where there was none.

THE EARLY YEARS OF BELGIAN RULE
(1916–1940)

W E HAVE seen that Rwidegembya sent his son Rwagataraka to Kinyaga to administer the Impara region in 1911, not long after the establishment of German civil administration in Rwanda. Initially, the young chief left the region south of the Mwaga River to his father's delegates, of which the most prominent was Seekabaraga. He established his main residence at Ishara peninsula in northern Impara (present Kagano commune), and in that area he moved to appoint his own clients to hill chief positions.

Wartime conditions soon fortified his power. In 1914, after war had broken out in Europe, the German administration in Rwanda organized a regiment of Rwandan soldiers, called the Indugaruga. Rwagataraka and one of his clients, Gisazi, chief of Bugarama region, were each authorized to recruit men who would receive training in the use of guns and other basic military knowledge.[30] But in April 1916, Belgian-led troops crossed the Rusizi River and swept across Rwanda.[31] After putting up a brief resistance, German forces retreated, leaving Rwanda to the Belgians. Rwagataraka and his Indugaruga initially also retreated. But once Belgian authority had been established, after the departure of the Germans, Rwagataraka approached the victors, requesting reinstatement to his post. This was granted, and before two months had passed Rwagataraka had returned to his command in Impara. His unchallenged preeminence, however, was yet to be confirmed.

The Ibaba Revolt

UNDER GERMAN rule, Kinyagan notables such as Seekabaraga and Nyankiiko had gained power and wealth. Although nominally the local representatives of Rwidegembya, Rwagataraka's father, they were not closely supervised. Rwidegembya, who had other regions to command as well, spent much of his time at court and did not pay much attention to local matters in Kinyaga. Both Seekabaraga and Nyankiiko, his nominal subordinates, also had clientship ties to the royal court, and they aspired to become direct representatives of the central government without the intermediary of a chief like Rwidegembya. But from around 1914, and particularly after the Belgian victory in 1916, Rwagataraka began taking affairs into his own hands. These efforts threatened the local position of the Kinyagan chiefs.

During the first year of Belgian rule, the military administration regarded the Rwandan king, Yuhi Musinga, with strong suspicion. Prominent regional chiefs saw their chance and, defying royal authority, took it upon themselves to deal directly with the Belgians. Musinga was unable either to discipline those chiefs who dealt directly with the Belgians or to protect those whom the Belgians sought to punish. As the king's prestige and control over the chiefs declined, his political power was undermined. Furthermore, initially Belgian policy favored the Hutu, particularly in the northwest (a region recently and only imperfectly incorporated into the Rwandan polity).[32]

These alterations in the power equation, along with the hardship caused by a severe famine (referred to as "Rumanura") in the northwest,[33] stimulated discontent and hostility against the Belgians. Frightened by rumors of imminent revolt, the occupying force reacted with severe and arbitrary action. Rwidegembya was imprisoned in December 1916, apparently to instill respect, and hopefully order, through the simple demonstration of Belgian power directed against one of the greatest of the land. It was reasoned that such a show of force would dampen rumors and the will to revolt.[34]

Two months later, Musinga himself was jailed briefly because of allegations (said by some to have been promulgated by Rwagataraka) that the king had been in contact with Germans. The accusations were subsequently judged false and Musinga was released. Not long after, the Belgians planned to bring Musinga to trial (and were even prepared to execute him) following an accusation that the king and some of his chiefs had poisoned the milk and butter of Belgian officers. But this too remained unsubstantiated, and the trial never took place. Nonetheless the accusations were known, rumors flew, and Musinga's standing was severely tarnished. Preeminent among those who stepped in to take advantage of the king's weakened position were Rwidegembya, Kayondo, and Rwubusisi—all three members of the queen mother's lineage (Abakagara), which since Rucunshu had been consolidating its control over hills and cattle throughout Rwanda.[35]

When Major Declerck was installed as the first Belgian Resident of Rwanda (in May 1917) he reversed previous policy as part of an effort to gain Musinga's support, and permitted the king to arrest the Abakagara chiefs who had flouted royal authority. On Musinga's orders the three chiefs were imprisoned in Kigali and released only after they had formally requested the king's pardon.[36] It was in this atmosphere of intrigue and treason that Kinyagan chiefs made their move. Led by Seekabaraga and Nyankiiko, members of the Abadegede, Abeerekande, and several other lineages in Kinyaga sought to free themselves of Rwagataraka's authority. Rwagataraka hastily took to his canoe and fled out on the lake to escape attack.[37]

In planning their revolt, the Kinyagans probably took into account Rwagataraka's former support of the Germans, Rwidegembya's apparently weakened position, and Musinga's declining power in the face of recent Belgian administrative actions. The Kinyagan chiefs might have hoped for Belgian support of their bid for local autonomy (implicitly against central court power); they may at the same time have sought support from the king by pledging direct dependence on the court, without the intermediary of a discredited Rwidegembya and his son. Such a strategy would have been no more than the continuation of earlier policies of Kinyagan chiefs relative to central court politics: to seek protection and in effect local autonomy through direct clientship to the king.

But the Kinyagan revolt, known as Ibaba, met with only temporary success. Rwagataraka appealed to his father (recently released from prison and reinstated at the court) and Musinga. Rwidegembya held several important posts in central politics and had clients throughout the country. And Rwagataraka's great-aunt, Kanjogera, had used her position as queen mother to acquire a key role in decision-making at the center. The Kinyagans who led Ibaba could hardly claim such powerful contacts. Not surprisingly, the king upheld Rwagataraka's suzerainty, and the chief resumed his stewardship of Impara.[38] In the face of superior Abakagara influence at the court, the attempt by local Tuutsi to assert their autonomy had failed. Seekabaraga and Nyankiiko had gained power within the Kinyagan context by accepting and manipulating central institutions of clientship. Yet their very acceptance of central Rwandan customs and support made them vulnerable. Once they were incorporated into the central political arena, the institutions they had accepted and used to their advantage could be turned against them.

In the aftermath of Ibaba, Rwagataraka purged many Kinyagans, notably members of the Abadegede and Abeerekande lineages. He strove to centralize power, eliminating potential rivals and appointing chiefs loyal to him to fill the vacated positions. Those deposed had little recourse; to regain status and wealth, they needed a patron, and often that patron would be Rwagataraka himself.[39] The turnover in personnel reflected a tightening of control from above, a pattern which continued in the years following Ibaba.

The Increasing Powers of Patron-Chiefs

THE POLICIES and use of clientship practiced by Rwagataraka were replicated at lower levels of administrative structures in Kinyaga, as hill chiefs, sharing in the power of the chief, their "patron," used clientship to reinforce their control. During the period after 1917, as the Belgian rulers began to organize colonial administration in the kingdom, a number of new demands were made on rural people. For most of the new demands, the administration relied on the chiefs, particularly the hill chiefs, as intermediaries to the population. Political authorities thus gained additional power; as the demands of the administration increased, so too did the chiefs' coercive capacity; what were intended as administrative tools by the Belgians were all too easily and frequently turned into political weapons in the hands of the Tuutsi chiefs.

Kinyagans were called upon to supply food and cattle for European needs,[40] serve as porters, and build roads. Token salaries were paid to workers on principal roads, but "paths and secondary roads" were to be maintained by the residents of each hill, as a form of corvée (akazi).[41]

The head tax, introduced in 1917, increased regularly from 1926. Meanwhile, during the 1920s expansion of European settler enterprises in Kinyaga and in Kivu to the west created growing demands for workers.

It was common practice for a chief who collected goods or cattle or who recruited porters and road workers during this period to keep for himself any remuneration paid; the individuals who actually provided the food or did the work often received nothing. The chiefs used these resources for accumulation (building up their herds) or consumption (buying cloth, for example). They also diverted people into working in the chiefs' own fields. A 1930 administrative directive instructing Territorial Administrators to put an end to such practices singled out numerous abuses:

> In the territories where food supplies are requested from the chiefdoms, the notables sometimes proceed in the following manner: In the case of beef, cattle are requisitioned from various hills or from a variety of abagaragu. The notable who requisitions these animals delivers one to the [administrative] post where he collects the payment, and places the others in his herds or else sells them to the traders. A similar method is used in the case of food supples. . . . With the profits obtained the persons concerned buy cloth.
>
> When porters are requested from the chiefdoms, it happens that a certain number of these are not used. These are sometimes used by the notables for cultivating the latter's fields.[42]

Since refusal to comply with any of the demands the hill chief made would expose a person to the possibility of losing his land, cultivators experienced a significant decline in security of tenure. As we have seen, it was often in the interests of a chief to expel a local landholder and install others who then became directly dependent on the chief for land; the previous tenant had to move, hoping to obtain land from another chief elsewhere. Should such incidents be brought to the attention of the authorities, the chief could plead that the victim had refused to comply with some order which the chief was "entitled" to give according to colonial regulations (to pay taxes, to work for Europeans), or "traditional" practice (ubuhake service, land prestations, ubureetwa). A Territorial Administrator with several years of experience in Rwanda openly acknowledged the difficulty of judging in such cases—but he was willing to give the benefit of the doubt to the chiefs for the sake of administrative expedience.[43]

Many Kinyagans remarked upon the tyrannical practices of the politico-administrative authorities during this period; their comments are exemplified in the following accounts.

That man [hill chief at Nyamavugo] commanded like the others; when someone didn't have beans to give as prestations, he expelled him from his land, and likewise for someone who didn't have mats to give.[44]

In fact there was no recourse to the courts; a chief could take someone's goods and could chase him away or have him "killed" by another chief.[45]

They would come to take your cow on the pretext that you were a rebel, and you couldn't say anything. . . . You would let your cow go, for at the least resistance you would be put in chains or sometimes killed. And in such a case you could not introduce a court case to claim your rights on the cow.[46]

After the cows of Gisazi (Chief of the Bugarama region) had perished in the Iragara epidemic (1920–1921) he went around seizing cattle from people, both those who were clients and those who were not. The informant's lineage lost a cow in this manner.[47]

Another source of power for chiefs was the abolition of *igikingi* domains begun in 1926.[48] We have noted that an *igikingi* consisted of land held by cattle owners, in which the proprietor controlled the use of pasturage and the distribution of agricultural land. But *ibikingi*, regarded as "anomalies" by the Belgian administration, were eliminated as part of the European policy of regroupment; abolition of *ibikingi* was also viewed by the administration as a means of providing plots to cultivators who had insufficient land.

In one sense, Belgian policy merely extended a practice that had begun well before 1926, when hill chiefs appointed from outside attempted to gain control over land within their administrative domain.[49] But through standardization efforts under colonial rule, subchiefs now obtained a "legal" right to take over *igikingi* land. The major victims, cattle-owners who did not themselves hold any political office, found their pastures being turned into agricultural plots, distributed by the subchiefs.[50]

Presumably the former land clients of *igikingi*-holders would have found it necessary to seek some form of linkage with the subchief (the new "land patron"), often through *ubuhake* clientship. *Ubuhake* cattle clientship also became important for those who had or acquired cattle and lived in regions of high population density. With the reduction in amount of pasturage, and the control by subchiefs over that land, persons without an *ubuhake* patron often could not find pasturage for their cattle. This was particularly true on the Nyamirundi peninsula, where cattle density in relation to population was the highest of any area of Kinyaga.[51]

Ubuhake

UNDER THESE conditions of growing personal insecurity, it is not surprising that *ubuhake* clientship became more widespread in Kinyaga. In Impara and Abiiru regions, people who had not been clients before, and whose fathers had not been clients, acquired patrons. Moreover, after Rwagataraka's conquest of Bukunzi and Busoozo, the clientship institutions of central Rwanda were extended to those two regions as well. The process which had begun to gain momentum during the period of German rule continued, whereby individuals who had not formerly been clients often found themselves obliged to seek a patron. Such growth of cattle clientship, observable for several Kinyagan lineages, is illustrated in figures 3–5 and 7–10, chapter 5.

Ubuhake clientship during this period took a variety of forms, but two major types can be distinguished. The first of these approximated the model of clientship most commonly associated with the Rwandan political system. Maquet, for example, assumed that all Rwandans were involved in *ubuhake* cattle clientship.[52] This form involved the transfer of a cow from patron to client. The client was entitled to the cow's milk, and to the usufruct of the cow's offspring. After the cow had given birth three times, the client sometimes would give the patron a female calf.[53] Before receiving the *ubuhake* cow, the prospective client would in some cases give the patron a cow, but this occurred mainly when the client was of relatively high status in relation to the patron.[54]

In fact, *ubuhake* cattle clientship never affected more than a small percentage of Rwanda's population, but in Kinyaga, and in other regions of the kingdom, the number of clients did grow markedly during the first three decades of colonial rule; men of the generation living under the reign of Musinga (1897–1931) were more likely to adopt clientship than their fathers. Recent research by Saucier in Butare Prefecture, south of Nduga, has shown that the percentage of men there who received cows as *ubuhake* clients doubled during the colonial period; yet clients still did not exceed 17 percent of the adult male population and there was a significantly higher proportion of Tuutsi clients than Hutu.

Saucier's data show that *ubuhake* cattle clientship in earlier periods included only a small proportion of the population, certainly less than ten percent, at least in southern Rwanda.[55] Although quantitative data from Kinyaga are not available, interviews there indicate that similarly low figures prevailed for the pre-European period, and that there was a marked growth of clientship in the early colonial period.

These data and the results of research by others[56] seriously challenge earlier assumptions about universal clientship as a primordial institution, which served to integrate Rwandan society (and thus reduce barriers between ethnic groups). According to this perspective, cattle clientship was the principal cultural element forming an unvaried seamless pattern from top to bottom, a structure in which everyone but the king himself was the client of another. But the evidence from Kinyaga and other areas now makes it clear that rather than seeking clientship, many successfully evaded it; and (at least in areas outside central Rwanda) cattle clientship grew significantly only with colonial rule. It is argued here that it was in part the very recent nature of *ubuhake*, and the increasingly involuntary nature of it, which contributed to the depth of feeling against Tuutsi chiefs in mid-century.

The benefits for the client in *ubuhake* cattle clientship included the use of a cow. Where pasture was scarce an important "advantage" of the client tie was the right of the client to graze his cattle on the patron's land. This would help to explain the high proportion of people who became clients in the area around Shangi-Nyamirundi. The disadvantages of this form of clientship included the danger of losing one's personally owned cattle, should client ties subsequently be severed. A client was expected to visit his patron regularly and to carry out personal services for him. The very nature of the relationship was diffuse; the demands made at different times to the same or different clients could vary considerably. Some clients bore such humiliation as taking a beating in place of their patron,[57] others worked as domestic help at the patron's residence. More favored clients repaired the reed fence surrounding the patron's homestead[58] or carried his tobacco pouch and pipe during the daily round of visits.

A second form of *ubuhake* clientship differed from the first in that no cow was transferred from the patron to his client. Yet, although the client received no cow, he had a similar relationship to the patron and performed services similar to those required as in the first form of *ubuhake* clientship. Kinyagans refer to such clientship as *guhakwa y'ubutaka* (to pay court for the land—land clientship). As might be expected, the patron in such a relationship was often the local hill chief (later, subchief), who controlled much of the land during this period. This type of clientship bore strong similarities to *ubureetwa*, but implied a special status for clients which *ubureetwa* did not convey.

Advantages for the client included higher status than simple cultivators who were constrained to *ubureetwa* service. In addition, a client sometimes gained protection against arbitrary actions by the hill chief. The disadvantages included the performance of services for the patron, but no corresponding usufruct of a cow. On the other hand, the patron, who had given no cow to the client, could claim no "legal" rights over any personal cattle the client happened to own.

The differences in the two forms of *guhakwa* described above help to illuminate more clearly the nature of such clientship. A major reason for seeking a patron was to protect one's property and to preserve or improve one's status. For patrons, *ubuhake* clientship provided greater control over individuals, assuring a following and services. Where transfer of a cow was involved, the patron obtained control over cattle, and *ubuhake* thus replaced *umuheto* clientship in some respects. For people who owned cattle, *ubuhake* clientship was a means of "protecting" that cattle. For those who did not own cattle, *ubuhake* could serve as a means of obtaining a cow to be used for bridewealth or for increased status; a cow was not an end in itself, but rather a means to a social goal.[59] As more Kinyagans were drawn into *ubuhake* clientship, the character of client ties was modified. Status differences between clients and non-clients widened and the exigencies of protection increased, so that clientship became more necessary—and less voluntary; the element of coercion had markedly increased.

This more oppressive character of clientship was linked to three developments. The first was the gradual disappearance of the old form of *umuheto* clientship. We have seen that early *umuheto* clientship had provided protection for the cattle of Kinyagan lineages while requiring few services in return; moreover, the lineage fulfilled obligations to an *umuheto* patron in common, as a corporate unit, thus reducing the imposition on any single individual. Separated from the cohesiveness of the larger kin unit, the individual client had fewer political resources with which to face his patron.

A second factor was the extension of clientship to less powerful members of the population. Greater inequality in the relative positions of patron and client meant less negotiating power for the client.

Third (and most important), the penetration of the administrative system was more effective during this period. With greater concentration of political authority in the local hill chief and the provincial chief and the disappearance of alternative authorities, many people found it necessary to seek a favorable position vis-à-vis the chiefs. Consequently, there was a trend toward combining the position of patron with that of hill chief.

Under these circumstances, the dilemma of a potential client was severe. In considering whether to become a client of the local chief, a person owning cattle faced a difficult choice: Should he resist the pressure to become an *ubuhake* client, he would thereby risk losing his cattle (and perhaps even his land), since cattle unprotected by a patron was regarded as fair game for powerful political authorities. Even if he were not deprived of his cattle and his land, he would be liable for assignment to *ubureetwa* work (if he were Hutu), and perhaps also to *akazi* or other undesirable tasks.

Should he request the protection of an *ubuhake* patron, probably his local subchief, he would gain protection for his cattle; no one would dare to deprive him of his cattle and risk the wrath of his patron. Moreover, should he achieve a favored client status, he would probably escape burdensome tasks, and be assigned to some of the prestigious functions of *ubuhake* clients, such as carrying the patron's pipe and tobacco pouch. The disadvantage of the *ubuhake* bond, however, was the authority over the client's personally owned cattle that the patron would acquire (in practice, if not legally). Once an individual had accepted a cow symbolizing his client status, the patron (the donor of the cow) assumed rights over all of the client's cattle, even those which, from the client's point of view, were his own property.[60]

The reasons why people entered into clientship during this period highlight the coercive character the relationship acquired. The most important of these reasons was the need for protection. But the need for protection arose from the political circumstances of the time. The increased power of the chiefs and their arbitrary use of this power created conditions of great insecurity; consequently the motivation to accept clientship often resulted from direct or indirect coercion. For example, Kaamuhanda, a resident of Murehe (Abiiru region) recounted that his cows were seized by Rwagataraka and he was forced to become a client of the hill chief, Rusasura, in order to repossess these cows.

> When I complained to Rwagataraka that I had never received any cattle from Rusasura he told me that if I was unwilling [to become a client] they would take my cattle or imprison me. I had to recognize the new patron because I was threatened with losing both cows and the land given me by my father.[61]

Subsequently Rusasura gave Kaamuhanda two cows, and the latter became an *ubuhake* client. The informant's father, who possessed *imbaata* (personally owned) cattle had not been an *ubuhake* client.

A man at Shangi recounted a similar incident involving his great grandfather, who became a client to protect his personally owned cattle. This Kinyagan noted that it was commonly believed that if someone refused to accept the *ubuhake* cow, the chief would "kill" (attack or dislike) him.[62]

A resident of Muramba (Cyesha region) explained why people accepted *ubuhake* clientship:

> Someone who had no patron, but who had *imbaata* cattle would sometimes (lose these) through spoliation. They would take them all from him. They would seize him and even put him in chains. Someone who was client of a powerful patron, knowing that a certain person had cows, and that the person had no patron, would go and ask his patron to give him so-and-so's cows. He would attack this person and appropriate his cows. . . . One had to pay court *(guhakwa)* to protect any cattle which came from the gift of a friend.[63]

Some of the difficulties clients encountered with their patrons are illustrated in the following examples:

> A man at Nyamirundi explained that his father Rubango, who owned some 400 cows, became a client of Rwabirinda to protect those cows. Later Gashuuhe, one of Rwagataraka's clients, attacked a prominent member of the lineage, Nyamugura, seizing all his cattle and deposing him from his position as hill chief at Nyamirundi and as representative for the Akamarashavu *(umuheto)* group. Rubango also lost all his cattle in the affair. Nyamugura was arrested, bound, and mistreated, and he eventually died as a result. The case is well known in Kinyaga, since Nyamugura was one of the few Hutu hill chiefs at the time.[64] He was attacked "because he was rich; and they disliked rich men."[65]

> Birara, father of an informant at Shangi, obtained more than 25 cows with money he received from a German who had married his sister. He became an *ubuhake* client of Seekabaraga in order to protect these cows. Birara's brother, Mutengeri, was attacked by Ntaabukiraniro (younger brother of Seekabaraga) because he did not want to become a client. Mutengeri, a strong blacksmith, resisted and succeeded in driving away Ntaabukiraniro's men; they took

three cows from him, but Mutengeri kept the rest. This incident occurred while P. Dryvers was A.T. at Cyangugu (late 1920s or early 1930s).[66]

At Rukunguri in Abiiru, a certain Rubaba became a client of Gisazi to protect his three cows; had he not become a client, he would have risked losing the cows.[67] And Seekayanje, grandfather of a Kinyagan in Abiiru region, lived at Mururu when Rubago was hill chief there. Seekayanje found it necessary to become a client of Rubago because the chiefs and patrons at that time "were like robbers." The man named three members of his lineage who had been arrested and had their belongings seized.[68]

An account by Mudaage asserts that such conduct by chiefs was a general phenomenon, with but few exceptions:

> With the exception of Mugenzi son of Nkombe and Nyankiiko, "all the other chiefs would come with a young small heifer and would give it to you supposedly as a sign of friendship. Then for some little fault, [the chief] would take all your cows, saying that All of them had come from him."[69]

Not only was coercion a common stimulus to entering *ubuhake* clientship, it also often characterized subsequent relations between the patron and client. Some of the difficulties inherent in having a hill chief for patron are dramatized in an account by Munda, a resident of Nyamirundi hill in the Impara region.

> Munda's *ubuhake* patron was Kajonge, the local hill chief. When Kajonge was deposed by Rwagataraka, all his cattle were seized, including the cow he had given Munda, and Munda's personal cattle as well. To recover his cattle, Munda became client of Mukimbiri, who succeeded Kajonge as hill chief and thus had received Kajonge's cattle. Mukimbiri was later deposed. Munda then became client of Seemuhunyege, Mukimbiri's successor. When Seemuhunyege was deposed, his successor Birikunzira became Munda's patron. But Birikunzira seized Munda's cattle (including two cows Munda had received from Seemuhunyege). After taking his case to the king, Munda was reinstated as Birikunzira's client. But when he returned to Kinyaga, Birikunzira again seized his cattle.[70]

Munda's experience points to a common pattern in clientship to the hill chief: When a patron-chief was deposed or transferred, the client would normally become client of the chief's successor. Since the turn-over of hill chiefs came to be fairly frequent, a client often went through several different patrons. This practice weakened the importance of affective ties between patron and client, and under these conditions little remained of the former personal alliance character of clientship.

Kinyagans quite rightly perceived that clientship was becoming in-creasingly identified with the administration. Indeed the importance which Belgian colonial authorities placed on the *ubuhake* ties of pro-vincial chiefs only confirmed that perception. As the two networks— administrative hierarchy and clientship ties—became more closely in-tegrated a chief's client ties outside his own administrative domain were seen to compromise the integrity and effectiveness of administra-tive structures. Hence in Kinyaga and elsewhere in Rwanda during the 1930s, the European administration instructed chiefs to terminate *ubu-hake* links to clients outside their chiefdoms. Rwagataraka's many client linkages outside his "official" domain now represented irregular channels of administration, as noted in a 1937 report:

> The chief Rwagataraka has continued his intrigues and his efforts to meddle in the affairs of provinces which are no longer under his authority. His major means of intervention was concluding cattle contracts with "clients" residing outside the Impara and Bukunzi [provinces]. Measures have been taken to have these [contracts] rescinded.[71]

And in 1938:

> Rwagataraka . . . has continued his sordid intrigues, rendering the situation difficult for certain of his colleagues.[72]

Ubureetwa

FOR HUTU, with or without cattle, the calculation of advantages and disadvantages of *ubuhake* clientship had to take account of *ubureetwa*, a relationship in which reciprocity was entirely absent. Whereas *ubu-hake* symbolized special status in relation to the patron (however un-equal the bargaining position of the partners became), *ubureetwa* symbolized low status. And while *ubuhake* clientship affected mainly (though not exclusively) those of Tuutsi status, *ubureetwa* service was (by colonial law) made incumbent on all Hutu men. But some managed to escape. Those constrained to do *ubureetwa* service were those whose lineage, or who individually, had not achieved favored status with the local chief or some other powerful person: *Ubureetwa* was a residual category for the powerless.

It is difficult to exaggerate the exploitative character of *ubureetwa*. The services performed were usually of the most menial kind—collecting and drying firewood for the use of the hill chief's household, serving as night watchman, fetching water, cultivating the hill chief's fields. Hutu were not only expected to perform such services without pay, but were often subjected to mistreatment as well. One of the most hated duties was that of nightwatchman *(ukurarira)*. A missionary with many years experience in Rwanda described this in the following terms:

> This is the one the Hutu complained about the most. In effect, they had to go in pairs, taking turns, to spend the night in the chief's hut, standing guard. Each was required to bring a faggot of dry wood, which would be used to keep a fire going throughout the night. One wasn't permitted to rest; blows would rain heavily on anyone caught sleeping.
>
> Certain chiefs abused their authority and found ways to make this already odious duty even more irksome. It is recounted that several were so cruel they kept nightwatchmen outside the hut, exposed to the cold and the rain. . . . Others, when morning came, would oblige the unhappy watchmen to go to the spring, often far away and at the bottom of the hill, to fetch water. . . . They also had to go and cut grass. Only after such harassment were they permitted to leave.[73]

Among Hutu, a common term used for *ubureetwa* was *ubunetsi*, meaning "an obligatory corvée from which a person cannot escape and from which he receives no profit for himself."[74] For *ubureetwa* directly affected the peasants' relation to their principal economic resource: Noncompliance could provoke loss of one's land. Of the various services performed for chiefs, *ubureetwa* was "the most hated and humiliating. . . . It symbolized the servitude of the Hutu vis-à-vis the dominant minority."[75]

For many years the colonial administration resisted abolishing *ubureetwa*. This was the only "traditional obligation" which continued to enjoy legal status. Even when *umuheto* prestations and land *(ubutaka)* prestations had been replaced by money payments to the chiefs and subchiefs, *ubureetwa* was retained in its nonmonetary form. The rationale for this was in part political: "Considering that the principle of workdays owed by the Hutu to a notable was an expression of the latter's obedience, the Administration decided not to authorize a money payment in place of [this type] of corvée."[76]

Pressure from chiefs and subchiefs was undoubtedly important in this decision, and there were major economic reasons for this. In 1931 a program was inaugurated by the Administration to encourage (if not require) the cultivation of coffee for export. Chiefs and subchiefs were to be the principal planters. The initial goal of the coffee program was 1000 coffee plants for each chief, 250 plants for each subchief, and 54 plants for each rural cultivator.[77] As colonial policy encouraged the entry of political authorities into the money economy, their need for agricultural workers increased. Chiefs were also expected to plant trees to fight erosion; firewood from these woodlands produced additional income. Many chiefs also undertook cultivation of other marketable crops such as fruits and vegetables. The unpaid labor available through *ubureetwa* could thus contribute substantially to enrichment of the chiefs. Colonial policy provided both the labor and the market for chiefs to accumulate wealth.

R. Bourgeois, an idealistic young territorial officer who served as Territorial Administrator in Kinyaga (then called Kamembe Territory) in 1933–1935, noted, with chagrin, the exploitative behavior of Tuutsi chiefs:

> A Hutu came to complain to me about how the subchief Rwanya-bugigira is treating him: When he was busy maintaining his coffee field, a representative of the subchief came and requested that he go and work for the direct profit of . . . [the subchief]; he refused, only his wife went there [to work]. The Tutsi of the territory of Kamembe continue, it seems to me, to consider the Hutu as subject to corvée at their discretion ["corvéable à merci"]; it won't be long before I discover that . . . [the chiefs also] view them as subject to tax at their discretion ["taillables à merci"].[78]

Clearly, the introduction of coffee cultivation and other measures exacerbated the burdens on Hutu cultivators, who were expected to care for their own fields while the chiefs made increasing demands for labor. Often it was women who felt the brunt of these exactions. Bourgeois tried to restrict such practices, though with only limited success. His efforts were recognized by Hutu in Kinyaga who gave him the nickname "Rukiza" (shortened form of "Rukizaboro"—he who cures the poor).[79]

Belgian policy and energetic administrators such as Bourgeois did attempt to regulate and "humanize" this system of labor requisition, but when a conflict arose between the human and administrative elements, the humanitarian elements were often ignored; the attempt to humanize an institution shaped largely by Belgium's own policies was impossible without the transformation of the entire system.

The elevation of *ubureetwa* to the realm of colonial law meant that it affected more people and in a more burdensome fashion than in the past. Moreover, as the experience of Bourgeois indicates, regulations restricting *ubureetwa* were difficult to enforce; if Hutu peasants knew of the restrictions, they were often unable to benefit from them. Were a Hutu to go to court, he had to testify before Tuutsi judges against his own chief. The chief usually won, since he was accustomed to "dealing" with the European system and he often knew the judge. Even by daring to come before the court, the plaintiff risked certain retaliation on the part of the chiefs. With powers in the hands of the chiefs increasing and opportunities for legal redress curtailed, even Hutu *ubuhake* clients *(abagaragu)* found themselves compelled to perform manual labor for their patron in some areas of Rwanda after 1930.[80]

The pattern of previous periods continued during the 1930s, whereby chiefs used measures of the colonial administration to their benefit. Recruitment of workers for *akazi* was used as a weapon; so was recruitment of people for other purposes, such as work for Europeans or for participation in a program of planned emigration. Beginning in the 1930s the Belgian administration in Rwanda sponsored a program to recruit Rwandan families for "transplantation" to Gishari, a sparsely populated highland area west of Goma in the Kivu Province of the Belgian Congo (now Zaïre). In Rwanda, the primary rationale advanced for the program was the need to reduce overpopulation. The major impetus behind it, however, was the fact that increased settlement in this sparsely populated region would assure labor and low cost food supplies to European settler enterprises in the vicinity of Gishari.[81]

Consequently the administration mounted a vigorous campaign to persuade Rwandans to emigrate. In 1938, for example, the Resident of Rwanda instructed territorial administrators to make this project a major priority, warning them that the annual evaluation of their performance would be based in part on their success in finding people to emigrate. The Territorial Administrators were told that they "should not neglect any opportunity to speak about this to Hutu natives and explain to them the advantages they would find upon settling in Gishari."[82]

Decisions by Rwandans to relocate in Gishari were supposed to be made on a voluntary basis. But Kinyagan accounts suggest otherwise. For example, Karihanze, a resident of Rukunguri in Impara, associated the loss of much of his lineage's land with the Gishari program. According to Karihanze, his two brothers were forced to leave their homes when the local subchief appropriated their land to plant a eucalyptus grove (required by the administration) and obtain plots to distribute to his favorites. One brother fled to Zaïre; the other, whom the subchief planned to send to Gishari ("the place where chiefs sent people they didn't like") fled to a nearby subchiefdom where he became a land client of the subchief.[83]

Cases such as this one speak eloquently for the need of protection, but the "protection" of clientship was, as we have seen, of an ambiguous kind. The dangers of not having a patron and the harshness of client status led many Kinyagans to seek escape through employment at European plantations or enterprises. Work for Europeans had begun earlier, but during the 1930s and 1940s there occurred a substantial increase in labor demands. In some respects, work for Europeans served as a functional substitute for clientship. Just as *ubuhake* clientship in the past had sometimes exempted the client from undesirable tasks, so contract labor offered a means of escaping *ubureetwa* or *akazi* services. Rather than fulfill the exactions of a subchief in order to ensure continued occupation of their land, many Kinyagans sought economic security through wage labor. Rather than relying on the precarious "protection," which had become exploitation, of a patron-chief, many put themselves under the patronage of a European employer.

The patron–client analogy cannot be extended too far, for a variety of arrangements evolved. Among workers within Kinyaga who did not leave their homes to work, some had *ubuhake* patrons while also holding a job. This could presumably have served as a means of "protection" of any cattle they might have had or been able to buy while working— or of their land. Others, even those who bought cows with earnings from their work, tended not to become *ubuhake* clients. Some workers who contracted out to work but left their wives behind found that their wives were forced to keep up obligatory cultivation of crops and the provision of services to the subchief, and to perform other duties reminiscent of *ubureetwa*. Although an "illegal" practice, this was difficult for the Administration to control.

FROM THE WAR YEARS TO THE ABOLITION OF UBUHAKE (1940–1954)

IN 1943, a severe famine devastated many areas of Rwanda. Food shortages were less severe in Kinyaga, but Bunyambiriri and other areas to the north and east of the region were hard hit. This famine, called Ruzagayura, is remembered by Kinyagans as a time when many Rwandans from other regions moved to Kinyaga, fleeing the famine and seeking better conditions. There was also increased immigration from Bushi in the west during this period. Subchiefs apparently welcomed the new immigrants, for in the 1940s the salary of a subchief depended at least in part on the number of taxpayers under his jurisdiction.[84] Pressure on land increased as plots were distributed to the new immigrants. One sign of increasing population pressure was the departure of significant numbers of Kinyagans toward Uvira (Zaïre) apparently in search of pasturage.[85] During and after World War II, as the colonial administration became more efficient, compulsory cultivation of such crops as manioc, sweet potatoes, and coffee was enforced more rigorously. *Akazi* became more burdensome as the number of roads to build and maintain augmented, and demands for salaried workers also increased substantially. The old forms of clientship were transformed, since the principal patrons were the chiefs and subchiefs, who enjoyed a monopoly of power conditional upon the execution of demands made by Europeans. These demands they passed on to the common people, and, as we have seen, added their own exactions, which varied according to the character of the chief involved and the nature of his relationship to a particular individual. The general tendency therefore was to use power arbitrarily; in acting thus toward their relatively powerless "clients," the patrons undermined the institution itself. During the 1940s and 1950s, young men whose fathers had submitted to clientship did their best to escape such ties, taking advantage of opportunities outside the system, and acquiring access to resources beyond the control of local chiefs.

Efforts to abolish *ubuhake* cattle clientship gained momentum after World War II, reflecting the declining importance of the institution. Earlier, the colonial authorities had opposed abolition on the grounds that any such measure would undermine the authority of chiefs.[86] But in 1951, prodded by the United Nations Trusteeship Council (particularly its Visiting Mission to Rwanda of 1948), the administration stated its intention to abolish *ubuhake*.[87] And in 1952 *Umwami* Rudahigwa issued a circular explaining why he planned to put an end to *ubuhake*. Citing the increased volume of litigation in the courts between patrons and clients, he emphasized positive social and economic effects to be gained through abolition. Two years later, while the 1954 U.N. Visiting Mission was in Rwanda, the king and the national Conseil Supérieur issued a decree providing for the progressive dissolution of *ubuhake* ties and distribution of cows to former clients.[88]

It was politically expedient for chiefs to disassociate themselves from the stigma of identification with discredited practices.[89] And they may have wished to eliminate an obvious focus for potential protest, since they had acquired other and more effective means of perpetuating their dominance. The discrimination against Hutu introduced in Rwanda's Catholic schools from the late 1920s meant that it was primarily the children of Tuutsi who attended secondary school, entered the priesthood, worked in the administration, and benefited in myriad other ways from the system, even without *ubuhake*. Thus abolition of cattle clientship did not substantially threaten Tuutsi power.

The abolition of *ubuhake* did, however, contribute to further erosion of chiefly legitimacy. For the measure abolishing *ubuhake* did nothing to eliminate the exploitation characterizing the role of patrons. The patron-chiefs preserved control of land, since the edict abolishing *ubuhake* made no provision concerning pasturage rights for cattle ceded to former clients. Thus although clients acquired rights to private ownership over a portion of the cattle which they formerly held in usufruct, they had no means of pasturing these cattle, except through dependence on former patrons who controlled pasturage.[90] *Ubuhake* land clientship was not affected by the decree. And even though the hated *ubureetwa* was abolished in 1949, replaced by a mandatory money payment, this work for chiefs continued to be required in many areas of the country.[91] Hutu in Kinyaga recall that they continued to perform *ubureetwa* services until the late 1950s.[92]

The intense anti-chief and anti-Tuutsi sentiment generated by these institutions is reflected in a series of articles published during the late 1950s in Rwanda's vernacular newspaper, *Kinyamateka*. Inequality of land distribution was a central issue: Several articles pointed out that the abolition of *ubuhake* in 1954 could hardly be effective if people still depended on chiefs for land to pasture cattle and to cultivate food or cash crops.[93]

The abolition of *ubuhake* cattle clientship and *ubureetwa* occurred when the institutions were already under attack, and had very few defenders. On both ideological and practical grounds, some action became necessary. By 1950, the structures of Rwandan society and particularly the nature of political power had greatly altered from earlier times and therefore it was possible (officially) to abolish the most evident symbol of exploitation under Tuutsi colonialism, but to leave the essential structure of this exploitation intact. Abolishing the institution still left power in the hands of Tuutsi chiefs. Pasturage was still controlled by Tuutsi, so a person could not own cattle without coming to those with power over land on their terms. Also, the nature of political power had changed so that new forms of control had been incorporated at the very heart of the body politic in colonial Rwanda. These included control over labor, land, educational opportunities, wealth, and, most important, access to the state apparatus and to opportunities for consolidating power in the hands of a few. Class differentiation was not determined by ownership of the means of production per se, but by access to power over distribution, allocation, and accumulation.

The new resources of the administrative elite far exceeded what had been available in an earlier period as a result of clientship ties. Now power was based on colonial forms of production and status, rather than on institutions such as clientship. Consequently when protest came, it was articulated in general ethnic terms or in concepts such as "demo-krasi" rather than being focused on specific institutions and individuals.

The changes in patterns of governance and clientship described in this chapter led rural people to seek alternatives to the system. Colonial policy in Zaïre, oriented toward European settler plantation production in Kivu (neighboring Kinyaga to the west) provided one potential outlet; economic changes within Rwanda provided another. The next chapter will discuss how Kinyagans responded to the European labor market. In choosing clientship to Europeans over clientship to Tuutsi under these conditions, many Kinyagans forged new ideological perspectives toward their own society. The material and ideological resources they acquired from outside the local context made it possible for them to challenge the system from within—and, ultimately, with success.

PART III

THE COHESION
OF OPPRESSION

8

KINYAGA AND THE
KIVU COMPLEX

As WE have seen, two decades of German presence in Rwanda substantially altered the political processes and the dynamics of clientship. After the Belgian victory in World War I, the new Belgian administration concentrated on consolidating political power; from the mid-1920s they strove to streamline and organize the administrative system based on rule by Tuutsi chiefs. This process brought about a substantial increase in the demands that chiefs were required to (and were able to) make on the population at large. Increasingly these demands, and the larger process of which they were a part, had a corrosive effect on patron–client bonds. Belgian authorities attempted to "humanize" and "civilize" the rule of Tuutsi chiefs—they hoped to maintain the system by sanitizing it, by removing the "abuses." The problem was, of course, that such abuses were central to the way the system of chiefly rule functioned; they were not occasional aberrations, products of individual moral "lapses." In fact, as the Belgian administration recognized, harsh conditions in the rural areas served other, economic goals of the colonial state—such as producing food surpluses or cash crops for export, or "motivating" people to work for wages as a means of escaping multiple exactions in their rural communities.

The problem of establishing a viable colonial order was not, of course, a question of administrative structure alone. In Rwanda, as elsewhere in Africa, colonial statebuilding was propelled and shaped by economic concerns. Colonialism served as a vehicle for the introduction of a type of dependent capitalism. And administrative power in the colonial state was used to create one of the essential features of capitalist social formations—a class of people who lacked secure access to the basic means of production (in this case the land). The economic transformations

accompanying this—in markets, commercial networks, crops cultivated, and in the social relations of production—are important for
understanding the demands made by the Belgian administration on
Rwandan chiefs, and the exploitative goals for which chiefs used their
power. In Rwanda generally, the economic policies of the colonial
state—often themselves contradictory—contributed to the contradictory nature and impact of chiefly rule, and fostered the growth of political consciousness among rural dwellers. This chapter will outline
some of the major features of Belgian economic policies toward
Rwanda, and, more broadly, toward the combined administrative entity
of Ruanda-Urundi—a very small, resource-poor colony adjacent to (and
administered as a part of) the Belgian Congo. The discussion will then
explore the particular ramifications of Belgian economic policies and
the system of labor control which developed at the local level in
Kinyaga.

BELGIAN COLONIAL ECONOMIC POLICIES

L IKE COLONIAL administrations elsewhere, the Belgian administration in Ruanda-Urundi had to confront the problem of how the
colony was to support itself; obtaining revenues to support the colonial
enterprise became particularly critical during the global economic crisis
of the 1930s. Under German rule, the export taxes on various products,
especially hides, had served as an important source of revenue; localized
attempts to introduce a hut tax (after 1913) had met with only limited
success. Hides continued to be an important revenue-producing export
in the early years of Belgian rule. In the 1930s, these revenues were
supplemented by taxes levied upon mining installations established in
the colony (primarily in the eastern area of Rwanda). But gradually,
Belgian colonial revenues came to rest on individual taxation and on
the extension of export taxes on food and cash crops (produced principally by smallholders). Key features of Belgian economic structures in
Ruanda-Urundi from the mid-1920s were tax collection (carried out by
the chiefs), as well as, in some areas, labor recruitment, and the encouragement of food and cash-crop production. From the mid-1920s
both food and labor were exported to serve the interests of economic
order in the Congo.

The system of tax collection imposed by the Belgian administration
was relatively effective: By 1931–1932 revenues from direct taxes on
rural people constituted about 50 percent of revenues for Ruanda-

Urundi.[1] And early official reports stressed this region's agricultural potential. The high population density, fertile land, and abundant rainfall of Rwanda and Burundi were seen to offer enormous possibilities for providing food to the much larger and less densely populated Congo. For example, a 1923 report by the Belgian administration in Ruanda-Urundi praised the inclusion of the colony in a customs union with the Congo, which, it claimed, had already "had a profound impact on the agricultural development of the country which will soon be able to provide enough local foods to feed the industrial centers of the Congo."[2] The report noted the emphasis in earlier reports on the potential of agriculture as the most important economic resource of the country, and commented, "This possibility has become a reality, and the role of this country as a source of food for Katanga [the copper-mining region in the southern part of the Congo] is being increasingly confirmed."[3] In addition to food, however, the people of Ruanda-Urundi were to supply the Congo with labor as well. We have seen that recruitment of workers for the mines of Katanga began in Ruanda-Urundi in 1925, with a small group of 216 men and a few wives and children.[4] The number of recruits increased rapidly during the next five years, reaching a total of more than 7000 by 1929.[5] Many Rwandans also went to Kivu province in eastern Congo to work on plantations or in service jobs in the embryonic urban centers.

Recruitment for the Katanga mines was halted in 1930 (it would not be resumed until 1949), and exports of food from Ruanda-Urundi to the Congo were temporarily suspended in the late 1920s in the wake of widespread famine. Food shortages had appeared in some local areas of Burundi in 1922 and 1923 with devastating impact.[6] Famine spread to other areas of Burundi in 1924 and hit the eastern and central regions of Rwanda as well. While the worst of the famine ended in 1926, famine conditions recurred in various local regions of Rwanda and Burundi for several years thereafter.[7] Nevertheless, food was exported from Ruanda-Urundi to the Congo in 1924 (3308 tons) and, in diminished quantities, in 1925 (2615).[8]

The famine of the 1920s and the worldwide depression which followed closely on its heels mark an important turning point for Belgian policy in Ruanda-Urundi. Ostensibly to counteract the famine, the administration introduced a series of programs that required vastly increased demands on rural manpower and set forth an explicit policy of reinforcing the power of the chiefs, who were responsible for seeing that each directive was carried out in all its details. The measures included the imposition of compulsory cultivation of famine-resistant

food crops (cassava, sweet potatoes and, in some areas, European potatoes), reclamation of marshes to provide additional land for cultivation, the introduction of required cash crop production (primarily
coffee) and reforestation programs. In addition, the administration introduced an ambitious program of roadbuilding.[9]

Introduced in Rwanda in the mid- and late-1920s, these measures
were substantially intensified during the Depression and in 1937 began
to be supplemented by an anti-erosion program. This was really much
more than an anti-famine campaign. It can best be understood as part
of a larger effort on the part of the state to control and channel African
labor, directing it toward projects that would contribute to the revenues
of the state, either directly (through the head tax and taxes on exports)
or indirectly (through facilitating the operations of European companies
and, in Kinyaga, of settlers, whose activities were regarded as important
to the economic growth of the colony).

The emphasis on forced peasant production reflected in part the outcome of an intense debate in Belgian colonial circles, a debate precip-
itated by the Depression, on the economic future of the Belgian Congo.
Boom conditions in the 1920s had resulted in rapid expansion of commerce and industries in the Congo. The depressed prices of the 1930s
led to massive layoffs in the industrial sector and a reevaluation of the
economic policies of the colony.[10] One result was a renewed interest
in peasant agricultural production in the Congo, to be based on coerced
labor regulated by the state.[11] Proponents of policies requiring Africans
to grow minimum acreages of food or non-food cash crops saw these as
humanitarian and "educational" measures.[12] The goal, they asserted,
was to guard Africans against famine and to provide incomes for smallholders. Critics, while accepting the need for greater emphasis on agriculture, deplored the resort to coercion. Some pointed out that
production levels had not been a problem in the 1920s when prices paid
to producers were high enough to constitute incentives.[13] Others alleged
that the main purpose of the policy of forced production was to ensure
availability of local products at very low prices, which European ex-
porters in the Congo could buy cheaply (and still sell for a profit on the
depressed world markets) or, in the case of food crops, which would
provide regular supplies of food cheaply to industrial enterprises such
as mines.[14] As Merlier has pointed out:

> Obligatory crop cultivation (referred to as "educational") was used
> to stabilize the balance of trade which still brought in four billion
> [francs] from 1931 to 1937: in contrast to the policy of mineral

production, a drop in the world agricultural markets was met with an increase in production and especially with a reduction in peasant incomes.[15]

In Ruanda-Urundi, a crucial component of policies for mobilizing rural labor was a renewed commitment on the part of Belgian authorities to "respect and reinforce" the power of "indigenous authorities" (by which was meant Tuutsi chiefs). Articulated in the program of Governor Voisin in 1930, the policy instructed European administrative personnel to keep in mind that "without the collaboration of indigenous authorities, the occupying power would find itself powerless and faced with anarchy." The Voisin program called for more careful supervision of chiefs "to avoid abuses in the area of prestations and customary corvées," and specified that the chiefs who were judged "incompetent" would be dismissed and replaced.[16] By the mid-1930s, the chiefly cadre in Rwanda was smaller in number and better educated than in the past: in 1935, 60 percent of the 969 chiefs and subchiefs in Rwanda were literate, and over 80 percent of them were Christians (overwhelmingly Catholic).[17] Chiefs were also more closely supervised and supported by the European administration, particularly in the area of obligatory work, tax collection, and labor recruitment.

The system was not, however, designed to limit abuses. The chiefs were expected to supervise and enforce the system of obligatory cultivation; they were to mobilize labor for roadbuilding, reforestation and building various installations for state activities (such as rural hospitals and dispensaries). And now chiefs were also to become major coffee growers, presumably by making use of "traditional" tribute in labor *(ubureetwa)* on the part of the general population.[18] Finally, one of the most important roles of the chiefs and subchiefs was to collect taxes. From the point of view of the Belgian colonial authorities, the streamlining of administrative structures, accomplished through the regroupment program of chiefdoms and subchiefdoms and the removal of "incompetent chiefs," was an important means of improving the efficiency of tax collection. Census records were compiled more precisely, and chiefs were instructed that tax collection was a central feature of their job.

The removal of *Umwami* Musinga from office in 1931 coincided, not accidentally, with these efforts to increase the ability of chiefs to impose state-mandated demands upon the population. Musinga's son Rudahigwa was designated as successor to his father, not according to Rwanda tradition but by the Belgian colonial authorities and the Catholic Church in Rwanda. One of Rudahigwa's first official acts (for which he was lavishly praised by the administration) was to abolish prestations in kind made to the chiefs and the king. These were replaced by a money payment (with a portion allocated to an official at each level: subchief, chief, and king) to be collected at the same time as the annual head tax.[19] This change provided additional incentives for Rwandan chiefs and subchiefs to collect taxes, since their own income was determined directly as a proportion of the taxes they collected.

By 1937 an estimated 41,000 hectares of marshland had been drained and prepared for irrigated cultivation; of these more than 30,000 hectares had been planted with crops. Some 7000 hectares of reforestation plots had been planted, and the road network in Rwanda and Burundi had been increased to more than 6000 kilometers of primary and secondary roads. More than 20 million coffee trees had been planted in the two countries by 1937; of these, 50,000 belonged to chiefs, 700,000 to subchiefs, and 19.8 million to peasants. While in 1927 coffee production from Ruanda-Urundi was about 10 tons, this had risen to 2000 tons in 1937.[20]

One consequence of the forced mobilization of rural manpower and more effective collection of taxes was a marked improvement in the financial situation of Ruanda-Urundi, despite the economic vicissitudes of the Depression. As a result of the world economic crisis and the drastic decline in world prices for primary products, the value of exports from Ruanda-Urundi had plummeted, with a direct impact on the colonial state's income from customs duties. In both Rwanda and Burundi (as in the Congo) the state weathered the crisis by squeezing the rural population. During the 1930s, the volume of hides and other exports from Rwanda and Burundi rose substantially (making up in part for the reduced value of these exports), and during the same period, the proportion of income for the Ruanda-Urundi state budget coming from head and cattle taxes rose significantly.[21]

In 1936 the territory of Ruanda-Urundi achieved a balanced budget for the first time. Income that year totaled 35 million francs, expenditures 31,200,000 francs. Revenues from the head tax, cattle tax, and money payments for "traditional" prestations amounted to 16 million francs, some 45 percent of the governmental receipts. Income from export and excise duties and contributions from mining operations provided the major part of the remaining income. Not counted in the budget were the important contributions in unpaid labor provided by cultivators in the chiefdoms that drained marshes, maintained the roads and footpaths, and carried out the reforestation programs.[22]

Impositions on the rural population were further increased after 1937, with intensification of the coffee campaign and an associated program for constructing anti-erosion ditches (rural people were constrained to terrace steep hills to inhibit erosion).[23] Between 1937 and 1945 coffee production rose further, from 2000 tons to 4800 tons.[24] But such export crop production was viewed by many Rwandans as "a European scheme for their own enrichment at the expense of the African."[25]

Under these conditions, "work" came to be the byword of the dual colonial state during the interwar period and after:

> Thus for several decades the country became a vast camp of forced work of a new type. The very notion of work came to be practically synonymous with corvée, to the point that the representatives of Authority themselves, natives as well as Europeans, understood it as such and interpreted it with this transformed nuance.[26]

Harsh rural conditions, particularly the multiple demands enforced on the population by the chiefs, were important in pushing rural Rwandans to migrate in search of work. In most areas of Ruanda-Urundi, opportunities for earning money were relatively limited, and work conditions and pay were poor relative to neighboring regions in East Africa and the Congo. From the central, southern, and northern areas of Rwanda, many migrated to Uganda or Tanganyika to escape rural exactions and to obtain higher earnings than could be got at home:

> This explains the massive emigration of men and able-bodied youth to the British Protectorate of Uganda: they went to look for work as *free labor.* This exodus reached dramatic proportions in certain areas of the country, such that young women also had to emigrate because they were no longer able to marry, so drained of young men had these regions become.[27]

In Kinyaga and the regions north of Kinyaga along the shore of Lake Kivu, people went west to the Congo or found jobs locally with European settlers in the area. Consequently, those left behind found it all the more difficult to cultivate the required obligatory fields and also fulfill the heavy demands for labor on "public works."

During World War II the colonial authorities called upon Rwandans to make significant contributions to the war effort. The conditions of the League of Nations Mandate prohibited the recruitment of Africans in the territory for military service. Instead, the Belgian administration required Rwandans to provide cheap food and cows for slaughter to assure supplies for the industrial centers in the Congo, where stepped-up production was seen as crucial to the war effort. Cattle-owners were forced to sell their cattle at ridiculously low prices; some men apparently committed suicide seeing their herds decimated in this way. And despite a two-year drought, cultivators were forced to sell beans to European middlemen for less than one franc per kilo; the middlemen later sold these products for enormous profits (beans for at least 5 francs per kilo) in the Congo.[28]

In these conditions, people migrated in larger numbers than ever before to Uganda, leaving behind (in some areas) mainly old people and children. The prolonged drought, labor migration, "harassing corvées which caused serious loss of time," and the "fléau de profiteurs de guerre" were key elements in the Ruzagayura famine that struck Rwanda in 1943.[29] Relief food supplies from the Congo were not brought in until the end of 1943, a year after the onset of famine; during the course of this food crisis, which lasted two years, at least 300,000 people died.[30] Like the Gakwege famine in the 1920s, the 1943 famine gave rise to intensified impositions on the population: in a decree of 1944, the colonial government ordered that all cultivators were to plant at least 35 ares of seasonal food crops (such as beans, peas, corn); in addition, they were to plant and maintain 25 ares of non-seasonal food crops (a substantial increase over the earlier 10 ares which had been mandated in 1926), which were to include 15 ares of manioc except in regions above 1900 meters, where sweet potatoes, potatoes, or other approved root crops could be substituted.[31]

In Kinyaga, as elsewhere in Rwanda, obligatory cultivation was enforced, roadbuilding and reforestation were pushed, anti-erosion ditches were imposed, and taxes were collected. The demands on chiefs to execute these programs have been noted in much of the literature on colonial Rwanda; oral and archival data from Kinyaga confirm such accounts. Little attention has been given in the published sources, however, to the conflicting relationship of these demands with the role of chiefs as labor recruiters for European enterprises. In Kinyaga, because of the region's proximity to the Congo, such labor demands contributed substantially to the oppressive character of chiefly rule. At the base of these conditions were contradictory views among European administrators, missionaries, and settlers over the extent to which labor should be "free" or coerced.

Earlier chapters have noted that Kinyaga's distance from central Rwanda and proximity to different peoples in the west contributed to cultural heterogeneity in the region and affected attitudes of Ndugans toward Kinyagans. Central chiefs tended to disdain Kinyagans and flaunt their "superiority" over them. Kinyagans resented the extension into their region of central administrative forms and institutions. Aside from differences in customs and attitudes, however, Kinyaga's peripheral location added an important dimension to the nature and impact of economic change in the region. The fertile soils and abundant rainfall in the areas near Lake Kivu, as well as the moderate climate and availability of transport on the lake, served as a strong attraction for European settlers and enterprises. During the 1920s and after, an expansion of plantations and mines in Kivu province of the Congo and in Kinyaga led to opportunities both for the development of smallholder production of marketable food commodities by Africans and for involvement in commerce, as well as to massive demands for labor. These different facets of economic change placed contradictory pressures on local labor supplies, pressures exacerbated by the development of coffee growing in the region by both European settlers and African smallholders. The conflicting demands for *main d'oeuvre* (manpower) dramatized the incompatible demands being made on chiefs. The active role of the European administrators and chiefs in recruiting labor added to the harshness of demands on the population (already overburdened by various required cultivation schemes and work projects), while at the same time wage labor provided to some Kinyagans channels of escape from administration at home. Both the harshness of administration and the escape which implied participation in wage labor elsewhere contributed to the later growth of overt organized protest against clientship and chiefly rule.

EUROPEAN SETTLERS IN KINYAGA AND KIVU

THE ESTABLISHMENT of European settlers in Kinyaga began during the 1920s. The largest employer during this period was the Protanag Company *(Société Coloniale des Produits Tannants et Agricoles)*, a large undertaking whose staff included nineteen Europeans in 1929. Protanag initi.lly planted coffee, gradually introducing black walnut trees to be exploited for tannin. The company had received authorization to occupy 981 hectares (slightly over 2400 acres); by 1929 it had planted 480 hectares and was employing 1500 Kinyagans.[32] Labor recruitment for Protanag was highly localized; in areas surrounding the company's concessions (located in Impara chiefdom, near to Lusunyu and Kibazi in present Kamembe and Karengera communes, respectively), it was estimated that more than 80 percent of the available men were employed.[33] In addition to the Protanag operations, toward 1929 the Compagnie de la Rusizi began to introduce cotton in the Bugarama region of Kinyaga. There was also a government-run model farm at Ntendezi and an industrial school at Kamembe.[34]

While the European settler population in Kinyaga was still quite small during the 1920s, it was already developing rapidly in the Kivu province of the Congo (until 1933 a "district" of the larger Orientale Province). After World War I, Europeans in considerable numbers came to Kivu, setting up plantations of coffee, tea, and quinine, and later undertaking mining enterprises. In 1925 there were about 192 European settlers in Kivu; by 1929 the number had risen to some 943.[35] These figures include all of Kivu, but a large proportion of the early Europeans settled near Lake Kivu. Demands for labor in the area increased so sharply between 1926 and 1929 that the colonial administration in Kivu "closed" several territories to recruitment.[36] Kinyagans were recruited to supplement the insufficient labor force on the western side of the lake. As noted with some alarm in a missionary's report of 1929,

> New economic conditions, created by the establishment of large agricultural companies in the District [Cyangugu] and especially the proximity of numerous settlers in Kivu . . . are a real difficulty for our work. . . . A lot of young people, for love of lucre or to flee the work requisitioned by the State, go to take on long term service. Christians often lose their morals if not their faith, the catechumens and pagans become indifferent to [Christian teachings].[37]

The World Depression resulted in a general reduction in labor demands and a lowering of wages in Kivu, although agricultural expansion continued: the estimated amount of land planted in coffee in Kivu more than doubled during the period 1929–1936, increasing from 5528 to 11,655 hectares.[38] After the Depression large-scale commercial agriculture and mining enterprises continued to expand in Kivu, and demands for labor increased as well. In 1935–1937 the European administration in Kivu again closed several territories to labor recruitment, advising European settlers and companies to seek workers outside those areas.[39]

In Kinyaga, the Depression arrested the activities of Protanag, but by 1939 there were some 11 European settlers with agricultural concessions and two agricultural companies in Cyangugu Territory, holding a total of about 1200 hectares. (From 1936 to 1953 Cyangugu included Rusenyi chiefdom, the area north of the Kilimbi River, which was formerly a part of Kibuye territory; therefore, these figures include European holdings in Rusenyi.)[40] In 1946, the number of Europeans holding agricultural concessions had risen to 35 and the area of their concessions to almost 2000 hectares. By 1948, some 50 Europeans held about 2500 hectares in Cyangugu Territory.[41] Most of these concessions were located in Kinyaga, south of the Kilimbi River; they were particularly numerous in Cyesha chiefdom, where fertile soils suitable for coffee-growing and the ease of transport on the lake were important in attracting settlers. Gold mining activities opened in 1936 in northeast Kinyaga, in the Nyungwe forest, adding further to the demands for labor. These activities were supplemented during the 1940s by the development of smaller mining operations for extracting cassiterite and small-scale industrial undertakings such as brick factories.

LABOR DEMANDS

THE GROWTH of plantations and other enterprises in Kinyaga led to a progressive augmentation in the wage labor force. Labor demands from Europeans in Kinyaga had to compete with demands from European establishments west of the lake. The development of an urban center at Bukavu (opposite Cyangugu in the Congo) from the late 1920s and higher wages paid in Bukavu and Kivu further exacerbated the labor drain on Kinyaga.

No precise figures are available for the number of Kinyagans employed as wage earners in their own region. Colonial government statistics are available for some years, but not from the same sources for each year.[42] Categories of workers included in the figures for one year sometimes do not appear for other years, making it difficult to compare figures. The colonial government depended on employers to supply statistics on numbers of employees, and upon occasion certain employers did not submit this information. (Table 3 provides an approximate idea of the growth of the wage labor force within Cyangugu Territory during the period 1930–1958, although the caveats mentioned above should be kept in mind.)

Similarly, few reliable figures are available on the numbers of Kinyagans who went to work in the Congo, but data from oral accounts and comments in administrative reports indicate that large numbers of Kinyagans went west to work on the plantations of Kivu and in the mines of Kivu and Katanga (now Shaba) in the Congo. Recruitment in Ruanda-Urundi by the Union Minière du Haut Katanga mining company began in 1925 and continued until 1929.[43] During the five-year

TABLE 3: Wage workers in Cyangugu Territory, 1930–1958

Year	Administration	Missions	Other[a]	Total
1930[b]	225	419	1,469	2,113[b]
1931	266	400	1,175	1,841
1935	65	279	1,402	1,746
1941[b]				5,440[b]
1942				6,616
1943	1,990	892	3,997	6,879
1944	1,309	731	4,446	6,486
1947				8,800
1948[c]	no fig. avail.	997	5,401	6,398[c]
1949	"	955	6,087	7,042
1950	"	1,055	6,365	7,420
1951	"	900	5,150	6,050
1952				5,690
1953[d]	no fig. avail.	800	4,325	5,125[d]
1954				12,465[e]
1955	no fig. avail.	500	4,250	4,750
1956				7,081
1958	no fig. avail.	511	6,070	6,581

[a]The category "other" includes workers in mining enterprises, agricultural establishments and industrial operations; in some years it includes employees of traders (less than 200 workers).

[b]The figures for 1930–1935 apply only to Kinyaga. From 1936 through 1952, Rusenyi Province was added to Cyangugu Territory so that the figures given here for 1941–1952 include Rusenyi as well as Kinyaga.

[c]For 1948 and subsequent years (with the exception of 1952, 1954, and 1956) the figures do not include employees of the administration.

[d]Figures for 1953 and after do not include Rusenyi.

[e]This figure, from the "Rapport Annuel AIMO" (Territoire de Shangugu) includes categories that are omitted from figures in other years. In the source used for most other years, the figure for 1954 is given as 4,750 (Territoire de Shangugu, "Estimation des Ressources des indigènes pour l'année 1954).

SOURCES: *Rapport sur l'administration du R-U,* 1930, 84.
Rapport sur l'administration du R-U, 1931, 88.
Loose page giving number of workers in Shangugu Territory, 1941–1944 (probably from Territoire de Shangugu, "Rapport annuel, AIMO, 1944.")
Rapport sur l'administration du R-U, 1947, 61.
Territoire de Shangugu, "Estimation des ressources des indigènes pour l'année," 1948, 1949, 1950, 1951.
Territoire de Shangugu, "Rapport annuel, AIMO, 1952," 38/1.
Territoire de Shangugu, "Estimation des ressources des indigènes pour l'année," 1953, 1955, 1959.
Territoire de Shangugu, Effectif maximum de travailleurs, "Rapport annuel, AIMO, 1954," 33.
A. T. Shangugu to Director Provincial de l'Economie à Bukavu, 91/R.A., 8 January 1957.

period, UMHK sent more than 7000 workers from Ruanda-Urundi to mines in Katanga (Zaïre); there is evidence that a large proportion of the recruits came from Rwanda. No statistics are available as to the number of Kinyagans recruited, but the zone of recruitment did include Cyangugu Territory (excluding the Rusizi Valley).[44]

From 1930, Bukavu grew in importance as a center of services and supply for settlers in Kivu and Kinyaga, adding to demands for labor.[45] Workmen were needed to build and maintain Bukavu's buildings; skilled and semi-skilled workers in trades such as mechanics, masonry, and carpentry were in great demand for the service industries of the town. Jobs as domestic servants were abundant, and in later years demand grew for clerks in various businesses. Even though the area around Bukavu was heavily populated, the large number of European plantations in the vicinity added to heavy labor demands there, and workers from other areas (such as Kinyaga) were called on to supplement the local labor supply.[46]

Government reports from the 1930s and later invariably note the significant impact on Kinyaga of the economic changes and labor demands in Kivu. In 1938, an official report noted that the region

is ... in the zone of attraction of the Congolese district of Kivu, to which it already supplies considerable labor and a variety of products.[47]

The report for 1939–1944 commented in a similar vein:

Kivu ... has continued to exert strong economic attraction on this Territory. This has resulted in the ongoing transformation of the activities of the natives of the western region of Shangugu, many of whom prefer to devote themselves to petty commerce or to offer their services to large companies.[48]

Despite their heavy involvement in commerce and wage labor, Kinyagans were still expected to maintain compulsory cultivation of crops and to perform various types of akazi. In 1946 the Territorial Administrator at Cyangugu assembled the chiefs and subchiefs of the region to give them the following instructions:

1. ... we appeal to the spirit of collaboration [of the chiefs and subchiefs] to "work better, work more."

2. We inform the subchiefs who are present of the results of yesterday's meeting with the settlers and the chiefs. We expect more firm collaboration from the subchiefs so that the indisci-

pline so evident among the Bahutu will cease. It is necessary that the native authorities become aware of the fact that they represent the State, and they must rule those they administer with justice and firmness. And in this regard, they must require from all Bahutu [who are] not working for Europeans the completion of all duties with regard to [obligatory] crops, the struggle against erosion, and the maintenance of the roads.

3. The collection of taxes must be intensified.[49]

In 1947 the colonial government's annual report noted that

The administration of the chiefdoms of this Territory is rendered more difficult by the proximity of Costermansville [Bukavu] and the arrival of European settlers at Shangugu which gives rise to substantial demands for local labor. Thirty percent of able-bodied men are working for European enterprises.[50]

Again, in 1952:

As in the past, the Territory of Shangugu continues to maintain very close relations with Kivu Province. Each morning hundreds of workers from Shangugu cross the bridge over the Ruzizi to go to work in Costermansville [Bukavu] and return to their homes in the evening.[51]

Official estimates of the number of "seasonal emigrants" from Cyangugu Territory working in Zaïre were 2000 in 1948, 3000 in 1953, 2500 in 1954 and 1955, 2900 in 1958.[52] The official figures for the total number of Kinyagans working in Zaïre in 1952 (including both "permanent"—on contract—and "non-permanent"—employed on a daily basis) was 4178.[53] In 1958 it was estimated that more than 2000 Kinyagans crossed daily from Cyangugu to work in Bukavu alone.[54]

Although these figures provide some indication of the extent of labor demands, they are probably underestimates. In spite of attempts to control and register labor recruitment and labor migration, colonial officials could not have known of all those who went away to work. The efforts of administrators in this regard were complicated by the common practice among Rwandans of using a new name when they undertook contract work.[55]

Comparison of statistics on wage earners with figures on population is likely to be misleading. Population mobility was high in Kinyaga during the colonial period, and therefore the figures on "hommes adultes valides" (able-bodied men registered in the administration records) were probably overestimates. This possibility is given credence by the situation in Cyesha chiefdom during 1942, at the height of wartime impositions. In a report deploring the harsh exactions being levied on the population, missionaries at the Catholic Mission of Nyamasheke noted that although official figures put the number of taxpayers (able-bodied men) at about 6000, the number actually present in the chiefdom during 1942 was only 3050. In that year, a total of 1520 men were employed on a daily (non-contract) basis. This figure, which did not even include those employed on contract, constituted nearly 50 percent of the actual adult population of the chiefdom at the time (3050), although according to official population figures, it would have amounted to only about 25 percent.[56]

Moreover, even if the population figures could be taken as accurate, comparison of statistics on workers with population figures for all of Cyangugu Territory need be regarded with circumspection. Participation in wage labor was much higher in the western parts of the Territory, near the lakeshore and on the hills bordering the Rusizi River.[57] Therefore, a figure showing the number of adult men employed as a percentage of the total number of "hommes adultes valides" in Cyangugu Territory would underrepresent the actual proportion of workers recruited on many particular hills.

The Belgian Administration and Labor Recruitment

IT WAS an integral part of Belgian colonial policy to aid in—if not to organize outright—the recruitment and control of labor. "European enterprise" was regarded as desirable, if not essential, to the functioning of the colony, and members of the administration were expected to facilitate the smooth operation of the settlers' activities. The administration stipulated regulations for employment of labor, including the terms of labor contracts, and administrators took an active role in recruiting. Indicative of Belgian policy in this regard was a letter sent in 1940 by the Resident of Rwanda to the Territorial Administrator at Cyangugu concerning the months when temporary workers "would be particularly welcomed by the coffee planters of Kivu." The communication gave the following instructions:

> Please take note of the above [instructions] and do what is necessary so that no obstacle be placed in the way of the hiring of natives under your jurisdiction, especially during the above-mentioned periods.[58]

The instruction that "no obstacle be placed in the way of recruiting workers" carried implications that the Territorial Administrator well understood: the population was to be informed of the "opportunities" to work for wages, and measures designed to encourage or pressure people to work for Europeans (such as higher taxes) were to be vigorously enforced. When the hiring of workers on contract was involved, the local officials were to ensure that various incentives favoring contract workers were in fact applied, such as exempting them from *akazi* and allowing (in fact obliging) them to make payment in lieu of *ubureetwa* service. A letter of 1938 from the Territorial Administrator in Cyangugu to three subchiefs regarding labor for the Nyungwe mines reflects these concerns:

> I am sending you herewith a copy of an extract from the note dated 30 March 1938 from Monsieur Le Resident du Ruanda, following a labor shortage at the Nyongwe [mine], where the situation, [which is] extremely irksome for the smooth operation [of the mine], should command your full attention:
>
> 1) the workers ["*engagés*"] at Nyongwe have the moral and legal obligation to complete their contract without interruption, even if they have not signed a regular contract, for they have all received equipment.
>
> 2) The chiefs and sub-chiefs have absolutely no right to recall to their hills any natives who have signed on to work for this enterprise.
>
> 3) The chiefs and sub-chiefs do not have the right to require that the wives and children of the workers carry out [obligatory] cultivation as provided for by Regulation 89.
>
> 4) The chiefs and sub-chiefs have no right to require the workers at Nyongwe to perform forced labor associated with *ubuletwa*; it is sufficient to remind them that the mine workers living in the workers' camps pay their *ikoro*, *ibihunikwa* and *ubuletwa* taxes in money and that the obligatory work duties thus paid for will be paid in money to the rightful claimants.
>
> 5) The chiefs and sub-chiefs are obliged to return immediately to the mine all those from their administrative domain who have left work without having successfully completed their contract.[59]

European settlers in Kivu would sometimes write to Kigali requesting permission from the Resident of Ruanda to recruit workers in Cyangugu; the Resident would then send instructions to the Territorial Administrator at Cyangugu to provide assistance in labor recruitment.[60]

European administrative authorities in Bukavu and Kivu province also used Cyangugu Territory as a labor pool. Several requests for workers addressed to the Territorial Administrator in Cyangugu during 1947 illustrate this point. In May 1947 the Territorial Administrator at Bukavu requested that Cyangugu send 20 workers to help prepare administrative buildings of the town for a visit by the Prince Regent and the Minister of Colonies from Belgium.[61] In November of the same year, Cyangugu was called on to supply workers for preparation of the Bukavu racetrack before a horse race,[62] and in December the Governor of Kivu Province wrote to the Territorial Administrator at Cyangugu requesting a force of 120 workers to be "used for upkeep of the gardens of Costermansville and paid at the normal rate."[63] An order was then sent from Cyangugu to Biniga, the Chief of Abiiru Province, instructing him to send twenty of the workers, which the Governor of Kivu wished to have immediately:

> To meet a request from the Governor [of Kivu], it is your responsibility to supply *as soon as possible* 20 workers to the [government] Agricultural Officer . . . in Costermansville.[64]

As the labor force grew in size, the attempts to control contract labor required increasing attention on the part of colonial officials in Cyangugu. Regulations governing contracts imposed sanctions for any worker who "deserted" before the expiration of his contract;[65] the government was to pursue and return to the employer any Rwandan known to have broken a work contract. Employers (in Kivu, Kinyaga, and elsewhere) filed complaints with the Territorial Administrator at Cyangugu about residents of Cyangugu Territory who had left before terminating their contracts, and the volume of such complaints came to dominate the work of the Territorial Administration at Cyangugu during the 1950s.

Chiefs and Labor Recruitment

CHIEFS WERE expected to play an active role in labor recruitment. A 1929 report noted that the administration encountered no difficulty recruiting workers; the A.T. would establish a list for each of the hills adjoining an area where work was in progress on construction or roadbuilding, and the chiefs of the area would be instructed to deliver a specified number of workers.[66] Until about 1930 it was common practice throughout Rwanda for chiefs who recruited workers to take the wages for themselves.[67] Several Kinyagans confirmed this; one claimed

that during the 1920s a delegate of Rwagataraka had recruited him to
work on a European enterprise at Kamembe. About 150 men worked
there, making cigars and operating machines to produce sacks. The
wages were taken by the recruiter; the workers received nothing.[68] By
collaborating in recruiting workers for European settlers, chiefs also
gained additional discretion over the population; it was left to the chiefs
and subchiefs to decide who had to go and who would be allowed to
stay.

Although European administrators were aware of such problems, the
abilities of Rwandan authorities to circumvent any controls were generally more effective than the controls themselves. In fact, the system
worked also to the benefit of the European community, including the
administrators themselves. Consequently, the colonizer was caught in
the contradictory position of attempting to assure "adequate" administrative authority in the hands of the Tuutsi chiefs on the one hand,
and professing the desire to control abuses on the other. The administrative system was predicated on the basis of chiefly power; only individual administrators were concerned about abuses.

But in sending people to work for Europeans the chiefs were under-
mining their own authority over the long term. Working as wage earners gave some Kinyagans a chance to gain economic independence and,
eventually, a certain autonomy vis-à-vis the chiefs. A growing awareness of this and an unwillingness to relinquish rural manpower from
local projects (including the cultivation of chiefs' fields) may help to
account for the reluctance of chiefs to cooperate with labor recruitment
efforts during the 1930s. As demands for labor increased, some chiefs
tried to hinder recruitment in their areas by making life extremely
uncomfortable for people who went to work for Europeans; this occurred even in the face of increasing demands on government administrators to provide greater numbers of workers. A circular issued by
the Resident of Ruanda in 1934 indicates some of the means used by
the chiefs to discourage workers:

> It has come to my attention that in various territories the native
> authorities sometimes impede the hiring of people under their ju-
> risdiction for work in European establishments.
>
> This obstruction takes a great variety of forms: sometimes a sub-
> chief evicts a native from his hill because the latter has been hired
> for a long term [contract] by a neighboring enterprise; sometimes
> another [subchief] opposes engagements [for wage labor] because
> his people have [already] paid the [head] tax; in other cases the

customary authorities claim the right to deny authorization for wage employment to natives who have not fulfilled their required labor obligations or who have not completed the work imposed by the Administration.

This obstruction must cease and every muhutu must remain free to sign a contract whenever he wishes with an enterprise within the country or in the Belgian Congo.[69]

Although the circular was intended as a general statement applying to all of Rwanda, specific incidents in Cyangugu suggest its particular relevance to conditions of that region. In 1937, a Kinyagan who had signed a contract with Symétain at Kalima (Zaïre) lodged a complaint that a cow he had left behind with a friend had been confiscated by the chief Rwagataraka.[70] In 1947, the employer of a Kinyagan from Abiiru Province sent a complaint to the Territorial Administrator at Cyangugu charging that his employee's wife had been beaten by the local sub-chief's representative in order to force her to carry out a *corvée*.[71] Kinyagans consulted during the research referred frequently to the "abuses of the chiefs" who would often force the wives of men who were away working to carry out *ubureetwa* services, and administrative documents confirm that such practices were a constant source of complaints.[72]

A subchief who did not produce labor for Europeans, failed to produce work gangs for *akazi*, or did not succeed in making people carry out the obligatory cultivation of manioc, coffee, and so on was liable to lose his position.[73] But the chiefs imposed exactions on their people far exceeding that that was "legally" permitted by colonial regulations. This could be traced in part to the difficulties of reconciling the capabilities of the system with contradictory demands, and to the blind enforcement of sometimes mutually incompatible requirements.

For example, in 1946 a subchief complained to the Territorial Administrator of Cyangugu that he found it difficult to mobilize sufficient workers both to perform *akazi* work and to maintain the roads in his subchiefdom. He noted that 130 of the 320 registered taxpayers under his jurisdiction were employed under contract in European enterprises (and were therefore exempt from *akazi*). The Territorial Administrator conveyed the complaint to the Resident at Kigali, and asked what exceptions could be made.[74] The response was terse and showed no understanding of the situation:

The duties imposed on the native circumscriptions for road maintenance do not constitute such a burden that they cannot be easily carried out. . . . The case you raise is far from unique. [Elsewhere this problem] has been resolved easily enough by applying organizational skills and common sense.[75]

Another important factor conditioning the actions of the chiefs was the implicit (and sometimes explicitly stated) conviction in colonial policy that requiring Africans to work for Europeans was basically "good" for them in some abstract moral sense; if harshness of administrative measures contributed to a desire to work for wages, then such harshness was itself beneficial and justified. From this perspective the excessive demands of the "neo-traditional prestations" due to chiefs admirably served the goals of the administration. Such thinking appeared quite early in Belgian official documents on Rwanda, as illustrated in the following comment from a 1921 report:

> In a population as numerous as that of Ruanda-Urundi, there are always sufficient [numbers of] bold individuals who are impatient with the authority of the chiefs and dissatisfied with the limited horizon of village life: a long-term engagement in a European enterprise or a [government] post releases them from their customary obligations.[76]

To "traditional" prestations, the administration added other demands—taxes, akazi, obligatory cultivation. By excusing contract workers from akazi, giving them a tax break, and permitting them to fulfill ubureetwa services through a money payment, the administration hoped to attract more people into the labor market.

The chiefs were backed by European authority, giving them the power to impose exactions; at the same time their freedom of action was ("legally") circumscribed with regard to the kinds and quantity of exactions permitted and the individuals on whom these could be imposed. In fact, these legal specifications seem to have been only unevenly enforced so long as a chief met the requirements placed on him. The chiefs viewed the demands they made on the population not from a legal point of view, but from the perspective of power and accumulation.[77] Maximization of power conditioned politics in Kinyaga, and "legal" prescriptions were merely devices to be manipulated or gotten around as it suited the ambitions of the power holders. It is true that the Belgian administration could depose those chiefs judged to be "abusing" their power, and there were cases of such deposition, particularly during the mid-1950s, when greater efforts were made to exercise supervision. But actions could be taken only when "abuses" were brought to the attention of the administration; probably many such cases simply went unreported.[78]

For cases of abuses that were reported, European administrators often tended to show leniency toward the chiefs. A report prepared in 1932 by the Territorial Administrator at Cyangugu suggests some of the reasons for this:

> Let us examine ... what the Administration requires of the chiefs and ... consider what benefit a chief still gets from [the position of] command that we have "generously" given or left to him.
>
> We harass the chiefs without respite: have all your men paid the head tax; has the collection of the cattle tax been completed on your hill; has your population planted the required acreages of manioc, sweet potatoes, ... cotton, ... coffee, trees, etc.? Have you carried out the reforestation program to the specified amount, given me porters, workers, etc., ... etc. ...
>
> The chief ends up thinking to himself that the Administrator is very demanding with regard to work but not very generous in [offering] rewards. ...
>
> Under current conditions chiefs who lack the prestige of wealth in cattle, especially young chiefs [thus] often find themselves in a very difficult situation materially. Given these conditions, is it any wonder that the mututsi prefers the former system and has a tendency to commit certain unjust practices?

The author of this document counseled restraint in dealing with such abuses: he suggested urging the chief in private to return the appropriated goods in such a way that it appears to the person that this results from "the munificence of the chief." Since the administrator will have refrained from taking the case to the public tribunal, "the chief will appreciate the fact that I have not wounded his pride."[79]

KINYAGANS AND WAGE LABOR

WORK FOR Europeans within Kinyaga offered only minimal economic advantages; salaries were on the whole low, particularly when compared to benefits to be gained through the sale of livestock and food. With the growth of Bukavu and the expansion of mining activity in Nyungwe forest the demand for these goods rose steadily, resulting in a spiral of rising food prices—a farmer's paradise.[80] Kinyagans did not fail to see the advantages in farming, trading, and later (after initial reluctance), growing coffee. The economic good sense of these people was a source of continual frustration to government agents faced with the demands for workers. In 1942 the Territorial Administrator at Cyangugu commented that:

> The extraordinary ease by which the natives of this Territory obtain money no doubt explains why the settlers of the Territory have such difficulty obtaining local workers, and why anything which requires corvée meets with so little enthusiasm.[81]

The same report proposed higher taxes in order to combat this "problem":

> Might it not be advisable to restore the appetite for work in the natives and for the development of the economic resources of the Territory by raising the tax rate substantially?[82]

Use of higher taxes to force Africans into wage labor was a common practice of European colonial governments in Africa. The application of this policy to Kinyaga meant that the taxes for Cyangugu Territory were consistently among the highest in the country. When the Belgian administration first introduced taxes in Rwanda in 1917, the tax was 5 francs for each household head in all areas of the country;[83] this was lowered to 3.50 francs in 1922[84] but restored to 5 francs in 1926. In 1927 the tax was raised to 7.50 francs, and it continued to rise thereafter.[85]

An additional tax was imposed on cattle-owners. In 1920 a man owning more than five head of cattle was taxed 10 francs for the head tax (5 francs more than people with no cattle or less than five cows); in 1921 only those owning more than ten head paid an additional tax, fixed at 7.50 francs, so that a man having ten head of cattle or more would have paid 10 francs for the head and cattle tax combined. By 1926 the cattle tax was levied on the basis of 1 franc for each head of cattle; this was raised to 2 francs per head in 1927.[86] These taxes continued to increase in subsequent years, supplemented by additional taxes introduced after 1930 (some as money payment for prestations that had formerly been paid in kind, others to finance the running of the chiefdoms).

During the 1930s different tax levels were introduced for individual territories; by 1940, the taxes demanded of Kinyagans were higher than for any other territory except Kigali. Gisenyi, similar to Cyangugu in its proximity to the Congo and also the object of heavy labor demands, had the same tax levels as Cyangugu. The head tax for Kigali Territory in 1940 was 42 francs, and the "supplementary" tax (levied on men with more than one wife) was 21 francs. The head tax for Cyangugu and Gisenyi Territories in 1940 was 32 francs, while the supplementary tax was 15 francs. However, a special lower tax rate was applied in Cyangugu for workers at the Nyungwe mines; they paid only 25 francs head tax and 12.50 francs supplementary tax.[87]

In 1947, tax rates for most people in Cyangugu Territory were the highest in the country, but for contract workers, taxes were among the lowest. It can be seen in table 4 that a man living in Cyangugu Territory with no more than one wife and no cattle would have paid a total tax of 80 francs (65 francs head tax for the central government, 10 francs head tax for the chiefdom, 5 francs payment for prestations in kind). In the territories of Kigali, Nyanza, Astrida, and Gisenyi (those having the second highest taxes), a monogamous man with no cattle would have paid 69 francs (55 francs head tax for the government, 9 francs head tax for the chiefdom, 5 francs payment for prestations). A man with more

TABLE 4: Taxes in different territories of Rwanda, 1947

Territory	GENERAL			CHIEFDOM		
	Head	Polygamy	Cattle[a]	Head	Polygamy	Cattle[a]
Kigali	55 FR	37 FR	18 FR	9 FR	6 FR	1 FR
Nyanza	55	37	18	9	6	1
Astrida	55	37	18	9	6	1
Cyangugu						
a) contract workers	35	23	18	10	7	1
b) others	65	43	18	10	7	1
Gisenyi	55	37	18	9	6	1
Ruhengeri	50	34	18	8	5	1
Byumba	50	34	18	8	5	1
Kibungu	35	23	18	6	4	1

Payment for prestations in kind: king   1 FR
     chiefs   1
     subchiefs   3

[a]The cattle tax did not apply to cows less than six months old at the beginning of the year, or to castrated animals and breeding bulls.
SOURCE: Resident to A. T. Shangugu, 2018/Fin., 12 December 1946.

than one wife paid additional taxes: 50 francs for each wife after the first in Cyangugu; 43 francs in Kigali, Nyanza, Astrida, and Gisenyi Territories. The taxes on cattle and for prestations were the same for all territories.

Workers in Cyangugu Territory who were employed on contract in a mining, industrial, or agricultural enterprise received a substantial tax break. This policy, proposed some years earlier by the Territorial Administrator at Cyangugu, was authorized at the end of 1946 and applied in Kinyaga from 1947.[88] To qualify for the lower taxes, a man had to have been "in service for at least six months or . . . be in possession of a contract specifying a minimum duration of six months."[89] The language is ambiguous; when the special tax is listed, however, it is usually described as applying to workers under contract.[90] Presumably, then, in 1947 the tax break applied principally, or only, to the 6500 men of Cyangugu Territory who were employed on contract in that year.

If the contract worker was monogamous and had no cattle, he paid 50 francs (34 francs government head tax, 10 francs chiefdom head tax, 4 francs payment for prestations in kind)—or 30 francs less than other taxpayers. For each additional wife, he paid a 30 franc supplementary tax. The tax differential for contract workers in Cyangugu was abolished in 1949, and a new form of tax reduction for contract workers applying to all territories in Rwanda was introduced in 1950. Those who were employed by a non-African for a work contract of at least 300 days and which would be carried out within 15 months from the signing of the contract could claim a 50 percent reduction of the head tax; however, only contract workers who were single or had no more than one wife were eligible.[91]

The presence of European enterprises and the consequent demand for labor had a dual impact on relations of the population with their chiefs. First, it increased the harshness of demands, contributing to resentment against the patron-chiefs. This was particularly true in Cyesha and Impara, the chiefdoms bordering Lake Kivu, which had the best land in the region for coffee growing, and where proximity to the lake facilitated transport. Second, for some people, wage labor provided an alternative to clientship and other exactions of the chiefs: it allowed them to acquire a material base outside the control of Tuutsi chiefs. These two factors were closely related, but work for Europeans was not always an "escape," so both aspects need to be considered.

One source of particular hardship was the recruitment of people to work on a daily basis. A distinction between workers hired by contract, usually for six months to three years, and those hired on a daily basis

Umwami Musinga (center), his half-brother Rwabilinda (left), and his maternal uncle Ruhinankiko, c. 1900. [Source: Von Parish, "Zwei Reisen durch Ruanda 1902 . . . ," *Globus* Nos. 85–86 (1904).]

Musinga and (to his right), his maternal uncle Kabaare, 1907.   [Source: Gift from Mme. J. Liebmann to MRAC.]

Musinga, his mother Kanjogera, and four of his wives.

The Belgian administrative post at Cyangugu, on the shores of Lake Kivu, 1918.

Cyangugu market, c. 1923
[Source: Barns, *Across the
Great Craterland,*
facing p. 164.]

Exchanging *amatega* bracelets, Cyangugu market, c. 1923. [Source: Barns, *Across the Great Craterland*, facing p. 166.]

Mwami Musinga on a visit to a Belgian administrator, c. 1925. He is accompanied by his son Rudahigwa (left), his scribe, and an aide (far right). [Source: from an album donated by M. Delhaye to the Musée Royal de l'Afrique Centrale.]

Umwami Charles Mutara Rudahigwa, 1955.

Rwagataraka, chief of Impara in Kinyaga, c. 1923. [Source: Barns, *Across the Great Craterland to the Congo*, facing p. 162.]

Tuutsi notable.

The burial of *Umwami* Rudahigwa at Mwima, July 28, 1959. Chief A. Kayumba announces that the new king will be Jean-Baptíste Ndahindurwa, while Vice Governor-General Jean-Paul Harroy and the Resident of Rwanda, André Preud'homme look chagrined. The person at left of photo holding a briefcase is François Rukeba.

Crowds waiting for the United Nations Visiting Mission, displaying placards calling for democracy, support of PARMEHUTU, and an end to Tuutsi colonialism.

Aloys Munyangaju, one of the leaders of APROSOMA. He was founder of the newspaper *Soma* at Cyangugu (1956), and in 1958 became editor of the newspaper *Temps Nouveaux d'Afrique* in Bujumbura.

Joseph Habyarimana Gitera, founder of APROSOMA.

Grégoire Kayibanda, founder of PARMEHUTU. During the 1950s he served as editor of the periodical *L'Ami*, and from 1955 editor of *Kinyamateka*. He was President of Rwanda from 1961 to 1973.

Colonel BEM Guy Logiest, Military Resident of Rwanda (November 1959) and then Special Resident (from December 3, 1959).

Cultivated fields and pastures in Kinyaga, with homestead and banana groves in foreground. [photo by D. Newbury, 1970]

Hut of traditional beehive construction.   [photo by D. Newbury, 1971]

Elderly Kinyagan couple in
front of their house, 1971.
[photo by C. Newbury]

Intensively cultivated marshes, on the shores of Lake Kivu, 1971.　[photo
by D. Newbury]

View of the city of Bukavu, in Zaïre, taken from Cyangugu in 1971.
[photo by C. Newbury]

greatly favored the former; contract workers received better wages (if the rations provided by employers are taken into account), were often lodged by their employer, paid lower taxes, and were supposed to be excused from both *ubureetwa* obligations (for which they made a money payment) and *akazi*. Non-contract workers were entitled to none of these privileges.

The situation in Cyesha chiefdom in 1942 provides an illustration of some of the difficulties that recruitment of day workers could cause for the recruits.[92] In the western part of Cyesha, a number of men from the hills bordering the Nyungwe forest worked in the mining installations at Nyungwe and near the Mwaga River; these workers were usually under contract or hired by the month. Normally, such people worked at places close enough to their homes for them to return home at night.

By contrast, day workers often encountered much more difficult conditions. Several European enterprises concentrated in a relatively small area close to the lake created heavy labor demands. Statistics on day workers in Cyesha in 1942 (at the height of the wartime exactions in other spheres) were as follows:

three brick factories	1150
three plantations	160
two missions	210
	1520

The adult male population actually present in Cyesha chiefdom in 1942 was estimated at 3050, so that the number of workers employed on a daily basis was nearly 50 percent of the adult male population.[93]

Conditions were especially harsh at two of the brick factories, which each employed 500 men. These factories were located only 90 minutes apart; unable to find enough workers in areas close by, the two establishments resorted to recruitment of men living some distance away. Two subchiefs whose subchiefdoms were located at three to four hours walk in the mountains west of the lake were ordered to produce 200 men each; the predecessors of these subchiefs had recently been deposed for not having produced sufficient numbers of workers. Because of the distance involved, workers had to find lodging near the brick factories during the week. After working full days Monday to Friday, and a half-day on Saturday, they could return to their homes only for Saturday night and Sunday. The employers apparently provided neither lodging nor rations. Workers coming from the higher altitudes often fell ill while living near the lake, and mortality among them was high.

The average wage paid to workers was one franc per day, but at one of the brick factories it was normal practice for the employer to withhold a part of the workers' wages as punishment for various infractions; some individuals received only ten francs in 24 days. In addition to poor wages and unhealthy conditions, the workers at that same brick factory frequently suffered physical abuse; they had to be retained at their jobs by force. The morale among workers at the factory was so low that this establishment employing 500 workers produced no more bricks than a third factory in the region (with less harsh working conditions) that employed only 150 workers.

The salary of one franc per day in 1942 appears exceptionally low; in 1929, the Protanag company was paying workers 1.50 francs per day, at a time when the colonial government paid ordinary laborers (employed in roadwork and construction) a daily wage of one franc.[94] Moreover, inflation from 1929 to 1942 had reduced the value of the franc; colonial reports often referred to decreased value of money as a justification for yearly tax increases.

The plight of the workers at the brick factories in Cyesha dramatizes the extent of wartime exactions in the region. Although spending the week away from home at their jobs, these workers were still expected to maintain obligatory cultivation, coffee plants, and reforestation projects. They were obliged to ask their wives to fulfill these duties or hire *mudeyideyi* to do it for them. A *mudeyideyi* was a Rwandan who hired out his services to another Rwandan; he received one franc per day, as well as food and lodging—better conditions than the day workers employed by Europeans. Missionaries at Nyamasheke Mission in Cyesha, appalled at the exactions being made on people in the region, sharply criticized the government policies, but to little avail.[95]

To escape work in the brick factories, many men left the two subchiefdoms where local labor recruitment was so high. Some went north to Rusenyi (in present Kibuye Prefecture) where there were fewer European settlers and fewer roads to maintain than in Cyesha. Some went to work in the mines as contract laborers or day workers; others went to hire out as *mudeyideyi* in other areas of Kinyaga (Impara and Abiiru chiefdoms). This emigration, of course, only made conditions more difficult for those who remained.

In the years after World War II, the Belgian administration introduced measures to stabilize the labor force—to reduce the numbers of workers employed by the day while increasing the proportion hired on contract. A report from Cyangugu in 1947 expressed satisfaction at the administration's success in this regard. As we have seen, by the end of 1947 there were 6500 workers on contract in Cyangugu Territory. Of 2300 workers employed on a daily basis, 1000 had been hired by the government for work on roads.[96]

Although coercion was often used in labor recruitment, some Kinyagans went "voluntarily" to work for Europeans as a means of escaping the demands of the chiefs, or they sought employment on their own (e.g., as contract workers) in order to avoid forcible recruitment on less favorable terms. Given conditions in the subchiefdoms, work in certain European enterprises was viewed by many as the lesser of two evils. For those who wished to escape the chiefs, work to the west in the Congo posed a particularly strong attraction, for it took them outside the region. Some Kinyagans signed on for three-year contracts to work in mines or construction firms in Kivu or Katanga; many sought work as domestic servants or skilled and semi-skilled workers in Bukavu.

Kinyagans interviewed for this study often mentioned arbitrary actions of the powerful as a principal reason they and others went to work for Europeans.[97] In the 1920s, a man from Muramba Hill (Cyesha chiefdom) left for Katanga on a three-year contract to escape his *ubuhake* patron:

> Seeing that I could not flee elsewhere, and that I could not make myself a client of someone else and [still] continue to live . . . so it was that I went to the Europeans [to work on European installations] in Katanga to do heavy jobs: to split rocks.[98]

Rurangwa, a Kinyagan who later became an activist in Hutu party politics, said he left his home at Mugera Hill to work at the mines in Katanga (Congo) in 1937; he and several others who accompanied him wished to escape the demands of the chiefs.[99] A man from Shangi (Impara chiefdom), also an activist in Hutu protest of the 1950s, recounted that his brother fled and went to work in Bukavu after the chief had taken his land and tried to seize his cattle. Another member of the same lineage was an *ubuhake* cattle client for a time; finding this unacceptable, he left to work at Kamituga in the Congo.[100]

From the hills near the forest in Kinyaga, considerable numbers of men went to work in the Nyungwe mines to escape *akazi* and other exactions.[101] As expressed by one informant:

> I went there because they were making my wife work and whenever I had some [banana] beer the *abamotsa* [subordinates of the subchief] would come and take it; but when I got to Nyungwe, no one asked me for anything any more.[102]

From this man's account, it would seem that the exemptions given to workers on contract (exemptions from *ubureetwa* and *akazi*) were enforced. The extent to which this occurred, however, varied from one subchiefdom to another and between different individuals as well.

Regardless of the reasons for which Kinyagans went to work for Europeans, participation in wage labor later provided certain of the workers a basis for opposing the system. Whether recruited by direct or indirect coercion, or whether they went "willingly" to escape what they considered an intolerable situation at home, these men were exposed to new experiences and came into contact with ideological alternatives to the Rwandan system. They became aware of different perspectives in social situations where they were not at the mercy of a local chief's exactions and where they could gain status and economic security outside the sphere of local political power in Kinyaga. In this sense, employment offered to some an alternative to submission to the chiefs. Kinyagans' participation in the Kivu complex meant that, through jobs or commerce, it became possible to gain an economic base relatively autonomous from the chiefs' monopoly over the formerly crucial economic resources—cattle and land. Many of the early leaders of Hutu protest activity in Kinyaga were former wage earners who had taken up trading enterprises of some kind—gaining both economic security and a network of contacts that later proved useful for political party organization.

The alternatives open to Kinyagans in the west conditioned the kind of elite that eventually emerged among Hutu of the region, as well as the attitudes of this elite. The peripheral position of Kinyaga contributed to harsh administrative demands, particularly in Cyesha; at the same time, the frontier position of the region afforded access to ideological alternatives to the Rwandan social system and the possibility of external social security and financial assistance. At the least, the openness to the west provided a chance for certain Kinyagans to remove themselves from the web of local entanglements and hence to achieve some independence of thought and action.

This case study of the Kivu complex shows that the labor control system developed in Kinyaga was particularly intense. But recruitment of workers occurred in other areas of Rwanda as well (see table 5), and Belgian economic policies fostered transformations throughout the country, not just in Kinyaga.[103] As a result, rural dwellers were incorporated into a money economy; some became semi-proletarianized through wage labor, and for many their relationship to the basic means of subsistence was altered. Throughout Rwanda the dual colonial state,

ruled by Europeans and by Tuutsi, imposed taxes, compulsory cultivation of certain crops, regulation of the labor force, and forced labor
(corvée) which served to make chiefly rule more oppressive and to define the primary objects of this oppression (the Hutu) in ethnic terms.

The fact that virtually all the chiefs were Tuutsi helped to create the
popular view that "Tuutsi" meant those who were wealthy and powerful and could treat others, especially Hutu, abusively. "Hutu" was
synonymous with subordinate, those who were excluded from political
power and who were particularly vulnerable to the depredations of the
chiefs. One result of these conditions was the development of political
consciousness among the rural masses, based on discontent at the treatment meted out by the chiefs. Thus, the dual colonial system, while it
attempted to promote the power of chiefs, eroded their legitimacy. Over
time, changing relations of production made resources available to
some who could use them, in the 1950s, to combat oppressive conditions which were in large part the product of political and economic
transformations over the previous half-century.

TABLE 5: Wage workers in Rwanda by territory, 1959[a]

Territory	Contract Workers	Gov't & Chiefdom	Total	Est. Pop.[b] 1956	Percentage Employed
Kigali	8,426	2,271	10,698	245,672	4.4%
Nyanza[c]	4,462	1,523	5,985	349,034	3.3
	(8,464)	(3,057)	(11,521)		
Astrida	6,995	2,158	9,153	324,056	2.8
Cyangugu[a]	4,686	1,581	6,267	121,534	5.2
Kibuye	3,992	1,844	5,836	105,041	5.6
Gisenyi	6,939	1,581	8,520	213,755	3.8
Ruhengeri	6,550	1,369	7,919	266,221	3.0
Byumba	2,170	1,179	3,349	182,687	1.8
Kibungu	4,073	1,007	5,080	156,501	3.2
Gitarama	4,002	1,534	5,536		

[a]These figures do not include workers employed outside Rwanda.

[b]Figures for total population by territory in 1959 were not available. The figures given here
(for 1956) would obviously underestimate the 1959 figures.

[c]The Territory of Nyanza had been subdivided into Gitarama and Nyanza Territories by
1959. The figures in brackets, therefore, represent the total for Nyanza-Gitarama.

SOURCE: *Rapport sur l'administration du R-U,* 1959, 451–452; Belgium, Gouvernement
Belge, Office de l'Information et des Relations Publiques pour le Congo Belge et le Ruanda-
Urundi, *Le Ruanda-Urundi* (Brussels: M. Weissenbruch, 1959), 35.

9

PRE-INDEPENDENCE POLITICS AND PROTEST

THE RWANDAN Revolution was most visible in the heroic events of central Rwanda—the focal point of the kingdom. In many renditions the Revolution has come to be represented in the actions of a visible and articulate Hutu leadership at the center. These were men of courage, perception, intelligence, and commitment. But while leadership was important in the politics that led to the Revolution of 1959–1961, it was not leadership that caused rural discontent. Instead the leaders drew on the energies derived from the Hutu experience.

During the 1950s in Rwanda there developed an alliance between three groups with convergent (though not identical) interests: the Hutu *evolués* (the word used in Belgian colonies for educated white-collar workers), local level Hutu leadership (transporters, traders, shopkeepers, catechists, etc.), and peasants. It is widely recognized that the formation of inter-class alliances is often crucial to a successful revolutionary movement,[1] but such organization may be inhibited by the conditions under which peasants live, where they are subject to powerful persons who can threaten their security and even their lives:

> Poor peasants and landless laborers . . . are unlikely to pursue the course of rebellion, *unless* they are able to rely on some external power to challenge the power which constrains them.[2]

External resources are important, but so may be a sense of autonomy from the pervasive cultural hegemony which backs state power. In some contexts, peasants have been able to preserve or create moral autonomy stemming from an awareness of alternative conceptions of social organization, different from the one forced on them. This can provide the essential justification (and impetus) on the part of peasants to resist the powerful and even risk rebellion against the state.[3] In Rwanda both types of situations were to be found, varying among different regions.[4]

The effects of colonial statebuilding, transformations in clientship, and labor-control policies discussed in previous chapters fostered political consciousness among rural people; some of these same changes also made available resources that could be used for effective protest. Aspirant Hutu leaders needed to link up with the simmering rural discontent which began to be overtly expressed after World War II, and which by the mid-1950s was reaching a boiling point. It was this rural anger which gave energy to the emergent national Hutu leadership and party organization. Hutu leaders in Rwanda were able to gain the attention of the European colonial government to the extent that they could claim to represent, (and to control), the rural masses. The leaders did not create rural political consciousness, however; they articulated and channeled it, even while being pushed to make particular demands by their rural constituencies.[5]

Hutu leaders, of course, had their own concerns and frustrations. Discrimination against Hutu in favor of Tuutsi in the schools, in institutions of the Church, and in employment practices of the state heightened awareness of ethnic distinctions among would-be Hutu elites, just as exploitative behavior of the chiefs angered the rural masses. But it was also in the mission schools that many who later became leaders in the Revolution acquired skills and contacts useful for articulating protest. At the local level, mission-educated Hutu schoolteachers often played key roles. And many of the Hutu who exercised leadership at a national level had studied at the Catholic major seminary at Nyakibanda. Such leaders could call upon a dense network of communication with the population through the Catholic press, church organizations throughout the country, contacts to Catholic groups outside Rwanda, and in the 1950s at least (although not always in earlier times), encouragement from European missionaries for the pursuit of "social justice" in opposition to the abusive rule of the Tuutsi oligarchy.

In the national political arena, increasing polarization into groups based on ethnic appellations gave the conflict of the late 1950s the appearance of an ethnic revolution. And so it was, in part. But that interpretation appears to accept implicitly the primordial nature of ethnicity; it fails to account for the variation over time and variability at any one time of ethnic identity and awareness. At the local level, regional differences in the nature of Hutu–Tuutsi relations and the extent of ethnic cleavage were reflected in substantial variations in the intensity of anti-Tuutsi sentiment. Clearly, considerations of class and power were important at this level. An analysis of voting returns in Kinyaga for the 1960 commune elections will be drawn on below to illustrate that variability and serve as the basis for suggesting the nature of local alliances and cleavages associated with revolutionary activity.

THE EMERGENCE OF POLITICAL PARTIES

ORGANIZED POLITICAL activity in Kinyaga emerged only slowly in the 1950s. Political cleavages increasingly came to be based on ethnic identity, but initially they were more precisely drawn along class lines—many "poor Tuutsi" considered themselves part of the populist movement. Hutu political organization in Kinyaga was launched during 1956 by the appearance of *Soma*, a newspaper oriented toward publicizing the arbitrary use of power by the chiefs and the discrimination in the society against the powerless. The paper was founded and edited by Aloys Munyangaju, a former seminarian from Save (near Astrida). Munyangaju's background illustrates how the socioeconomic transformations discussed in previous chapters shaped the Hutu leadership.

Although originally from central Rwanda, Munyangaju had moved to Kinyaga in 1947 to work for a private company in Bukavu. Perhaps in part because of his "outside" experience (both in central Rwanda and in the Congo) he quickly came to identify with the plight of Hutu in Kinyaga; in 1953 he was one of only two Hutu to serve on the Shangugu Territorial Council. He was a prime figure in the initial articulation of dissent in Kinyaga, looked to as mentor by many of the early Kinyagan Hutu activists. Moreover, Munyangaju's educational background in Catholic mission schools and at the Grand Séminaire of Nyakibanda acquainted him with ideological alternatives to the Rwandan system of exploitation. Similarly, his "old boy ties" in the Catholic mission network provided an important network of relations with Hutu leaders in other areas of the country who themselves had come through mission schools.

Munyangaju's employment in Bukavu reinforced this sense of intellectual autonomy, and also made material resources available to him, independent of the politico-economic structures of Rwanda. A degree of economic independence, enhanced status, and (probably) ambitions for greater mobility were one dimension of this: neither family ties nor employment was under the scrutiny of Kinyagan chiefs. In addition his

contacts in Bukavu provided access to other Hutu and to printing fa-
cilities. The newspaper *Soma* was printed in Bukavu, and distributed
through a network of people sympathetic to Munyangaju's ideas, many
of whom themselves had been forced to seek work in the Congo.[6] Economic autonomy outside Rwanda was thus instrumental in the ability
of these Hutu leaders to seek autonomy from Tuutsi rule within the
country.

There were similar pockets of identity-autonomy within Kinyaga itself. These were especially important in areas only recently placed under central control, where the memory of independence was strongly
alive and where the structures of the colonial state were closely identified with Tuutsi rule. In 1958–1959 a series of articles appeared in
the Catholic weekly *Kinyamateka*[7] castigating the system of unre-
strained chiefly power and the exploitation by Tuutsi, particularly in
the Bukunzi-Busoozo-Bugarama chiefdom of Kinyaga. What is particularly interesting is that the articles were written by a man who had
been born and raised in Bukunzi and who was currently residing there.
It will be recalled that the inhabitants of Bukunzi and a neighboring
(ex)-kingdom, Busoozo, were exclusively Hutu until Tuutsi chiefs were
introduced from 1925. After the conquest of Bukunzi and Busoozo by
Belgian-led troops in 1925, the Tuutsi chief Rwagataraka had been authorized to send in his clients to rule these areas—a good example of
collaboration between Tuutsi and Belgians for complementary but not
necessarily identical goals. The people of these areas had tenaciously
maintained their identitive autonomy, and their resentment against
Tuutsi control was particularly strong. In this respect Bukunzi and Busoozo resembled the northwestern areas of Rwanda (Gisenyi and Ruhengeri) where Tuutsi were few and their rule insecure. In such areas,
the Rwandan central court exercised only a nominal presence before
the European arrival; Tuutsi power in the area was extended (often in
brutal ways) under European rule, but was never very secure.

The author of the articles in *Kinyamateka* had been educated at
mission schools and was a primary-school teacher at the time the articles appeared. Teaching, like wage employment, provided economic
and ideological outlets similar to those available through work in Bukavu. The articles also illustrated the active role of the Catholic Church
in providing material resources, a distributive infrastructure for the
paper through the mission network, and moral support and encouragement for those who sought to question the system.

Administrative innovations during the 1950s introduced by Rwanda's
king and the Belgian administration (in response to growing rural dis-

content within Rwanda as well as pressure from the United Nations Organization) had heralded the later emergence of open debate over the Hutu–Tuutsi problem. At three-year intervals from 1948, the Trustee-ship Council of the United Nations sent a Visiting Mission to tour Ruanda-Urundi for several weeks. The reports of these Visiting Mis-sions expressed shock at the inequalities in Rwandan social and polit-ical structures and called on the Belgian authorities to undertake a program of progressive "democratization" to prepare the population for self-government. The 1948 Visiting Mission urged the Administration to

> democratize the whole political structure as far as possible and as speedily as circumstances permit. The masses must by degrees be led to take part in the choice of their leaders, and in sanctioning important decisions, the final aim being to achieve an increasingly widespread electoral system.[8]

The 1954 Visiting Mission's report noted the cleavages in the social and political structures of the Trust Territory:

> The factors which normally unify a society, such as a common status, suffrage, racial equality, human rights and freedoms, have yet to be fully established in Ruanda-Urundi.[9]

A decree issued on July 14, 1952 by the Belgian administration rep-resented a step toward reform. The decree provided for the introduction of councils at the levels of the subchiefdoms and Territories and the retention of existing councils at the chiefdom and country levels. In accordance with the 1952 decree and a measure of application issued on July 10, 1953, electoral colleges at the subchiefdom level were se-lected in 1953 for each subchiefdom by the local subchief, with the consent of his chief (Chef de Chefferie) and the Territorial Administra-tor. The subchiefdom electoral colleges chose from among their number the members of the subchiefdom councils. Members of the councils at higher levels of the administrative hierarchy were then selected from this base by a complicated series of indirect elections.[10] As Jacques Maquet and Marcel d'Hertefelt have pointed out, the reform initiated by the 1952 decree was really quite modest—the elections did not in-volve a popular consultation (since the basic unit, the subchiefdom electoral college, was formed on the basis of nomination by the sub-chief), and the councils were therefore hardly representative of popular sentiment.[11] But in many areas some Hutu were selected to serve on the subchiefdom council; later these same people often played an active role in the party politics of the late 1950s.

Three years later, in the 1956 councilor elections, subchiefdom electoral colleges were chosen by popular vote; however, the councils themselves were chosen indirectly, through the electoral colleges.[12] The period of preparation for the election of the subchiefdom electoral colleges in 1956 was also quite brief. In Cyangugu Territory, for example, only twenty-seven days elapsed between the time when the Territorial Administrator met with the chiefs and subchiefs to explain the purpose and procedures of the elections and the day on which voting began (September 30, 1956).[13] Munyangaju's newspaper, Soma, carried some pre-election coverage in Kinyaga,[14] and in some areas the Catholic missions played a role in informing the population and influencing the choice of candidates. The pre-election period was so brief, however, that many people may not have understood the meaning of the vote,[15] and there was little opportunity for organization or campaigning in support of candidates.

The 1956 councilor elections were nevertheless important in terms of the emergent Hutu political activism, with a particularly significant impact on the cadre of Hutu local leaders. Hormisdas Kanyabacuzi, one of the early Kinyagan Hutu activists, is a good example of this. First selected to serve on his local subchiefdom and chiefdom council in 1953, Kanyabacuzi was later elected for a second term on both councils in 1956. He found his work as a councilor to be a radicalizing experience and a major impetus to join APROSOMA:

—What led you to think about joining the [Aprosoma] party?

Before, when I was on the subchiefdom and the chiefdom councils and I saw what the Tuutsi were doing against the Hutu, I said to myself: if ever we had a place where we could speak out so that they would let the Hutu free, . . . if only we had someone to listen to us. . . .

One day at a chiefdom [council] meeting the chief brought a letter stating that a Hutu who normally cultivated for a Tuutsi did not have to do this [anymore], unless the latter gave him money. Then one of the subchiefs said, "Why do you say that, since Kanyabacuzi is there and so he is going to prevent our subjects from working." Then they said to him, "Chief, why do you say that, when you should have told us this only among ourselves?"

Then I said, "Since this has become a law, then I will not tell lies, and I will go to notify my fellows." That other one [the subchief] remained annoyed, very annoyed that I had heard that. It was I alone who was on the chiefdom council, I was the only Hutu. All the others were Tuutsi. And even on the subchiefdom council I was alone with only one other Hutu.[16]

In 1956 only the members of the electoral colleges at the lowest level of the administrative hierarchy (the subchiefdom) were chosen by popular vote. In 1956 as in 1953, the councils themselves (at the subchiefdom, chiefdom, territory, and country levels) were chosen by indirect vote, and this tended to favor the incumbent authorities. Given the lack of grassroots organization, the control of voting procedures by the subchiefs, and the limited experience of the population in general with the meaning and mechanisms of popular elections, the 1956 results are not fully representative. However, certain general observations can be made.

In Kinyaga the proportion of Tuutsi elected to the subchiefdom electoral colleges in 1956 was 46.3 percent—higher than the all-Rwanda figures (see table 6). This might be explained in part by the proportionately larger percentage of Tuutsi in the Kinyagan population,[17] and the "multiplier effect" of greater Tuutsi organization and political control in areas of higher Tuutsi concentration. Still, significant regional differences in voting patterns were evident in Kinyaga, patterns manifested even more clearly later in the 1960 communal elections.[18]

At the national level, the results of the 1956 elections indicated that the Tuutsi still controlled powerful political resources. The percentage

TABLE 6: Ethnic Composition of Subchiefdom Electoral
Colleges in Kinyaga by Chiefdom, 1956

Chiefdom	Tuutsi	Hutu	Other*	Number of seats
Impara	157 (58.6%)	104 (38.8%)	7 (2.6%)	268
Cyesha	60 (40.5%)	88 (59.5%)	—	148
Abiiru	52 (54.2%)	44 (45.8%)	—	96
Bukunzi	16 (15.4%)	85 (81.7%)	3 (2.9%)	104
Total	285 (46.3%)	321 (52.1%)	10 (1.6%)	616

*Includes Swahili (Muslims) and Congolese.
SOURCE: A. T. Shangugu to Resident, 3544/A.I., 16 October 1956; Maquet and d'Hertefelt, *Elections*, 111.

of Tuutsi elected to the subchiefdom electoral colleges, for example, was twice their percentage of the population as a whole; while they constituted only 16.5 percent of the population, Tuutsi held 33.08 percent of the places on the subchiefdom electoral colleges. On the other hand, Hutu, who made up 82.74 percent of the population, held only 66.72 percent of the electoral college places.[19] Clearly, a significant percentage of Hutu had voted for Tuutsi candidates.

Nevertheless, the 1956 elections were far from encouraging for Tuutsi powerholders. The representation of Tuutsi on the electoral colleges at the subchiefdom level had declined significantly from 1953 (by 20 percent[20]), and the explosive potential of ethnic voting blocks in direct popular elections could not be ignored. The politics of the next four years were greatly conditioned by this realization, by the anticipation of elections scheduled to be held again in 1959, and by the expectation that the end of colonial rule was imminent.

Perhaps in anticipation of these changes, Belgium appointed a new Governor-General of Ruanda-Urundi in 1955. He was Jean-Paul Harroy, an astute and dynamic administrator who was only 45 years old at the time. Harroy was appalled at the conduct of Tuutsi chiefs in Rwanda. He deplored the fact that many Tuutsi authorities showed no interest in development of the welfare of their people; their major concern was to enrich themselves. To this end, Harroy observed, they used various forms of extortion to extract from rural dwellers everything but the "strict minimum the latter needed to survive."[21] In the early 1950s, Harroy discovered, tensions in the rural areas were already much more serious than official reports let on. By the mid-1950s, conflicts had become even more severe:

Violent incidents involving some deaths, although localized, cannot have been rare.

On this subject I heard many stories in which, for example, in the hills the safety of a [European] agricultural agent or a physician carrying out a vaccination program was not assured, for the Hutu population—aroused by whom?—wanted to attack their Tuutsi assistant. . . .

"Order" then had to be reestablished by a police action during which the traditional authority [Tuutsi] would profit from the occasion, which he had sometimes himself provoked, to "teach [them] a lesson." . . . Certain of these lessons gave rise to many cruel acts.

And unfortunately, lacking the power to do otherwise, or sometimes for the sake of convenience, the Belgian official on the spot closed his eyes to such brutal practices.[22]

Galvanized by such conditions, Hutu leaders began to take an increasingly assertive public stance. They demanded political, economic, and cultural changes and democratization of the political system. Tuutsi "traditionalists" at court reacted vociferously in defense of established privilege; the king, rather than serving as an impartial mediator, tended to side with these Tuutsi. This, in turn, generated more aggressive verbal attacks from Hutu leaders. The main Hutu participants in the political infighting at the national level were literate men; most of them were connected with the church network, and they shared a common educational background in church mission schools and common grievances over blocked mobility.[23]

The success of their campaign would depend on the extent to which they could claim and use mass support. By 1954, the writings of one of the more prominent Hutu leaders, Grégoire Kayibanda, had begun to recognize the importance of linkages between educated elites ("évolués") and the concerns of rural people. Kayibanda argued that the Catholic elites, rather than rejecting rural people, should attempt to help them "to struggle against their moral, intellectual, and economic distress." Ideally, according to Kayibanda, a rural évolué "spend[s] time with [people on the hills], chats with them often, knows their aspirations better, their distress, their complaints, and sees better the injustices of which they are the victims."[24] Such an approach was important not only to combat Tuutsi hegemony, but also to protect Hutu leaders from being implicated as accomplices of the oppressive system. Kayibanda warned his fellow Hutu évolués not to take on airs and separate themselves from the concerns of the masses:

> These islands of Europeanized intellectuals could sooner or later find themselves uprooted by pitilessly mounting waves of the exasperated popular masses. This "populace" which supposedly is "dormant" also poses a problem and if the rural évolués were not there, their absence would hasten the day when the "populace," harrassed and worn out, not discerning very clearly any more "the brothers who do nothing for them," would be opposed not only to exoticism, but also, and even more intensely, to their brothers of the same race.[25]

Kayibanda recognized and was attempting to respond to a growing consciousness of oppression among rural people, the majority of whom were Hutu. To make these connections the national leaders often relied on people such as Kanyabacuzi in Kinyaga. Such activists, although often still linked to the land, were also engaged in other forms of work, as catechists, primary school teachers, truckdrivers, traders, artisans. They were, as Lemarchand suggests, a form of "rural proletariat."[26]

An important resource for protesters at both the national and local levels was access to the press through which critics of the system could make their views known. Two of the men who later became major Hutu leaders, Grégoire Kayibanda (later President of the PARMEHUTU party) and Aloys Munyangaju (Vice President and later President of APROSOMA) achieved prominence as journalists/editors for Catholic periodicals. While a schoolteacher in Kigali during the late 1940s, Kayibanda published a series of articles in L'Ami, a monthly journal published by the Catholic diocese at Kabgayi. In 1953 Kayibanda moved to Kabgayi to become Secretary in the Education Inspection division and editor of L'Ami. From 1955 through 1957 he served as lay editor of Kinyamateka. Munyangaju, who in 1956 had founded and edited Soma in Kinyaga, assumed in 1958 the editorship of Temps Nouveaux d'Afrique, a French-language daily newspaper published by the Catholic press in Bujumbura.[27]

Through articles in these publications, Kayibanda, Munyangaju, and other Hutu publicized their cause among Europeans, particularly the Belgian administration, the Catholic missionary hierarchy, and external observers such as the United Nations. They strove to raise the consciousness of the rural poor, to "gutega amatwi" (open their ears), giving voice to rural dwellers' complaints and suggesting ways to combat oppressive conditions.[28]

The debates published in Kinyamateka gave voice to attitudes and discussions that were occurring at the grassroots level in many areas of the country. Evidence presented in earlier chapters of this study belies a view of Hutu peasants as unaware that they were being oppressed and exploited. Local-level data from Kinyaga corroborate the conclusion reached by Ntezimana, a Rwandan scholar who has studied the role of the press in the Rwandan Revolution:

Not to be attributed to an "intelligentsia" which would have played the role of catalyzing element, the [protest] movement engaged in Kinyamateka and in Temps Nouveaux d'Afrique did not arise as instantaneously as it may seem. It did not come out of a vacuum. The spectacular increase of articles from year to year, the diversity of subjects considered, the extension of the phenomenon to the whole country, the receptivity on the part of readers and, as a corollary, the growth in numbers of copies printed, show that *Kinyamateka*, without following a preconceived plan ..., responded to a long-awaited [need] on the part of the people and addressed their long-standing concerns. The press did no more than bring out into the open and canalize, directly or indirectly, a climate which preceded it by many years, or even decades.[29]

In addition to the press the Hutu counter-elite[30] skillfully used organizational networks and political ties forged through the Catholic Church. Through their activities in the church, educated Hutu lay leaders found opportunities to gain status and recognition denied them in the sphere of state politics. Large church celebrations were an occasion for such leaders from different regions to come together; for example, the celebration in 1950 of Save Mission's Fifty-Year Jubilee is remembered by many Hutu leaders as the first occasion when Hutu from different areas discussed together the issues of political and economic inequalities and Tuutsi discrimination against Hutu. This was also the year in which the Legion of Mary was introduced in Rwanda. The Legion, of which Kayibanda was president in the late 1950s, provided a ready context for communication. By 1959 the Legion had established a chapter at each of the Catholic missions in the country and could claim a total of 6000 members.[31]

After the 1956 elections, the Belgian government and Tuutsi authorities failed to introduce reforms, and protesting Hutu began to doubt possibilities for peaceful political change. Positions became increasingly polarized, and opportunities for compromise diminished. As Theda Skocpol has observed, the reaction of the state in times of crisis is a crucial variable in the growth and outcome of revolutionary protest, and external power considerations (the situation of the state in the international context) are often critical to the capacity of the state to deal with revolutionary challenges.[32] These considerations are applicable in the Rwandan case, all the more so because of the dual character of rule in the country—Belgian and Tuutsi.

Neither the king nor the High Council (Conseil Supérieur) of Rwanda used their power and prestige to respond to Hutu demands. *Umwami* Rudahigwa, apparently influenced by the more traditionalist Tuutsi at court, helped to defeat a proposal in 1956 to provide separate representation for Hutu on the Governor's Council of Ruanda-Urundi.[33] Like the *umwami*, the High Council took the position that the main issues to address in Rwanda were economic and social; they refused to define the problem as one of ethnic discrimination. The composition of the Council was in itself not reassuring to Hutu. During the crucial period 1956 to 1959, this group (the highest advisory body of the state) included only three Hutu, less than 6 percent of its membership. Such Hutu underrepresentation is especially significant if one considers that the High Council was expected to assume legislative functions when Rwanda was granted self-government by Belgium.[34]

The High Council's position was articulated in 1957, shortly before the visit of the United Nations Visiting Mission. In its "Statement of Views," the Council called for accelerated progress toward self-government, with emphasis on extension of educational opportunities, broadening of political participation, and social and economic reforms. But the statement recognized only one type of discrimination in Rwanda— the segregation between Africans and Europeans; there was no mention of the Hutu–Tuutsi problem.[35] The High Council thus followed the *umwami*'s lead by not recognizing discrimination against Hutu.

Hutu leaders replied to the High Council's statement with the "Manifesto of the Bahutu" signed by Kayibanda and eight other Hutu. This document was sent to Governor Harroy in Bujumbura in March 1957. The signatories, noting that they could have included the signatures of a million other Hutu, vociferously asserted the centrality of the "Hutu–Tuutsi problem" and the need for Belgian government recognition of it. They opposed elimination of legal distinctions between Hutu, Tuutsi, and Twa on identity cards, for this would make it impossible, the Manifesto argued, to determine what progress was being achieved toward more egalitarian political structures. The Hutu–Tuutsi problem, claimed this Manifesto, lay primarily in the political, socioeconomic, and cultural monopoly held by Tuutsi:

> The problem is above all a problem of political monopoly which is held by one race, the mututsi; political monopoly which, given the totality of current structures becomes an economic and social monopoly; political, economic, and social monopoly which, given the *de facto* discrimination in education, ends up being a cultural monopoly, to the great despair of the Bahutu who see themselves condemned to remain forever subaltern manual laborers and still worse, in the context of an independence which they will have helped to win without knowing what they are doing. The buhake is no doubt abolished, but it is replaced even more by this total monopoly which is largely responsible for the abuses about which the population is complaining.[36]

The Manifesto pointed to disaffection among rural Hutu youth (and some Tuutsi who had become impoverished) who wandered about, "fleeing the *travail-corvée* (work-corvée), [which is] no longer adapted to the situation and psychology of today. [Such youths] no longer accept the discipline of coercion which in any case gives rise to abuses which the authorities seem to ignore." Fathers were finding it difficult to feed their families: "a substantial number are not without thinking that the Belgian Government is linked to the nobility for their total exploitation." But on the other hand, the European was important as a constraint on Tuutsi exploitation, "not because [people] think the European is perfect, but because it is necessary to choose the lesser of two evils. Passive resistance to many of the orders of subchiefs is only a consequence of this disequilibrium and this malaise." Finally, the Manifesto noted the chagrin of the Hutu seeing themselves "quasi-systematically relegated to subordinate positions."[37]

As solutions to these problems the Manifesto recommended rapid changes in Rwanda's political and social system. A change in attitude was required, away from the view that only Tuutsi could serve as elites. Specific policies to remedy the poverty and powerlessness of Hutu should include the abolition of corvées (workers on roads and other public works should be hired regularly, paid wages, and protected by social legislation) and the legal recognition of land rights, with each person having land sufficient for agriculture and pasturage: "the bikingi [pasturages of the bourgeoisie] would be suppressed." Other demands of the Manifesto called for establishment of a rural credit fund to help agriculturalists and artisans, codification of laws and customs, a lowering of social (ethnic) barriers in school admissions and distribution of scholarship funds, and the establishment of social centers for women and girls in the rural areas.[38]

In mid-1957 Kayibanda formed an organization, Mouvement Social Muhutu (Hutu Social Movement), designed to promote the objectives articulated in the Hutu Manifesto. Several months later, Joseph Habyarimana Gitera, one of the signatories of the Manifesto, formed his own group, l'Association pour la Promotion Sociale de la Masse. Gitera, like Kayibanda and Munyangaju, had attended school at the Petit Séminaire of Kabgayi and the Grand Séminaire at Nyakibanda. But unlike Kayibanda, who was a teacher and leader of several organizations, Gitera was a small-businessman with a brickworks near Astrida. Gitera founded his own journal, *Ijwi rya Rubanda Rugufi (Voice of the Little People)* in which he engaged in impassioned, vitriolic attacks on the monarchy and the *Kalinga* drum, symbol of royalty. He called upon rural people to oppose their Tuutsi oppressors, by force if necessary.[39]

The tone of Gitera's protest was more vindictive and messianic than the writings of Kayibanda; it was Gitera whom the Tuutsi conservatives most feared. Yet Kayibanda was the better tactician, quietly building an organization at the grass roots, based on a structure of local cells, with a party organizer on each local hill. From Kabgayi Mission, Kayibanda was in a strategic position to contact Hutu in the areas around the mission and in the north, where the Tuutsi population was small; in both areas, anti-Tuutsi sentiment ran high.

MSM and APROSOMA represented two substantially divergent approaches in their ideology and tactics. Kayibanda's association, later transformed into the Parti du Mouvement de l'Emancipation Hutu in 1959, stressed liberation of Hutu and took a strongly anti-Tuutsi stance. APROSOMA, by contrast, called for freedom of all oppressed groups in Rwanda, Hutu as well as poor Tuutsi. For both groups, of course, the monopoly of power and wealth held by Tuutsi chiefs and the abuses perpetrated by them were a central issue, but the differences between the leaders were real. Further study is needed of the roots of this cleavage among the Hutu counter-elite. Regional considerations were undoubtedly important; Munyangaju and Gitera, the major leaders of APROSOMA, were both from Astrida region, and Munyangaju lived for a decade in Kinyaga. Kayibanda and Bicamumpaka, leaders of PARMEHUTU, were from the central and northwestern regions of the country, respectively.

On July 25, 1959, *Umwami* Mutara Rudahigwa died in Bujumbura of what was officially reported as a brain hemorrhage. His successor, Kigeri Ndahindurwa, was chosen by conservative Tuutsi elements, who named him without consulting the Belgian authorities. The death of Rudahigwa and the subsequent choice of Ndahindurwa can be considered as an "accelerator" to revolutionary activity, as defined by Chalmers Johnson, for these events exposed the inability of the Belgian administration to impose its will; the failure of the administration to influence the choice of a new *umwami* made it clear that the Belgians were no longer in full control of the situation. The death of Rudahigwa acted as an accelerator also in that it convinced the Hutu that they had to organize more rapidly in preparation for violent confrontation.[40]

Rwanda was a simmering caldron from August through October 1959. Tension was heightened by expectancy. The report of a parliamentary commission from Belgium, which had visited Rwanda earlier in the

year, was expected to appear soon, and elections were due at the end
of 1959. Many speculated over what form the elections would take; a
flurry of party organization took place in expectation of the announce-
ment. Meanwhile, both Tuutsi and Hutu protesters tried to build up
their coercive capabilities.[41] APROSOMA and PARMEHUTU, the two
major Hutu parties, escalated their demands for social justice and the
redistribution of power and privilege. Feeling their own position threatened by the Hutu stand, leaders of the newly formed Tuutsi monarchist
party, the Union Nationale Rwandaise (UNAR), resorted to coercion
and violence to prevent people from joining the Hutu parties. A moderate Tuutsi party was organized by younger educated Tuutsi évolués,
many of them employees of the administration. This party, the Ras-
semblement Democratique Rwandais (RADER) called for progressive
reforms, a constitutional monarch, and democratization of political
structures.

THE HUTU UPRISING OF NOVEMBER 1959

THE FIRST blows of the revolution were struck in November 1959
in the vicinity of Kabgayi Mission (Marangara and Ndiza chiefdoms). The igniting spark occurred on Sunday, November 1, when a
gang of Tuutsi youths attacked the Hutu subchief Dominique Mbon-
yumutwa. Although he escaped with his life, rumors spread that he had
been killed. Local Hutu moved quickly to retaliate. On Monday
November 2, Hutu gathered for a protest outside the house of the Ndiza
chief, Gashagaza; they attacked four Tuutsi notables who had sought
refuge in the chief's house, but spared Gashagaza. Among those attacked was the subchief Nkusi, who had on two previous occasions
publicly threatened retribution against supporters of the Hutu parties.

Hutu in Marangara and the neighboring Ndiza chiefdom thus spear-
headed the violent protests which set Rwanda on the path of revolution.
Violent incidents spread from Ndiza and Marangara to other areas of
Gitarama territory, then on November 6 to Ruhengeri and Gisenyi territories in the northwest. By November 7, the rural violence had
reached Byumba (northeast Rwanda) and Kibuye (west-central Rwanda).
On Sunday November 8 and Monday November 9, the raids extended
into Nyanza and Kigali territories (where Tuutsi influence was predominant). Only three districts did not experience widespread Hutu attacks
against Tuutsi during the November uprising: Astrida (seat of
APROSOMA), Cyangugu, and Kibungo.[42]

The violence spread first in the areas of strong PARMEHUTU influence (Gitarama, Ruhengeri, Gisenyi, Byumba Territories). Similar tactics were used by Hutu in these different areas, but even so most analysts of these events consider the violence to have been spontaneous. The rapidity with which this protest spread gave evidence of intense resentments against Tuutsi rule and a desire for change among many rural people. It was directed primarily against Tuutsi chiefs, and not (at least at this stage) against the *umwami*. Many of those participating in the raids claimed they thought that European authorities and the *umwami* had ordered destruction of Tuutsi homes.[43] The violence was limited mainly to the burning and looting of Tuutsi dwellings while, on the whole, Tuutsi lives were spared:

> Incendiaries would set off in bands of some ten persons. Armed with matches and paraffin, which the indigenous inhabitants used in large quantities for their lamps, they pillaged the Tuutsi houses they passed on their way and set fire to them. On their way they would enlist other incendiaries to follow in the procession while the first recruits, too exhausted to continue, would give up and return home. Thus day after day, fires spread from hill to hill.

> Generally speaking the incendiaries, who were often unarmed, did not attack the inhabitants of the huts and were content with pillaging and setting fire to them. The most serious incidents involving tragic wounding and death occurred when the Tuutsi were determined to fight back, or when there were clashes with the forces of order.[44]

The Hutu uprising of November 1959 was important because it demonstrated the depth of rural discontent with Tuutsi domination, and the ability of Hutu to destabilize the state. The Hutu protests also provoked a Tuutsi counterattack, better organized and more brutal than the Hutu initiatives, which forced the Belgian administration to act. As Reyntjens has pointed out, the Hutu Revolution was directed not against the Belgian administration, which claimed a monopoly of coercive force, but against the Tuutsi, who did not control the main instruments of coercion available to the state.[45]

In its campaign appeals the UNAR party consistently called for rapid moves toward independence from Belgium. The UNAR position was based on the realization that the Hutu needed time to organize and mobilize their political resources—but that once this mobilization was achieved, the political tide would be running strongly against Tuutsi powerholders. The longer the Belgians remained in the country, the greater the chance that the Hutu protest movement would succeed in dislodging the Tuutsi from power. Thus, to the extent that the European administration was not entirely neutral (and from November 1959 it decidedly was not), the continued presence of Belgian rule in Rwanda tended to aid the Hutu.[46] In this context, the intensity of Tuutsi efforts to seize independent control of the state apparatus without delay is understandable. Yet it was these efforts which, in turn, generated strong counter-action on the part of Hutu leaders and the Belgian administration.

On Friday November 6 the *umwami* requested permission to reestablish order with his own army. The Belgian administration denied his request, but he ignored the order. The Tuutsi reaction began, with orders from the court to arrest certain Hutu leaders and bring them before the king. Beginning on Saturday November 7, units of the earlier Tuutsi army organization were dispatched, and a number of Hutu leaders were killed. Gitera, a prime target, was protected by Belgian-led forces; Kayibanda went into hiding. Captured Hutu were taken to the *Ibwami* at Nyanza, where many were then tortured by UNAR leaders.[47] The Tuutsi regime intended to eliminate Hutu leaders in the hope that this would squelch the movement of rural radicalism and agitation in the countryside.[48]

The Belgian administration was not caught unprepared. Several weeks before the violence erupted Governor Harroy had contacted a friend of his, Colonel B. E. M. Guy Logiest, who was at that time an officer of the Force Publique in the Congo. Harroy asked Logiest to evaluate the military forces available to the government in Rwanda and make recommendations for sending reinforcements if necessary. An initial detachment was sent to Rwanda from Bujumbura on October 24. Additional Force Publique soldiers and Belgian paratroopers, as well as Logiest himself, came to Rwanda on November 4, after the violence erupted.[49]

Logiest's troops tried to prevent violence and reestablish order. But once the Tuutsi counterattack began, a major concern of the Belgian military operations in Rwanda was to protect Hutu leaders. Governor Harroy and the *umwami* issued a joint proclamation calling upon the population to assist in maintaining calm in the country. A state of emergency was declared (November 11), military rule was imposed throughout Rwanda (November 12), and Colonel Logiest was appointed as Special Military Resident. By November 14, relative calm had been restored; this proved, however, to be only a temporary lull. Gradually passive resistance, as well as overt opposition to the Tuutsi chiefs, spread from central and northern Rwanda to other regions.[50]

Harroy claims that he encouraged Colonel Logiest to install structures of administration staffed by Hutu in the aftermath of the November uprising; such measures were necessary, he and Logiest believed, to ensure that Tuutsi supporters of UNAR would not regain control of the state. Whatever the role of Harroy, Logiest clearly became an active partisan aiding the Hutu. As he later explained, at the time he believed he had to choose between two possible courses of action: Either he could support the Tuutsi structures (this would mean moving rapidly toward independence for Rwanda and, in his view, would be harmful for the popular masses in the country) or he could opt for democratization. Logiest consciously chose the latter option, knowing full well that this would "require . . . the establishment of a republic and the abolition of Tutsi hegemony."[51]

After the November conflicts opposition to Tuutsi in many areas was so great that the population refused to obey Tuutsi authorities. Logiest instructed local Belgian administrators to depose as many such chiefs as possible. Other Tuutsi chiefs and subchiefs fled from their posts, often seeking refuge in neighboring areas outside Rwanda. Logiest and his delegates then appointed new, interim chiefs, who were supporters of the Hutu parties (PARMEHUTU and APROSOMA) or, in some cases, of the progressive Tuutsi party, RADER. The results of this policy were dramatic: By the beginning of March 1960, Hutu interim authorities already headed 22 of Rwanda's 45 chiefdoms, and 297 of the 531 subchiefdoms. Logiest's policy was intended to prevent a return to power by Tuutsi. It gave Hutu leaders access to valuable political resources, and put them in a favorable position to campaign for the important Commune elections scheduled for June–July 1960.[52]

The Rwandan Revolution was thus launched in November 1959, with the Hutu uprising and the Tuutsi counterattack. The Revolution ended 22 months later, when legislative elections and a referendum on the monarchy were held in September 1961.[53] Sporadic violent incidents punctuated this period of transition, becoming particularly severe in the weeks before the commune elections of 1960 and the legislative elections of 1961. In the 1961 legislative elections, supervised by the United Nations, Hutu parties won an overwhelming majority of the votes. A referendum held at the same time resulted in a decisive rejection of the monarchy. Nine months later Rwanda regained formal independence from European rule, on July 1, 1962. It is beyond the scope of this study to analyze the intricate negotiations that occurred during this period between Belgian authorities, Hutu leaders, the United Nations Organization and various factions of Tuutsi groups. The events of the Rwandan Revolution have been covered in detail by other authors such as Lemarchand, Murego, Linden, Reyntjens, and Harroy. Therefore I will limit my discussion of this period to one major milestone in the Hutu struggle to gain control of the state: the commune elections held in June–July 1960, nine months after the Revolution began.

THE 1960 COMMUNE ELECTIONS

ON A national level the commune elections of 1960 marked an important gain for Hutu. The elections were to select burgomasters and councilors for the newly created communes—administrative entities designed to replace existing subchiefdoms (restructured into larger units) and chiefdoms (provinces), which were to be abolished. The Hutu parties, especially PARMEHUTU, won an overwhelming victory at the polls, with 83.8 percent of the vote. Hutu parties won a majority of the votes in 211 of the 229 communes, and of the 2896 councilors elected, 2623 were candidates of Hutu parties. The results of these elections demonstrated widespread support for the Hutu leadership and program. The victory at the polls also placed Hutu leaders in critically important positions; henceforth they could exercise control over key resources, and engage in daily contact with the population.[54]

In Kinyaga, a core of some fifteen APROSOMA adherents began organizing among the local population during the early months of 1960. These Hutu held a number of meetings, planning organizational strategies and preparing for the upcoming commune elections.[55] The leaders developed a friendly rapport with the Belgian Territorial Administrator at Cyangugu, who apparently gave them moral and even some organizational support. As the emphasis of the administration shifted from a primary concern with effective administration under colonial rule to a desire to leave an honorable legacy of an independent country, individual sympathies also adjusted to these new perspectives, and many administrators, led by Special Resident Logiest, proffered support to the majority ethnic group.

Such help was particularly important given the open Tuutsi (UNAR) efforts at intimidation of Hutu who attempted to explain the meaning of the elections to the population.[56] For example, several Hutu traders with shops at Bushenge market near Shangi were attacked and their shops looted—a punishment for their activities in support of the Hutu parties. As a result of such challenges, Hutu leaders at times found it necessary to hold clandestine meetings in the forest, so that they would not be perceived by the chiefs.[57]

Party organization in Kinyaga had been initiated by Aloys Munyangaju, under the aegis of APROSOMA. As we have noted, this party called for social and economic changes to help all disadvantaged groups in Rwanda, not just Hutu. Although in the majority comprised of Hutu, APROSOMA initially welcomed Tuutsi who shared its goals of working for social and political changes and an end to the arbitrary power of the chiefs.[58] PARMEHUTU, which did not commence activities in Kinyaga until May 1960, espoused a more frankly radical ethnic ideology than APROSOMA, ruling out the possibility of cooperation with Tuutsi. As we have seen, Kayibanda focused the initial organizational efforts of PARMEHUTU around Gitarama in the center of the country and in the northern regions of Ruhengeri–Gisenyi. APROSOMA activities were centered principally at Astrida (now Butare), under the leadership of Gitera, and in Kinyaga. When PARMEHUTU commenced activities in Kinyaga in May 1960, the party gained adherents in some areas from among APROSOMA supporters. As one Belgian administrator commented at the time, "A virulent APROSOMA [member] becomes PARMEHUTU."[59]

Many of the Kinyagan Hutu who played leading roles in early protest activities were men who had mobility (they were often truckdrivers or traders), access to instruments for communication (e.g., printing presses or mimeograph machines in Bukavu for putting out circulars and party membership cards), and an acquaintance with ideas of organizing which they used to mobilize protest. And some of the local Hutu leaders were schoolteachers or catechists who enjoyed a wide network of local ties and prestige associated with their work. Often the activists were from Hutu lineages that had enjoyed high status, wealth, and prestige before Abanyanduga Tuutsi and European rule were imposed in Kinyaga. For example, one of the Hutu founders of APROSOMA in Kinyaga, and later the party's regional president, was Philippe Sarukondo, a man whose lineage had a long history of independence and resistance to Tuutsi rule. Sarukondo's ancestors had cleared their land on the northern extremity of Nyamirundi peninsula (Impara province); during Rwabugiri's attacks against Ijwi Island, a member of the lineage had been killed for alleged treason. In the 1950s, Sarukondo was a trader-transporter living at Kamembe; he had access to a truck and therefore was in a key position to assume a role of leadership in Hutu protest activities.[60]

Included among those who aided Sarukondo in publicizing APROSOMA views were a court clerk, a teacher, a catechist, and several trader-shopkeepers. The party cards were printed in Bukavu by a Kinyagan Hutu who worked as a typesetter at one of the printing presses there. These Hutu activists and the assistants they recruited distributed the newspaper *Soma* and sold APROSOMA membership cards (at 5 francs each); more important, through their general mobility, visibility, and outspoken political views they were able to articulate deep-rooted and widespread grievances of rural residents. During the months just before the July 1960 commune elections, the two predominantly Hutu parties united to form a cartel for the elections, and Hutu organizers toured Kinyaga holding meetings to explain the significance of the parties and the voting to the population. For a brief period, there even occurred a modest form of cooperation between the two Hutu parties and RADER (a cooperation reminiscent of the earlier Ibaba revolt), which was the party favored by many Kinyagan Tuutsi, particularly the *évolués*. RADER participated jointly with APROSOMA and PARMEHUTU in several of the pre-election meetings. The leaders of all three parties found commonality of interest against UNAR. In Kinyaga, UNAR attracted support mainly from the Abanyanduga Tuutsi (those from central Rwanda) who viewed Kinyagans in general and Hutu in particular with undisguised disdain.[61]

For the commune elections of 1960, APROSOMA and PARMEHUTU candidates ran on a common ticket in Cyangugu Territory, obtaining a large majority of the positions of burgomaster and communal councilor. Of the nineteen burgomasters elected, only two were Tuutsi; one of these, the son of the chief of Abiiru, never assumed office, but stepped aside in favor of a Hutu runner-up.[62] All of the new burgomasters had had some primary-school education and were (or had been) traders, teachers, or wage-earning employees. Most of them, understandably, had played central roles in the organization of Hutu party activity.

One of the interesting aspects of the election results in Kinyaga and elsewhere in Rwanda was the variation among different areas in the extent of pro-Hutu (or anti-Tuutsi) voting. The variations can be explained in part by the nature of party organization, the role of personalities, the degree of political awareness on the part of the population, and the last-minute boycott called by national UNAR party leaders.[63] However, it appears that these factors, especially the latter two, did not vary greatly between the different provinces of Kinyaga. It will be suggested here that the nature of Hutu–Tuutsi relations and the extent of perceived exploitation in a given area were the key variables accounting for variations in the voting, and these considerations influenced party organization in important ways. While actual voting percentages are not available for the chiefdom (province) level, the figures on numbers of seats won by each party are generally valid for making comparisons between the different provinces of Kinyaga.[64]

The percentage of seats won by Hutu was very high (93% or more) in both Bukunzi and Cyesha provinces. Cyesha was characterized by a relatively large Tuutsi population, relatively long-standing and highly developed forms of clientship, and relatively intense Western social, cultural, and economic penetration. A large area of Bukunzi province was composed of the two former Hutu kingdoms (Bukunzi and Busoozo), which were characterized by a very limited Tuutsi population, and recent introduction of central government (Tuutsi) norms and institutions. Thus Bukunzi proper and the Bugarama portions of the chiefdom showed a relatively high degree of "social change" indicators. The common feature accounting for the similar voting patterns of these two provinces might appear to be that both had experienced relatively high levels of Western economic and cultural contact. But the "social change" factor as a possible explanation for a high Hutu vote in the region needs to be examined more closely.

Bukunzi chiefdom, though a mountainous region far from central Rwanda, was near two of the four Catholic missions in Kinyaga at that time; one of these (Mibirizi) was the first mission founded in Kinyaga and one of the earliest missions in Rwanda. In addition, Bukunzi included an area of early introduction of cotton (in the Bugarama Valley, the low plain surrounding the Rusizi River) and coffee (in the mountains), as well as a commercial tradition of mobility through historical ties with Bushi (Bukunzi) and Burundi (Busoozo and Bugarama).

Cyesha was the site of the second Catholic mission in Kinyaga (Nyamasheke, founded in 1928) and was an important educational center. Extensive involvement in the Western economic network was also characteristic of Cyesha, as reflected in the presence of a large number of European enterprises, brick factories, mining operations, and plantations. In some circumstances this served as a potential "escape" from administrative exactions. But in Cyesha the "escape" element was severely diminished by several factors: the control of this form of employment remained in the hands of foreigners with an influence on administrative policy (particularly for labor demands), and in certain areas there was considerable land alienation. Therefore, in Cyesha "social change" tended to create increased possibilities (and pressures) for exploitation on the part of the chiefs. Exploitation in Cyesha intensified because of the close mesh of European labor demands and chief–patron administrative power. In this context, then, social change and exploitation cannot fairly be portrayed as independent variables.

Thus two somewhat different types of "social change" characterized these areas of intense pro-Hutu vote. Bukunzi and Cyesha also differed in the forms of client institutions, the degree of central political penetration, and the size of their Tuutsi population. Therefore it is difficult to explain the common high Hutu vote in the two regions on the basis of any one of these factors alone.

In Abiiru province, also an area of high participation in the market through labor migration to the Congo, the Hutu percentage of the vote was relatively low (43%). But through most of the colonial period there was little European enterprise in Abiiru itself, and hence land alienation and the demands for local labor and food supplies (administrative demands which were often used for exploitative purposes elsewhere) were relatively less harsh—or at least (given the access to the Kivu complex outlets) these demands may have been *perceived* as less harsh by the population.

The element that seems to differentiate Abiiru from Bukunzi and Cyesha (areas which are themselves dissimilar in some respects) was a high degree of perceived exploitation. In Cyesha this was associated with intensive Tuutsi and European presence, and in Bukunzi with a long-standing tradition of independence and the brusqueness with which central norms were imposed. It is significant in this regard that PARMEHUTU, the more radically anti-Tuutsi party, focused its organizational efforts mainly on Nyamasheke and Nyakabuye communes (located in Cyesha and Bukunzi provinces, respectively).[65]

Impara province represents an intermediary case, between Cyesha and Bukunzi on the one hand, and Abiiru on the other. In Impara province the number of seats won by Hutu was very high (93% or more) in three communes, but somewhat lower (60–80%) in the remaining five communes. Impara in general was an area of old and highly developed client forms associated with relatively intense land pressure, and in the areas near the lake, a scarcity of pasturage. European enterprise was less developed in the region compared to the situation in Cyesha (with the exception of the original concession to Protanag, which was located in Impara near the lake). But in many areas of Impara, Western economic penetration tended to take the form of coffee cultivation by chiefs and smallholders, and labor emigration to the Congo, often of a short-term nature.

One of the communes in Impara province with a very high Hutu vote (100%—comparable to that of communes in Bukunzi) was Nyamirundi, home of Sarukondo, the regional president of APROSOMA. The Nyamirundi peninsula is the area in Kinyaga with the highest population density in the region and the highest density of cattle relative to population; in that respect Nyamirundi differs from Bukunzi but resembles Cyesha. But like people in Bukunzi, the Hutu of Nyamirundi preserved memories of past status and autonomy, free from Tuutsi control. The other two communes in Impara with a very high pro-Hutu vote were also areas of high population and cattle density, where coffee cultivation was highly developed.[66]

In the five communes of Impara where the pro-Hutu vote was moderately high, local factors (such as the nature of Tuutsi lineages in the area) were important, and land pressure was apparently somewhat less intense. The influence of Mibirizi Mission, staffed at the time by Rwandan clergy, may have contributed to the election results in Mibirizi commune, where 61 percent of the commune council seats went to the Hutu parties, 15 percent to RADER, 15 percent to UNAR, and 7 percent to MUR (a party related to UNAR). Clientship forms in Impara were similar to those in Cyesha; forms of labor exploitation were more similar to those in Abiiru. Further research is needed to assess adequately how coffee cultivation in Impara affected clientship and perceived exploitation.[67]

Voting patterns in Abiiru differed markedly from those in other provinces of Kinyaga. The proportion of seats won by candidates of the Hutu parties was low (43%) in Abiiru; and, more than in any other province, the Abiiru vote was fragmented. Five different parties each received 5 percent or more of the seats, and three coalitions each received at least 20 percent. In addition, Tuutsi parties received a much higher proportion of the seats in Abiiru than in other areas. In the other three provinces, UNAR and RADER together with their related parties won an average of about 10 percent of the seats; in Abiiru, 20 percent of the seats went to extremist monarchist parties (UNAR and the related MUR).

Furthermore, Abiiru was the only area of Kinyaga where seats were won by an independent party, Intérêts Communaux du Kinyaga (INTERCOKI). This party, led by young members of the white-collar elite who worked in Bukavu, claimed no formal ethnic affiliation, but was widely considered to have been a local front for RADER.[68] INTERCOKI

and RADER together captured 32 percent of the seats in Abiiru. Therefore, the nonexclusively Hutu vote was markedly greater than the total
Hutu vote—55 percent as opposed to 43 percent—in all three of the
communes in Abiiru.[69] Elsewhere in Kinyaga, UNAR (the extremist
Tuutsi party) gained 5 percent of the seats in Cyesha, 3 percent in
Impara (concentrated in the five communes with moderate pro-Hutu
vote), and no seats in Bukunzi. The moderate Tuutsi party, RADER,
captured 9 percent of the seats in Impara and 5 percent in Bukunzi.

The non-Hutu vote, and particularly the extremist Tuutsi UNAR
vote in Abiiru, needs further explanation, as it varied significantly from
other areas of Kinyaga. First, it should be noted that Abiiru was the
home of François Rukeba, one of the three "most ardent supporters of
the crown."[70] A principal organizer of UNAR at the national level,
Rukeba was regarded as the "emotional" element of that party; it is
likely that his charismatic character alone attracted a certain number
of UNAR votes in Abiiru. This may also account in part for the intensive organization of UNAR in Abiiru and the relatively low turnout of
voters for the election.

Second, the client system and local-level exactions were relatively
less harsh in Abiiru than in Impara–Cyesha. In Kinyaga intensity of
social change in terms of new forms of economic activities, largely
introduced from outside (e.g., plantations, mines, cash crops, labor recruitment), generally was less directly reflected in voting patterns than
the ways these changes interacted with pre-existing social institutions
(though often in Kinyaga these two forms of social change were com-

TABLE 7: Ethnic Composition of Communal Councils in
Kinyaga by Province, 1960

PROVINCE	PARMEHUTU-APROSOMA	UNAR	MUR	RADER	INTER-COKI	INDE-PENDENTS	TOTAL SEATS
Bukunzi	42 (93%)	—	1 (2%)	2 (4%)	—	—	45
Cyesha	51 (93%)	3 (5%)	—	—	—	1 (2%)	55
Impara	78 (82%)	3 (3%)	1 (1%)	8 (9%)	—	5 (5%)	95
Abiiru	19 (43%)	6 (15%)	2 (5%)	1 (3%)	12 (29%)	2 (5%)	42
Total	190	12	4	11	12	8	237

SOURCE: Territoire du Ruanda-Urundi, Service des Affaires Politiques et Administratives,
"Elections communales, résultats pour l'ensemble du Ruanda."

plementary). The characteristics of Tuutsi governance (relatively harsh or relatively mild) were at least as important in influencing perceived exploitation as was social change per se. To the degree that the two elements can be distinguished for analytic purposes, it can be said that it was the changing structures of the state, clientship, and labor control practices that brought the system down as much as the fact of introduced economic change.

Part of the reason for the relatively less harsh client conditions in Abiiru can be traced to the different history of clientship there compared to that of Impara–Cyesha and Bukunzi. From the late eighteenth century, certain lineages in Abiiru retained ties of direct clientship to the royal court. Although this changed during the colonial period as clientship changed, many of the people of Abiiru considered themselves "the king's men" more than did the populations of other regions of Kinyaga. This may help to explain the relatively large UNAR vote in Abiiru, for one of the major tenets of UNAR propaganda was that a vote for (or membership in) the Hutu parties represented direct opposition to the king.[71] In Abiiru such an appeal, combined with an intensive UNAR organization and lack of polarized political atmosphere, was apparently well-received.

Abiiru also exhibited somewhat lower population density than Impara, which, as pointed out above, appears to have had a direct relationship to the harshness of client forms. Where land pressure was severe, the protection of one's land and especially pasturage became an important concern; hence clientship tended to become more necessary and more exacting. Land pressure in Impara and Cyesha was exacerbated by growth in cultivation of coffee plants. In Abiiru, although population density was very high in some areas, the predominant cash crop was bananas.[72] Coffee cultivation implied a panoply of regulations administered by local chiefs and agricultural officers to force cultivators to tend their coffee plants according to particular, colonially mandated criteria. By contrast, cultivators growing bananas could gain a cash income through brewing banana beer or selling bunches of bananas, while avoiding the administrative impositions associated with coffee. Banana producers also had more control over the sale of their product; the price of coffee was controlled by the government.

Abiiru generally had a higher percentage of chiefs who were native to Kinyaga than did other regions. This meant that through cognatic, affinal, neighborhood, and other affective and institutional ties, the population had more numerous potential lines of access to their chiefs to redress or moderate grievances. Moreover, the common cultural heritage between chiefs and subjects may have meant there was less of the resentment found among Hutu in other areas in reaction to central chiefs (Banyanduga chiefs) who viewed Hutu peasants in general and Kinyagan peasants in particular with scorn.

Finally, and most important, the Abiiru results reflect the relatively less-developed class divisions between Hutu and Tuutsi in Abiiru. A 1956 report commenting on the large percentage of Tuutsi elected to the 1956 subchiefdom electoral colleges in Abiiru noted that

> In Biru . . . there are very few true batutsi pastoralists with clients and who were elected for this reason. Almost all the batutsi elected are small cattle owners who are at the same time cultivators.[73]

Moreover, although data on individual candidates are not available, it appears that those gaining seats in Abiiru were largely Tuutsi innovators and progressives. If INTERCOKI is taken to be a Tuutsi party, it is clear that ethnic lines were transgressed on a large scale in the Abiiru voting: RADER and INTERCOKI received 32 percent of the seats; UNAR and MUR, 20 percent. The hypothesis may therefore be advanced that an absence of clear class divisions between Tuutsi and Hutu in Abiiru led to a pattern of voting based more on persons and programs than on ethnic orientation and Hutu–Tuutsi polarization.

10

CONCLUSIONS

THE GROWTH of royal power in Rwanda during the nineteenth century concentrated increased control over land, cattle, and people in the hands of Tuutsi who derived their power from their association with the state apparatus. During the twentieth century this process intensified as Tuutsi manipulated new material and coercive resources introduced by Europeans. In collaboration with European rulers, but not always with their explicit knowledge, Tuutsi political agents utilized these resources in pursuit of private goals. They sought to tighten their grip over land, cattle, and labor and managed to exclude most Hutu from access to education, higher status jobs, and positions of responsibility in government structures. The impact of colonial statebuilding in Rwanda was thus to elaborate and intensify a system of political oppression and economic exploitation dominated by a group that defined itself, and others, by ethnic criteria.[1]

For most rural people in Rwanda, growth of the colonial state meant greater intrusion into their daily lives and increased exactions. Meanwhile, transformations in patron–client politics undermined access to land and cattle, threatening the security of many. The development of labor control practices intensified exploitation even while creating opportunities for combatting it. Therefore, colonialism in Rwanda fostered not just the emergence of new forms of competition and new ideologies, but also the creation of new forms of oppression and exploitation, as well as the intensification of older ones. For many Rwandans, social, economic, and political changes under colonialism meant loss of land, loss of security, and extraction of new forms of taxes and requisitions for labor. The group awareness that emerged among the victims of these processes (most of whom were Hutu) came as a response to the ways in which Tuutsi used the state apparatus to forward their own interests.[2]

CHANGING ELEMENTS OF OPPRESSION

THE CONCLUSIONS to be drawn from the changes in one region of Rwanda are relevant for other regions as well. We have analyzed how the growing power of the state undermined kin groups, transformed patron–client ties, and created new forms of ethnic identities. These changes occurred in the context of, and interacted with, alterations in the social relations of production. Transformations in state power, clientship relations, and labor control mechanisms helped to create the social preconditions to revolution, by contributing to a heightened political consciousness and solidarity among Hutu.

The growth of self-conscious identity among groups of Tuutsi had emerged in the central core of the state before the onset of European colonialism. The rich oral literature of the court and its highly developed ritual embodied in the Esoteric Code[3] served as effective catalysts in the ideologization of Tuutsi identity; these were perhaps more effective in some ways than writing because of the participatory aspects of oral recitations and ritual and because such oral presentations could adapt to changing circumstances and perceptions. During the colonial period, Tuutsi self-awareness was further enhanced and articulated in the writings of educated Tuutsi. Since writing was a skill limited to a relatively small number of Rwandans—many of them Tuutsi—the fact of literacy, as well as the content of the written work, became an important element (as both implement and symbol) of class differences and hence of Tuutsi elite identification.

Group awareness among Hutu came later. This was partly because Hutu relationships to the central structures of political power were both diffuse and distant: as Hutu were increasingly included in a common structural role within a single state apparatus, they also developed an "ethnic" identity, which was no less powerful than that of Tuutsi. This book has told the story of how that identity emerged.

A national political role for Hutu leaders was delayed, relative to that of Tuutsi, partly because of the structural obstacles to obtaining modern "leadership" skills in a restrictive colonial context. There were always political leaders who were "Hutu," but they were leaders of localized kinship, neighborhood, or regional groups, who may have coordinated local resistance to the changing impositions of Tuutsi control but did not appear to mobilize Hutu more generally. Many of the Hutu who became prominent during the colonial period were educated in mission schools. They played an important role in articulating Hutu demands in the 1950s, using the printed news media to propagate their cause. Leaders were also central in organizing coordinated manifestations of discontent. Such leaders were important throughout the period of the expansion and changing nature of Tuutsi power, but especially in the 1950s and early 1960s.

Hutu political identity, articulated in the Hutu party politics of the 1950s, constituted a vehicle of revolutionary protest and ultimately led to the overthrow of Tuutsi hegemony. Yet Hutu leaders did not "create" Hutu ethnic consciousness. The grievances that formed the basis of this consciousness and provided the motivating force of its political effectiveness were already there, products of the realities of everyday life for non-Tuutsi. In many ways, the grievances were felt more deeply by the peasants in the hills than by the Hutu elite. In fact, for Rwanda it would be more accurate to argue that Tuutsi chiefs, through their use and abuse of power, created Hutu consciousness. It is in this sense that the analysis concerns the "cohesion of oppression." It was in fact oppression in its many different forms that brought about the cohesion among Hutu that contributed to the revolution and its outcome.

THE EMERGENCE OF POLITICAL PROTEST

THE LATE nineteenth and early twentieth centuries saw the erosion of kin group status and solidarity in Kinyaga, while the extension of clientship ties brought together men of various kin groups in a common position of political subordination. These two developments, linked to the expansion of state power, served to broaden corporate identity beyond kin criteria to embrace ethnic criteria. Such changes reflected the increased power available to Tuutsi during the colonial period and the transformation of clientship linkages from ties of alliance to instruments of exploitation.

Also important in the emergence of protest were the presence of ideological alternatives to the central Rwandan system (both old—from memories of an earlier autonomy—and new—the result of European mission and educational influences or experiences with different conditions outside Rwanda, as in the Congo), and the possibility, for some people, of gaining economic autonomy from the system. The geographical location of Kinyaga played a role in this regard. During the earlier period, distance from the central court provided a certain amount of political autonomy to Kinyaga, so that the hierarchical patterns of stratification and subordination as they emerged in central Rwanda came late to the region.

Later, during the colonial period, Kinyaga's frontier position assumed significance with the development of the "Kivu complex." Proximity to Kivu meant that colonial exactions in the form of high taxes, forced labor on public works, obligatory cultivation, and recruitment of workers for European enterprises were very severe. These conditions served to heighten antagonism against Tuutsi intermediaries. At the same time, changing relations of production provided some economic independence to wage workers and, thereby, escape from clientship. Proximity to Bukavu provided ideological alternatives and a certain amount of economic autonomy to a small Hutu "elite" who found clerical or skilled workers' jobs in the town (and could thus free themselves from personal dependence on chiefs). These leaders used such resources as mimeograph machines and organizational skills (acquired outside the system) to articulate and channel the grievances of rural dwellers.

Thus, the mechanisms of protest were acquired at least in part through external contacts. Economic autonomy provided both independence vis-à-vis local authority and impetus for leaders to change their situation of blocked mobility. Moreover, through external contacts (including the church networks) the future leaders of protest gained skills essential for effective organization.

The establishment of an identity group determined by its members' relations to an oppressive system, the perception of viable ideological alternatives to this system, and the acquisition of external material bases independent of the system itself were key developments in the organization of effective protest in Kinyaga. This Kinyagan model cannot be extrapolated directly to other regions of the Rwandan state. It does appear, however, that similar elements were present even though different conditions weighted their importance differently.[4]

The northern regions (Gisenyi, Ruhengeri) were similar to Kinyaga in that the introduction of central Tuutsi rule coincided roughly with the arrival of European colonial rule. Moreover, in these areas as in Kinyaga, a frontier location and memories of earlier times facilitated access to alternatives to the central Rwandan political norms. But in the north, Tuutsi–Hutu relations differed in certain respects from those in Kinyaga because the Tuutsi were proportionately fewer,[5] and central power had been only very recently and imperfectly established. Even after fifty years of contact with central institutions, political activity in the north during the terminal colonial period may be seen more as resistance than as revolution. Anti-Tuutsi sentiments in this region were fostered not only by the experience of a viable political alternative, but also (in Gisenyi) by the oppressive administrative measures taken to encourage labor migration to Zaïre (Rutshuru and Gishari), which paralleled those in Kinyaga.

On the other hand, intra-Hutu cohesion on issues other than opposition to the Tuutsi has been problematic in the northern regions. A tradition of very large sub-clans that have retained a considerable degree of corporate autonomy is one element that cuts through pan-Hutu cohesion. A second is the well-developed system of land clientship in the north involving Hutu landowners and other Hutu who are their land clients. The land clientship system constitutes a potential source of cleavage among northern Hutu, and in the early post-independence period, the issue of land reform in the north was a continuing source of tension between Hutu leaders from the north and those from the central regions of the country.[6]

As in the north, ethnic differences were clearly drawn in central Rwanda, but Tuutsi domination was long-established and harsh. Here, as in Kinyaga, economic change (forced cultivation and *akazi*, as well as cash crop production) was important in the development of more exploitative relationships, and in creating a potential for resistance. But an important ingredient in the articulation of dissent seemed to be material and moral support from sources outside the Tuutsi system. In this regard, the Catholic Church played a key role through schools, publications, and employment, and also by providing an organizational network and skills. Political protest in the center was organized by a highly educated Hutu elite who were unable to attain a higher status.

Gisaka, located far from central Rwanda on the eastern frontier of the country (in southern Kibungo Prefecture) and characterized by a relatively large Tuutsi population,[7] would seem to constitute a case in some ways quite similar to that of Kinyaga. As in Kinyaga, the conquest of Gisaka by the Rwandan central court did not long pre-date the reign of Rwabugiri. In some respects, the area was not fully incorporated before Rwabugiri's time. Major resistance occurred even in this century. Contact with Rwandan cultural norms, however, was of longer duration and generally greater in intensity than in Kinyaga. Tuutsi control was probably relatively well-developed, and this may have impeded the expression of Hutu dissent. (More research at the local level is needed before any firm conclusions can be drawn.)

Opportunities to acquire an independent economic base and awareness of alternatives were not as easily accessible to residents of Gisaka as to Kinyagans. Protest in Kibungo, therefore, was perhaps manifested less in Hutu political activity than by the relatively high rate of long-term labor emigration to Uganda or Tanzania.[8] The frequency of voyages by Hutu in search of work and the length of time they spent abroad may have reduced the potential political impact of external contacts. Such a pattern of migration implies that the emigrants lost their local base in Rwanda; therefore, migration was apparently more important as a form of escape than as a means of introducing alternatives to the Gisaka social system.

More data are needed on the impact of colonial changes in Gisaka to explain why emergence of overt protest there was delayed. Gisaka's relatively low population density with a relatively high proportion of Tuutsi and its more fully developed clientship institutions may have impeded effective organization. Moreover, in Gisaka the problem of "cohesion" among the Hutu was compounded by "escape" through long-term or frequent labor migration. In Kinyaga, the proximity of the Kivu complex meant that the ultimate escape was to be sought in overturning the system.

The empirical material presented in this study supports a number of historical propositions that are clearly incompatible with the functionalist model of Rwandan society and politics described in chapter 1. The propositions include the following:

1. Statebuilding does not always promote integration; it may generate profound social cleavages.
2. Dependency relationships (analyzed here as clientship ties) do not proliferate only in the absence of strong state structures, as studies of feudalism in Europe often suggest. Clientship may gain importance in the context of a strong, growing state.
3. Moreover, clientship relations do not necessarily promote vertical integration between social strata; patron–client ties which become highly exploitative may foster cohesion among subordinates.
4. Ethnicity in Africa is not primordial. It is a historical, socially constructed category that can experience significant change. Changes in ethnic identities and solidarities are related to other broader societal transformations.
5. In Rwanda, oppression created by clientship and policies of labor-control fostered the growth of political consciousness and pan-Hutu ethnic solidarity.

6. Social revolutions in Africa are not generated exclusively by outside forces undercutting traditional beliefs. Outside resources may be important, but so are internal structural transformations—the long-term processes which produce the preconditions for revolution.

There were elements of both class and ethnic conflict in the struggles of the 1950s. But the "ethnic" element was not just a primordial relic from the precolonial period; it was shaped and transformed as a result of colonial changes. Economic grievances were a critical factor in rural unrest, as was the struggle over access to the means of production (land and labor). But for the majority of the population, ethnic status and class overlapped—that is, most of the people who were poor and exploited were categorized as Hutu. Among Hutu, however (as among Tuutsi), there were differences. For example, some Hutu (such as school teachers, traders, artisans) were better off than others. Yet in the context of the Rwandan state, based on ethnic discrimination, all Hutu were viewed as, and to a certain extent were, "subordinate."

Not all Tuutsi were rich, powerful, and wealthy. Data from Kinyaga indicate that many nonpolitical Tuutsi had their grievances against the system (probably many of these became adherents of RADER or local independent parties during the late 1950s). Then why did the conflict of the late 1950s take the form of a Tuutsi–Hutu confrontation? The salient fact was that virtually all those who controlled the state—the chiefs and subchiefs—were Tuutsi, and here is where the ethnic factor becomes important. We have seen that even within Kinyaga the extent of Hutu–Tuutsi cleavage varied according to historical and colonially introduced factors. But ultimately, an appeal to Hutu solidarity became, for Hutu leaders, the most effective rallying point for revolutionary activity. Although Hutu could and apparently did distinguish among Tuutsi of different types and attitudes, the fact that chiefs and other African agents of the state were seen as exploiters, and that virtually all of these were Tuutsi, made an appeal to ethnic solidarity potent where an appeal to "all poor people" may have been less so. Because colonial policies had repeatedly pressed upon Hutu their inferior, excluded status, even poor Tuutsi did not experience quite the same forms of discrimination as did those classified as Hutu.

This book has focused on Rwanda, but I would like to think that the approach used here is relevant for the study of politics elsewhere in Africa as well. Such an approach is particularly useful for understanding the evolving interactions between changing state structures and economic inequality that occurred (in various forms) in colonial Africa and that are occurring today, in other forms, in post-colonial African states.

An important general point that is reaffirmed when a historical approach is used concerns the meaning of "traditional" when applied to institutions, offices, or roles in Africa. We cannot assume, for example, that where chiefs retain titles that predate European colonialism, the powers and prerogatives of those chiefs (and the constraints on their power) have remained unchanged in the face of colonial political transformations and the growth of capitalist economic relationships. In other words, if we are to understand the impact of colonialism on class structures we need to look beyond surface manifestations of power to ways in which control over key resources (such as land, cattle, labor, education, jobs) may change, how those changes are related to state power, and how they may affect rural political consciousness.[9]

The empirical emphasis of this approach also demonstrates, in contrast to some of the early dependency writing on Africa, that local leaders in a colonial or neocolonial situation are not just puppets of external forces (such as European colonial rulers, international capital, or, more recently, the World Bank and the International Monetary Fund). What local collaborators with external powers are able to do is substantially constrained and circumscribed by the reality of dependence. Yet such local leaders can and do shape these circumstances in important ways, as we have seen in the case of Tuutsi authorities in Rwanda.[10]

Similarly, if an emphasis on history and empirical analysis is combined with field work and collection of oral data, it will be possible to discover more about the ways that non-elites have attempted to shape the conditions of their subordination. Research of this type has already begun to show that non-elites have not been just passive recipients of the policies of leaders in colonial or post-colonial African states.[11] This is an important area of research and one that political scientists cannot afford to neglect if they are to understand the dynamics of contemporary state formation and decline in Africa.[12]

Until recently, much of the work of political scientists studying the third world has privileged the study of elites. In the 1960s this orientation took the form of viewing government leaders as benevolent "modernizers." Growing state power ("government penetration") was seen as positive because it reflected an increasing capacity on the part of leaders to get people to do what they wanted them to do.[13] That approach has since been questioned; it is now recognized more generally that we need to look behind the rhetoric of leaders to how they are using power, to what ends, and to whose benefit.[14] An approach such as the one used in this study, combining theoretical inquiry with historical, empirical research and a local-level perspective,[15] helps to illuminate such interactions between state and people.

APPENDIXES

APPENDIX I

MODERN KINYAGA

THE ECOLOGICAL CONTEXT

KINYAGA IS nestled in the southwestern corner of Rwanda, separated from the rest of the country by a high range of mountains and dense forest. Numerous peninsulas and islands of Lake Kivu constitute the western limit of the region, with the border continued by the Rusizi River flowing south from the lake. Topographical variety is an important aspect of Kinyagan terrain; in the past this made communications difficult and contributed to a high degree of autonomy between different areas even within Kinyaga itself. The mountains running north–south in the eastern part of Kinyaga descend into steep hills as one moves westward toward the lake. In the extreme south is a vast flat region called the Bugarama Valley, part of the river plain of the Rusizi River which empties into Lake Tanganyika. The plain is significantly lower in altitude than the rest of Kinyaga,[1] and there is a corresponding increase in the mean temperature as well as rainfall differences.

Scattered homesteads dot the slopes and tops of hills, but are not generally found in the valleys. This settlement pattern with homesteads linked by footpaths helps to define a hill (rather than a valley) as the residential unit. There is no "village" as such, but a hill or a portion of a hill has some of the characteristics of a village in that families are often linked by historical ties and common residence. I follow conventional usage in the literature on Rwanda, using the term "hill" to describe an administrative unit which often coincided with a residential unit, rather than a topographical feature alone.

CROPS AND CATTLE

THE KINYAGA landscape gives an impression of high population density and intensive agricultural exploitation, an impression heightened by the luxuriant aspect of the banana groves. In general, the productivity of Kinyaga's soils is superior to that of the central regions of Rwanda, where longer and denser settlement has resulted in exhaustion and erosion of soils. The region's abundant rainfall contributes both to the high productivity and to the green lushness of the countryside.

A homestead *(urugo)* consists of one or several huts and is often enclosed by a reed fence. Normally each homestead is surrounded by a banana grove, and beyond the bananas are located the household's plots of beans, maize, squashes, sweet potatoes and, in some areas, peanuts, peas, or sorghum. Manioc is also grown, and some fruits and vegetables. Besides the fields close to the home, other fields are often cultivated in the swamps. Many farms have plots of coffee, and in some areas tea, for which smallholder production was introduced in the late 1960s. Cultivated plots are worked by the entire family; both men and women participate together in the major agricultural activities of cultivation and harvesting, and during the rainy season much of their time is spent in their fields. Otherwise the care of fields and home are the domain of women, while care of livestock (cattle, goats, sheep) and the maintenance of lineage ties fall to men.

While there are variations from region to region and year to year, the agricultural year is roughly divided into a rainy season and a dry season. The rainy season lasts from October to late May, consisting of two maxima, which are separated by a short dry season varying from two or three weeks to more than a month (December–January). The rainy season is long enough to permit two bean harvests, while the short dry season is brief enough so that it does not cause significant alterations in social or farming activities. During the long dry season (from early June to mid-September) work in the fields is minimal, and this is the time used particularly for weddings, housebuilding, and other social events.

In the past cattle played an important social role. They were used for bridewealth, for establishing social ties, in contracting political alliances, in family ritual, in purchase of land, in commerce with areas to the west and central Rwanda. The most frequent reminder one has today of the role of cattle is the characteristic wooden milk pots accompanying processions honoring a newly married couple. There are also numerous economic uses of products related to cattle: manure for fertilizer and cement, meat, milk, and hides. Cattle continue to hold an important economic place in the life of some families. Yet, except for beef, very little that has to do with cows appears in the local markets. The pattern of exploitation of such products follows either socially determined or new commercial routes (e.g., the exportation of hides).

For most people today, however, cattle do not appear to be a very high priority orientation. This is partly because cattle are fewer per capita now than in the past.[2] Money has taken over some of the functions cattle fulfilled, and cattle are the possession of a single man and not a lineage. Land for pasturage has diminished considerably as demands for agricultural land have increased with population growth.

In the mountains of eastern and southeastern Kinyaga cattle are found less frequently. In other respects, too, these areas differ culturally from the regions nearer the lake.[3] These regions are referred to by other Kinyagans as "Rukiga," and the people there are called "Abakiga" (a general term referring to people of the mountains, "montagnards," implying the common stereotypes usually attributed to mountain people—physical strength, stubbornness, rugged independence, love of autonomy, and reserved social life). The cultural distinctions are strongly drawn in the minds of Kinyagans; people living nearer to the lake generally consider themselves of superior culture and upbringing to those of the mountains, as (in their view) they themselves approach more closely the manners and cultural attributes of central Rwanda.

LOCAL GOVERNMENT

R EFERRED TO for administrative purposes as Cyangugu Prefecture, Kinyaga forms one of ten such administrative units in contemporary Rwanda. In 1970 Kinyaga's population of some 250,000 amounted to almost 15 percent of Rwanda's total population at the time (3.7 million);[4] the average population density for the prefecture (113 km²) was lower than that of all but three of the other prefectures in the country (see table 8).[5] However, within Kinyaga the distribution of population varies considerably with the highest density located near the lake and along the northeastern bank of the Rusizi River. Only two communes showed a population density lower than 124 per km²: Bugarama Commune, made up principally of the Bugarama Valley, which was relatively unpopulated in the past because of sleeping sickness;

and Karengera Commune, which includes an inaccessible mountainous region where the forest is being progressively cleared and settled. (See table 9 and map 4 for the population density by commune in 1970).[6]

Each prefecture in Rwanda is headed by a prefect appointed directly by the central government. Prefectures are divided into communes (11 in Kinyaga)[7] each presided over by a burgomaster and an elected communal council. At the time of the research, burgomasters and their councils were selected through direct popular elections (with secret ballot) held in each commune at three-year intervals from 1960.[8] For most citizens, the commune organization constitutes their closest and most frequent contact with government. The commune registers birth, deaths, and marriages; it issues the identity card which every adult must carry, and other papers essential for entry to post-primary school or job applications, and it collects nationally imposed taxes. The commune also constitutes a focus for commercial activities and a center for social activities, particularly the work of the "foyers sociaux"—local branches of the government-funded women's agency that undertakes to diffuse information about basic sanitation, nutrition, homemaking, etc. to women; in some places the women's social centers offer literacy courses for adults. The commune organizes local festivities for national holidays, and groups representing each commune (dance troupes, singing groups, etc.) are sent to represent the commune at the prefectoral or national manifestations.

TABLE 8: Population density in Rwanda by Prefecture, 1970

Prefecture	Population	Area	Density (pop./km²)
Butare	570,650	1,830 km²	312
Byumba	456,810	4,987	92
Cyangugu	251,310	2,226	113
Gikongoro	272,290	2,192	124
Gisenyi	444,870	2,395	186
Gitarama	436,690	2,241	195
Kibungo	214,220	4,134	52
Kibuye	250,660	1,320	190
Kigali	352,860	3,251	109
Ruhengeri	430,220	1,762	244
Rwanda	3,680,580	26,338 km²	140

SOURCE: République Rwandaise, *Etude démographique du Rwanda*, 1970, 16, 26.

In 1970, a burgomaster typically had been born in and was a resident of his commune. He had had several years of primary school, perhaps a few years of secondary education, and he spoke some French. His lifestyle did not differ greatly from that of the rest of the population; although his home may have been slightly more elaborate, there were few other signs of great wealth distinguishing him from others. It was unusual for a burgomaster to have a car, although I knew of one who had a small motorbike. In the nomination of candidates for the communal elections of 1971, there was apparently a conscious effort to favor those with several years of secondary school, and where incumbents were replaced after the election, the educational level of the new burgomasters was significantly higher than that of their predecessors.[9]

At that time, the burgomaster was pre-eminently a local man; his primary base was the commune, and there were pressures on him to represent the needs and interests of his commune.[10] He filled multiple roles—administrative, political, and judicial. Administratively, he was responsible for tax collection, road maintenance, record-keeping, supervision of development projects, and a variety of other tasks. Politically, he was the intermediary from his people to the prefectoral

TABLE 9: Distribution of population in Cyangugu Prefecture by Commune, 1970

Commune	Population	Area*	Density (pop./km²)
Bugarama	18,533	176.3 km²	105
Cyimbogo	25,157	113.0	223
Gafunzo	40,099	133.9	299
Gatare	28,599	169.2	169
Gishoma	22,639	69.3	327
Gisuma	27,301	99.4	275
Kagano	23,455	143.9	163
Kamembe	24,483	87.4	280
Karengera	27,332	329.5	83
Kirambo	23,202	82.6	281
Nyakabuye	23,238	95.1	244
Total	284,038	1,499.6 km²	189

*These figures exclude lake and forest areas.
SOURCE: Based on CINAM, *Etude du développement de la région du lac Kivu*, II (March 1973), Annexe, Tableau I.

Population Density in Cyangugu Prefecture by Commune, 1970

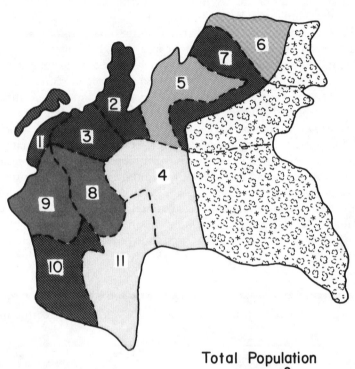

1. Kamembe
2. Gafunzo
3. Gisuma
4. Karengera
5. Kagano
6. Gatare
7. Kirambo
8. Nyakabuye
9. Cyimbogo
10. Gishoma
11. Bugarama

Total Population Per Km²

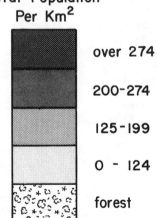

over 274

200-274

125-199

0 - 124

forest

authorities, as well as from the prefectoral authorities to the people—hearing complaints and mobilizing support. In some communes, the burgomaster also served as local representative of the MDR-PARME-HUTU ruling party; even where he did not hold the official party position he was expected to mobilize interest in party activities. In the judicial realm, the burgomaster was called upon to arbitrate local conflicts too minor to be brought before the formal Tribunal de Canton—a district court which depends on the appeals court at Cyangugu (Tribunal de Première Instance).[11] In 1969, the majority of cases introduced at the commune level concerned banditry *(urugomo)*, land litigation or requests for land *(amasambu)*, theft *(ubujura)*, and divorce *(ubwahukane* or *ubutangukane).*[12]

The power of the burgomaster lay largely in his ability to rally support. Although each commune had a small police force of from 8 to 14 men, this was insufficient to rely on coercive power alone for administrative and other functions. Of much greater importance was the burgomaster's control over various services needed by the population and his ability to manipulate these to attract a following. The patron-client relationships that resulted differed in some important ways, however, from the Tuutsi–Hutu clientship of the past.[13]

Linkages to powerful people outside the commune, although not sufficient in themselves, were nevertheless necessary for the burgomaster to maintain his position. Although the population of the commune elected the burgomaster, the Prefect and the national minister from Cyangugu Prefecture had the final word in the lists of candidates for the communal elections; they often took an active role in the choice and listing of candidates on the slate.[14] A clientship network continued to operate in that the links of a burgomaster to superiors could greatly influence his tenure; a shift of power at higher levels, such as a change of minister or change of prefect, could modify substantially the standing of a burgomaster who was viewed as being under the patronage of the official in question. Similarly, links to superiors affected the security of tenure of a prefect, while he attempted to ensure that his subordinates (burgomasters in particular) were loyal to him.[15]

MISSIONS AND SCHOOLS

I N 1970 there were six Catholic[16] and two Protestant[17] missions in Cyangugu Prefecture. The Catholic missions are older and more numerous; the percentage of Christians who are Catholic is correspondingly greater than those who are Protestant. Small communities of Muslims are found at Kamembe, the major commercial center of the Prefecture (located near the lake just a few kilometers from the major urban center of Bukavu, Zaïre), and at a small commercial center in the Bugarama Valley. The Christian missions maintain a network of schools, which in 1970 offered the only primary school education in the region. Post-primary education did not begin to develop in Kinyaga until after independence, and was still quite limited in 1970.[18] A report from Cyangugu in 1970 noted that parents in the region were discouraged by the very small number of places in secondary school for their children; the number of places was decreasing relative to the number of pupils completing the final year of primary school.[19] Kinyagans found it difficult to send their children to attend the more numerous secondary schools of central Rwanda, partly because of government policy, partly because of the expenses involved.

Access to education was only one of several domains in which Kinyagans (in 1970 at least) saw themselves as disadvantaged relative to the central regions of the country. Ambivalent relationships between Kinyaga and central Rwanda, not without tension and mutual distrust, have long historical roots (as discussed in Part I). From the perspective of the central government, in 1970 Kinyaga was still remote culturally as well as geographically; consequently, for government administrators posting to Kinyaga was sometimes seen as a form of exile. But as this study shows, their geographical position has been critically important to Kinyagans. It helped to define their autonomy in the period before European rule, to intensify their oppression during the colonial period, and to provide access to ideological alternatives and material resources during the political struggles of the 1950s.

APPENDIX II

NOTE ON METHODS
AND SOURCES

THE MOST important sources for this study consist of oral accounts. Since my major interests focused on the colonial period, and I preferred where possible to consult eyewitnesses, most of the respondents were over 60 years old. Respondents were selected from different regions, classes, clans, occupational categories, and from both of the two major ethnic groups. Interviews were conducted in all 11 communes of Cyangugu Prefecture, but particular attention was concentrated on the former provinces of Impara and Abiiru. For specific topics such as family histories, data on chiefs, and the political events of the 1960s, other suitable criteria were employed in the choice of informants.

Two basic types of interviews were conducted. Both types included standardized questions pertaining to an estimation of the informant's genealogy, lineage, clan, approximate age, and a brief life-history. The remainder of the first type of interview then consisted of open-ended questions on a variety of topics, which varied according to the local region and the respondent's interests. Before each interview I prepared general questions to be discussed, attempting to focus these on topics with which an informant would be most familiar; then additional questions arose in the course of the interviews.

The majority of interviews were of this first, unstructured type; conducted in Ikinyarwanda with the assistance of a Rwandan interpreter, they were later translated verbatim into French. The unstructured interviews usually lasted about an hour and a half, sometimes stretching to three or four hours. Individual interviews were most common, but group interviews including up to four persons were also employed. I often scheduled return meetings with particularly good informants and made three or four visits to some of the exceptional ones.

A second type of interview, administered mainly in the Impara and Abiiru regions, involved the use of a standardized questionnaire on family traditions and client ties. From selected lineages on different hills and from a variety of clans, I tried to interview the lineage head or the oldest member of the lineage. In some cases I consulted several members of the same lineage. Although questions from this standardized questionnaire were sometimes administered in the course of a taped interview of the unstructured type, much of the material on family history and client ties was collected through separate, more structured interviews, which were shorter than the unstructured ones.

To complement the oral data, I consulted written sources where available. For general information about Rwandan history and culture, there are abundant published materials. The major bibliographies are those of Joseph Clément, "Essai de bibliographie du Ruanda-Urundi" (Usumbura, 1959), and of Marcel Walraet, *Les Sciences au Rwanda, Bibliographie* (Butare, INRS, 1966). Useful bibliographies are also found in Marcel d'Hertefelt, "Le Rwanda"; René Lemarchand, *Rwanda and Burundi*; and, more recently Filip Reyntjens, *Pouvoir et Droit au Rwanda*. The most exhaustive bibliography, providing valuable annotations is Marcel d'Hertefelt and Danielle de Lame, *Société, culture et histoire du Rwanda. Encyclopédie bibliographique, 1863–1980/87* (Tervuren, 1988).

Documents of the Belgian colonial period preserved in Belgium and in the Prefecture archives at Cyangugu are useful for information on colonial policy and its implementation; they are also a rich source of statistics. Important lacunae in the Cyangugu Prefecture collection hindered extensive use of unpublished colonial documentation on the region, but several administrative reports and other writings relevant to Kinyaga are found in the papers of the Derscheid Collection.

Records preserved by Catholic missionaries in Rwanda are an invaluable source for the period from 1900. The missions staffed by fathers of the Société des missionnaires d'Afrique (White Fathers) normally maintained a Diary recording notable events of interest to the mission. Up to the 1940s, the diaries for the early Kinyagan missions (Mibirizi and Nyamasheke) often refer to political events and sometimes contain ethnographic or historical studies carried out by the missionaries. Other mission documents (reports, letters, missionary writings) are preserved in the archives of the Archdiocese of Rwanda at Kigali and at the White Fathers center in Rome.

APPENDIX III

CHRONOLOGY OF THE KINGS OF RWANDA

Name	Approximate Date of Death	Century
Ndahiro Ruyange	1386 (±20)	14th
Ndoba	1410 (±18)	
Samembe	1434 (±16)	
Nsoro Samukondo	1458 (±14)	15th
Ruganzu Bwimba	1482 (±12)	
Cyirima Rugwe	1506 (±10)	
Kigeri Mukobanya	1528 (±12)	
Mibambwe Mutabaazi	1552 (±14)	16th
Yuhi Gahima	1576 (±16)	
Ndahiro Cyaamatare	1600 (±18)	
Ruganzu Ndoori	1624 (±20)	
Mutara Seemugeshi	1648 (±22)	17th
Kigeri Nyamuheshera	1672 (±20)	
Mibambwe Gisanura	1696 (±18)	
Yuhi Mazimpaka	1720 (±16)	
Karemeera Rwaaka	1744 (±14)	
Cyirima Rujugira	1768 (±12)	18th
Kigeri Ndabarasa	1792 (±10)	
Mibambwe Sentabyo	1797 (±10)	
Yuhi Gahindiro	1830 (±10)	
Mutara Rwogera	1860 (±5)	
Kigeri Rwabugiri	1895	19th
Mibambwe Rutarindwa	1896	
Yuhi Musinga	1931 (deposed; died in 1940)	
Mutara Rudahigwa	1959	20th
Kigeri Ndahindurwa	1960 (deposed)	

SOURCE: Based on Jan Vansina, *L'évolution du royaume Rwanda des origines à 1900* (Brussels: ARSOM, 1962), 56.

APPENDIX IV

GENEALOGIES OF RWANTERI AND NYARWAYA

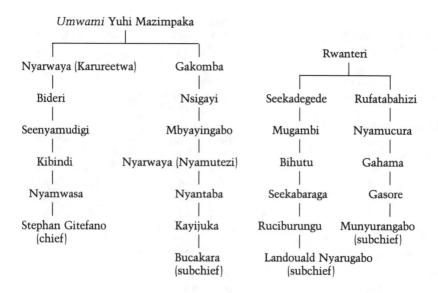

Umwami Yuhi Mazimpaka

Nyarwaya (Karureetwa) — Gakomba

Rwanteri

Bideri — Nsigayi — Seekadegede — Rufatabahizi

Seenyamudigi — Mbyayingabo — Mugambi — Nyamucura

Kibindi — Nyarwaya (Nyamutezi) — Bihutu — Gahama

Nyamwasa — Nyantaba — Seekabaraga — Gasore

Stephan Gitefano (chief) — Kayijuka — Ruciburungu — Munyurangabo (subchief)

Bucakara (subchief) — Landouald Nyarugabo (subchief)

SOURCE: Delmas, *Généalogies*, 61–62, 129; Nyarugabo 10/8/70, 1 and 10/9/70, 11.

APPENDIX V

NON-*UBUHAKE* TRANSFERS
OF CATTLE

INGWATE COWS (the term comes from the verb *kugwatiriza*) were obtained in the following fashion:

X gives Y a bull-calf. In return, Y loans X a cow. Each time that the cow loaned to X gives birth to a bull-calf, X must take this bull-calf to Y, who becomes its owner. But when the cow loaned to X gives birth to a heifer, there are two possible courses of action. If X is poor, he might keep the heifer, and return the cow to Y. Alternatively, X gives the first heifer to Y. When the cow loaned to X gives birth to a second heifer, X keeps the heifer, and then returns the cow to Y. The heifer which X keeps belongs to him as personal property—*impahano*. Should he pass the impahano on to his descendants, it and its offspring become *imbaata*.[1]

Ugushega is a contract involving a friendship exchange of cattle which is still practiced today in Bushi, and between Kinyagans and Shi. Bourgeois specifies that in Kinyaga the exchange is made between two Hutu who are normally (Bourgeois says always) linked first by the blood pact, *kunywana*. A gives to B a heifer or a cow, called *ishega*. B gives to A a gift, varying from several goats and a bull-calf to two bull-calfs or even just one bull-calf. The gifts given by B become the personal property of A. But the *ishega* cow is kept by B only on the performance of certain conditions.

After every third calf is born to the *ishega* cow, B must send A a heifer. This heifer returned to A (the owner of the *ishega* cow) is called *inyiturano* in Ikinyarwanda, *uburonde* in Mashi. As Bourgeois noted

---

1. Bourgeois, "Moeurs et coutumes," 143–144.

in 1935, the obligation of returning the *uburonde* heifer was often ignored, giving rise to continual litigation in the courts.[2]

An institution similar to *ugushega* is known as *ubugabire* in Buhavu.
In the past, Havu residents of Ijwi Island often formed *ubugabire* contracts with their Kinyagan neighbors to the east, and this practice has
continued up to the present.[3]

2. Bourgeois, "Moeurs et coutumes," 144–145.
3. Personal communication from David Newbury.

APPENDIX VI

LIST OF INFORMANTS

FOLLOWING EACH name, the individual's lineage and clan are indicated in parentheses. There then follows the name of the hill on which the person lives (or used to live), the code number for interviews with the informant, and the date on which the interview occurred:

Name. (lineage, clan) hill; code, date.

For example, in the first citation, Bagara belongs to the Abaroha lineage, Abazigaaba clan; he lives at Mugera hill; the code of the interview with him is M-1, and he was interviewed on 9 July 1971. Note that for dates the form day/month/year has been used. If an individual did not provide a lineage name this is indicated by a dash (——).

B = Abiiru   G = Bugarama   K = Bukunzi   M = Impara
S = Busoozo   F + another letter = Interview not taped

Bagara. (Abaroha, Abazigaaba) Mugera; M-1, 9/7/71.
Bagaruka Thadée. (Abarindi, Abashambo) Ishara; C-1, 11/2/71, 13/7/71.
Bahenda. (Abarindi, Abashambo) Rukunguri; M-44, 2/11/72.
Bahufite Pierre. (Abakara, Abeega) Butambara; C-2, 12/7/70.
Bakengura Paulin. (——, Abasinga) Rusunyu; M-2, 23/8/70.
Bakomeza Paul. (Abarari, Abahima-Abashambo) Murehe; R-1, FR-1, 27/7/70, 27/11/70, 23/12/70, 12/5/71.
Barera Ankeri. (Abanywa, Abashambo) Isha; FM-1, 8/5/71.
Barihuuta. (Abahinga, Abagesera) Mwezi; K-1, 3/2/71.
Baaruguriyiki Simon. (Abahinga, Abagesera) Mwezi; K-2, 3/2/71.
Bigirimaana Mburamatare. (Abageera, Abanyiginya) Muramba; C-3, 19/2/71.

Bigumba. (Abakabara, Abashambo) Nyamagana; R-2, 26/11/70.

Bihame. (Abatabya, Abazigaaba) Bunyereli; S-1, 21/1/71.

Bikamba Nsibura (——, Abatsibura) Butambara; C-27, 12/10/72.

Bikaari Clavier. (Abarindi, Abashambo) Rukunguri; FM-2, 27/5/71.

Bikolimaana Daniel. (Abacuku, Abasindi) Mwezi; K-2, 3/2/71.

Biniga Léonidas (Abahanya, Abeega) Nyakarenzo; R-4, 17/10/70, 12/10/70.

Birara Denis. (Abarundi, Abacyaba) Gashonga; FR-3, 19/5/71.

Birikunkomo Antoine. (Abajanga, Abeenegitori, Abanyiginya) Ruganda; R-3, FR-2, 4/12/70, 8/1/71, 12/5/71.

Birimwiyundo Michel. (Abakoobwa, Abanyiginya) Shangi; FM-3, 18/6/71.

Birori. (Abahimbwa, Abasinga) Nkanka; FM-4, 4/12/71.

Birumbi. (Ababuzi, Abagesera) Ibanda; C-4, 18/2/71.

Biseruka François. (Abahanya, Abeega) Bushenge; M-3, 9/7/71.

Bishashaari. (——, Abeega?) Gasambu; R-5, 1/12/70.

Biizimaana Charles. (Abashango, Abanyiginya) Nyamasheke; C-5, 13/2/71.

Booyi. (Abashaaki, Abashambo) Kazinda; G-1, 13/1/71.

Booyi Paulin. (——, Abacyaba) Nyamavugo; M-4, M-36, 28/9/70, 28/10/70.

Bucuti. (Abatonyi, Abiitira) Nyamavugo; M-5, 28/9/70, 28/10/70.

Buuda Pierre. (Abateganya, Abakoobwa) Rukunguri; F-4, 27/5/71.

Bulimumbali Nkwakuzi. (Abahanga, Abanyiginya) Nyarwungo; C-14, 18/2/71.

Burumbuuke Charles. (Abagahi, Abasinga) Ishara; C-1, 11/2/71, 13/7/71.

Buyooga Zacharie. (Abarinzi, Abagesera) Mwezi; K-15, 3/2/71.

Bwazire Gabriel. (Abageshi, Abiitira) Cyete; FR-5, FR-10, 17/5/71.

Byumva Nicodème. (Abarundi, Abacyaba) Gashirabwoba; FM-5, 19/6/71.

Cyigwira. (——, ——) Mubumbano; C-6, 17/7/70.

Fashaho Claver. (——, Abeega?) Butambara; C-7, 12/2/71.

Gafaranga Evard. (Abajenje, Abasinga) Burenga-Nyamirundi; FM-6, 16/6/71.

Gahayira Anatole. (Abaziguura, Abagesera) Biguzi; M-6, 2/7/71.

Gahima Jean. (——, ——) Cyibumba; M-9, 25/8/70, 28/8/70.

Gahogo Basile. (Abasheeri, Abashambo-Abanyiginya) Mushaka; R-6, FR-6, 26/7/70, 22/5/71.

Gahwijima. (Abahande, Abashambo) Mutongo; R-7, 28/11/70, 6/1/71.

Gakuru Augustin. (Abahabe, Abasambo) Giti; G-2, 15/1/71.

Gashiibonde Michel. (Abiishaza, Abiitira) Tyazo; C-25, 17/2/71.

Gashyamangali. (Abahunde?, Abanyiginya) Ruharambuga; K-7, 5/2/71.

Gasimba Raphael. (Abenemugunga, Abanyiginya) Gashonga; R-8, 26/7/ 70.

Gatozi. (Aboozi, Abiitira) Muhwehwe; G-3, 20/1/71.

Gihura Michel. (Abaruruma, Abongera) Cyete; R-10, 10/7/70, 15/6/71, 22/6/71, 25/6/71.

Gishungu. (Abacooca, Abongera) Cyete; R-21, FR-7, 1/12/70, 14/5/71.

Gishungu Jean. (Abatangize, Abasinga) Kiranga; FR-8, 21/5/71.

Gisiribanyi. (Abahoozi, Abiitira) Shangi; M-7, FM-7, 30/9/70, 22/10/70, 12/6/71.

Habagati Michel. (Abaliro?, Abashambo) Gihinga; M-8, 5/2/71.

Habarugira Joseph. (——, ——) Cyibumba; M-9, 25/8/70, 28/8/70.

Habimaana. (Abacuura, Abeega) Bumazi; FM-8, 19/6/71.

Habimaana Pierre. (Abagosi, Abazigaaba) Cyibumba; M-9, 25/8/70, 28/ 8/70.

Habumugisha, Ferdinand. (Abagisha, Abashambo, Abareera) Gashura; M-31, 7/1/71.

Hakizimfura Ladislas. (Abatege, Abanyiginya) Biguzi; M-6, 2/7/71.

Kabahizi Raphael. (Abahabuura, Abasinga) Mugera; M-10, 9/7/71.

Kaabo. (Abakanani or Abanyandwa, Abatsoobe) Mururu; R-11, FR-9, 30/ 11/70, 15/5/71.

Kabooyi. (——, ——) Muhari; M-11, May 1970.

Kadugano. (——, ——) Murangi; R-12, 17/6/70.

Kaamazaana. (——, Abatsoobe) Mururu; M-13, 28/11/70.

Kamooya. (Abagande, Abasinga) Nyamubembe; K-3, 1/2/71.

Kampara Joseph. (——, Abakono) Muramba; C-8, 19/2/71.

Kaamuhanda. (Abakulingoma, Abashambo) Murehe; R-14, 27/11/70, 23/12/70.

Kanyabacuzi Hormisdas. (Abaramira, Abagesera) Shagasha; M-12, 8/7/ 71.

Kanyabashi Zacharie. (Abazirankende, Abagesera) Karambi; C-9, 20/2/ 71.

Kanyamasovu Athanase. (Ababambo, Abiitira) Isha; FM-9, 19/6/71.

Kanyangurube Trojan. (Abahanya, Beega) Cyete; FR-10, 17/5/71.

Kanyanzige. (——, Abazigaaba) Mutongo; R-15, 28/11/70, 6/1/71.
Kanyarubira. (Abashumbuusho, Abeega) Muhwehwe; G-4, 20/1/71.
Kanyarubungo. (Abanyabyiinshi, Abanyiginya) Gasambu; R-16, FR-11, 1/12/70, 6/1/71, 13/5/71.
Kanyarubungo Jean. (Abatogoogo, Abashambo) Gashonga; FR-12, 18/5/71.
Kanywabahizi. (Abaliro, Abasinga) Bitare; C-11, 13/2/71.
Karahoze. (Aboozi, Abiitira) Muhwehwe; G-5, 20/1/71.
Karamaga. (——, Abatsoobe) Winteeko; R-17, 7/12/70.
Karamira Théodomir. (Abango, Abashambo) Shangi; FM-10, 17/6/71, 18/6/71.
Karibu. (Abaramira, Abagesera) Nyamagana; R-18, FR-13, 26/11/70, 22/12/70, 13/5/71.
Karihanze Nicodème. (Abahande, Abasinga) Rukunguri; FM-11, 1/6/71.
Karorero Léonidas. (Abahwehwe, Abatsoobe) Giti; G-6, 15/1/71.
Karubanda. (——, Abasinga) Mubumbano; C-10, 13/7/70, 17/7/70, 19/7/70.
Kaaryo. (Abaserezi, Abeega) Muboori; K-4, 4/2/71.
Kayirara Canisius. (Abacundura, Abiitira) Tyazo; C-25, 17/2/71.
Kayumba Callixte. (Abazina, Abanyiginya) Gafuba; M-33, 6/10/71.
Kibibi. (Abahinda, Abagesera) Munyinya; M-13, 10/12/70.
Kibuye Joseph. (Abatega, Abasindi) Rurama; K-4, 4/2/71.
Kigunda. (Abatiihinda, Abatsoobe) Rango; FR-14, 21/5/71.
Kivumu. (Abeeru, Abacyaba) Muhwehwe; G-7, 19/1/71.
Koogi. (Abashambo, Abanyiginya) Mukoma; M-15, 26/9/70.

Maasomaaso. (Abasiine, Abacyaba) Bitare; C-20, 13/2/71.
Mabamba. (Abahima, Abashambo) Nyakarenzo; R-19, 25/11/70.
Mabumbuli. (Abayombo, Abasindi) Mwezi; K-1, 3/2/71.
Majoro. (Abavumbi, Abasindi) Nkanka; M-14, 19/8/70.
Makoma. (Abanenge, Abashambo) Nyakarenzo; R-20, FR-15, 26/11/70, 15/5/71.
Makwaruza Paulin. (Abashongore, Abiitira) Gashaaru-Shangi; FM-12, 18/6/71.
Marekabiri Simon. (Abafanga, Abongera) Gafuba; FM-13, 17/6/71.
Masenge Elias. (Abiirorerwa, Abatsoobe) Nyamubembe; K-5, 2/2/71.
Matabaaro. (Abareego, Abasinga) Bitare; C-11, 13/2/71.
Mbonyiyeeze Théonis. (Abafanga, Abongera) Gafuba; FM-13, 17/6/71.
Mboonyuburyo Ildefonse. (Abashongore, Abiitira) Mukoma; M-15, FM-14, 26/9/70, 17/6/71.
Mirambi. (Abageshi, Abiitira) Cyete; R-21, FR-16, 1/12/70, 15/5/71.

Misigaro. (Abagogo or Ababunda, Abasinga) Nyamirundi; M-16, 30/9/ 70.

Mpakanyi. (Abacamunkoni, Abasinga) Cyato; M-17, FM-15, 10/12/70, 7/1/71, 12/5/71.

Mudaage Vunabandi. (Abahinda, Abagesera) Munyinya; M-18, 10/12/ 70, 11/1/71.

Mudibiri Laurent. (Abateganya, Abakoobwa) Gashonga; FR-17, 29/5/71.

Mudomo Pierre. (Abakara, Aboozi, Abiitira) Nyamirundi; M-28, 1/10/ 70.

Mugorozi Ntaamakeero. (Abagarukira, Abashambo) Shangi; M-19, 24/ 9/70.

Muhindangiga. (Abahinda, Abasinga) Winteeko; R-22, 7/12/70.

Mukara Mathias. (Aboori, Abasindi) Muboori; K-8, 4/2/71.

Mukarugina Pascasie. (Abagina?, Abanyiginya) Muyira, C-12, 7/6/70.

Muke Gérard. (Abeenegitori, Abanyiginya) Gabiro; M-20, 1/10/70, 5/ 10/71.

Mukeeshimaana Augustin. (Abaseego, Abasindi) Rwimbogo; S-2, 21/1/ 71.

Mukeeza Sylvestre. (Abasiizi, Abeega) Rukunguri; FM-18, 1/6/71.

Mukuzo. (Abasangabo, Abazigaaba) Nyaruteeja; S-3, 6/12/71.

Munda Pierre. (Abageza, Abasinga) Nyamirundi; M-21, FM-16, 30/9/70, 16/6/71.

Muneene. (——, Abashambo) Mururu; R-23, 30/11/70.

Munigankiiko Christophe. (Abakwira, Abiitira) Bugarama; FG-1, 25/5/ 71.

Murekumbanze. (——, Abagesera) Bumazi; M-22, 5/7/71.

Mushinzimaana. (Abasoni, Abiitira) Isha; FM-17, 8/5/71.

Mutabazi Mathias. (Abasiizi, Abeega) Rukunguri; FM-18, 1/6/71.

Mutarambirwa Cyprien. (Abasigwa, Abanyiginya) Gafuba; FM-19, 3/6/ 71.

Mutwarangabo. (Abaavu, Abacyaba) Bunyangurube; M-23, 28/9/70.

Muyobozi Hungulimaana. (Abasiigi, Abacyaba) Nyarwungo; C-4, 18/2/ 71.

Mwemerankiiko Charles. (Abahanuka, Abagesera) Bunyereli; S-4, 22/ 1/71.

Ndarabutse Anastase. (Abahuuga, Abaganda) Butambara; C-13, 12/2/71.

Ndarabutse Bernard. (——, Abazigaba) Muhanga; K-6, 1/7/70.

Ndaruhuutse Didace. (Abanyabyinshi, Abanyiginya) Gafuba; M-24, 1/ 10/70, 29/10/70, 31/10/70.

Ndaseezeye Athanase. (Abajyujyu, Abashambo) Ruhoko; FR-18, 21/5/71.

Ndaziimanye. (Abatandura, Abashambo) Nyakarenzo; R-24, 25/11/70, 22/12/70.

Ndegeya. (Abayobe, Abasinga) Nyabintare; G-8, 13/1/71.

Ndimubanzi. (Abagonde, Abanyiginya) Ruherambuga; K-7, 5/2/71.

Ngendahiimaana Casimir. (Abashenyi, Abiitira) Shagasha; R-25, 10/7/71.

Ngirumpatse Donat. (Abadondi, Abashambo-Abanyiginya) Nyamirundi; M-28, 1/10/70.

Ngiruwonsanga Jean. (Abashooza, Abacyaba) Mukoma; M-26, 30/9/70.

Ngurube. (——, Abasinga) Nyarwungo; C-14, 18/2/71.

Ngwijabarezi Michel. (Abatega, Abasindi) Nyantomvu; S-5, 21/1/71.

Nkiikanyi Elias. (Aboozi, Abiitira) Mubumbano; C-15, 12/2/71.

Nkomati. (——, Abagesera) Bumazi; M-22, 5/7/71.

Nkundiye Papias. (Abanyamagana, Abazigaaba) Bunyangurube; M-25, FM-20, 28/9/70, 29/10/70, 11/6/71.

Ntaabwoba. (Abajwanga, Abasinga) Gitongo; C-16, 17/2/71.

Ntakiyimaana (Abahiri, Abasinga) Bitare; C-11, 13/2/71.

Ntashuti. (Abahinga, Abadasumbwa-Abagesera) Nyaruteeja; S-6, 6/12/71.

Ntemabiti Michel. (Abazirankende, Abagesera) Gikundamvura; S-7, 14/1/71.

Ntibashimwa. (Abashengere, Abasinga) Muboori (Mwezi); K-8, 4/2/71.

Ntongo Antoine. (Abahande, Abanyiginya) Gihinga; M-27, 5/2/71.

Ntuuro. (Abasunga, Abiitira) Nyamirundi; M-28, M-29, 1/10/70, 23/10/70.

Ntuuro Mashirakinyoma. (Abakeeshi, Abagesera) Mwiyando; K-8, 4/2/71.

Ntuuro Raphael. (Abaroha, Abazigaaba) Ngoma; S-8, 27/12/70.

Nyagasega. (Abagoboka, Abashambo) Nyamagana; R-26, 26/11/70.

Nyamabwa Pierre. (Abatare, Abanyikarama) Biguzi; M-6, 2/7/71.

Nyamajanja Jacques. (Abadiri, Abasinga) Cyiya; C-17, 20/2/71.

Nyaminaani. (Ababondo-Aboozi, Abiitira) Nkungu; K-9, 1/2/71.

Nyamutezi. (——, Abakoobwa) Cyamuti; FM-30, n.d.

Nyarugabo Landouald. (Abadegede, Abeega) Gafuba; M-30, 10/9/70, 11/9/70.

Nyirakabiliizi Yulita. (Abeenegahuliro, Abashambo) Giti; G-9, 15/1/71.

Nyiramandwa Anna. (Abagahi, Abasinga) Nyamasheke; C-18, 11/7/70.

Nyirandenzi. (Abatsuri, Abiitira) Buhokoro; FM-21, 11/6/71.

Nyiranjajure Cécile. (Abanangu, Abashambo) Gasura; M-31, 7/1/71.

Nyiringango Paul. (Abanagwa, Abanyiginya) Murangi; R-27, 11/12/70, 8/1/71.

Nzeeyimaana. (Abateeko, Abazigaaba) Ruyonga; R-28, FR-19, 27/11/70, 11/5/71.

Nzogiroshya Faustin. (Abahuuga, Abanda) Bushenge; FM-22, 19/6/71.

Polisi Paul. (Abajyujyu, Abashambo) Butambamo; FR-20, 19/5/71.

Rekeraho Noel. (———, Abashambo) Runyanzovu; K-10, 1/8/70, 3/8/70.
Rivuze Octave. (Abatango, Abashambo) Gashonga; FR-21, 18/5/71.
Rubangiza. (Abarwenga, Abasambo) Ruhoko; FR-22, 19/5/71.
Rubanza Raphael. (Abasinzi, Abasinga) Gitongo; C-21, 17/2/71.
Rubayiza Gabriel. (Abakara, Abasinga) Gitambi; K-13, 25/1/71.
Rubwebwe Sylvestre. (Abashumbuusho, Abeega) Muhwehwe; G-10, 19/1/71.
Rufali. (Abeenegitore, Abanyiginya) Ruyonga; R-29, 27/11/70, 23/12/70.
Rugambarara Paul. (Abayombo, Abasindi-Abashambo) Nyakabuye; K-11, 1/2/71, 2/2/71.
Rugata Paul. (Abagamba, Abazigaaba?, Abagesera) Muganza; S-9, 14/1/71.
Rugati Bandora. (———, Abashambo) Cyimpundu; K-12, 29/1/71.
Rugemanandi Sixbert. (Abagina, Abashambo) Nyamubembe; K-3, 1/2/71.
Rugendashyamba Nicodème. (Abatambuuka, Abashambo) Nyamubembe; K-9, 1/2/71.
Rugerero Charles. (Abahanya-Abaswere, Abeega) Shangi; M-34, 18/7/70, 25/9/70, 23/10/70, 30/10/70.
Rugigana Joseph. (Ibigina, Abashambo) Cyato; M-35, 2/8/70.
Rugimbanyi Pierre. (Abageshi, Abiitira) Cyete; FR-23, 17/5/71.
Ruhanika Bihore Paulin. (Abanyaruke, Abasindi) Rwimbogo; S-10, 22/1/71.
Ruhengehenge. (Abahwehwe, Abatsoobe) Muhwehwe; G-11, 19/1/71.
Ruheeshyi Pierre. (———, Abasinga) Nyarwungo; C-14, 18/2/71.
Ruhuguura Bernard. (Abatanganshuro, Abasiita, Abunguura?) Ishara; C-1, 11/2/71.
Rukaburacumu Corneille. (Abahande, Abanyiginya) Mubumbano; C-19, 10/2/71.
Rukebeesha (Abaturagura, Abacyaba) Bitare; C-20, 13/2/71.
Rukebeesha Raphael. (Abanyakarendezi, Abasinga) Mwegera; S-11, 22/1/71.

Rukemampunzi Alexis. (Abarari, Abahima-Abashambo) Rango; FR-24, 18/5/71.
Rukeeratabaro Théoneste. (Ababambo, Abiitira) Bumazi; FM-23, 10/7/71.
Rukezambuga Bernard. (Abagabiro, Abasinga) Gafuba; FM-24, 12/6/71.
Rukubashyamba. (Abakaragata, Abacyaba) Nyakarenzo; R-30, FR-25, 25/11/70, 13/5/71.
Rupfuura Pascal. (Abaziga, Abacyaba) Kaboza; K-13, 25/1/71.
Rurangwa Théonise. (Abaganda, Abagesera) Mugera; FM-25, 11/6/71.
Rusangwa. (——, Abashambo) Muganza; G-12, 13/1/71.
Rutete Amos. (Abiishaza, Abasinga) Bunyangurube; M-36, 28/9/70.
Rutungwa Trojan. (Abaganzu, Abanyiginya) Gitongo; C-21, 17/2/71.
Ruvugama. (——, Abasinga) Nkanka; M-37, 24/8/70.
Ruvuvu Simon. (Abimuye, Abashambo-Abanyiginya) Nkanka; M-38, 14/8/70, 18/8/70.
Ruvuzacyuma Médard. (Abajyujyu, Abashambo) Butambamo; FR-26, 29/5/71.
Rwagasore Vénuste. (Abaaka, Abanyiginya) Nkanka; M-39, 13/8/70, 22/8/70.
Rwajekare Dominique. (Abaziga, Abacyaba) Kaboza; K-13, K-14, 25/1/71.
Rwambikwa. (Abazirankende, Abagesera) Ibanda-Yove; C-22, 18/2/71.
Rwamiheto Gabriel. (Abaramira, Abanyiginya) Mutuusa; C-7, 12/2/71.
Rwamukikanyi Dominique. (Abarenda, Abatsoobe) Mwezi; K-15, 3/2/71.
Rwemera. (Abajenje, Abasinga) Nyamirundi; M-40, 1/10/70.
Rwigimba. (Abaranga, Abashambo, Abanyiginya) Mugera; M-1, 9/7/71.
Rwivanga. (Abanyambiriri, Abasinga) Nyarwungo-Rangiro; C-22, 18/2/71.

Sabuhoro. (Abahwika, Abashi) Shangi; M-41, 18/7/70, 25/9/70.
Sagatwa Louis. (Abakungu, Abashambo) Gihundwe; R-31, 11/12/70.
Saake Ruyenzi. (Abarangu, Abasinga) Nyarwungo; C-4, 18/2/71.
Sarukondo Philippe. (Abageza, Abasinga) Bugeza-Nyamirundi; FM-29, 14/10/72.
Seebagore Michel. (Abajonge, Abasinga) Rugano; C-23, 19/2/71.
Seebaja Jean. (Ababago, Abasinga) Buhoro; C-24, 19/2/71.
Sebasare Narcisse. (Abeerekande, Abasinga) Nyamugari; FM-26, 30/6/71.
Sebiyorero. (Abaharabugi, Abongera) Bunyangurube; FM-27, 16/6/71.

Seehuuri Simon. (Abacuku, Abagesera, Abazirankende) Ryazo; C-16, 17/2/71.

Sekabuhoro. (——, Abazigaaba) Nyamagana; R-32, 26/11/70, 22/12/70.

Seekarahennye Gervais. (Abahande, Abanyiginya) Gafuba; M-42, 1/10/70, 23/10/70.

Seekimondo. (Abakoobwa, Abashambo?) Nyakanyinya; R-33, 4/12/70, 8/1/71.

Seemarora Charles. (Abahengu?, Abanyiginya) Cyiya; S-12, 20/2/71.

Seemigabo Selesi. (Abakumbi, Abasinga) Tyazo; C-25, 17/2/71.

Seemirama. (Abakwiye?, Abazigaaba) Cyete; R-34, FR-27, 1/12/70, 14/5/71.

Sempiga Claver. (Ababuga, Abasinga) Butambara; C-13, 12/2/71.

Seemusaho. (Abakagenyi, Abanyiginya) Isha; FM-28, 8/5/71.

Seemuyeego. (Abasheri, Abatsoobe) Nyamagana; R-35, 26/11/70.

Seenuma. (Abaziguura, Abagesera) Biguzi; M-6, 2/7/71.

Seenyanzobe. (——, ——) Shangi; M-43, 24/9/70.

Seeruhojojo Dominique. (Abanyandwi, Aboozi-Abiitira) Cyiya; C-17, 20/2/71.

Seerusaaza. (Abayobe, Aboozi-Abiitira) Gabiro; M-20, 1/10/70.

Shabani Idi. (Abarenge, Abasinga) Bugarama; G-13, 14/1/71.

Suubwango Joseph. (Abatagara, Abeega) Giti; G-14, 18/1/71.

Tegeko Jean. (Abakabara, Abashambo) Shagasha; M-32, 2/7/71.

Yoboka Ananias. (Abazirimo, Abanyabutumbi, Abashambo, Abanyiginya); Muramba, C-26, 7/7/71, 14/7/71.

Zikamabahari. (Abahuuha, Abongera) Ruyonga; R-36, FR-28, 27/11/70, 11/5/71.

NOTES

CHAPTER I

1. Jacques J. Maquet and Marcel d'Hertefelt, *Elections en société féodale: une étude sur l'introduction du vote populaire au Ruanda-Urundi* (Brussels, 1959), 86.

2. Maquet mentions other factors as well but tends to emphasize these three. Jacques J. Maquet, *Le Système des relations sociales dans le Ruanda ancien* (Tervuren, 1954), 171–183. This study was published in English in slightly modified form as *The Premise of Inequality in Ruanda* (London, 1961). See also his "Rwanda Castes" in Arthur Tuden, and Leonard Plotnicov, eds., *Social Stratification in Africa* (New York, 1970), 93–124.

3. Maquet classified Rwanda as a caste system on the basis of four overlapping criteria; the presence of different groups characterized by endogamy; hereditary membership in these groups; hereditary occupational specialization within the groups; and arrangement of the groups in a hierarchical social structure. Maquet, *Relations sociales*, 157–158. Maquet later stressed the rigid and "closed" character of the strata as his main justification for describing them as castes. See his "Rwanda Castes," 110–111.

4. "The Rwandan principle of inequality could be expressed in the following terms: people born in different castes are unequal in inborn endowment, physical as well as psychological and have consequently fundamentally different rights." Maquet, *Premise of Inequality*, 165.

5. For some examples, see Jacques J. Maquet, "La participation de la classe paysanne au mouvement d'indépendance du Rwanda," *Cahiers d'Etudes Africaines* 4.4 (1964): 552–568; René Lemarchand, *Rwanda and Burundi* (London, 1970); Leo Kuper, *The Pity of It All* (Minneapolis, 1977).

6. The major exception in this regard was the north of Rwanda. But these were areas recently conquered by Tuutsi and therefore incompletely integrated into Tuutsi ideological hegemony; for Maquet, such areas were precisely the exception that "proved the rule" since to him no struggle was apparent in other regions.

7. Jan Vansina's history of state development in Rwanda was the first to challenge this view in a sustained comprehensive manner. See Jan Vansina, *L'évolution du royaume rwanda des origines à 1900* (Brussels, 1962). Later, Marcel d'Hertefelt stressed the importance of regional cultural variations in his "Le Rwanda," Marcel d'Hertefelt et al., eds., *Les anciens royaumes de la zone interlacustre méridionale,*

Rwanda, Burundi, Buha (Tervuren, 1962), 9–112. A particularly important reassessment is found in Claudine Vidal, "Le Rwanda des anthropologues ou le fétichisme de la vache," *Cahiers d'Etudes Africaines* 9.3 (1969): 384–401. For a critical review of studies on Rwandan state development see M. Catharine Newbury, and Joseph Rwabukumba, "Political Evolution in a Rwandan Frontier District: A Case Study of Kinyaga," *Rapport de l'INRS* (Butare, 1971), 93–119. In his study of the Rwandan Revolution René Lemarchand recognized regional variations in Tuutsi control as an important factor in Hutu protest of the 1950s. However, he did still accept Maquet's synchronic portrayal of the premise of inequality and *ubuhake* clientship for the central regions of the country. Lemarchand, *Rwanda and Burundi*. In a more recent analysis Lemarchand acknowledges the perspective presented here. See his "The State and Society in Africa: Ethnic Stratification and Restratification in Historical and Comparative Perspective," Donald Rothchild and Victor A. Olorunsola, eds., *State Versus Ethnic Claims: African Policy Dilemmas* (Boulder, 1983), 44–66.

8. For a perceptive critique of Maquet's functionalist approach, see Gerald Studdert-Kennedy, *Evidence and Explanation in Social Science: An Interdisciplinary Approach* (London, 1975), 3–20.

9. "As might have been expected, the more competent persons on political organization were Tuutsi and in fact more than 90 percent of our informants were Tuutsi. Since the number of Hutu and Twa was too small to be of any significance their interviews were not taken into account in the computation of the results." Maquet, *Premise of Inequality*, 3.

10. Maquet has denied the charge of overrepresentation of the central regions in his sample of informants. Maquet, "Rwanda Castes," 122. But there could have been and appears to have been overrepresentation in terms of the ideas and normative values of the center.

11. See Vansina, *L'évolution du royaume Rwanda,* and d'Hertefelt, "Le Rwanda." Two primary sources are particularly important for material on regional differences. See *Historique et chronologie du Ruanda* (Kabgayi, 1956) and I. Reisdorff, "Enquêtes foncières au Ruanda," (mimeo, 1952). Note also that most of northern Rwanda (what is today included in Gisenyi and Ruhengeri Prefectures, as well as a large part of Byumba Prefecture) and the southern part of Kinyaga remained outside the administrative control of the Rwandan kingdom. Jacques J. Maquet and Marcel d'Hertefelt, *Elections en société féodale; une étude sur l'introduction du vote populaire au Ruanda-Urundi* (Brussels, 1959), 8–9.

12. Ikinyarwanda, a Bantu language, is spoken as a first language by Rwandans in all areas of the country. Rwanda is one of the few present-day states in Africa with such a single, truly national language. The small size of the country (it is about the size of the state of Vermont) is, of course, important. There are lexical variations and differences in accent among different regions (for example, the Ikinyarwanda spoken in Kinyaga shows the influence of longstanding historical contacts with peoples to the west in Zaïre), but all three of Rwanda's ethnic groups—Tuutsi, Hutu, and Twa—speak Ikinyarwanda. The language at the royal court and among upper-class Tuutsi exhibited certain distinct characteristics, and the type of Ikinyarwanda spoken by Twa in certain areas shows some marked differences from the Ikinyarwanda used among other groups. (André Coupez, personal communication). The language of instruction in secondary schools and at the university level is French; government documents are often printed in both Ikinyarwanda and French.

13. For a more complete consideration, see my "Ethnicity in Rwanda: The Case of Kinyaga," *Africa* 48.1 (1978): 17–29.

14. For a consideration of this difference in identity on Ijwi, see David Newbury, "Rwabugiri and Ijwi," *Etudes d'Histoire Africaine* 7 (1975): 151–175; and also his "The Clans of Rwanda: An Historical Hypothesis," *Africa* 50.4 (1980): 389–403.

15. This point is made by Vidal, "Le Rwanda des anthropologues," 400.

16. Marcel d'Hertefelt proposed this interpretation, revising his earlier views on the caste character of Rwandan society; see Marcel d'Hertefelt, *Les Clans du Rwanda ancien: éléments d'ethnosociologie et d'ethnohistoire* (Tervuren, 1971), 75, n. 1. d'Hertefelt retained two of Maquet's criteria (endogamy and hierarchy) but substituted for "caste" a description of Rwandan social groups as "classes endogamiques et hiérarchisées."

17. Léon Classe, "Le Ruanda et ses habitants," *Congo* 1.5 (May 1922): 681, fn. 2.

18. Louis de Lacger, *Le Ruanda* (Kabgayi, 1961), 60.

19. An influential statement of this position was that of Clifford Geertz, "The Integrative Revolution: Primordial Sentiments and Civil Politics in the New States," Clifford Geertz, ed., *Old Societies and New States* (New York, 1968), 105–157. Although Geertz recognized that ethnic identities were being broadened and transformed as a result of political and social changes, it is his stress on the "primordial" character of such ethnic ties that has been most cited.

20. See Karl Deutsch, "The Growth of Nations: Some Recurrent Patterns of Political and Social Integration," *World Politics* 5.2 (1952): 158–195; and Deutsch, *Nationalism and Social Communication* (Cambridge, MA, 1953) for an example of this type of thinking. The disruptive effects of modernization were stressed by Samuel Huntington, *Political Order in Changing Societies* (New Haven, 1968), esp. Ch. 2. Huntington, assuming that "traditional" societies had low levels of participation, defined "political modernization" as increased political participation (resulting from economic and social changes). "Political development" in his analysis was reflected in the growth of capacity on the part of the state to preserve order in the face of demands for participation stimulated by political modernization.

21. Anthropologists were the first to articulate this dynamic view of ethnic solidarities. For a few examples among many, see J. Clyde Mitchell, *The Kalela Dance* (Manchester, 1958); Edmund R. Leach, *Political Systems of Highland Burma* (Boston, 1965); Aidan Southall, "The Illusion of Tribe," *Journal of Asian and African Studies* 5.1/2 (1970): 28–50; Elizabeth Colson, "Contemporary Tribes and the Development of Nationalism," June Helm, ed., *Essays on the Problem of Tribe* (Seattle, 1968), 201–206.

22. Paul R. Brass, "Class, Ethnic Group and Party in Indian Politics," *World Politics* 33.3 (1981): 451, n. 2.

23. Examples of studies that use an instrumentalist perspective include Robert Melson and Howard Wolpe, *Nigeria: Modernization and the Politics of Communalism* (East Lansing, 1971); Nelson Kasfir, *The Shrinking Political Arena: Participation and Ethnicity in African Politics, with a Case Study of Uganda* (Berkeley, 1976); Crawford Young, *The Politics of Cultural Pluralism* (Madison, 1976); Marguerite R. Barnett, *The Politics of Cultural Nationalism in South India* (Princeton, 1976); Myron Weiner, *Sons of the Soil: Migration and Ethnic Conflict in India* (Princeton, 1978). For examples of the functionalist approach to ethnicity, see Paul R. Brass, "Ethnicity and Nationality Formation," *Ethnicity* 3 (1976): 225–241; Brass, "Class, Ethnic Group and Party"; Crawford Young, "Patterns of Social Conflict:

State, Class, and Ethnicity," *Daedalus* 3.2 (Spring 1982): 71–98; and Young, "The Temple of Ethnicity," *World Politics* 35.4 (1983): 652–662. For a recent survey of issues relating to ethnicity in Africa, see Crawford Young, "Nationalism, Ethnicity, and Class in Africa: A Retrospective," *Cahiers d'Etudes Africaines*, 26.3 (1986), 421–495.

24. The term is used by John Lonsdale. See his perceptive theoretical analysis in "States and Social Processes in Africa: A Historiographical Survey," *The African Studies Review* 24.2/3 (June/September 1981): 139–207.

25. My view on this aspect of state power is convergent with that of Richard Joseph in his study of ethnicity in Nigeria. I have found Joseph's work useful in helping to situate my study in the context of the field at large. See Richard A. Joseph, "Ethnicity and Prebendal Politics in Nigeria: A Theoretical Outline," (paper presented at the Annual Meeting of the American Political Science Association, Denver, Colorado, September 1982); and Joseph, "Class, State, and Prebendal Politics in Nigeria," *Journal of Commonwealth and Comparative Politics* 21.3 (1983): 21–38.

26. Gavin Williams, and Teresa Turner, "Nigeria," John Dunn, ed., *West African States: Failure and Promise* (Cambridge, 1978), 133, cited in Joseph, "Ethnicity and Prebendal Politics," 2.

27. As Cynthia Enloe writes, transformations in ethnic identities often result from "calculated decisions made by government officials. . . . Political power does not just react to ethnicity: power can shape ethnicity." Cynthia Enloe, *Police, Military and Ethnicity* (New Brunswick, NJ, 1980), 14.

28. For examples of studies in which clientship is seen to inhibit horizontal solidarity-formation, see Carl Landé, "Group Politics and Dyadic Politics: Notes for a Theory," in Landé, *Leaders, Factions and Parties: The Structure of Philippine Politics* (New Haven, 1965), 141–148; and Luigi Graziano, "A Conceptual Framework for the Study of Clientelistic Behavior," *European Journal of Political Research* 4.2 (1976): 149–174. Such a view of clientship, not always explicit, is often linked to a conceptualization of patron-client ties as a source of equilibrium (or "immobilism") for a political system. For a critique, see Robert R. Kaufman, "The Patron-Client Concept and Macropolitics: Prospects and Problems," *Comparative Studies in Society and History* 16.3 (1974): 284–308.

29. This definition is adapted from the one in James C. Scott, "Patron-Client Politics and Political Change in Southeast Asia," *American Political Science Review* 66.1 (March 1972): 91–113.

30. In their analyses of colonial Kenya, Lonsdale and Berman have suggested that the colonial state's interventionist role in labor-control policies was shaped significantly by contradictory pressures to assure both accumulation and legitimation. See J. M. Lonsdale and B. J. Berman, "Coping with the Contradictions: The Development of the Colonial State in Kenya 1895–1914," *Journal of African History* 20.4 (1979): 487–505; and B. J. Berman and J. M. Lonsdale, "Crises of Accumulation, Coercion and the Colonial State: The Development of the Labor Control System in Kenya, 1919–1929," *Canadian Journal of African Studies* 14.1 (1980): 37–54.

CHAPTER 2

1. Although these areas were not at that time politically subordinate to the Rwandan court, their peoples shared elements of Rwandan cultural norms. On the role and significance of these norms in the western regions of what is today Rwanda

(including Kinyaga) see David Newbury, "'Bunyabungo': The Western Rwandan Frontier, c. 1750–1850," Igor Kopytoff, ed., *The African Frontier: The Reproduction of Traditional African Societies* (Bloomington, 1987), 162–192.

2. "Histoire des provinces de l'Impara et du Biru (Kinyaga) sous le règne de Kigeri III Ndabarasa," according to the notes of Father Léon Delmas, 1929 (J. M. Derscheid Collection of documents on Rwanda and Burundi). Father Delmas collected a wealth of historical and ethnographic material during his long period of missionary work in Rwanda. He spent several years in Kinyaga, where he founded the Mission of Nyamasheke in 1928.

3. The Abasinga are a very old clan in Rwanda concentrated particularly in the western regions. It is significant that the other two territories with a large percentage of Abasinga are Kibuye (19.55%) and Nyanza (18.26%). (d'Hertefelt, *Clans*, Annexes, Tableau 2.) These two territories bordered on or included parts of Bunyambiriri.

4. For an analysis of the process by which political transformations may foster changes in clan identities see David Newbury, "Kings and Clans on Ijwi Island (Zaïre), c. 1780–1840," (Diss., University of Wisconsin–Madison, 1979); and "Clans of Rwanda."

5. For example, one account asserts that the Abahande were the first inhabitants of Kinyaga. They were said to have come from Bupfureero (south of Bushi) to settle in Kinyaga, but originally their ancestor, Rukiramiro, had come from Gisaka. (Muke, 5/10/71, 1.) [Citations of interviews include the name of the informant, the date of the interview, and the page number of the typed translation of the interview. Thus the present citation refers to p. 1 of an interview with Muke, on 5 October 1971. More complete identification of informants is provided in Appendix VI.]

6. Rwandan control was first introduced to Ndorwa in the eighteenth century during the time of *Umwami* Kigeri Ndabarasa. Gisaka, however, was not placed definitively under Rwandan rule until the reign of Mutara Rwogera in the mid-nineteenth century. The campaigns of Rwandan armies against Ndorwa and Gisaka during the reigns of Cyirima Rujugira and Kigeri Ndabarasa are described in Alexis Kagame, *Un abrégé de l'ethnohistoire du Rwanda précolonial*, vol. 1 (Butare, 1972), 117, 144–153, 156–157. Further references to the wars are found in Alexis Kagame, *Les milices du Rwanda précolonial* (Brussels, 1963), 58, 104–105, 108, 113–114, 118. See also Vansina, *L'évolution du royaume Rwanda*, 98. On the history of Ndorwa, see Jim Freedman, *Nyabingi: The Social History of an African Divinity* (Tervuren, 1984); and Iris Berger, *Religion and Resistance: East African Kingdoms in the Precolonial Period* (Tervuren, 1981).

We lack evidence on whether immigrants coming from regions to the north and northeast of central Rwanda spoke Ikinyarwanda; but traditions in Kinyaga do view people coming from the general direction of Rwanda (north and east of Kinyaga) as "Rwandan" and distinguish them from people of Shi and Havu culture.

7. Bakomeza 27/7/70, 1.

8. Bagaruka and Burumbuuke 11/2/71, 2.

9. Rwambikwa and Rwivanga 18/2/71, 1.

10. Rurangwa 11/6/71.

11. Rugata 14/1/71, 1, 6.

12. Birikunkomo 12/5/71.

13. Kagame, *Milices*, 63, 129–130. Alexis Kagame was a Rwandan Catholic priest and one of the country's earliest "Westernized" intellectuals. For more than four decades, until his death in 1982, he enjoyed the position of foremost historian of the

Rwandan state. A prolific writer, he published a large body of work that is invaluable for reconstructing precolonial political developments. It is important to use a critical perspective toward Kagame's work, however; his perspectives on Rwandan history reflect the ideological views of the central court, making him an apologist for Tuutsi culture and power. For a consideration of Kagame as mediator between an oral genre and a written genre of knowledge, and an assessment of his work from this perspective, see Jean-Pierre Chrétien, "Confronting the Unequal Exchange of the Oral and the Written," in Bogumil Jewsiewicki and David Newbury, eds., *African Historiographies: What History for Which Africa?* (Beverly Hills, 1986), 75–90.

14. Nyarugabo 10/8/70, 1, 3. A similar version is also found in two written accounts: Delmas, "Impara et Biru sous Ndabarasa," in the Derscheid Collection; and *Historique et chronologie du Ruanda* (Kabgayi, 1956), 96. These three sources are probably not independent. The earlier written account was recorded by a Catholic missionary (Father Delmas). The later written account of Rwanteri's arrival in Kinyaga was compiled by Belgian administrators who had access to the missionary writings. The oral account comes from a former subchief who was educated at the Belgian school for sons of chiefs and was one of the most prominent members of his lineage during the Belgian colonial period. His grandfather Seekabaraga spoke to Delmas about the history of Kinyaga, as noted in "Notes Préliminaires" of the Diary of Nyamasheke Catholic Mission, (hereafter referred to as "Diaire Nyamasheke"); Seekabaraga could well have been the source for the written accounts. Moreover, Nyarugabo would have had access to the account published by the Belgian administration.

15. Rurangwa 11/6/71; Muke 5/10/71, 1. Rurangwa's account is corroborated by the fact that the people of Ijwi retain no oral record of Bijeli or his family, despite extensive questioning on this point. References to "Ijwi origins" are often used in Rwandan and Rundi traditions to connote unknown (and slightly dangerous) western origins. (Personal communication, David Newbury.)

16. The exact identity is not clear. Nyarwaya-Karureetwa, a son of *Umwami* Yuhi Mazimpaka, lived during the eighteenth century; his son Vuningoma was a renowned warrior during the succession struggle following the death of Kigeri Ndabarasa. Another Nyarwaya (Nyarwaya-Nyamutezi), son of Mbayingabo and great-grandson of *Umwami* Yuhi Mazimpaka, is said to have died toward the end of the reign of *Umwami* Mutara Rwogera (c. 1865). (Kagame, *Milices*, 43, 45, 108.)

A comparison of the genealogies of descendants of the two Nyarwaya with that of Rwanteri's descendants (see Appendix IV) makes it appear unlikely that Nyarwaya-Nyamutezi and Rwanteri were contemporaries. But Nyarwaya-Karureetwa and Rwanteri could have been. Since Nyarwaya would have lived during the time of Cyirima Rujugira and Kigeri Ndabarasa (son and grandson of Mazimpaka), this would place Rwanteri's arrival in Kinyaga in the eighteenth century.

17. A person whose ancestor came to Kinyaga as a follower of Rwanteri's wife explained that the wife was Rugondana, daughter of *Umwami* Cyirima Rugwe (sic). (Bagara and Rwigimba 9/7/71, 1.) If the reference is to Cyirima Rujugira, the account is plausible. Another Kinyagan suggested that Rwanteri was married to Nyiramandwa, the daughter of a Rwandan king, but could not specify which king. (Muke 5/10/71, 1.)

18. Bagaruka and Burumbuuke 11/2/71, 17.

19. Bagaruka and Burumbuuke 11/2/71, 13–14, 17; Bagaruka 13/7/71, 2–3.

20. Bucuti 28/10/70, 12; Ndaruhuutse 29/10/70, 12; Yoboka 14/7/71, 3.

21. Kaamuhanda 27/10/70, 3, 6.
22. Seemusaho, Barera, Mushinzimaana 8/5/71.
23. Nyamutezi, n.d.
24. Bagara and Rwigimba 9/7/71, 1.
25. Bahufite 12/7/70, 1–2.
26. Sebasare 30/6/71.
27. Karubanda 13/7/70, 1.
28. Ngendahiimaana 10/7/71, 1–3.
29. Makoma 15/5/71.
30. Midibiri 29/5/71.
31. Gasimba 26/7/70, 1.
32. Ruvuvu 14/8/70, 3.

33. As noted above, the Abasinga may have been among the earliest occupants of Kinyaga, and their numbers were probably swelled by others coming from Bunyambiriri where food shortages had been frequent; more recently, Bunyambiriri was one of the regions hardest hit during the Ruzagayura famine of 1943. Bunyambiriri, an area of very high population density, appears to have been a point of dispersion for people going farther west.

34. Matabaaro, Kanywabahizi, Ntakiyimaana 13/2/71, 2.
35. Karamira 17/6/71.
36. Biseruka 9/7/71, 2.
37. Mutarambirwa 3/6/71.
38. Ruvuzacyuma 29/5/71. Mugenzi was killed on orders from the royal court. *Historique et chronologie,* 102.

39. Diary of the Mibirizi Catholic Mission, 16 August 1908 (hereafter referred to as "Diaire Mibirizi").

40. Kaaryo and Kibuye 4/2/71, 1; Gahogo 22/5/71, 1; R. Bourgeois, "Notes sur l'administration du Territoire de Shangugu," (1934), ch. 1, in the Derscheid Collection (hereafter referred to as "Notes Shangugu"); Paul Masson, *Trois siècles chez les Bashi* (Bukavu, 1966), 28–32. Also, interviews with Ndimubanzi and Gashyamangali 5/2/71, 1; Ntuuro Mashirakinyoma, Mukara, Ntibashiimwa 4/2/71, 1. There is no comprehensive history of the Shi kingdoms, but of a vast literature some of the more important works include P. Colle, *Monographie des Bashi* (Bukavu, 1971); J. B. Cuypers, *L'alimentation chez les Shi* (Tervuren, 1970); Richard D. Sigwalt, "The Early History of Bushi. An Essay in the Historical Use of Genesis Traditions" (Diss., University of Wisconsin-Madison, 1975); Elinor D. Sosne, "Kinship and Contract in Bushi: A Study in Village Level Politics" (Diss., University of Wisconsin-Madison, 1974); Bishikwabo Chubaka, "Histoire d'un état Shi en Afrique des Grands Lacs: Kaziba au Zaire (ca. 1850–1940)" (Diss., Louvain-la-Neuve, 1982); Bishikwabo, "Le Bushi au XIXe siècle: Un peuple, sept royaumes," *Revue Française d'Histoire d'Outre-Mer* 67.246/247 (1980): 88–98; Bishikwabo, "Essai sur l'exercice du pouvoir politique au Bushi (1890–1940)," (Mémoire de Licence, UNAZA, Lubumbashi, 1973); Njangu Canda-Ciri, "La résistance Shi à la pénétration européenne, 1900–1916" (Mémoire de Licence, UNAZA, Lubumbashi, 1973); C. Bashizi, "Processus de domination socio-economique et marché du travail au Bushi (1920–1940), *Enquêtes et Documents d'Histoire Africaine* 3 (1978): 1–29; David Newbury, "Bushi and the Historians: Historiographical Themes in Eastern Kivu," *History in Africa* 5 (1978): 131–151.

41. R. Bourgeois, "Notes Shangugu," ch. 1.

42. Barihuuta and Mabumburi 3/2/71, 1; Mwemerankiiko 22/1/71, 1; Ntaashuti 6/12/71, 1; Ntuuro Mashirakinyoma, Mukara, Ntibashiimwa 4/2/71, 1–2. The clearest account of the gradual movement from Gisaka to Busoozo via Burundi was given by Bihame 21/1/71, 1. André Coupez, linguist at the Institut National de la Recherche Scientifique (Butare, Rwanda) and the Musée Royal de l'Afrique Centrale (Tervuren, Belgium) has determined that the language spoken in Busoozo shows close affinities to Kirundi. (Personal communication.)

43. "Whoever didn't eat mutton or other bad (inedible) things, that person came from this side. All the other big families who came from the other side would eat everything." Gihura 15/6/71, 6.

44. For a historical analysis of the use of such stereotypes in the central court traditions see D. Newbury, " 'Bunyabungo.' "

45. *Ubutega* (pl., *amatega*), a woven bracelet fashioned from forest lianas, was a prized item of apparel for Rwandan women. *Amatega* were usually worn on the legs, covering the calf from ankle to knee, so that a woman required several hundred in order to be considered "well dressed." *Imikaaka*, a particularly finely woven type of *ubutega*, were worn only by the wives of rich and powerful men; they therefore had a kind of snob appeal. Neither *amatega* nor *imikaaka* were produced in Rwanda; they were imported from regions to the west. The Tembo, who live just west of Buhavu, were specialists in *ubutega* production, and the *amatega* were an important item of trade between Tembo areas and the east, particularly Rwanda. See David Newbury, "Lake Kivu Regional Trade during the Nineteenth Century," *Journal des Africanistes* 50 (1980): 6–30. Other references to the trade in *amatega* are found in Antoine Nyagahene, "Les activités économiques et commerciales du Kinyaga dans la seconde partie du XIXe siècle" (Mémoire de Licence, Université Nationale du Rwanda, Butare, 1979); and Bernard Lugan and Antoine Nyagahene, "Les activités commerciales du sud Kivu au XIXe siècle à travers l'exemple de Kinyaga (Rwanda)," *Cahiers d'Outre-Mer* 36.141 (1983): 19–48.

CHAPTER 3

1. On Rwanda's royal history, see Alexis Kagame, *Abrégé*, vol. 1; idem, *Histoire du Rwanda* (Leverville, 1958); idem, *L'histoire des Armées-Bovines dans l'ancien Rwanda* (Brussels, 1961); idem, *Milices*. The major analytical study of Rwandan expansion remains that of Vansina, *L'évolution du royaume Rwanda*. For a later analysis presenting perceptive new insights, see J. K. Rennie, "The Precolonial Kingdom of Rwanda: A Reinterpretation," *Transafrican Journal of History* 2.2 (1972): 11–53; and Alison L. Des Forges, "Court and Corporations in the Development of the Rwandan State" (unpublished essay). Other important sources for early history include de Lacger, *Le Ruanda*; Léon Delmas, *Généalogies de la Noblesse du Ruanda* (Kabgayi, 1950); A. Pagès, *Un royaume hamite au centre de l'Afrique* (Brussels, 1933).

2. Kinyagans maintain that early political authority in the region was based on kinship units. This may in fact be an idiom they use to describe a locus of authority that differed from later forms; it is possible, for example, that kinship was less important in determining political units than was common residence. This study will use informants' concept of the kinship group as the early political unit and residential group, with the caveat that this may be more an "ideal" (or model) than a valid representation of the actual situation. Note also that "kinship" in this context

implies social recognition of membership in a group rather than strictly biological ties.

3. This description is based on interviews I conducted in Bukunzi and Busoozo during 1970 and 1971 and on *Historique et chronologie*, 98–102; de Lacger, *Ruanda*, ch. 2, especially 82–88; d'Hertefelt, "Le Rwanda," 61; E. Ntezimana, "Coutumes et traditions des royaumes du Bukunzi et Busozo," *Etudes rwandaises* (avril 1980): 15–39; and Ntezimana, "L'arrivée des Européens au Kinyaga et la fin des royaumes hutu du Bukunzi et du Busozo," *Etudes rwandaises* (juin 1980): 1–29. For a roughly analogous situation see Marcel Pauwels, "Le Bushiru et son Muhinza ou roîtelet Hutu," *Annali Lateranensi* 31 (1967): 205–322; Ferdinand Nahimana, "Les Bami ou roîtelets Hutu du corridor Nyabarongo-Mukingwa avec ses régions limitrophes," *Etudes rwandaises* 12 (mars 1979): 1–25; and Nahimana, "Les principautés hutu du Rwanda septentrional," *La civilisation ancienne des peuples des Grands Lacs* (Paris, 1981), 115–137.

4. Marcel d'Hertefelt, and André Coupez, *La royauté sacrée de l'ancien Rwanda: texte, traduction et commentaire de son rituel* (Tervuren, 1964), 151, 277–279

5. For descriptions of Rwabugiri's reign see R. Bourgeois, *Banyarwanda et Barundi*, vol. 1 (Brussels, 1957), 145–168; de Lacger, *Ruanda*, 112–114, 120–121, 341–360; Delmas, *Généalogies*, 87–91; Kagame, *Armées-Bovines*, passim; Kagame, *Milices*, passim; Kagame, *Un Abrégé de l'Histoire du Rwanda du 1853 à 1972*, vol. 2 (Butare, 1975), 13–105; Pagès, *Royaume hamite*, 152–195; Vansina, *Evolution*, 90–91; Des Forges, "Court and Corporations," 46–57.

6. David S. Newbury, "Les campagnes de Rwabugiri: chronologie et bibliographie," *Cahiers d'Etudes Africaines* 14.1 (1974): 181–191.

7. Ndaruhuutse 29/10/70, 8–9; Murekumbanze 5/7/71, 3–4; Ndaziimanye 22/12/70, 9.

8. Murogozi 24/9/70, 6.

9. See Alexis Kagame, *Le code des institutions politiques du Rwanda précolonial* (Brussels, 1952), 95–96, 116–117, 119–120, 124, fn. 77; Alexis Kagame, "La possession du sol et l'administration dans l'ancien Rwanda," *Compte rendu des travaux du séminaire d'anthropologie sociale tenu à Astrida en juillet 1951* (Astrida, 1952), 71–72; Maquet, *Relations sociales*, 123–128; Vansina, *Evolution*, 57–58.

10. Kabahizi 9/7/71, 3; Mugorozi 24/9/70, 6; Murekumbanze 5/7/71, 3–4; Ndaruhuutse 29/10/70, 11; Seekarahennye 23/10/70, 13; Bakomeza 23/12/70, 4; Kaamuhanda 23/12/70, 12; Karibu 22/12/70, 6; Ndaziimanye 22/12/70, 9; Ngendahiimaana 10/7/71, 5; Nyiringango 11/12/70, 8; Ruhengehenge 19/1/71, 5.

11. Nkundiye 28/9/70, 6.

12. Bakomeza 23/12/70, 4. Some informants trace the division of *ubutaka* and *umuheto* to the desire of the chiefs to extract more from the population. For example, Ngendahiimaana 10/7/71, 5.

13. There was no particular geographical basis for such selection; the major criterion was that the lineage be wealthy in cattle or, later, in agricultural produce or luxury goods.

At Shagasha hill a man recounted that his lineage had been selected for *umuheto* by the chief Rwata, acting on authorization from Rwabugiri. But he also portrayed the selection as an agreement between Rubuga and Rwata: "Then Rubuga, seeing an opportunity, said to himself: 'These men cannot remain there with just a land chief.' They were given an *umuheto* chief. . . . [who was] Rwata." Ngendahiimaana 10/7/71, 5.

14. Rwata, also appointed by Rwabugiri, may have preceded Ntiizimira as chief of Impara; some accounts say he also commanded in Abiiru. He did not stay in power for long, and memories of him are vague. He held authority mainly for *umuheto*, but some accounts say he commanded certain hills for *ubutaka* as well. Biseruka 9/7/71, 5; Gisiribanyi 22/10/70, 3–4; Ndaruhuutse 29/10/70, 3; Nyarugabo 10/9/70, 6; Byumba 19/6/71; Bakomeza 27/7/70, 3; Birikunkomo 4/12/70, 1; Kaamuhanda 23/12/70, 5; Ngendahiimaana 10/7/71, 5–6; Seekimondo 4/12/70, 10; Bagaruka and Burumbuuke 11/2/71, 20; Bizimaana 13/2/71, 14; Pauwels, "Bushiru," 288; Delmas, *Généalogies*, 89.

15. The term *umunyamukenke* is little known in Kinyaga, but the term *umunyamuheto* to refer to the *umuheto* chief or his representative is common. My analysis is based on the recollections of Kinyagans interviewed in 1970–1971. Their version is corroborated by a description given in 1902 by a German officer, F. R. von Parish. He recounted that in "Mukinjaga" the chief of "kubutaka" was Rwabirinda, and the chief of "kumuheto" was Rwidegembya. He further explained that, in Kinyaga and in the other western provinces of Rwanda near Lake Kivu,

> the Kubutaka receives the tax of products from the land, . . . Kumuheto receives the tax of butega. . . . This Kumuheto also has all the large and small livestock under his command. . . . In former times there was only a category of Kubutaka; it was only with Luabugiri that the governmental power of tax-collecting was divided; Luabugiri introduced this to supply his numerous Watussi.

F. R. von Parish, "Zwei Reisen durch Ruanda 1902 bis 1903. Aus Tagebüchern, Briefen und hinterlassen Papieren des Oberleutnants F. R. von Parish," *Globus* 86 (1904): 74.

16. *Historique et chronologie*, 97. Rwidegembya's victory was linked to the ascendance of the Abakagara lineage (Abeega clan) after the Rucunshu Coup of 1896.

17. Bakomeza 23/12/70, 4.

18. Kagame, *Abrégé*, vol. 1, 158.

19. Pagès, *Royaume hamite*, 160.

20. Habarugira, Habimana, and Gahima 25/8/70, 7; Nkundiye 29/10/70, 5; Ruvuvu 14/8/70, 5; Bakomeza 27/7/70, 4; Nyiringango 11/12/70, 1; Gihura 25/6/71, 3; Bizimaana 13/2/71; Yoboka 7/7/71, 10.

21. Kanyarubungo 6/1/71, 3, 11; Ngendahiimaana 10/7/71, 5; Ndegeya 13/1/71, 8–9.

22. Pagès, *Royaume hamite*, 160.

23. Vansina, *Evolution*, 90; Jacques J. Maquet, "Les pasteurs de l'Itombwe," *Science et Nature* 8 (1955): 3–12.

24. Booyi Paulin 28/10/70, 8; Sabuhoro 18/7/70, 3; Gihura 25/6/71, 10; Seekimondo 4/12/70, 10.

25. Gihura 15/6/71, 11 and 22/6/71, 6; Bucuti 23/9/70, 1–2; Habarugira, Habimaana, Gahima 25/8/70, 14; Nyarugabo 10/8/70, 2; Rugerero 25/9/70, 2; Ruvuvu 14/8/70, 3; Nyiramandwa 11/7/70, 4.

26. Yoboka 14/7/71, 7–8.

27. Booyi Paulin 28/10/70, 10.

28. Karubanda 13/7/70, 2 and 17/7/70, 3.

29. Such fears persist even today, along with many of the cultural stereotypes

about Kinyagans. One of my research assistants, from Nduga, had been warned by her mother not to eat food prepared by local people. Kinyagans, she had been told, were inclined to poison outsiders. For further discussion of these stereotypes, see D. Newbury, "'Bunyabungo.'"

30. Their distrust was sometimes justified as, for example, when Kinyagans on the Nyamirundi peninsula set off signal fires to warn friends and relatives on Ijwi Island of an impending attack by Rwabugiri's armies. R. Bourgeois, *Banyarwanda*, vol. 1, 153. A study based on data from Ijwi provides details of this incident:

> Mugogo lived near the northern tip of Nyamirundi. Women from his family had married for two successive generations with a family on Ijwi, and his sons had received fields on Ijwi near to their 'brothers' of the same clan. As Rwabugiri prepared for the attack, several men from Nyamirundi, including Mugogo, came to Ijwi to ask their daughters to return temporarily to Nyamirundi and thus to escape the imminent battle. Mugogo's daughter refused to return to Nyamirundi but promised to flee to a secure place on Ijwi if she were given warning of the attack; and thus a system of signals was set up. Mugogo built a house on the northern tip of Nyamirundi—clearly within sight of Ijwi across one kilometer of water—which he burned, to warn the Bany'Iju, shortly before Rwabugiri launched his attack. Mugogo and a neighbor who had helped him build the house were later killed by Rwabugiri for their treasonous demonstration of family solidarity.

See D. Newbury, "Rwabugiri and Ijwi," 163.

31. Accounts of the Kanywiriri battle are found in interviews with Ruvugama 24/8/70, 1; Rwagasore 22/8/70, 1; Bakomeza 27/11/70, 6; Gahwijima 6/6/71, 1; Gihura 25/6/71, 2; Kanyarubungo 6/1/71, 11–12; Karibu 26/11/70, 1; Seekimondo 8/1/71, 2–4. Kagame reports that it was common practice to give the truth potion to spies sent to reconnoiter foreign territory. *Institutions politiques*, 56–57. Kinyaga and Kinyagans were at the center of an extensive trade network linking regions to the west with central Rwanda. Because of these trading activities (as well as kin ties), many Kinyagans were familiar with areas west of the Rusizi River and Lake Kivu. On the characteristics of these trade networks, see D. Newbury, "Lake Kivu Regional Trade"; Nyagahene, "Activités économiques et commerciales"; Lugan and Nyagahene, "Activités commerciales"; Bernard Lugan, "Les pôles commerciaux de lac Kivu à la fin du XIXe siècle," *Revue française d'histoire d'outre-mer* 64.235 (1977): 176–202.

32. Gahwijima 28/11/70, 1 and 6/1/71, 1, 5, 12; Gasimba 26/7/70, 5; Kaabo 30/11/70, 1; Kaamuhanda 23/12/70, 14; Seekimondo 4/12/70, 1; Pagès, *Royaume hamite*, 154–155.

33. Félix Dufays and Vincent de Moor, *Au Kinyaga. Les enchaînés* (Brussels, 1938), 13.

34. One man, attempting to explain the flexibility of ethnic categories, cited several "ennobled Hutu" in Abiiru province and said that "in fact whoever came from Nduga was called Tuutsi. Whereas whoever came from the Congo was called Shi." These terms were also subject to many different interpretations: "Actually all the Abiiru were called Hutu. There were no Tuutsi in Abiiru. All the Abiiru were called the Hutu [subjects] of Rubuga" (Gihura 25/6/71, 15). What Gihura seems to be arguing here is that, in Abiiru at least, "Tuutsi" did not have the hierarchical overtones associated with this category in some other areas. He was surely aware that (as

indicated in census figures) during the Belgian colonial period a significant proportion of the population in Abiiru identified themselves as "Tuutsi."

It is interesting that in central court traditions "Tuutsi" was sometimes defined on the basis of wealth, not birth. In the distribution of pasture land, every Tuutsi was entitled to receive land to pasture his cattle. But in this context, "according to pastoral law, whoever possesses many heads of cattle is called Tuutsi, even if he is not of the Hamitic race," Kagame, *Institutions politiques*, 96.

CHAPTER 4

1. The first European to enter Rwandan territory was Oscar Baumann, an Austrian who had been sent by a German antislavery group to explore possibilities for economic development in East Africa. After reaching Lake Victoria Baumann expanded the original goals of his mission to include traversing Burundi. In September 1892, during a brief detour from his journey through Burundi, Baumann spent several days in southern Rwanda. See Jean-Pierre Chrétien, "Le passage de l'expédition d'Oscar Baumann au Burundi (septembre-octobre 1892)," *Cahiers d'Etudes Africaines* 8.1 (1968): 48–95, esp. 60–62. Baumann published an account of his East African expedition in *Durch Massailand zur Nilquelle* (Berlin, 1894).

2. For two excellent critical analyses of approaches to the study of resistance, see Allen Isaacman, and Barbara Isaacman, "Resistance and Collaboration in Southern and Central Africa, c. 1850–1920," *International Journal of African Historical Studies* 10.1 (1977): 31–62; and Terence Ranger, "The People in African Resistance: A Review," *Journal of Southern African Studies* 4.1 (1977): 125–146. Isaacman and Isaacman stress the importance of considering the often divergent ways in which different social strata in a given society chose to resist or accommodate to colonial rule.

3. Details on the Abapari leaders and their activities in the Rusizi River Valley area are found in interviews with Habarugira, Habimaana, Gahima 25/8/70; Ndaruhuutse 1/10/70; Rugerero 25/9/70; and Ruvuvu 14/8/70. On the Force Publique see F. Flament et al., *La Force Publique de sa naissance à 1914* (Brussels, 1952), 101; and Bryant P. Shaw, "Force Publique, Force Unique: The Military in the Belgian Congo, 1914–1939" (Diss., University of Wisconsin-Madison, 1984).

4. In the Abiiru region, forces led by Magaja, Rushema, and Muhamyanjunga attacked the Abapari. Muhamyanjunga was shot in the arm; his colleagues and their followers fled. Farther north at Shangi hill (Impara province) Kinyagan forces again put up a brief fight, then scattered in disarray.

5. Rugerero 25/9/70, 10; Booyi Paulin 28/10/70, 4–5; Gisiribanyi 30/9/70, 1–2; Ndaruhuutse 1/10/70, 2; Rugerero 18/7/70, 2; Ruvugama 24/8/70, 8; Ngurube Ruheeshyi, Bulimumbari 18/2/71, 18.

6. The estimate is made by R. Ch. Bourgeois, but with no indication as to his source. "Le passage du premier Belge au Ruanda, le Lieutenant Sandrart (1896)," *Servir* 12.3 (1951): 143. According to Kagame, Nshozamihigo was commander of the expedition, but he ordered Bisangwa and Muhigirwa to take the forefront of the attack. (Kagame, *Milices*, 166). This may explain why Kinyagan accounts and also de Lacger identify Bisangwa or Muhigirwa as the main leaders. According to Rugerero, Bisangwa was the leader, designated through divination, but he shared this position with Muhigirwa (Rugerero 18/7/70, 1–2 and 25/9/70, 10). De Lacger iden-

tifies Bisangwa as leader of the expedition (*Ruanda*, 362), while Seekarahennye asserts that Muhigirwa led the expedition. (Seekarahennye 23/10/70, 1).

7. Muhigirwa thought that the Abapari guns would be of the muzzle-loading type, like those used by the Abanyankore, who had been defeated by Rwandans using spears and bows and arrows. Instead, the Abapari had breech-loading rifles (*uburyoko*, "little guns") against which the tactics which had succeeded in Rwabugiri's battle against the Abanyankore were of no use. Bagaruka and Burumbuuke 11/2/71, 11, 19; Kagame, *Milices*, 174; R. Bourgeois, *Banyarwanda* (1957), 164.

8. Bisangwa was the most famous of the warriors who perished at Shangi. It is said that he intentionally put himself at risk, to preserve his honor and avoid the wrath of the royal court, and perhaps also to encourage the king to act kindly toward his children. Bisangwa had sworn to bring back from the expedition the body of a European and knew he would face execution if he failed in his mission. Seekarahennye 23/10/70, 1; Bagaruka and Burumbuuke 11/2/71, 11.

9. This description of the encounter between Rwandan forces and the Abapari is based on accounts by Gisiribanyi 30/8/70, 3; Habarugira, Habimaana, Gahima 25/8/70, 21; Nyarugabo 10/8/70, 7; Rugerero 18/7/70, 12 and 25/9/70, 10; Ruvugama 24/8/70, 8; Seekarahennye 1/10/70, 1–2; Bagaruka and Burumbuuke 11/1/71, 10–11; Karubanda 13/7/70, 3. Another version adding some details is R. Ch. Bourgeois, "Premier Belge," 142–145. Several Kinyagans made the curious observation that there were European women present, whom they took to be the wives of the Abapari. As Des Forges has pointed out, stories about the presence of women reflect Rwandan opinions on how easily the Abapari defeated the royal armies. See Alison L. Des Forges, "Defeat is the Only Bad News: Rwanda Under Musiinga, 1896–1931" (Ph.D. Dissertation, Yale University, 1972), 20 (cited hereafter as "Musiinga").

10. "Diaire Nyamasheke," "Préliminaires."

11. de Lacger, *Ruanda*, 362; *Historique et chronologie*, 13, 105. According to de Lacger, the Abapari spent only about three weeks at Shangi. Kinyagan accounts suggest that the sojourn of the Abapari at Shangi lasted about three months. Later, from their base at Nyamasheke, the Abapari reconnoitered north as far as Rubengera, this time led by Rupari himself. R. Ch. Bourgeois, "Premier Belge," 140–141; "Diaire Nyamasheke," "Préliminaires." According to Delmas, writing in the "Diaire Nyamasheke," it was the second group of Belgians who were called "Abapari."

12. Gisiribanyi 30/9/70, 2; Ndaruhuutse 1/10/70, 4 and 31/10/70, 6; Seekarahennye 23/10/70, 1; Bigirimaana 19/2/71, 6; "Diaire Nyamasheke," "Préliminaires."

13. Karibu 26/11/70, 6. Alternatively, the cattle belonged to Rwabishuugi and the latter's successor as chief of Bugarama (Mugenzi son of Nkombe) had seized them (Gihura 25/6/71, 8–9). In either case Seevumba (Rwabishuugi's brother) could have asserted a claim on the cattle as property of the family.

Apparently, Seevumba had invaded the region and engaged in armed clashes with Kinyagans on one or several occasions before the Abapari arrival (Nyirangango 11/12/70, 9; Kanyarubira 20/1/71, 1; Bakomeza 23/12/70, 14; Gahwijima 6/1/71, 6).

14. Gahwijima 6/1/71, 6; Habarugira, Habimaana, Gahima 25/8/70, 19; Bigumba 26/11/70, 2.

15. Seekimondo 4/12/70, 11.

16. Literally, *Abagufi* means "the small ones." Other descriptions refer to these men as Abahiri or Abuuma, but it is not clear whether these terms describe the same group (Ndaruhuutse 1/10/70, 2 and 21/10/70, 1; Seekarahennye 1/10/70, 1).

In February, 1897, soldiers of the Force Publique commanded by Baron Dhanis staged a mutiny in northeastern Zaïre (then the Congo Independent State). A major goal of subsequent military operations by the Congo Independent State in the eastern part of the country was to capture and disarm these "rebels." (Flament, *Force Publique*, 383ff.). For an interesting study of the Dhanis revolt viewed as a case of early anti-colonial resistance, see D. K. Bimanyu, "A propos des premiers mouvements de résistance: cas de la révolte de l'expédition Dhanis (14 fevrier–19 mars 1897)," (Mémoire de Licence, Université Lovanium, Kinshasa, 1970).

17. The encounter between the Abapari and the Abagufi was recounted by many Kinyagans consulted for this study. Some sample accounts are found in the interviews with Mboonyuburyo and Koogi 26/9/70, 13; Ndaruhuutse 1/10/70, 2 and 21/10/70, 1; Bakomeza 23/12/70, 8, 14; Bagaruka and Burumbuuke 11/2/71, 10–11, 20; Bagaruka and Ruhuguura 11/2/71, 4, 12; Rutungwa and Rubanza 17/2/71, 15–16.

Among published sources, the fullest account of these conflicts is in Flament, *Force Publique*, which describes a skirmish between Lt. Evrard Dubois and Dhanis rebels led by Changuvu. On 12 November 1897, Dubois and a force of 100 African soldiers were ambushed, and 31 of Dubois's men were killed. Two days later Dubois himself was also killed by Changuvu and his men, and the Belgian forces pulled out of the area (Flament, *Force Publique*, 187, 419–420). See also de Lacger, *Ruanda*, 371–372.

18. de Lacger, *Ruanda*, 372.

19. *Historique et chronologie*, 17; William Roger Louis, *Ruanda-Urundi, 1884–1919* (Oxford, 1963), 79–91.

20. Bagaruka and Burumbuuke 11/2/71, 19. The same account notes that just before the attack at Shangi, Muhigirwa had bound Muvunyi (one of the Kinyagan collaborators) and suspended him from the entrance to his compound.

21. Delmas, *Généalogies*, 25; d'Hertefelt and Coupez, *Royauté sacrée*, 514; de Lacger, *Ruanda*, 356–357.

22. de Lacger, *Ruanda*, 358; d'Hertefelt, and Coupez, *Royauté sacrée*, 333–334.

23. Bisangwa had commanded the Ingangurarugo, Inkaranka, and Inyangakugoma armies. Ingangurarugo, which had in the past been Rwabugiri's principal army occupying the high position of royal escort, had suffered heavy losses from its Ibisumizi company at the battle of Shangi. After Bisangwa's death, his brother Sehene took over command of Ingangurarugo and Inkaranka armies. When Sehene was later assassinated, Bisangwa's son Balikage assumed command of the two armies, but he was young and inexperienced, and could not exercise the influence at court held by his father and uncle.

Mugugu commanded the Ababito and Abarasa armies. Upon his death, these armies were placed under two sympathizers of Kabaare's faction (Rutiishereka and his son Rwayitare), who both fought on the side of the Abeega at Rucunshu. See Kagame, *Milices*, 113, 162, 166–167, 171.

24. Descriptions of the Rucunshu Coup are found in de Lacger, *Ruanda*, 358–359, 361–369; d'Hertefelt and Coupez, *Royauté sacrée*, 333–334, Alexis Kagame, *La poésie dynastique au Rwanda* (Brussels, 1951), 47; Léon Classe, "Notes sur la famille de Musinga" (ms, n.d.). I am grateful to Père Hoffscholte of the Société des Missionnaires d'Afrique for making the latter document available to me. For details on the events at Rucunshu and the factions involved, see Des Forges, "Musiinga," 21–22, 26; Kagame, *Abrégé*, vol. 2, 117–126. Kagame, *Milices*, passim.

25. *Historique et chronologie*, 97.

26. Ndaziimanye 22/12/70, 1, 13–14; Bishashaari 1/12/70, 2; Seekimondo 8/1/71,

9. The date is from *Historique et chronologie*, 103, which states that Nyamuhenda was deposed by Musinga.

27. Examples of enclaves and *intoore* hills in Kinyaga taken over by Rwagataraka are found in R. Bourgeois to J. M. Derscheid, 6 December 1933 (Derscheid Collection); Senyanzobe 24/9/70; Tegeko 2/7/71, 5.

28. Nyarugabo 10/9/70, 7; Rutete and Booyi Paulin 28/9/70, 1; Burumbuuke 13/7/71, 5–6; Bizimaana 13/2/71, 13; Kampara 19/2/71, 4; Karubanda 13/7/70, 1–2.

Kinyagan accounts are contradictory as to the extent of Birasinyeri's jurisdiction, some saying it encompassed all of Impara, others that it was limited to the northern part of Impara. Possibly these accounts refer to different time periods. During Rwidegembya's ascendance after Rwabirinda's removal in 1905, the rise of Seekabaraga would seem to have reduced or eliminated Birasinyeri's role in southern Impara. The role of Birasinyeri as general "supervisor" for all of Impara was emphasized by Seemigabo, Kayirara, Gashiibonde (whose accounts were generally reliable) 17/2/71, 20. Others imply that the actual authority of Birasinyeri was limited to northern Impara. For example, Nkiikanyi 12/2/71, 4; Nyamajanja and Seeruhojojo 20/2/71, 7. Again, the type of authority is unclear, and it may have been that Birasinyeri exercised authority for *umuheto* in some areas of Impara, and for *ubutaka* in the same or other areas. In practice, there was undoubtedly a good deal of flexibility generated by efforts of one or another chief to attain direct links to Rwidegembya rather than passing through Birasinyeri.

It was reported in 1929 that when Rwagataraka arrived in Kinyaga (1911) Birasinyeri was "chief of Impara," and retained effective administration of the province until 1914, when Rwagataraka himself assumed direct control. Territoire de Kamembe, "Rapport établi en réponse au questionnaire addressé en 1929 par M. le Gouverneur du Ruanda-Urundi à l'Administrateur du Territoire de Kamembe," in the Derscheid Collection (hereafter cited as Questionnaire 1929, Kamembe"). Although this statement may have exaggerated the actual scope of Birasinyeri's power, it is indicative of the prestige he enjoyed.

29. Seekimondo 8/1/71, 7; Bagaruka and Ruhuguura 11/2/71, 3, 9; Kampara 19/2/71, 16. *Historique et chronologie*, 104.

30. "Questionnaire 1929, Kamembe," 3.

31. Kinyaga had its own administrative school (called "Ecole des Batutsi") until around 1930, when all activities were centralized in a single institution at Nyanza, later moved to Astrida (now called Butare) where the school was named the Groupe Scolaire. Initiative for the school in Kinyaga came in 1915, when Rwagataraka asked the European missionaries at Mibirizi to provide a secretary for him who would teach him how to read and write. This person, called "mwalimu," provided instruction at an "Ecole des Fils des Chefs" set up by Rwagataraka at Mubumbano (near Rwagataraka's residence at Ishara just north of Nyamasheke). In 1920 the Belgian administration moved this school to Cyangugu ("Diaire Nyamasheke," "Préliminaires"). In 1929 there were 23 pupils at the Ecole des Batutsi in Cyangugu; their number had recently been diminished by the departure of 20 who wished to study at mission schools, and 10 who were sent to the official school at Nyanza. "Questionnaire 1929, Kamembe," 16.

32. Gouvernement Belge, Ministère des Colonies, *Rapport présenté par le Gouvernement Belge au Conseil de la Société des Nations au sujet de l'administration du Ruanda-Urundi* (Geneva, 1931). The Belgian government's annual report on Administration in Ruanda-Urundi underwent a number of changes in name. To avoid

confusion, subsequent references to the annual reports for different years will use a single abbreviated title: *Rapport sur l'administration Belge du R-U.*

33. For examples of these exchanges, see Appendix V.

34. "Diaire Mibirizi," 28–29 April, 1 November 1907; 15 April, 2 July, 17–18 July 1914; 4 February 1918; Ntezimana, "Fin des royaumes hutu." Ntezimana includes fascinating material on the tactics used by the Abakunzi to protect their *umwami* and evade the European-led invading forces.

35. "Rapport d'ensemble sur la situation de la Résidence du Ruanda et sur l'activité de l'Administration," 10 October 1918, Gouvernement Belge, Ministère des Colonies, Services des Territoires des Colonies, Dossier AE/II No. 1847, portefeuille 3288x (Archives Africaines, Brussels). Hereafter cited as "Rapport sur Résidence du Ruanda."

36. Baaruguriyiki and Bikolimaana 3/2/71, 13; Kaaryo and Kibuye 4/2/71, 9; Masenge 2/2/71, 4.

37. "Diaire Mibirizi," April 1923; Ntuuro Mashirankoma, Mukara, and Ntibashiimwa 4/2/71, 20; Nyaminaani and Rugendashyamba 1/2/71, 2, 6, 8–9; Rugambarara 1/2/71, 2, 11 and 2/2/71, 10; Rugaati 29/1/71, 2; Rwamukikanyi and Buyooga 3/2/71, 708. One version asserts that Ndagano's deathbed instructions to his son Bigirumwera required that the two men be killed, because they were guilty of having told Nyirandakunze about the birth of an heir to the throne. Rupfuura 25/1/71, 10. Pauwels alleges that the ritual killing of Shyirakeera was carried out by a son of Ndagano. "Bushiru," 216.

38. "Diaire Mibirizi," 4 April 1923 and July 1923; Masenge 2/2/71, 4; Nyaminaani and Rugendashyamba 1/2/71, 8. It is not clear when Rwagataraka actually took command of Gashashi, but apparently, through secret agreement with Musinga, he did not act immediately on this authorization. Des Forges, "Musiinga," 300.

39. "Diaire Mibirizi," 8 and 30–31 January 1924, March-April 1924, 14 March 1925; Kamooya and Rugemanandi 1/2/71, 12; Nyaminaani and Rugendashyamba 1/2/71, 8.

40. "Diaire Mibirizi," 17 September 1924; Mwemerankiiko 22/1/71, 7.

41. "Diaire Mibirizi," 11 March 1925; Des Forges, "Musiinga," 301; Ndimubanzi and Gashyamangali 5/2/71, 8; Ntuuro Mashirakinyoma, Mukara, Ntibashiimwa 4/2/71, 6, 10, 14; Nyaminaani and Rugendashyamba 1/2/71, 8; Rekeraho 1/8/70, 1; Rugambarara 1/2/71, 4; Rugaati 29/1/71, 7.

42. Most Abakunzi interviewed maintained that Rwagataraka had wished to gain control of Bukunzi for a long time; from this perspective, the succession struggle and its resulting conflicts in Bukunzi provided Rwagataraka with an opportunity to muster European aid. Without such aid, the Abakunzi boast, Rwagataraka could never have dared to enter their kingdom. They view the invasion in March 1924, the subsequent military occupation, and the expedition which caused Nyirandakunze's death as the result of Rwagataraka's initiatives. See, for example, accounts by Rwamukikanyi and Buyooga 3/2/71, 9, 11; Barihuuta and Mabumbuli 3/2/71, 6–7; Baaruguriyiki and Bikolimaana 3/2/71, 13; Kaaryo and Kibuye 4/2/71, 9; Masenge 2/2/71, 4, 9–10; Rugambarara 1/2/71, 5 and 2/2/71, 5–6; Rwajekare 25/1/71, 9.

Viewed from the perspective of central court politics, the situation was more complex than this. Des Forges suggests that Rwagataraka's action in misleading the initial invading force in March 1924 may have reflected an attempt to please Musinga, who did not wish to have the royal family of Bukunzi captured. This view is seemingly contradicted by the assertion of one informant in Bukunzi that Musinga himself sent Rwagataraka to conquer Bukunzi as vengeance against Nyirandakunze. There was, this man pointed out, a great deal of friendship and respect between Musinga and Ndagano; Nyirandakunze's eventual defeat should therefore be traced to the anger of Musinga over the loss of his friend Ndagano (poisoned by Nyirandakunze). These two explanations, though apparently contradictory, may in fact be complementary. When Rwagataraka misled the invading force in March 1924, he prevented the capture of Bigirumwera (not Nyirandakunze, who was already safely in hiding anyway), the favorite son of Ndagano who had been named in his father's last testament to represent him to Musinga. Rwagataraka thus saved the person who could be viewed as a protégé of Musinga in the place of Ndagano. But later, Rwagataraka participated actively in the expedition which eliminated Nyirandakunze, who could be viewed as Musinga's enemy. See Des Forges, "Musiinga," 301; and Rupfuura 25/1/71, 6–7, 10.

43. *Historique et chronologie*, 100, 102.

44. "Questionnaire 1929, Kamembe," 4, 7.

45. The friendly relations between Rwagataraka and Europeans were noted by many of the Kinyagans interviewed, including, among others, Bakengura, 23/8/70, 5; Muke and Seerusaza 1/10/70, 8; Nyarugabo 10/8/70, 8–10; Kaamuhanda 23/12/70, 13; Karubanda 13/7/70, 4 and 17/10/70, 8. For additional evidence, see "Diaire Nyamasheke."

46. T. Alexander Barns, *Across the Great Craterland to the Congo* (London, 1923), 161–162.

47. "Questionnaire 1929, Kamembe," 4, 7.

48. For a description of Musinga's dismissal and the events leading up to it, see Des Forges, "Musiinga," esp. ch. 9; Kagame, *Abrégé*, vol. 2, 172–182. Briefer accounts are given by de Lacger, *Ruanda*, 531–539; and Antoine Van Overschelde, *Un audacieux pacifique: Monseigneur Léon Paul Classe, apôtre du Ruanda* (Namur, 1948), 152–158.

49. The rivalry between Rwagataraka and Musinga appears to have arisen as the former gained a stronger hold on his Kinyagan power base, using that and his positive relations with Europeans as a springboard for maneuverings in the central arena. It was also part of the larger Abeega–Abanyiginya rivalry. One sign of conflict with the king was the drawn-out power struggle between Rwagataraka and Birasinyeri. Another manifestation (or source) of their enmity was Rwagataraka's repudiation of his wife Musheeshimbugu, a daughter of Musinga. Several informants remarked on the conflict between Rwagataraka and Musinga: Booyi Paulin 28/10/70, 15; Rwagasore 13/8/70, 12; Rukebeeshya and Maasomaaso 13/2/71, 5. Some Kinyagans disposed to proffer aid and solace to the exiled king were restrained by fear of attracting Rwagataraka's disfavor; others did so surreptitiously. Seekimondo 8/1/71, 10. Rwagataraka's divorce from Musheeshimbugu was linked to his efforts to become a Catholic, at which point the fathers required that he retain only one wife. See "Diaire Nyamasheke," February 1931.

According to Des Forges' analysis, the rivalry between Rwagataraka and Musinga emerged in the open only after 1926; before that time, Rwagataraka was apparently allied to Musinga in opposition to his own father, Rwidegembya. (Des Forges, "Musiinga," 253, 320.) Rwidegembya died in August 1930. "Diaire Nyamasheke," 24 August 1930.

50. Kabooyi July 1971, 1; Bagaruka and Ruhuguura 11/2/71, 8.

51. *Historique et chronologie*, 98.

52. See *Historique et chronologie*, 98, 103. The Abaya, lineage of Etienne Gite-fano, descended from Yuhi Mazimpaka, who reigned in the late seventeenth century. Joseph Bideri's lineage, the Abahindiro, includes the descendants of Yuhi Gahindiro, who reigned in the early nineteenth century. Ambroise Gakooko could trace his ancestry to Yuhi Gahima (reigned during the sixteenth century), from whom the Abanama are said to descend. Delmas, *Généalogies*, 48, 51, 83, 231–234.

53. According to admission requirements promulgated in 1946, the Groupe Sco-laire admitted fifty students each year, divided equally between Rwanda and Burundi, and admission was based on a competitive examination. However, sons of chiefs could be admitted on the recommendation of the colonial administration, in which case the exam would be waived. In 1946 and 1947, only one Kinyagan was admitted to the Groupe Scolaire each year; the number rose to five Kinyagans admitted in 1948. "Admission au Groupe Scolaire," *Servir*, 7.3 (1946): 146; "Liste des étudiants au Groupe Scolaire de la Préfecture de Cyangugu, 1932–1969" (supplied by the Groupe Scolaire, Butare).

In 1949, total enrollment at the Groupe Scolaire was 293, including students fol-lowing the three year "école moyenne" and the specialized studies of four to five years which followed. In that year there were not more than nine students (about 3% of the student body) from Cyangugu Prefecture attending the Groupe Scolaire. In 1954 the total number of students at the school had increased to 450 (215 at the école moyenne, and 235 in the specialized sections). Not more than 16 students (3.5%) were from Cyangugu Territory. Six of the students from Cyangugu had been admitted during the previous year. Fred E. Wagoner, "Nation-Building in Africa: A Description and Analysis of Rwanda," (Diss., American University, 1968), 90; "Dis-cours prononcé le 24 octobre 1954 par le Résident du Ruanda à l'occasion du 25ème anniversaire de la fondation du Groupe Scolaire d'Astrida," *Servir* 15.5 (1954): 252. "Liste des étudiants au Groupe Scolaire de Cyangugu."

A prominent Kinyagan asserted to me that it was conscious policy of the Rwandan royal court to concentrate the development of educational opportunities in central Rwanda. This was to serve as a means of keeping Rwandans in peripheral regions such as Kinyaga from gaining access to posts in administrative or other offices. Conversely, the policy was to favor young people from central Rwanda in allocation of places in school, and hence in future access to influential positions.

CHAPTER 5

1. The integrationist view is most clearly presented in Maquet, *Relations so-ciales*. The coercive view is stated directly by Helen Codere, "Power in Ruanda," *Anthropologica* ns 4.1 (1962): 45–85. These and other studies of clientship in Rwanda have been critically examined by Jean-François Saucier in "The Patron-Client Relationship in Traditional and Contemporary Southern Rwanda," (Diss., Columbia University, 1974). For a seminal early critique see Claudine Vidal, "Le Rwanda des anthropologues," *Cahiers d'Etudes Africaines* 9.3 (1969): 384–401.

2. Some writers did recognize variations in types of *ubuhake* cattle clientship. Codere, for example, distinguished between clientship linking Tuutsi patrons and Hutu clients (which she characterized as generally exploitative) and patron–client ties in which both partners were Tuutsi (which she characterized as types of alliance). "Power in Ruanda," 54–55.

3. According to Maquet, all Tuutsi were linked together by *ubuhake* ties as both patrons and clients:

> The *umwami* was the only patron who was client of no one. His clients were the great Tutsi chiefs. These latter were the patrons of less important Tutsi, who, themselves, were the patrons of Tutsi who were even less important, etc. In this manner, the Tutsi constituted a homogeneous unity of individuals, linked to one another by ties of fidelity and protection. From this point of view, *ubuhake* contributed to the unity and solidarity of the aristocratic caste.

Moreover, through *ubuhake*, he continues, "almost every Hutu was linked to a Tuutsi and participated in the social power of the superior caste by identifying himself with a protector who was a member of the dominant group. *Relations sociales*, 161, 173.

4. See Scott, "Patron-Client Politics," 3.

5. Ndaruhuutse 1/10/70, 11; Bakomeza 27/7/70, 1 and 12/5/71; Ngendahiimaana 10/7/71, 1–2; Rukemampunzi 18/5/71; Reisdorff, "Enquêtes foncières," 51–52.

6. For example, Byumva 19/6/71, 3.

7. Yet the *ubuhake* clientship of one member of a lineage in Kinyaga sometimes sufficed to protect other members. Vidal indicates that group clientship of the *ubuhake* type was also found in southern Rwanda, when *ubuhake* was being introduced there. "Rwanda des anthropologues," 389.

8. See Kagame, *Institutions politiques*, 20–22, 26–27. According to Kagame, initial recruits for new armies were usually drawn from among the young men whose fathers were members of existing armies.

9. Maquet states that "Every Rwandan, Twa, Hutu, as well as Tutsi, was affiliated to an army *(ingabo)." Relations sociales*, 130. See also Kagame, *Institutions politiques*, 21; Kagame, "La possession du sol et l'administration dans l'ancien Rwanda," 71–72. For information on specific social armies, see Kagame, *Armées-bovines;* and Kagame, *Milices,* passim.

10. Among Kinyagans who indicate early *umuheto* ties for their lineages are Bakomeza 23/12/70, 5; Gihura 15/6/71, 9 and 22/6/71, 1–2; Makwaruza 18/6/71; Zikamabahari 11/5/71. Informants who cite *umuheto* patrons for their lineages only under Rwabugiri or later include Booyi Paulin 28/10/70, 8; Ndaziimanye 22/12/70, 17–18; Ngendahiimaana 10/7/71, 5, 8; Karorero 15/1/71, 6; Ruhengenge 19/1/71, 5.

11. Yoboka 14/7/71, 1. In the northernmost part of Kinyaga, where members of the Abazimya social army were numerous, non-cattle-owners were sometimes recruited as well and required to give beer as prestations. Yoboka 14/7/71, 6. It is not clear whether the recruitment of non-cattle-owners to which Yoboka refers occurred before the time of Rwabugiri; for other areas of Kinyaga there is no evidence for recruitment of non-cattle-owning lineages prior to Rwabugiri's reign.

12. Booyi 28/10/70, 8.

13. Yoboka 14/7/71, 5. Yoboka lived in Cyesha province, a region of relatively intensive and early central Tuutsi penetration, as compared with other areas of Kinyaga.

14. Bakomeza 23/12/70, 5; Ngendahiimaana 10/7/71, 5; Makwaruza 18/6/71. Sometimes the *umuheto* cow was replaced by a payment of luxury items special to Kinyaga; such was the case for the Abaruruma at Cyete, who gave belts of otter fur *(imishumi)* instead of a cow, or, if no otter fur was available, fiber bracelets *(amatega)*. Gihura 10/7/70, 2 and 22/6/71, 7.

15. According to most of the accounts collected, however, the *umuheto* obligation

was uniquely that of sending prestations to the patron, whereas military service was organized by the provincial chief holding authority over the land. The confusion may be explained by the fact that *umuheto* became widespread in Kinyaga only under Rwabugiri and by then there was a tendency to organize armies *(ingabo)* under provincial (land) chiefs. Military service by a Kinyagan lineage that may have been performed for an *umuheto* chief during the reign of Rwogera (father of Rwabugiri) is described in M. C. Newbury, "Deux lignages," 29.

16. Kagame, *Institutions politiques*, 37–39, 42, 87. Bourgeois defines *imbaata* cattle as being *impahano* cows which have been handed down from the original owners to heirs. *Impahano* cattle were obtained through purchase, through *ingwate* or *ugushega* contracts, or through marriage payment (if a marriage remains stable, the cows exchanged by the lineages involved become *impahano*). R. Bourgeois, "Moeurs et coutumes," 137–158. For an explanation of *ingwate* and *ugushega* contracts, see Appendix V.

17. Rugerero 25/9/70, 6; Gihura 15/6/71, 9 and 22/6/71, 4.

18. An account by Gihura provides clear evidence of such affective ties. Gacinya, chief of the Abakwiye social army and *umuheto* patron of Gihura's lineage, had come to accompany *Umwami* Rwabugiri to Buhimanryarya in Kinyaga. While at Buhimanryarya, Gacinya died. A last request of the dying chief was that he be buried by the descendants of Gishuuta, who had been "chosen" for *umuheto* by Gacinya's father, Rwabika. Thus it was that Gihura's father, Karabahanda (who was grandson of Gishuuta) and Karabahanda's paternal uncle had the honor of bearing Gacinya's body to the "tomb of the nobles" *(mury'iimfura)*. Gihura 22/6/71, 4. Kagame confirms that Gacinya died late in the reign of Rwabugiri, but says the death occurred in Bunyabungo (Bushi), and was caused by tuberculosis. *Milices*, 151.

19. On these and other forms of land tenure in Rwanda, see Jacques J. Maquet and Saverio Naigiziki, "Les droits fonciers dans le Ruanda ancien," *Zaire* 11.4 (1957): 339–359; Jan Vansina, "Les régimes fonciers Ruanda et Kuba—une comparaison," Daniel Biebuyck, ed., *African Agrarian Systems*, 348–363, (London, 1963); Rwabukumba and Mudandagizi, "Formes historiques de la dépendance," 6–25; Gaëtan Feltz, "Evolution des structures foncières et histoire politique du Rwanda (XIXe et XXe siècles)," *Etudes d'Histoire Africaine* 7 (1975): 143–154.

20. Bucuti 28/9/70, 2; Rutete and Booyi Paulin 28/9/70, 5; Gafaranga 16/6/71, 1–2.

21. Mboonyuburyo and Koogi 26/9/70, 10; Muhindangiga 7/12/70, 2; Ngenda-hiimaana 10/7/71, 2. The word *abagereerwa* is derived from the verb *kugereera*, to grant land. *Abagereerwa* is a term particularly common in northwestern Rwanda, where the *ubukonde* system of land tenure and land clientship was widespread. On land clientship in Bushiru, a formerly autonomous Hutu kingdom in northwestern Rwanda, see Pauwels, "Bushiru," 314ff.

22. Reisdorff, "Enquêtes foncières," 62–64.

23. For example Rwigimba (Abaranga lineage, Abanyiginya-Abashambo clan) received land at Mugera hill and a wife from the Abaganda lineage (Abagesera clan) who were already established on the hill. Rwigimba 9/7/71, 1. A similar process has been documented in southern Rwanda near Butare. Rwabukumba and Mudandagizi, "Formes historiques de la dépendance," 11–12.

24. Reisdorff, "Enquêtes foncières," 66.

25. R. Bourgeois, "Moeurs et coutumes," 148.

26. For example, at Muhwehwe hill in the Bugarama region of Kinyaga, the Aba-

shumbuusho distributed land to those who came later; there were no prestations involved, but the recipients would help the land donor in the production of banana beer. Kanyarubira 20/1/71, 4.

27. For a particularly clear presentation of the different types of *igikingi* beneficiaries see Vidal, "Rwanda des anthropologues," 393. Transformations of an *igikingi* on a hill during the nineteenth century are outlined in Rwabukumba and Mudandagizi, "Formes historiques de la dépendance," 14–15. It is significant that the authors of this article found that initially there were no prestations in food or cattle required from recipients of land on the *igikingi*. "It seems that at that time, the advantages of the manor arose mainly from the control over land which made it possible to reserve for oneself the lion's part and which made it possible to install and regroup one's followers" (p. 15).

28. Kagame, *Institutions politiques*, 97; Gahayira, Seenuma, Nyamabwa, Hakizimfura 2/7/71, 2–3; Tegeko 2/7/71, 2.

29. Reisdorff, "Enqêtes foncières," 51–52.

30. Maquet and Naigiziki, "Droits fonciers," 344; Vidal, "Rwanda des anthropologues," 397; Rwabukumba and Mudandagizi, "Formes historiques de la dépendance," 13.

31. Aside from land clientship, Tuutsi could procure agricultural labor for two days out of every five-day week in exchange for a cowhide or a hoe. When the object wore out the "employer" would replace it, thus continuing the relationship. Reisdorff, "Enquêtes foncières," 53. See also Claudine Vidal, "Economie de la société féodale rwandaise," *Cahiers d'Etudes Africaines* 14.1 (1974): 61.

32. Bagaruka and Burumbuuke 11/2/71, 1. On Bukunzi, which had its own specific land tenure practices, see Reisdorff, "Enquêtes foncières," 54–57.

33. This was sometimes referred to as the transfer of an *inka y'ubushuti* or *inka y'ubuntu*, the cow of friendship. On other contracts *(ingwate, ugushega, ubugabire)* see Appendix V.

34. See Reisdorff, "Enquêtes foncières," 51–52, 58–61. The importance of distinguishing pre-Rwabugiri Tuutsi from those who came later was reiterated by Sixte Butera, a physician and one of Kinyaga's leading intellectuals (interview, 8 November 1971).

35. From 1926, the Belgian administration conducted inquiries in all the "Territoires" of Rwanda to determine the succession of chiefs on each hill. The study was to aid the administration in its efforts to effect a consolidation and regroupment of hills into larger "subchiefdoms." Data contained in such studies are invaluable, as manifested in the documents on the subject available for Ruhengeri Territory. Unfortunately, the regroupment study for Cyangugu has disappeared; it is therefore difficult to provide statistics on the number of chiefs introduced from outside, but interview data indicate clearly that distribution of local hills to outsiders dates from the reign of Rwabugiri.

36. Habarugira, Habimaana, Gahima 22/8/70, 14.

37. Rwagasore 13/8/70, 7; Sabuhoro 25/9/70, 5.

38. Ruvuvu 14/8/70, 1, 5. The leprosy is said to have developed as punishment for Rwabugiri's having killed his mother, Nyiramavugo.

39. According to this version, Rwabugiri offered Ntiizimira cows as a reward, but Ntiizimira refused, asking instead for control over land. Rwabugiri said to Ntiizimira: " 'Since you are a courageous man, one of my heroes, I am going to give you many cows—enough to fill a valley.' The other refused and instead demanded *ubu-*

reetwa, permission to make the Tuutsi work for land. 'I am going to demand a cow from Tuutsi for the land they live on and for the pasture land for their cattle. Then this cow will be added to that of *umuheto.'* " Yoboka 14/7/71, 1.

40. Rwata son of Buhake (Abaha clan), a contemporary of Ntiizimira and also a favorite of the king, had a career similar to that of Ntiizimira. Both rose to power through the largesse of Rwabugiri. Both commanded in Kinyaga (Rwata commanded several hills, or all of Impara or Abiiru). Both succeeded in marrying one of their sons to a daughter of the king. And, ultimately, both were deposed and killed on Rwabugiri's orders. Bakomeza 27/7/70, 3; Birikunkomo 4/12/70, 1; Kaamuhanda 23/12/70, 5; Ngendahiimaana 10/7/71, 5–6; Seekimondo 4/12/70, 10; Bizimaana 13/2/71, 14; Biseruka 9/7/71, 5; Habarugira, Habimaana, Gahima 28/8/70, 6. *Historique et chronologie,* 103; Delmas, *Généalogies,* 89; Kagame, *Milices,* 64; Kagame, *Armées-bovines,* 78.

41. Kagame, *Milices,* 170. Ntiizimira himself called the social army Imbanzagukeba, but the name Imbanzamihigo became common later when the group was commanded by Rwidegembya; Imbanzamihigo is the name most often used today. Habarugira, Habimaana, Gahima 25/8/70, 19; Nyarugabo 10/8/70, 5.

42. For example, Ntiizimira appointed his brother Nyanuzi (son of Musuhuuke) and Nyanuzi's son, Sagahara, to command Buhoro, Karambi, and Mugomba hills; he appointed his own son, Gasheegu, to represent him at Korwa and Mubumbano hills. Kizima, a native of Bufundu (Abasinga clan) and a son-in-law of Ntiizimira, received responsibility for Nyarwungu and other hills near the forest (Ibanda, Yove, Rwumba, Karunga, etc.). Rwabigwi and Nyakagabo, both sons of Mutsinzi (Abacyaba clan), nephews of Ntiizimira (SiSo) were appointed to command Bitare, Butambara, and Mubumbano. Habarugira, Habimaana, Gahima 25/8/70, 11 and 28/8/70, 4–5; Nyarugabo 10/8/70, 5.

43. Habarugira, Habimaana, Gahima 25/8/70, 11; Rutungwa and Rubanza 17/2/71, 9, 11; Yoboka 14/7/71, 12, 15. Rukeezamuheto was son of Seemuhangamucyamu, of the Abanaama lineage, Abanyiginya clan. Muragizi was a member of the Abaganzu lineage, Abanyiginya clan.

44. Ntiizimira controlled at least five official herds, in addition to his personal cattle. His official herds included Impara, Imitagoma, Akaganda (an *inyambo* herd of special cows reserved for the king), Abazatsinda (inherited from his father), and Intulire I. Kagame, *Armées-bovines,* 26, 28, 50, 56, 78.

45. Biseruka 9/7/71, 8; Ndaruhuutse 19/10/70, 8–10; Rugerero 23/10/70, 7; Ruvuvu 14/8/70, 3; Kanyarubira 21/1/71, 3–4. The ethnographer Jan Czekanowski described *umuheto* as a "war tax" introduced by Rwabugiri. Czekanowski conducted studies in central, eastern, and northern areas of Rwanda in 1907–1908, focusing particularly on Bugoyi and Mulera in the northwest. Czekanowski, *Forschungen im Nil-Kongo-Zwischengebiet,* vol. 1 (Leipzig, 1917), 271.

46. Booyi Paulin 28/10/70, 9.

47. Booyi's account is ambiguous. It is not clear whether Nyankiiko was acting on the authority of Rwidegembya or of Rwabirinda. Probably Nyankiiko had links to both chiefs, since Rwidegembya and Rwabirinda commanded simultaneously in Kinyaga; theoretically authority over land *(ubutaka)* was under the jurisdiction of Rwabirinda. Nyankiiko, as a hill chief, would have had links to Rwabirinda for that purpose. A question remains as to whether Nyankiiko's authority for *umuheto* derived also from Rwabirinda. This is not impossible, as there are indications in the accounts of other informants that Rwabirinda commanded *umuheto* companies (for

example, Habarugira, Habimaana, Gahima 28/8/70, 2). Thus, if Booyi's grandfather was attempting to escape from an *umuheto* company that was under Rwabirinda's authority, the incident became an example of competition between two *umuheto* chiefs both of whom sought authority over the same lineage.

48. For example, Habagati 5/2/71, 1; Mudaage 11/1/71, 7–11; Rugerero 25/9/70, 2; Ruvuvu 14/8/70, 3; Ruhengehenge 19/1/71, 5; Bizimaana 13/2/71, 14.

49. I am indebted to Rita Van Walle for pointing out the resemblance between *ubureetwa* duties and the work agriculturalist residents of an *igikingi* were expected to perform for the *igikingi* proprietor (personal communication).

50. At the time of the Umuryamo cattle epidemic (early 1890s), Yoboka was a child old enough to herd cattle; he remembers having seen Ntiizimira.

51. Yoboka 14/7/71, 1, 3–4, 9–10, 15 and 7/7/71.

52. Yoboka 14/7/71, 1, 9, 15.

53. For example, the clients of Bigaruranshuro and later of his son Seebakungu (Abadegede, Abeega) were called Abatagoma; the followers of Rwanyamugabo (Abeerekande, Abasinga) were known as Abahuurambuga.

54. Gisiribanyi 22/10/70, 3.

55. Nyarugabo 10/8/70, 2. Seerutabura was a member of the Abareganshuro lineage, Abanyiginya clan.

56. Data from Kinyaga thus support Vidal's findings regarding the development of *ubuhake* in central and southern Rwanda. See Vidal, "Rwanda des anthropologues," 396–397.

57. Sebasare 30/6/71.

58. Sebasare 30/6/71; Habarugira, Habimaana, Gahima 28/8/70, 4; Seekarahennye, 23/10/70, 3.

59. Sebasare 30/6/71.

60. Sebasare 30/6/71; Habarugira, Habimaana, Gahima 28/8/70, 4–5; Ndaruhuutse 1/10/70, 2; Nyarugabo 10/9/70, 2–3; Tegeko 2/7/71, 3; Ruvugama 24/8/70, 4; Ruvuvu 14/8/70, 2, 5–6; Seekimondo 8/1/71, 1, 3; Ruhuguura and Bagaruka 11/2/71, 5; Bizimaana 13/2/71, 13; Karubanda 17/7/70, 6; Bakomeza 23/12/70, 8; Karibu 22/12/70, 8.

61. Seekarahennye 23/10/70, 4.

62. Sebasare 30/6/71; Habarugira, Habimaana, Gahima 25/8/70, 11; Ntonga 5/2/71, 5–6; Ruvuvu 18/8/70, 4; Seekarahennye 23/10/70, 5; Rufali 27/11/70, 2; Matabaro, Kanywabahizi, Ntakiyimaana 13/2/71, 9; Seemigabo, Kayirara, Gashiibonde 17/2/71, 13.

63. Sebasare 30/6/71, 2; Booyi Paulin 28/10/70, 6–7; Bucuti 28/9/70, 11; Ruvuvu 18/8/70, 4.

64. Sebasare 30/6/71, 2.

65. Sebasare 30/6/71, 2; Habagati 5/2/71, 2.

66. Sebasare 30/6/71, 2; Booyi Paulin 28/10/70, 6; Bucuti 28/9/70, 11 and 28/10/70, 8; Rutete and Booyi Paulin 28/9/70, 5; Ruvuvu 18/8/70, 4.

67. Sebasare 30/6/71, 2; Nyarugabo 11/9/70, 7.

68. Sebasare 30/6/71.

69. Sebasare 30/6/71, 1; Bakengura 23/8/70, 3; Gahayira, Seenuma, Nyamabwa, Hakizimfura 2/7/71, 4–5; Habagati 5/2/71, 2; Habarugira, Habimaana, Gahima 25/8/70, 11; Nkundiye 29/10/70, 5; Rugerero 23/10/70, 4.

70. Cyigwira 17/7/70, 1; Karubanda 13/7/70, 1 and 17/7/70, 4, 9; Rukaburacumu 10/2/71, 1–2, 8, 10, 12–13; Rutungwa and Rubanza 17/2/71, 3; Seemigabo, Kayirara,

Gashiibonde 17/2/71, 14; Habarugira, Habimaana, Gahima 28/8/70, 11, 14; Mudaage 11/1/71, 16; Muke 5/10/71, 2; Nyarugabo 11/9/70, 7; Ruvuvu 18/8/70, 6.

71. Gahayira, Seenuma, Nyamabwa, Hakizimfura 2/7/71, 5, 12; Habagati 5/2/71, 2; Habarugira, Habimaana, Gahima 25/8/70, 11, 22 and 28/8/70, 4, 11; Mpakanyi 7/1/71, 2; Muke 1/10/70, 2; Ntonga 5/2/71, 3; Ntuuro 23/10/70, 9; Ruvuvu 18/8/70, 6; Rugerero 30/10/70, 1; Seekarahennye 23/10/70, 3, 6; Rufali 27/11/70, 4–5; Delmas, Généalogies, 169.

72. Ntonga 5/2/71, 6; Senyanzobe 24/9/70, 2.

73. Ntonga 5/2/71, 6; Senyanzobe 24/9/70, 2.

74. Bagaruka and Burumbuuke 11/2/71, 13; Kampara 19/2/71, 5; Habagati 5/2/71, 2; Nkundiye 29/10/70, 6; Rugerero 30/10/70, 1.

75. Nyarugabo 11/9/70, 7; Rugerero 30/10/70, 4.

76. Nyarugabo 11/9/70, 5; Rwagasore 13/8/70, 5; Birikunkomo 8/1/71, 4–5; Ndaziimanye 22/12/70, 7, 22; Nzeeyimaana 27/11/70, 4; Sagatwa 11/12/70, 2; Seekimondo 8/1/71, 14, 15; Delmas, Généalogies, 231.

77. Rukaburacumu 10/2/71, 8, 16.

78. Rukaburacumu 10/2/71, 6; Habagati 5/2/71, 2; Habarugira, Habimaana, Gahima 25/8/71, 11 and 28/8/70, 12–13; Ndaziimanye 22/12/70, 21; Rufali 27/11/70, 3; Territoire de Shangugu, "Rapport sur H.A.V. et gros bétail"; Delmas, Généalogies, 169.

79. Bakengura 23/8/70, 2; Tegeko 2/7/71, 8–9; Sagatwa 11/12/70, 2–3.

80. Seemirama 1/12/70, 12; Bagaruka 13/7/71, 12, 17; Rukaburacumu 10/2/71, 2, 8; Territoire de Shangugu, "Rapport sur H.A.V. et gros bétail."

81. Kanyabacuzi 8/7/71, 3; Mpakanyi 7/1/71, 2; Tegeko 2/7/71, 9; Senyanzobe 24/9/70, 2; Delmas, Généalogies, 231.

CHAPTER 6

1. Such scissions followed no regular pattern of segmentation, but depended on such factors as the numerical size of the group, residential mobility, the emergence of a particularly wealthy or powerful member within the lineage. The occurrence of such scissions is noted by d'Hertefelt, "Le Rwanda," 41.

2. In central Rwanda, the term inzu (now commonly used to designate a branch of a lineage) formerly denoted the basic kinship unit which mediated between an individual and political authorities. Although the term inzu is known in Kinyaga and is sometimes employed in reference to smaller portions of an umuryango, it does not seem to have been limited to the more specialized meaning attached to it in central Rwanda. Moreover, Kinyagans often use umuryango to designate the group which in central Rwanda would be called inzu. On the meaning and role of inzu in central Rwanda, see d'Hertefelt, Clans, 76, fn. 3; d'Hertefelt, "Le Rwanda," 41; Alexis Kagame, Les organisations socio-familiales de l'ancien Rwanda (Brussels, 1954), 84ff. In 1935, Bourgeois found that the designation inzu was used in Kinyaga, and normally referred to a group of twelve kinsmen and their families. His account does not, however, specify any functions for this group. "Moeurs et coutumes," 133.

3. d'Hertefelt, Clans, 3; D. Newbury, "Clans of Rwanda."

4. Members of certain clans did, however, perform ritual functions on occasion. For example, members of the Abazigaaba, Abagesera, and Abasinga clans might be called upon at times of hut-building, or termination of a period of mourning. See d'Hertefelt, "Le Rwanda," 42; and d'Hertefelt, Clans, 3–7.

5. For a discussion of the multi-ethnic character of Rwandan clans, and an evaluation of our present state of knowledge on the problem, see d'Hertefelt, *Clans*, 56–62.

6. A slightly different semantic construction is presented by Bourgeois. He defines *ikinege* as an individual adult man who establishes a home, and from whom other kin groupings *(inzu, umuryango)* descend. "Moeurs et coutumes," 133.

7. For this analysis, "corporate" refers to a group with specific rules of membership (in this case, kinship ties, real or assumed) and a formalized structure of authority. "Corporate action" refers to actions of the members of the group carried out in response to directions given by the recognized head of the group. See Max Weber, *The Theory of Social and Economic Organization*, Talcott Parsons, ed. (New York, 1964), 145–146.

8. Gihura 15/6/71, 13.

9. Ruhengehenge 9/1/71, 11. For a discussion of the consolidation of lineage land through marriage alliances see Pierre B. Gravel, *Remera: A Community in Eastern Ruanda* (The Hague, 1968), 170–179.

10. An analysis of the corporate role of lineages with regard to political authorities in general and *umuheto* obligations in particular is found in M. C. Newbury, "Deux lignages."

11. As one Kinyagan noted, "Anyone who dared to disobey the lineage head risked bringing on himself the curse of the whole lineage." Majoro 19/8/70, 3. On the limited nature of the powers held by lineage heads in northwestern Rwanda, see Czekanowski, *Forschungen im Nil-Kongo*, vol. 1, 246–247.

12. Rwidegembya took over the position of his father Cyigenza after the death of the latter on Ibinja Island (c. 1893). Delmas, *Généalogies*, 39; *Historique et Chronologie*, 97.

13. Nyarugabo 10/8/70, 7.

14. Seekadegede, from whom the Abadegede descend, and Rufatabahizi, ancestor of the Abafata, were brothers, sons of Rwanteri. Many Kinyagans do not distinguish the Abafata as a separate lineage, referring to all descendants of Rwanteri as Abadegede.

15. Bakomeza 12/5/71 and 27/7/70, 2 and 27/11/70, 7; Rukemampunzi 18/5/71.

16. Ndaseezeye 21/5/71; Polisi 19/5/71; Ruvuzacyuma 29/5/71.

17. Gihura 10/7/70, 15/6/71, 22/6/71, and 25/6/71, passim.

18. Yoboka 14/7/71, 1, 3–4, 9–10, 15, and 7/7/71.

19. *Historique et chronologie*, 25; A. T. Shangugu to Résident, 1144/a/P.I./ORG., 2 October 1933. Some ten years after the imposition of German rule, Czekanowski described the "ibiletwa" (people constrained to perform *ubureetwa* service) in northwestern Rwanda as men who had received land from a chief; they were distinguished from "free farmers" who lived on land cleared by their ancestors and who had not been forced off their land by Tuutsi authorities. Czekanowski, *Forschungen im Nil-Kongo*, vol. 1, 270–271.

20. *Historique et chronologie*, 24. The terms of the decree referred to *ingabo* chiefs, which is an alternative term (more current in central regions) for what most Kinyagans refer to as *umuheto*.

21. Résident Simon to A. T. Shangugu, 1691/P. I. divers, 28 December 1934.

22. From 1939, authorization to substitute money payment for *ubureetwa* was granted to a few categories of persons, such as catechists and workers engaged on contract. *Historique et chronologie*, 29.

23. Nyirandenzi 11/6/71, 1.
24. Rurangwa 11/6/71, 1.
25. Ruvuzacyuma 29/5/71, 3.
26. Kanyarubungo Jean 18/5/71.
27. Buuda 27/5/71; Mudibiri 29/5/71.
28. Birara 19/5/71, 2.
29. At least one Kinyagan stated that such a person without kin would sometimes pay land prestations in common with one of the large lineages on the hill. This does not appear to have been the case, however, for services such as *akazi* (corvée) during the Belgian period.
30. *Ubuhake* cattle clientship, which some have portrayed as a source of protection from such spoliation was often of little help. In cases of land seizure there was no guarantee of protection by one's *ubuhake* patron, because the jurisdiction of such a patron was formally limited to the protection of a client's cattle; in fact this depended to a great extent on the power and status of the patron and on his relationship to the client. In addition, a conflict with one's *ubuhake* patron (who was frequently hill chief as well) was often the reason a person moved to a different hill. Because of these factors, patrons tended to demand more and to do less for their clients than in previous times.
31. These leaders from formerly prominent Hutu lineages were marginal men as described by Murray Edelman, "identified with two social classes or other incompatible social groupings." *The Symbolic Uses of Politics* (Urbana, 1967), 89. However, they were "marginal" in a dual sense. Although their lineages had enjoyed high status in the past, they had been relegated to subordinate positions and thus rendered marginal by changes since the final years of the nineteenth century. Secondly, these Hutu leaders were marginal in that, by working for wages, they acquired economic independence and skills which could have given them higher social status, but they found their aspirations blocked by the existing political conditions. Thus they were marginal in both a time-depth sense, (relative to their former status) and in a synchronic sense, (relative to the society in general).
32. The use of kinship terms for general status relationships has been noted by other writers on Rwanda. In eastern Rwanda, for example, Gravel found that kinship terminology was often used to express status relationships outside the group of genealogically related kin. *Remera*, 125ff.
33. Ian Linden with Jane Linden, *Church and Revolution in Rwanda* (Manchester, 1977), 164. See also Alison Des Forges, "Kings Without Crowns: The White Fathers in Ruanda," Daniel F. McCall et al., eds., *Eastern African History* (New York, 1969), 193–195.
34. Gamaliel Mbonimana, "Christianisation indirecte et cristallisation des clivages ethniques au Rwanda (1925–1931)," *Enquêtes et Documents d'Histoire Africaine* 3 (1978): 138–143. Mbonimana found evidence of discrimination against Hutu during 1928 in schools at eight of the nine missions for which he collected data. (See table 2, p. 143 of his article.)
35. Mbonimana, "Christianisation indirecte," 142, 144. See also Linden, *Church and Revolution*, 163–164.
36. Mbonimana, "Christianisation indirecte," 146–151, 154–156.

CHAPTER 7

1. Bakomeza 27/7/70, 2.
2. Nyarugabo 10/8/70, 2.

3. Bakomeza 27/11/70, 6–7.

4. "Rwabugiri ordered an inspection of cattle *(kurundisha),* and then he emptied Kinyaga [of cows] by taking with him all the cows which had managed to survive Umuryamo. . . ." Mudaage 11/1/71, 7.

5. Ndaruhuutse 1/10/70, 3.

6. Karibu 26/11/70, 2–3.

7. Mudaage 11/1/71, 7. No data are available on previous rates of exchange for such purchases, but Mudaage implied that this was an inflated price due to the scarcity of cattle.

8. This pattern is indicated also in Reisdorff, "Enquêtes foncières," 59.

9. It is not clear to what extent Bushi and Buhavu were affected by Umuryamo, but Kinyagan accounts imply that the impact was milder west of the lake than in Rwanda.

10. The king had fallen ill during an expedition against the Shi; he died in his canoe before he could reach Rwandan shores. The royal corpse was brought to Rugaragara, near Nyamirundi peninsula, and from there was transported to central Rwanda for the royal rituals of burial. The kingdom entered a period of mourning which was to last four months—a time when the population shaved their heads and refrained from cultivation with iron tools.

11. Ndaruhuutse 31/10/70, 6.

12. Bagaruka and Burumbuuke 11/2/71, 17–19; Habarugira, Habimaana, Gahima 25/8/70, 21; Karubanda 13/7/70, 2. Gato may have been accompanying Rupari (Lt. Lange) who is said to have explored the western shore of the lake as far as Rubengera. R. Ch. Bourgeois, "Premier Belge," 140–141.

13. According to Kinyagan accounts, Gato had fled to Kirehe Island where he resisted attempts by local authorities to confiscate his cattle. He met his death only after Mihigo, the king of Ijwi Island, intervened. Mihigo, having asked Mwami Musinga for permission, sent a group of armed men to kill Gato and seize his cattle (Bigirimaana 19/2/71, 6).

Ijwi versions of this incident provide a different view of the relations between the two kings, Mihigo and Musinga. Ntambuka Barhahakana, Mihigo's son and heir to the throne, explained that his father sent men to attack Gato on the express request of Musinga. The Ijwi rulers regard Kirehe Island as part of their domain, so Musinga's request for assistance from Mihigo was interpreted as a request for Gato's extradition. Other oral accounts from Ijwi point out that this affair was evidence of Rwandan recognition of Ijwi's claims on the offshore islands. Moreover, as this incident occurred in the aftermath of Rwabugiri's conquest of Ijwi, the Gato affair is interpreted as a sign that Rwanda now accepted Mihigo's restoration to the drums of Ijwi and recognized him as "legitimate" king. The Ijwi accounts also suggest that Mihigo's action indicated his magnanimity in agreeing to cooperate with Rwabugiri's son. Gato's lineage is said to have come originally from Ijwi, which may help to explain Mihigo's interest in the affair (personal communication from David Newbury).

14. Bigirimaana 19/2/71, 7.

15. During Rwabugiri's campaigns against Bushi, Seemakamba, a son of Shumbusho and brother of Mugugu (an *Umwiiru* who had supported Rutarindwa) received several hills near the Rusizi River, where he had recruited several local clients. But, like other members of his lineage Seemakamba perished at Rucunshu. Thereafter, several of his local clients forged *umuheto* links with Seekabaraga's lineage, the Abadegede (Abeega clan); others paid court to Kabaare, who was a maternal uncle of Musinga and, as we have seen, a key figure in the coup mounted by the Abakagara.

Gihura 22/6/71, 8 and 25/6/71, 4; Bishaashaari 1/12/71, 1; Gahwijima 6/1/71, 2–3; Karibu 22/12/70, 1; Seekabuhoro 22/12/70, 6.

16. On Rwabugiri's authorization his son Rutarindwa had selected several hills in Kinyaga as personal enclaves (intoore hills, from the verb gutora, to choose) and he had appointed Kanyonyomba son of Ndarwubatse, a close associate of Rwabugiri, to administer the hills. Kanyonyomba appointed Kinyagan delegates as his umuheto or ubuhake clients. But after Kanyonyomba and his son Karahamuheto died fighting for Rutarindwa at Rucunshu, the dead chief's Kinyagan hills and clients were turned over to Kayondo, a nephew of Kabaare. Included among these hills were Rango in Abiiru and Nyamugari and Shagasha in Impara. Bakomeza 27/11/70, 2, 6 and 27/11/70, 6–7; Kaamuhanda 23/12/70, 9, 19.

17. Rutiishereka son of Sentama (Abeenegitori lineage, Abanyiginya clan) was another favored client of Rwabugiri who had received hills in Kinyaga. As chief of the powerful Abashakamba social army, at Rucunshu Rutiishereka had shifted support to the Abeega when the battle began turning in their favor. But, known to be a loyal supporter of the Abahindiro, Rutiishereka met his death three years after Rucunshu, in struggles occurring in the wake of the coup. Meanwhile, one of Rutiishereka's clients in Kinyaga appropriated his patron's former clients there. This man, Ntaabwoba son of Seekarimbwa, became a "representative" of the chief who succeeded Rutiishereka as chief of the Abashakamba. However, far from central Rwanda, Ntaabwoba could escape supervision from his superior. He substantially increased umuheto prestations and abused his umuheto clients. Biseruka 9/7/71, 5–6; Habarugira, Habimaana, Gahima 25/8/70, 17; Seekimondo 4/12/70, 1–5.

18. von Beringe, "Bericht über politische Lage im Bezirk Usumbura," 15 July 1902 USU II I/D/28, cited in Louis, Ruanda-Urundi, 121. For an account of Kandt's sojourn in the Kivu area, see his Caput Nili, vol. 2 (Berlin, 1919), esp. 246ff.

19. Ndaruhuutse 1/10/70, 4.

20. Ndaruhuutse 1/10/70, 4. Other accounts which cite the cattle raids against Ijwi and Burundi include Rugerero 23/10/70, 2; and Bucuti 28/9/70, 6.

21. Bucuti 28/9/70, 6. Another Kinyagan noted that certain Rwandans who served as interpreters for the Germans also gained access to new resources in cattle. Such men received cows not from Kandt but from the population, who gave them cows to buy immunity. "They demanded things and beat people and thus they could obtain cows by this type of coercion." Rukaburacumu 10/2/71, 3.

22. Gihura 22/6/71, 2. A similar process of regionalization in umuheto clientship occurred in Rusenyi, a region neighboring Kinyaga to the north. Reisdorff found that a lineage there, the Abaganzu, abandoned their former umuheto patrons early in this century to become members of the local umuheto group, the Abazimya. "Enquêtes foncières," 60.

23. Seekimondo identifies himself as a member of the Abakoobwa and Abashambo clans. He does not use a lineage name.

24. Seekimondo 4/12/70, 2.

25. Seekimondo 4/12/70, 1–2.

26. Ndaziimanye 22/12/70, 15.

27. Gahwijima 28/11/70, 4.

28. Ndaziimanye 22/12/70, 14.

29. Booyi Paulin 23/10/70, 11. For examples from other regions of political authorities using power arbitrarily during this period see A. Pagès, "Au Rwanda, droits et pouvoirs des chefs sous la souveraineté du roi hamite; quelques abus du système,"

Zaïre 3.4 (1949): 359–377; Jean-Pierre Chrétien, "La révolte de Ndungutse (1912).
"Forces traditionneles et pression coloniale au Rwanda allemand," *Revue Française d'Histoire d'Outre-mer* 59.4 (1972): 645–680; and Czekanowski, *Forschungen im Nil-Kongo*, vol. 1, 271. Chrétien cites the excesses of Abeega chiefs in northern Rwanda as an important factor in the Ndungutse revolt of 1912 (in which local Hutu and Tuutsi rebelled against chiefs from outside). Czekanowski observed that when Hutu were asked to provide food for Europeans, the local chief usually kept a portion for himself. Food requisitions thus became another tax that benefited the chiefs.

30. Bakomeza 23/12/70, 2; Kaamuhanda 23/12/70, 2; Rufali 23/12/70, 2; Seekimondo 8/1/71, 12.

31. In Kinyaga, after short battles at Cyangugu and Mibirizi, the Germans fled to Mashyuza during the night. Kanyarubungo 6/1/71, 16; Mirambi and Gishungu 1/12/70, 4; Rufali 23/12/70, 1; Louis, *Ruanda-Urundi*, 220. "Diaire Mibirizi," 21 April 1916.

32. Initially, the Belgians divided the country into two separate administrative "zones," thus threatening the country-wide cohesion of central court influence, the major political resource of the king. In a severe blow to Musinga's power, Belgian officers initiated the policy of dealing directly with the chiefs in each of the administrative zones. In the western unit, certain chiefs maneuvered to assert their independence from Musinga; moreover, Tuutsi notables who attracted the disfavor of the Europeans were mistreated and humiliated by the occupying force. Major Declerck, "Rapport d'ensemble sur la situation de la Résidence du Ruanda et sur l'activité de l'Administration," 10 October 1918. Gouvernement Belge, Ministère des Colonies, Service des Territoires des Colonies, Dossier AE/II no. 1847, portefeuille 3288x. Archives Africaines, Brussels. (Hereafter cited as "Rapport sur la situation.") See also Des Forges, "Musiinga," 206–208.

33. For a description of the origins and widespread impact of the famine, see Des Forges, "Musiinga," 210–211.

34. Des Forges, "Musiinga," 211–213.

35. Des Forges, "Musiinga," 214–216; Declerck, "Rapport sur la situation."

36. According to Declerck, Musinga maintained that these three chiefs "who ought to have been the support of the throne, abandoned him and refused all services since they believed that Musinga would be arrested and taken to Kigali." Declerck, "Rapport sur la situation."

37. Booyi Paulin 28/10/70, 14; Bucuti 28/10/70; Rugerero 23/10/70, 2 and 30/10/70, 4; Ndarabutse and Seempiga 12/2/71, 10; Rukebeeshya and Maasomaaso 13/2/71, 5; Seemigabo, Kayirara and Gashiibonde 17/2/71, 12; Bikamba 12/10/72, 5; Rufali 27/11/70, 5–6. The dating is not certain. Two facts suggest that this opposition to Rwagataraka may have occurred during an earlier imprisonment of Rwidegembya.

First, Kinyagans say that the insurrection occurred when Rwidegembya was in jail "at Gisenyi"; Des Forges notes that in December 1916 Rwidegembya was sent to prison in "the far northwest." Des Forges, "Musiinga," 213. This would seem to rule out the 1917 imprisonment, which was in Kigali.

Second, the Diary of Mibirizi Mission (the only mission in Kinyaga at the time) makes no reference during 1917 to such an incident. It is likely that the forceful expulsion of Rwagataraka from the region would have been recorded by the missionaries. But the diary was interrupted after the Belgian conquest of Rwanda in 1916, to be resumed only in February 1917. It is, thus, possible that Ibaba occurred before the resumption of the diary, during the initial imprisonment of Rwidegembya.

In 1918, in the entry for 24–25 May, the diary refers briefly to rumors that Rwagataraka had been deposed "au moins en partie"; the entry for 26 May 1918 states that Rwagataraka returned to Cyangugu on 25 May 1918, and comments "Seekabaraka n'a pu fournir le nécessaire." It is conceivable that informants telescoped two separate events into one, linking Ibaba to Rwidegembya's imprisonment when these were in fact separate incidents. Alternatively, the diary's 1918 entry may refer to a brief resurgence of the earlier opposition.

38. Birikunkomo 8/1/71, 1; Rufali 27/11/70, 6–7, 23/12/70, 1.

39. Rugerero 30/10/70, 4; Ndarabutse and Seempiga 12/2/71, 10; Bikamba 21/10/72, 5; Birikunkomo 8/1/71, 1; Bagaruka and Burumbuuke 11/2/71, 13; Birumbi, Muyobozi, Sake 18/2/71, 11; Kampara 19/2/71, 5; Nyamajanja and Seeruhojojo 20/2/71, 10; Seemigabo, Kayirara and Gashiibonde 17/2/71, 12–13.

40. As an example, several Kinyagans cite the ad hoc "Iwawa" affair. This involved the requisition by the Belgians of cattle which were supposedly to be sent to Iwawa Island (off the northern tip of Ijwi), for reasons that are obscure. The program obviously offered possibilities for self-aggrandizement on the part of chiefs. At Nyakanyinya hill, people remember having to give one cow per lineage (Iwawa is a very small island). Yet Ndabikunze, son of Birasinyeri who was chief of Abiiru region at the time, was flogged because he did not produce sufficient cows. Seekimondo 8/1/71, 12.

41. The administration conveniently (but mistakenly) viewed such work as "prestations dues aux chefs par leurs indigènes." "Questionnaire 1929, Kamembe," 14.

42. Résident Coubeau to all Délégués (Territorial Administrators), Kigali, 1966/Org. 5, 5 April 1926.

43. P. Dryvers, "Politique et justice," statement submitted on 25 November 1932 by the Territorial Administrator at Kamembe.

44. Booyi Paulin 28/10/70, 16.

45. Rusangwa 13/1/71, 7. Reference to a chief's having people "killed" in such contexts is usually figurative rather than literal.

46. Nyamujanja and Seeruhojojo 20/2/71, 7.

47. Booyi Paulin 28/10/70, 17.

48. In 1926, a measure was introduced providing that no new *ibikingi* could be granted and that when existing ones became vacant through decease of the occupant or for some other reason the domain would be placed under control of the hill chief. *Rapport sur l'administration du R-U* (1926), 67. This policy was later (from 1929) extended into outright abolition of all *ibikingi*.

49. For example, during the reign of Musinga, an Ndugan chief was appointed to administer Gashirabwoba hill in Kinyaga. Yeeze, lineage head of the influential Abarundi lineage, a man who had formerly also acted as hill chief of Gashirabwoba, found his position threatened by the Ndugan who set about trying to take over the *igikingi* of the Abarundi. Byumva 19/6/71, 2.

50. The Abacuura at Bumazi had their *igikingi* taken away from them while Bisanana was subchief on the hill, during the reign of Rudahigwa. The lineage was allowed to keep only a banana grove and some fields for planting crops. People who came to ask Bisanana for land would settle on the Abacuura's former *igikingi*. Birimwiyundo 18/6/71, 1.

Makwaruza cites several lineages deprived of their *igikingi* during the time when Rwagataraka was chief, 18/6/71, 2. Much depended on the discretion of the local hill chief, however. Some lineages retained sufficient land for the agricultural and pastoral needs of the lineage members and even, in certain cases, land occupied by land clients of the lineage.

51. CINAM, *Etude du développement,* vol. 2, Carte 17, based on "Rapports de Commissions Préfectorales," 1969.

52. Maquet, *Relations sociales,* 161, 173.

53. Nkundiye 28/9/70, 5.

54. Gravel also found this practice in eastern Rwanda. *Remera,* 165, 168. Among Kinyagan informants this was best described by Kampara 19/2/71, 10. The *umurundo* of the potential client's cattle would occur first, and the prospective patron would take one cow; only then would he give the client a cow.

55. Saucier, "Patron-Client Relationship," passim, and esp. 73, 88.

56. See Vidal, "Rwanda des anthropologues"; and Rwabukumba and Mudandagizi, "Les formes historiques de la dépendance."

57. Such was the experience of Bucuti 28/9/70, 2, and several others whom he mentions.

58. On the symbolic importance of repairing the enclosure *(kubaka inkiike),* see Gravel, *Remera,* 164.

59. As Gravel has demonstrated, the cow was the proof or "token" attesting to the existence of a relationship. Pierre B. Gravel, "The Transfer of Cows in Gisaka (Rwanda): A Mechanism for Recording Social Relationships," *American Anthropologist* 69.3–4 (1967): 322–331.

60. Kagame states that cows a client might receive as bridewealth for his sisters or daughters would be considered as cows belonging to the *ubuhake* patron. *Institutions politiques,* 42. Whatever the "legality" of such a practice, Kinyagans found it unfair and resented the loss of personal ownership over cattle. In fact, the reach of an *ubuhake* patron normally tended to encompass all cattle in possession of the client, no matter how the cattle had been obtained. The question was one of power, not of legality, and the client was relatively powerless in the matter.

Maquet noted a tendency of patrons to take over at least some of the personal cattle of their clients, should the *ubuhake* bond be terminated. Maquet, *Relations sociales,* 156.

61. Kaamuhanda 27/11/70, 6.

62. Birimwiyundo 18/6/71, 3.

63. Kampara 19/2/71, 9.

64. Gafaranga 16/6/71, 1–2; Yoboka 14/7/71, 12; Burumbuuke 13/7/71, 6; Bizimaana 13/2/71, 13.

65. Booyi Paulin 28/10/70, 10–11.

66. Karamira 17/6/71, 6.

67. Karihanze 1/6/71, 1.

68. Kanyamasovu 19/6/71, 2.

69. Mudaage 10/12/70, 8.

70. Munda 30/9/70, 4–5.

71. *Rapport sur l'administration du R-U* (1937), 72.

72. *Rapport sur l'administration du R-U* (1938), 77.

73. Pagès, "Droits et pouvoirs," 372.

74. Pagès, "Droits et pouvoirs," 377.

75. Rwabukumba and Mudandagizi, "Les formes historiques de la dépendance," 21. See also M. Catharine Newbury, "Ubureetwa and Thangata: Catalysts to Peasant

Political Consciousness in Rwanda and Malawi," *Canadian Journal of African Studies* 14.1 (1980): 97–112.

76. *Historique et Chronologie*, 27.

77. *Historique et Chronologie*, 26.

78. R. Bourgeois, *Témoignages* (Tervuren, 1982), 61. Bourgeois discusses other exactions imposed by chiefs as well (cf. pp. 66–70). I am emphasizing those noted most frequently by informants.

79. Bourgeois, *Témoignages*, 64.

80. Rwabukumba and Mudandagizi, "Les formes historiques," 24.

81. See R. Spitaels, "Transplantation des BanyaRuanda dans le Nord-Kivu," *Problèmes d'Afrique Centrale* 6.2 (1953): 110–116; and J. Kajiga, "Cette immigration séculaire des ruandais au Congo," *Bulletin trimestriel du Centre d'Etude des Problèmes Sociaux Indigenes* 32 (1956): 6–65. Some years earlier, a similar project had been devised for Katanga, in the copper mining area of southern Zaïre. Union Minière had proposed a project to provide agricultural plots to former mineworkers from Rwanda and Burundi, so that they would remain in the region and produce food for sale to the mining compounds. The social organization of these resettlement projects was planned in detail, even to the point of specifying that Tuutsi chiefs would be designated, and supplied with cattle and other resources so that they would not be obliged to engage in agricultural labor themselves. The project was never implemented. (Jean-Luc Vellut collection of documents on Zaïre, Memorial Library, University of Wisconsin, Madison).

82. Resident to all A.T.'s, No. 1252 AIMO, 6 May 1938. Hutu were particularly urged to emigrate, but initially Tuutsi were accepted as emigrants as well. Among the advantages cited in the Resident's letter were:

1. Abundant fertile land; same crops as in Ruanda but with a much higher yield.
2. Excellent pastures which remain green even during the dry season.
3. Presence in the region of 730 Banyaruanda families who are ready to help them get settled.
4. Gishari constitutes a province commanded by the munyaruanda chief Joseph Bideri; no interference possible by Bahunde chiefs.
5. Complete exemption from all taxes and all corvée for two years; then for 4 years, reduced tax.
6. Absolute freedom to return to Ruanda when they wish, for the Banyaruanda who go to Gishari do not cease being men of the Mwami.
7. The Banyaruanda of Gishari are commanded by a former Administrateur of Ruanda, Mr. Colinet, who is well acquainted with the culture and customs of Banyaruanda.
8. The Bahutu who are linked by a contract of ubugaragu, can obtain the withdrawal of this contract and leave with their personally owned cattle. . . .

83. Karihanze 1/6/71, 2. The arbitrary fashion in which recruitment was carried out drew the notice of Catholic missionaries at Nyamasheke Mission. Their report confirms the evidence from Kinyagans' accounts that local people were reluctant to emigrate to Gishari. ("Diaire Nyamasheke," 11 October and 1 December 1940). As noted, the Rwandan chiefs responsible for selecting emigrants treated this as a way of exiling opponents and of claiming additional land. The several hundred thousand emigrants were settled in an area of Hunde population. Today these emigrants and their offspring form 85 percent and more of the population of some localities. Al-

though they have lived there for some fifty years, they have not been granted full
Zaïrean citizenship; relations between Hunde and Rwandans remain strained. See
Bucyalimwe Mararo, "Une rationalisation? Les migrations rwandaises au Kivu,
Zaïre," Bogumil Jewsiewicki and Jean-Pierre Chrétien, eds., *Ambiguités de l'inno-
vation. Sociétés rurales et technologies en Afrique Centrale et occidentale au
XXème siècle* (Québec, 1984), 39–54.

84. Ndaruhuutse 1/10/70, 8–9. A salary scale introduced in 1945 provided that
chiefs with up to 3000 taxpayers in their chiefdom would receive a 1000 FR monthly
salary; for each 1000 taxpayers beyond 3000, 100 FR was added to this salary. In
addition, a chief was to receive 1 FR per year for each taxpayer as payment for
"prestations coutumières en vivres" and 0.50 FR for each tax on cattle collected in
his chiefdom during the year. For each taxpayer who made a money payment in lieu
of doing *ubureetwa* service ("rachat de la prestation *ubuletwa*"), the chief received
4.50 FR. Thus, as noted by *Servir*, a chief administering a chiefdom of some 10,000
taxpayers with 10,000 cattle, and assuming that 2000 people made a money payment
for *ubureetwa*, could earn approximately 44,400 FR in one year.

The monthly salary of a subchief consisted of 350 FR for subchiefs administering
200 taxpayers or less; the amount increased by 10 FR for each 100 taxpayers in excess
of 200. To this fixed monthly salary was added an annual payment to the subchief
of 3 FR for each taxpayer as "rachat des prestations coutumières en vivres" and 3 FR
for each head tax collected in the subchiefdom during the year. *Servir* estimated that
a subchief with 500 taxpayers under his jurisdiction, of whom 200 made a money
payment for *ubureetwa* (amounting to 15 FR per person) could earn some 10,560 FR
annually. "Note sur les traitements," *Servir* 5.6 (1944): 291–293.

Aside from the stated salary, a chief received income from his *inyarulembo* (a
subchiefdom under direct control of the chief, from which he received the revenues
that would normally have gone to a subchief) and from such enterprises as cattle-
raising, reforestation plots, and coffee. With the exception of *inyarulembo*, many
subchiefs had access to similar resources on a smaller scale. The remuneration of
chiefs and subchiefs was quite generous in light of the fact that in 1948 the salary
of laborers in Kinyaga was not more than 3.50 FR per day. Territoire de Shangugu,
"Estimation des Ressources des Indigènes pour l'année 1948." The stated goal of
raising the chief's salaries in 1945 was to encourage them to "abandonner toute
velleité de pressurer leurs administrés." "Note sur les traitements," 293.

85. "Bon nombre d'indigènes ont émigré vers le territoire d'Uvira, au Congo Belge.
Cet exode s'explique par le développement constant de la population et du cheptel
et la nécessité de rechercher de nouveaux pâturages." *Rapport sur l'administration
du R-U* (1939–1949), 37–38.

86. In 1938 the Administration commented that "to attempt to eliminate this
institution under pressure of a more or less liberal ideology, would be dangerous for
the peace and future of the Territory." *Rapport sur l'administration du R-U* (1938),
72.

87. Gouvernement Belge, Ministère des Colonies, *Plan décennal pour le développement économique et social du Ruanda-Urundi* (Brussels, 1951), 400.

88. See J. Vanhove, "Une réforme d'importance au Ruanda: la suppression du bail
à cheptel," *Journal des Tribunaux d'Outre-Mer* 10 (1954): 97–98; and Arrêté No. 1/
54 du 1er avril 1954, modifié par ceux du 3 août 1954 et du 1er février 1956. For text
of the edict, see R. Bourgeois, *Banyarwanda et Barundi: l'évolution du contrat de
bail à cheptel au Ruanda-Urundi* (Brussels, 1958), 19–22.

89. In a meeting of Tuutsi notables with *Umwami* Rudahigwa called to discuss *ubuhake*, one of the prominent central chiefs stated that *"Ubugaragu [ubuhake] as it is practiced in Rwanda is a type of mitigated slavery; so how is it possible that [such] an institution which reflects a characteristic of slavery continues to exist?"* R. Bourgeois, *Evolution du contrat de bail*, 13.

90. R. Bourgeois, *Evolution du contrat de bail*, 13, 19–22.

91. Previously, beginning in 1939, money payment in lieu of *ubureetwa* work had been permitted for certain categories of people and in 1945, the option of paying money for *ubureetwa* instead of performing services was officially extended to the entire population. See Décision du Gouverneur du Territoire du Ruanda-Urundi, Usumbura, 23 December 1948; *Historique et chronologie*, 29; "Note sur les traitements," 292.

92. This is attested to in detail by Seekimondo 8/1/71, 8.

93. See "Ingoyi y'ubuhake iracitse, dusubizwe inyuma ni y'ubutaka?" (Ubuhake is ended; should we then retrogress because of land?) in *Kinyamateka*, 1 February 1959; and "Nyirukugorerwa ibikingi yagororewe yakoze idi abandi batakoze?" (What has the owner of ibikingi done [to deserve] more than others?), *Kinyamateka*, 15 February 1959.

CHAPTER 8

1. Chrétien, Jean-Pierre, "Une révolte au Burundi en 1934," *Annales: Economies, Sociétés, Civilisations* 25.6 (1970): 1678–1717, esp. 1692.

2. *Rapport sur l'Administration du R-U* (1923), 5.

3. *Rapport sur l'Administration du R-U* (1923), 20.

4. The men were hired for contracts of 180 workdays; they were to be paid 1.50 francs per day net; the employer was to pay their capitation tax, and food and equipment were to be supplied to them free of charge. *Rapport sur l'Administration du R-U* (1925), 85–86.

5. O. Hakiba Buki, "Contribution à l'étude historique de l'importation de la main d'oeuvre du Ruanda-Urundi à l'UMHK (1926–1973)," (Mémoire de Licence, UNAZA, Lubumbashi, 1974). [Henceforth Hakiba, "Main d'ouevre," 95–96.]

6. A missionary in one of these areas reported that "we are told that starving people supposedly fall down on the roads, that birds of prey and dogs devour those who starved to death." "Diaire Kanyinya," 25 January 1922, cited in Roger Botte, "Rwanda and Burundi, 1889–1930: Chronology of a Slow Assassination," *International Journal of African Historical Studies* 18.1/2 (1985): 308.

7. Botte, "Rwanda and Burundi."

8. *Rapport sur l'Administration du R-U* (1925), 103.

9. The program was announced in a message sent to all administrators by Governor Voisin in September 1930. See Voisin, "Idées conductrices de la politique générale à suivre dans le Ruanda-Urundi," Usumbura, 25 September 1930. It should be noted, however, that imposed compulsory cultivation had been authorized earlier, in Ordonnance-Loi No. 52 of 7 November 1924. This was implemented in Rwanda at the end of 1926 when the Resident of Ruanda issued an edict ("règlement") requiring each able-bodied male cultivator in the country to plant and maintain 19 ares of manioc or sweet potatoes in addition to his other fields. (An are is equal to 100 m² or 1/100 of a hectare; a hectare is slightly less than 2.5 acres.) New land was to be made available for this purpose by draining marshes and through the appropriation

of pasture from Tuutsi. B. Habimana and J. P. Harroy, "Instauration et abrogation des cultures vivrières obligatoires au Rwanda," *Civilisations* 20.3/4 (1980): 179; Kagame, *Abrégé*, vol. 2, 199–200; Paternostre de la Mairieu, *Rwanda*, 130; more generally, see J. L. Vellut, "La misère rurale dans l'expérience coloniale du Zaïre, du Rwanda, et du Burundi" (paper presented at the 26th Annual Meeting of the African Studies Association, Boston, December 1983).

10. Copper production from Katanga comprised 50 percent of the Congo's exports in 1929. With the fall in world demand and the sharp drop in the price of copper (from 14 francs per kilo in 1928 to 4 francs in 1934) the mines cut back production drastically; Katanga mines produced 140,000 tons of copper in 1929 but only 54,000 tons in 1932. The mines laid off more than 100,000 workers; only about 20,000 of these were able to find alternate work on plantations. P. Merlier, *Le Congo de la colonisation belge à l'indépendance* (Paris, 1962), 142. See also B. Jewsiewicki, "The Great Depression and the Making of the Colonial Economic System in the Belgian Congo," *African Economic History* 4 (Fall 1977): 153–176; and Jewsiewicki, "African Peasants in the Totalitarian Colonial Society of the Belgian Congo," Martin A. Klein, ed., *Peasants in Africa* (Beverly Hills, 1980), 45–75.

11. E. LePlae, for many years the Director-General of Agriculture at Belgium's Ministry of Colonies, was responsible for the initial legislation (1917) authorizing obligatory cultivation in the Congo. He defined compulsory crops as "those which are imposed on natives by their Government, but the product of which belongs to those natives who consume them and sell them exclusively for their own profit." E. LePlae, "Les cultures obligatoires dans les pays d'agriculture arriérée," *Bulletin Agricole du Congo Belge* 18 (1927), 449. The "profit" derived from sale of such products was to provide income from which rural people would pay taxes to the colonial state. See Bogumil Jewsiewicki, "Notes sur l'histoire socio-économique du Congo," *Etudes d'Histoire Africaine* 3 (1972): 209–241.

12. For a discussion of this debate, see Roger Anstey, *King Leopold's Legacy* (Oxford, 1966), 82–84.

13. See O. Louwers, *Le Problème financier et le problème économique au Congo belge en 1932* (Brussels, 1933), 50–56.

14. G. Hostelet, *L'Oeuvre civilisatrice de la Belgique au Congo de 1885 à 1953,* vol. 1 (Brussels, 1954), 267–269, cited in Anstey, *King Leopold's Legacy*, 83; Merlier, *Le Congo,* 137ff.; Territoire [Zone] de Walikale, Zaïre, *Rapports Agricoles*, 1930s–1950s.

15. Merlier, *Le Congo,* 143; cf. also Jewsiewicki, "Great Depression," 160: "In general the colonial administration put as much of the burden of the Great Depression as possible on the 'traditional' rural societies. The price of agricultural products dropped abruptly while compulsory cultivation and taxes increased and the monopoly power of large trading companies expanded."

16. *Historique et Chronologie,* 25–26.

17. Of the 69 chiefs in the country, 53 were Catholics; of 900 subchiefs, 725 were Catholic, and 24 were Protestant or Adventist; the rest were non-Christian. During that year (1935), 28 chiefs were removed from office for "inefficiency" and replaced. This, as well as conversions, was undoubtedly a factor in the increase in the number of Catholic chiefs in 1936 to 54, and of subchiefs to 756. The number of Protestant or Adventist subchiefs increased to 25. (de Lacger, *Le Ruanda,* 557). From 1927 there had been a massive conversion of Tuutsi to the Catholic Church; in previous years Tuutsi had retained a strong reserve toward the Catholics. For an analysis of reasons

for this shift, see Linden, *Church and Revolution*, ch. 7; Mbonimana, "Christianisation indirecte."

18. Kagame, *Abrégé*, vol. 2, 199–200.

19. *Historique et Chronologie;* de Lacger, *Le Ruanda;* Kagame, *Abrégé,* vol. 2, 199. Bourgeois found that in 1932–1933 some subchiefs in Kinyaga made their people pay much more than the legally specified amount for such payments. See his *Témoignages,* 70.

20. Paternostre de la Mairieu, *Le Rwanda,* 132.

21. For an analysis of these trends, see Chrétien, "Révolte au Burundi," 1691–1693; Learthen Dorsey, "The Rwandan Colonial Economy, 1916–1941," (Diss., Michigan State University, 1983), 178.

22. de Lacger, *Le Ruanda,* 580–581.

23. Lemarchand, *Rwanda and Burundi,* 122.

24. Paternostre de la Mairieu, *Le Rwanda,* 132.

25. Memorandum of Protestant Alliance, 24 April 1944, cited in Linden, *Church and Revolution,* 206. Compare also two accounts collected by Dorsey from Butare Prefecture (in southern Rwanda): "We grew their coffee, planted their forests and built their roads without pay"; and "The Belgians joined force with the Batutsi, so we were powerless to revolt. Besides we were accustomed to forced labor and planting coffee was the same as all others." Dorsey, "Rwandan Colonial Economy," 217, 222.

26. Kagame, *Abrégé,* vol. 2, 205. Kagame is referring here to the use of the term *akazi* (literally, "work," derived from the Kiswahili word *"kazi"*) to refer to colonial forms of corvée.

27. Kagame, *Abrégé,* vol. 2, 206; see also Jean-Pierre Chrétien, "Des sédentaires devenus migrants: les motifs des départs des Barundi et des Banyarwanda vers l'Uganda (1920–1960)," *Cultures et Développement* 10.1 (1978): 71–101.

28. Kagame, *Abrégé,* vol. 2, 206–208.

29. Kagame, *Abrégé,* vol. 2, 207.

30. Linden, *Church and Revolution,* 207. For comparable conditions in the Congo, see Gilbert, *L'Empire du silence* (Brussels, 1947), 23–29, cited in Young, *Politics in the Congo,* 223: "In one place the food situation is becoming aggravated to the point of threatening famine; in another, the villages are disintegrating; elsewhere there is depopulation. The native populations have been deeply troubled by an ill-considered war effort and this has been singularly aggravated by the agitation amongst the whites."

31. Harroy and Habimana, "Cultures vivrières obligatoires," 179–180; Paternostre de la Mairieu, *Le Rwanda,* 175. For an explanation of "are," see note 9.

32. *Rapport sur l'Administration du R-U* (1929), 124.

33. "Questionnaire 1929, Kamembe," 14–15.

34. Delmas, "Station de Mibirizi-Nyamesheke," (typescript, 25 January 1929), Archives of the Société des Missionnaires d'Afrique, Rome.

35. Kalemaza, Kavuha, "Le développement de l'agriculture au Kivu colonial, 1903–1948," (Mémoire de Licence, UNAZA, Lubumbashi, 1973), 32.

36. Kalemaza, "Agriculture au Kivu," 56.

37. Delmas, "Mibirizi-Nyamasheke."

38. Kalemaza, "Agriculture au Kivu," 43.

39. Kalemaza, "Agriculture au Kivu," 61. On colonial labor policies and conditions of workers in Kivu, see Jean-Luc Vellut, comp., "Enquêtes sur la main-d'oeuvre au Kivu (1930)," *Enquêtes et Documents d'Histoire Africaine* 3 (1978): 30–38;

C. Bashizi, "Processus de domination socio-économique et marché de travail au Bushi (1920–1945)," *Enquêtes et Documents d'Histoire Africaine* 3 (1978): 1–29; Bishikwabo Chubaka, "Un aspect du colonat au Congo belge: le sort des travailleurs du Kivu (1900–1940)," *Genève-Afrique* 16.1 (1977–1978): 25–44.

40. To reduce administrative outlays, Kibuye Territory was divided among its three neighboring Territories as of January 1, 1936; the northern part was attached to Gisenyi, the eastern part to Nyanza, and the southern part (Rusenyi chiefdom) to Cyangugu. Kibuye Territory was reestablished in February 1953, at which time Rusenyi was again separated from Cyangugu. (*Historique et Chronologie*, 115.) Most of the Europeans in the area settled south of the Kilimbi River in Kinyaga proper. Thus although the figures include Rusenyi, only a small percentage of the settlers and land area conceded to them were located in that province.

41. Territoire de Shangugu, "Enterprises agricoles des non-indigènes, énumeration des entreprises et superficies," in "Rapport annuel agricole," 1946. Relève des concessions agricoles accordées au 31 decembre 1948," in Territoire de Shangugu, "Rapport Annuel Agricole," 1948, annexe submitted on 3 March 1949.

42. The best sources for such statistics are the annual reports submitted to Kigali by the Territorial Administrator at Cyangugu ("Rapport Annuel AIMO"); however, only a few of these reports were to be found in the cellar of Cyangugu Prefecture, where colonial documents from the region are stored. I was also unable to locate these reports in archives in Kigali.

43. For a description of the motivations behind the UMHK recruitment and the manner in which it was carried out, see Bruce Fetter, "L'Union Minière du Haut-Katanga, 1920–1940: La naissance d'une sous-culture totalitaire," *Cahiers du CEDAF* 6 (1973): esp. 12–20; Hakiba, "Main d'oeuvre," 63ff. The early recruitment in Ruanda-Urundi ended partly as a result of pressure from the League of Nations, but also because the desired quota of workers had been obtained. Recruitment was resumed for approximately a ten year period during 1949–1958. Hakiba, "Main-d'oeuvre," 10, 96, 112, 128.

44. Hakiba, "Main-d'oeuvre," 12–15, 95–96. Other areas located in Zone IV, the area of heaviest recruitment, included Rubengera, Gisenyi, Ruhengeri, and Kabaya Territories, and parts of Kigali, Gatsibo, and Rukira Territories.

45. On the early years of Bukavu's urban growth, see Pilipili Kagabo, "Contribution à la connaissance des origines du centre de Bukavu (Kivu) de 1870 à 1935," (Mémoire de Licence, UNAZA, Lubumbashi, 1973).

46. In 1934, there were at least 83 Europeans with enterprises centered in Bukavu and adjoining areas, of which 50 were engaged in agricultural activities ("colons agricoles"); and 7 were classified as "colons commerçants," 8 as "commerçants seulement," 5 as "colons industriels," 7 as "exerçant profession libérale," and 5 as "colons artisans." Most of those in the latter five categories were located in Bukavu proper. "Province de Costermansville, Liste des colons installés à la date du 8 mai 1934," *Congo* 1.1 (January 1935): 118–127.

47. *Rapport sur l'Administration du R-U* (1938), 76.

48. *Rapport sur l'Administration du R-U* (1939–1944), 38.

49. C. Bourgeois, Administrateur du Territoire, Procès-Verbal de la Réunion Plenière des autorités indigènes, Territoire de Shangugu, 31 octobre 1946.

50. *Rapport sur l'Administration du R-U* (1947), 61.

51. Territoire de Shangugu, "Rapport Annuel AIMO," 1952, 1.

52. Territoire de Shangugu, "Estimation des ressources des indigènes pour les

années 1948, 1958"; Territoire de Shangugu, "Rapport Annuel AIMO," 1945, 19. The *Rapport sur l'Administration du R-U* (1959), 192 provided combined figures for all of Rwanda on "spontaneous emigration" and "emigration through recruitment" as follows:

1949	10,992
1952	14,013
1953	3,851
1955	2,715
1958	1,013

The larger figures for 1949 and 1952 may have resulted from recruitment of workers for three-year contracts in those years.

53. Territoire de Shangugu, "Rapport Annuel AIMO," 1952, 38/1.

54. The size of the Kinyaga work force in Bukavu was substantial enough that plans had been prepared to construct housing for Africans on Mururu hill, located in Rwanda alongside the Rusizi River directly opposite Bukavu. (Personal communication from Jan Fransen.)

55. Résident to A.T. Shangugu, 2119/MOI, 19 December 1945; A.T. Shangugu to Résident 1323/MOI, 28 December 1945.

56. During a 1942 campaign to collect contributions for the war effort in Europe, it was estimated that every adult male in Cyesha chiefdom had been contacted— and this informal census yielded a figure of only 3050 men. "Quelques notes pour le Mwami du Ruanda à l'occasion de son passage au Kinyaga le 26 avril 1942," (typescript) [hereafter cited as "Quelques notes pour le Mwami"], Archives of the Société des Missionnaires d'Afrique, Rome.

57. For example, the annual report for 1954 noted that in Abiiru Chiefdom (bordering the Rusizi River), "chefs et sous-chefs rencontrent de grosses difficultés du fait de la proximité de Bukavu. Une bonne partie des HAV [hommes adultes valides] sont employés à Bukavu ou sur les chantiers de la RUVIR." Territoire de Shangugu, "Rapport Annuel AIMO," 1954, 9 ter.

58. Résident to A.T. Shangugu, 1316/AIMO, 4 June 1940.

59. A.T. Shangugu to three subordinates, 22/AIMO/Route, 19 April 1938.

60. Heus to A.T. Costermansville, 20 November 1947.

61. "As there is a shortage of labor in Costermansville, I would much appreciate it if you could send us 25 auxiliary workers by June 1." A.T. Costermansville to A.T. Shangugu, 379/A.O., 12 May 1947.

62. Agent Principal Territorial Shangugu to Chef Biniga, 25 November 1947. The chief was instructed to send 25 workmen accompanied by an "intelligent leader" to Bukavu the next morning.

63. Gouverneur du Kivu to A.T. Shangugu, 6515/Cab., 11 December 1947.

64. Agent Principal Territorial Shangugu to Chef Biniga, 18 December 1947.

65. In 1922, such sanctions involved from four to 12 lashes, or hard labor for one to 14 days. *Rapport sur l'administration du R-U* (1922), 22.

66. "Questionnaire 1929, Kamembe," 14.

67. "Notice sur le Ruanda," (typescript, with the handwritten addition "redigé en 1916 par un missionnaire du Ruanda pour servir aux troupes Belges"), in Gouvernement Belge, Ministère des Colonies, Service des Territoires des Colonies, Dossier AE/II, No. 1847, portefeuille 3288 (Archives Africaines, Brussels); Résident Coubeau to all delegates, 1966/Org., 5 April 1930.

68. Seemigabo, Kayirara, Gashiibonde 17/2/71, 78.

69. Circulaire du Résident Simon, 79/AIMO, 26 November 1934.

70. Direction Générale, Service MOI du Symétain to A.T. Shangugu, 14 December 1937.

71. Rycx to A.T. Shangugu, 23 July 1947.

72. A.T. Shangugu to three subordinates, 19 April 1938. In 1940 the Territorial Administrator at Cyangugu recommended a policy of deposing chiefs or subchiefs who required *ubureetwa* services from the wives or children of salaried workers who had made a money payment for exemption from such services. A.T. Shangugu to Résident, 555/AIMO, 3 April 1940.

73. de Lacger, *Le Ruanda,* 557; Kagame, *Abrégé,* vol. 2, 204.

74. A.T. Shangugu to Résident, 1412/AI, 31 October 1946.

75. Résident to A.T. Shangugu, 2193/AI, 22 November 1946.

76. *Rapport sur l'administration du R-U* (1921), 87.

77. The Administration was aware of this tendency but hoped to change the chiefs through education. A letter from the Resident in 1929 warned that

> We must ensure for workers an absolute respect of their [private] property, particularly with regard to land and cattle which they have been able to acquire through their work. . . . In allowing ownership rights over such wealth created outside their control to pass into the hands of batutsi chiefs or other notables, without their having contributed even a land concession or a cow as genitor, the [colonial] authority would in reality render itself accomplice to an usurpation, which neither customary practices nor tradition can justify. . . . If the native does not yet have a clear awareness regarding these juridical notions, it is up to us to educate him on this point, correcting his errors and shaping his mentality with patience and perseverance. (Résident to all Délégués, 5 October 1929.)

78. Pagès believed that by the late 1940s most abuses had been eradicated. However, his portrayal of chiefly avarice and arbitrariness in earlier periods would tend to cast doubt on his optimistic conclusions for the later period, since the conditions of power inequality giving rise to the earlier abuses had persisted. (See Pagès, "Droits et pouvoirs des chefs," passim.) Data cited in a study by Audrey Richards confirm the continued salience of such abuses. She points out that "beatings or other punishments" were cited as a reason for migrating by a number of labor migrants to Uganda interviewed in 1951 for her study. One man had returned to Rwanda three times (in 1938, 1941, and 1944) hoping to find that the beatings had ended; each time he was disappointed and left again for Uganda. Audrey Richards, *Economic Development and Tribal Change: A Study of Immigrant Labour in Buganda* (Cambridge, 1956), 70–71.

When Jean-Paul Harroy arrived in 1955, as newly appointed Vice Governor-General of Ruanda-Urundi, he observed a variety of exploitative (illegal) practices by the chiefs. See his *Rwanda: De la féodalité à la démocratie, 1955–1962* (Brussels, 1984), esp. ch. 4.

79. Dryvers, "Politique et justice."

80. In 1938, for example, Kinyagans furnished 250 tons of food to the Nyungwe center, *Rapport sur l'administration du R-U* (1938), 76.

81. Territoire de Shangugu, "Avis et considérations de l'Administrateur Territorial de Shangugu quant à l'établissement des prévisions des ressources des indigènes de son Territoire pour l'année 1943," 16 September 1942.

82. "Prévisions des ressources des indigènes pour 1943."

83. *Rapport sur l'administration du R-U* (1920), 22.

84. A commercial "crisis" during 1921 had resulted in a lack of buyers for local products such as food and hides; several trading establishments of Asians and Arabs had closed down that year. See *Rapport sur l'administration du R-U* (1921), 25, 33. Reduced rural incomes made it more difficult for people to pay the head tax, as reflected in a substantial decline in tax revenues (by almost 50%); hence the administration's decision to reduce the tax in 1922. *Rapport sur l'administration du R-U* (1922), 9, 18.

85. *Rapport sur l'administration du R-U* (1926), 19; (1927), 18.

86. *Rapport sur l'administration du R-U* (1920), 22; (1921), 33; (1926), 19; (1927), 18.

87. Chef du Secrétariat du Ruanda-Urundi Straunard, communicating Ordonnance du Gouverneur du Ruanda-Urundi, 22/Fin., 13 January 1940.

88. Territoire de Shangugu, "Avis et considérations de l'A.T. concernant les taux Impôts Indigènes proposés pour l'exercice 1944," 14 October 1943; and Ordonnance No. 65/AIMO, Gouverneur du Ruanda-Urundi, 2 December 1946.

89. Gouverneur du Ruanda-Urundi Simon, 1044/A.I./Imp. Ind., 26 February 1947.

90. *Rapport sur l'administration du Ruanda-Urundi* (1947), 61.

91. Telegram No. 33323/ r v t No. 194817, AIMO, Usumbura; Usumbura, Ord. No. 21/155, 1 December 1949, "fixant les taux de l'impôt de capitation et de polygamie pour l'exercice 1950."

92. The following information on labor recruitment and working conditions in Cyesha during 1942 is from "Quelques notes pour le Mwami."

93. See note 56 above.

94. "Questionnaire 1929, Kamembe," 14.

95. "Quelques notes pour le Mwami." In 1940, the Nyamasheke Diary records the unsuccessful efforts of a missionary to convince the Belgian Territorial Administrator from Cyangugu that the demands being made on the population in the domain of obligatory crops were excessive. The Catholic Father argued that given the depleted manpower of the region, the high demands for workers, and the poor local soil (not at all fit for the cultivation of potatoes, one of the required crops), the people of Cyesha were doing the best they could. The Administrator demonstrated a singular lack of understanding, viewing the population as lazy and the local chief as incompetent. "Diaire Nyamasheke," 10 December 1940.

96. *Rapport sur l'administration du R-U* (1947), 61.

97. Mudaage (10/12/70, 5), for example, claimed that large numbers of men left the Bugarama region to escape prestations demanded by Gisazi, the chief there; some went to Ijwi and Maramba, others went to Kamituga. Another person noted that people preferred to have wage work because those who did not have such work had to cultivate sweet potatoes, plant trees, and maintain the roads (without pay). Sagatwa 11/12/70, 5.

For people living in the eastern and central areas of Rwanda, both the exactions of the chiefs and economic hardship were key reasons for migrating to Uganda in search of work. Rwandan migrants interviewed in 1951 for Richards' study made the following types of comments to explain why they decided to leave home:

The people in Rwanda work all day long and the money they earn makes no difference because they go half-naked still.

In Nyanza the food is short and people are poor.

I left because in Ruanda a man and his wife have to work from early morning till late at night for his chief.

Ordinary men work for their chiefs and when they have nothing to wear, they leave their country to look for money.

Commenting on the situation in Rwanda, Richards notes that "it appears that women have separate gardens from their husbands and may also be asked to grow compulsory crops on them, and that women as well as men are liable to communal cultivation." Richards, *Economic Development*, 68–70.

Autobiographies of Hutu women recorded by Helen Codere also evoke the hardships suffered by wives left behind when their husbands migrated. Nyiramasuka, for example, recalled that "my husband had no employment. We lived solely by cultivating. . . . We lived together the first three years we were married, then, because the Hutu were meanly treated by the Tuutsi sous-chefs and were forced to do corvées, my husband decided to go to Uganda. He left me and our one child. He died and never returned to Rwanda." Helen Codere, *The Biography of an African Society: Rwanda 1900–1960* (Tervuren, 1973), 257.

98. Kampara 19/2/71, 8.

99. Rurangwa 11/6/71, 2. One of Rurangwa's fellow migrants had previously worked for Protanag as foreman of a work crew. When Protanag closed down during the Depression, he worked for several years inspecting coffee plants, until 1937 when he left for Lubumbashi. Rukezambuga 12/6/71.

100. Karamira 17/6/71, 5–6.

101. Birumbi, Muyobozi, Sake 18/2/71, 3.

102. Fashaho and Rwamiheto 12/2/71, 3–4.

103. See Codere, *Biography of an African Society*, and the material cited from Richards, *Economic Development*, in notes 78 and 97 above. See also Dorsey, "Rwandan Colonial Economy," 5–8, and ch. 6. Dorsey stresses the importance of the spread of coffee cultivation in these transformations.

CHAPTER 9

1. Eric Wolf, *Peasant Wars of the Twentieth Century* (New York, 1973, first published 1969), 289.

2. Wolf, *Peasant Wars*, 290.

3. James Scott, "Hegemony and the Peasantry," *Politics and Society* 7.3 (1977): 267–296.

4. For an analysis of these variations, see M. Catharine Newbury, "Colonialism, Ethnicity, and Rural Political Protest: Rwanda and Zanzibar in Comparative Perspective," *Comparative Politics* 15.3 (1983): 253–280.

5. See Herbert F. Weiss, *Political Protest in the Congo: The Parti Solidaire Africain During the Independence Struggle* (Princeton, 1967). Weiss is the principal exponent of the concept of "rural radicalism," derived from his study of nationalist political activity in the Congo. The concept is an excellent expression of Hutu protest politics in Rwanda as well, though the target of protest differed. While leaders of Hutu parties protested against Tuutsi domination, leaders of nationalist parties in the Congo made the European regime their major target. Later, during the Congo rebellions/revolution of 1963–1965 rural protest turned against Congolese agents of the (by then independent) state. On parallels and contrasts between rural protest in

Rwanda and Zaïre see Catharine Newbury, "Réflexions sur les racines rurales de la révolution: Rwanda et Congo oriental," Catherine Coquery-Vidrovitch et al., *Rébellions/Révolutions au Zaire, 1963–1965*, Vol. 2 (Paris, 1987), 195–205.

6. Munyangaju worked in Bukavu from 1947 until 1958 when he was named editor of the Bujumbura newspaper, *Temps Nouveaux d'Afrique*. (Paternostre de la Mairieu, *Le Rwanda*, 399; interview with Aloys Munyangaju, 11 November 1971.) An exposition of Munyangaju's assessment of the political situation in Rwanda is found in Aloys Munyangaju, *L'actualité politique au Rwanda* (Brussels, 1959).

7. *Kinyamateka* has been published in Ikinyarwanda since the 1930s by the Catholic press at Kabgayi, Rwanda. By 1955 the paper's circulation had reached 20,000; it was read by "la quasi-totalité des 'lettrés,'" and as conflicts escalated, many of the illiterate gained access to the contents of *Kinyamateka* by having the literate read it to them. Emmanuel Ntezimana, "*Kinyameteka, Temps Nouveaux d'Afrique* et l'évolution socio-politique du Rwanda (1954–1959)," *Etudes Rwandaises* 11 (mars 1978): 79.

8. United Nations Trusteeship Council, "Report of the U.N. Visiting Mission to the Trust Territory of Ruanda-Urundi under Belgian Administration," T/217, 4th Session, Supp. no. 2 (October 31, 1948), 13.

9. United Nations Trusteeship Council, "Report of the U.N. Visiting Mission to East Africa," T/1168, 15th Session, Supp. no. 2 (1955), par. 185.

10. Maquet and d'Hertefelt, *Elections*, 19.

11. Maquet and d'Hertefelt, *Elections*, 22–25.

12. Maquet and d'Hertefelt, *Elections*, 30–31. The authors note, however, that subchiefs still had the power to place on the subchiefdom electoral colleges persons of their choice who had not been elected by the population.

13. This was in fact a longer pre-election period than most other territories of the country experienced. Maquet and d'Hertefelt, *Elections*, 34.

14. See, for example, "Avant les elections," *Soma* (August 30, 1956), cited in Donat Murego, *La Révolution rwandaise, 1959–1962* (Louvain, [1975]), 826 & note 460, Annexes, p. 63. In response to a questionnaire in French distributed to Europeans and Rwandan "évolués" after the 1956 elections, a European agricultural agent noted that "On a l'impression que la presse ait joué un rôle sensible dans l'orientation des élections. Entre autres *Soma*."

15. A questionnaire in Ikinyarwanda concerning the conduct and impact of the 1956 elections was distributed to subchiefs and other notables in Cyangugu Territory; the responses of thirteen persons have been preserved in the Cyangugu Prefecture Archives. Two of the thirteen respondents mentioned that there was influence from the Catholic missions prior to the elections. A subchief mentioned that people in his subchiefdom were pleased to have the opportunity to choose the electoral college themselves (instead of having the subchief select members). Two other respondents noted that some segments of the population expressed dissatisfaction about the results of the elections. "Ibibazo byerekeye itora ryoherwerejwe abatware b'imisozi n'abanyacyubahiro" (Questionnaire on the elections, sent to hill chiefs and other notables), 1956.

Reports by members of the Belgian Territorial Service in Cyangugu insisted that for much of the population, the 1956 elections were regarded as just another census-taking. Maquet and d'Hertefelt note the presence of similar misconceptions about the voting. They point out that where discussion of candidates took place prior to the 1956 elections, this occurred most commonly within family or lineage groups.

They also believe that pressure was exercised by Tuutsi on Hutu but admit the difficulty of finding concrete examples of this. Maquet and d'Hertefelt, *Elections,* 36ff., 42.

16. Kanyabacuzi 8/7/71, 5.

17. In 1956 Tuutsi constituted 22.08 percent of the Kinyagan population, while in Rwanda as a whole Tuutsi were only 16.59 percent. The proportion of Tuutsi in Cyangugu Territory in 1956 was third highest in the country, ranking behind Kibuye and Astrida. The percentage of Tuutsi elected to the 1956 subchiefdom electoral colleges in Kibuye (46.1%) was similar to that of Kinyaga, while that of Astrida (36%) was closer to the all-Rwanda figures. Maquet and d'Hertefelt, *Elections,* 86, 113, 114.

18. No attempt is made here to present a full analysis of the 1956 elections. The results are not fully representative since the elections were organized and run by the subchiefs; the Tuutsi political elite was much more highly organized than the Hutu, and there was a good deal of misunderstanding among the population about the purpose and role of the elections. It is, however, interesting that the 1956 voting patterns within Kinyaga are similar to those of 1960 discussed below.

19. Maquet and d'Hertefelt, *Elections,* 86. For a consideration of why the vote was not entirely along ethnic lines, see *Elections,* 85ff.

20. Maquet and d'Hertefelt, *Elections,* 29.

21. Jean-Paul Harroy, *Rwanda* (Brussels, 1984), 91. Included in these extortions was a practice whereby chiefs would appropriate most of the income a cultivator might obtain from selling his coffee crop. Consequently, some coffee growers left their coffee unharvested.

22. Harroy, *Rwanda,* 92.

23. Official colonial policy in Rwanda favored graduates of the administrative school in Astrida in appointments for administrative positions. Therefore, graduates of mission schools with education comparable to that of the Astridians found their diplomas devalued. They were less likely to be hired for administrative positions, and if they did get hired, their salaries and benefits would be lower than those of their compatriots who had attended the administrative school. Since most of the students at the Astrida school were Tuutsi, this amounted to a visible, and grating, form of ethnic discrimination. See Linden, *Church and Revolution,* 232; and Kagame, *Abrégé,* vol. 2, 236.

24. *L'Ami* No. 110 (February 1954), 57, 59; *L'Ami* No. 118 (October 1954), 352, cited in Linden, *Church and Revolution,* 233–234.

25. *L'Ami* No. 110 (February 1954), 60, cited in Murego, *Révolution rwandaise, 1959–1962,* 694.

26. Lemarchand, *Rwanda and Burundi,* 7, 141, 479.

27. Linden, *Church and Revolution,* 232–235, 245, n. 115; Paternostre de la Mairieu, *Rwanda,* 391, 399.

28. Linden, *Church and Revolution,* 253.

29. Ntezimana, "*Kinyamateka,*" 81. On the role of the press in the emergence of revolutionary protest, see also Murego, *Révolution rwandaise,* 790–829.

30. This term is used by Linden; it is adopted here as an appropriate description of the national-level Hutu activists. Linden, *Church and Revolution.*

31. Linden, *Church and Revolution,* 258 and n. 75, 276.

32. Theda Skocpol, *States and Social Revolutions: A Comparative Analysis of France, Russia, and China* (Cambridge, 1979).

33. The Governor's Council was the highest advisory body in Ruanda-Urundi. After March 1957, it was called the *Conseil Générale*. In 1959, only 12 of the 45 members of the Council were Africans; of these, only two were Hutu. The Council had no legislative authority; it examined budgetary proposals, considered questions submitted by the Government, and addressed *voeux* to the government. F. Nkundabagenzi, ed., *Rwanda politique, 1958–1960* (Brussels, 1960), 14; Belgium, Corps Législatif, *Rapport du Groupe de Travail*, No. 342, 19.

The 1956 proposal for reform of the Governor's Council was made by M. Maus, a settler from northern Rwanda. When it came to a vote, the Council voted unanimously against adoption of the measure, except for Maus's single vote in favor. Maus reacted bitterly; castigating the shortsightedness of Council members, he submitted his resignation. Nkundabagenzi, *Rwanda politique*, 14.

34. The system of electoral colleges and the distribution of *ex officio* seats resulted in 24 of the 32 seats on the High Council being held by Tuutsi. The other 8 seats were to be filled by appointment. In 1957, when the High Council was constituted following the 1956 elections, only one of the members appointed was Hutu. The figure of 6 percent Hutu representation on the High Council during the 1956–1959 period is used because, during this time, one Tuutsi member of the High Council resigned, and a Hutu was appointed in his place. Thus, by 1959 there were two Hutu on the High Council. The number of Hutu on the council had decreased since 1953, when after the elections in that year the 32-member High Council included three Hutu. Maquet and d'Hertefelt, *Elections*, 205.

35. An English translation of the "Statement of Views" is reproduced in U.N. Trusteeship Council, Report of the Visiting Mission T/1402 (1957), Annex II.

36. Nkundabagenzi, *Rwanda politique*, 21–22.

37. Nkundabagenzi, *Rwanda politique*, 23–24.

38. Nkundabagenzi, *Rwanda politique*, 24–28. For an analysis of the demands in the Hutu Manifesto and its significance, see Murego, *Révolution rwandaise*, 760–764.

39. Lemarchand, *Rwanda and Burundi*, 151–152; Linden, *Church and Revolution*; Nkundabagenzi, *Rwanda politique*; Paternostre de la Mairieu, *Rwanda*, 394.

40. Johnson defines an accelerator as "Some ingredient, usually contributed by fortune, which deprives the elite of its chief weapon for enforcing social behavior, or which leads a group of revolutionaries to *believe* that they have the means to deprive the elite of its weapons of coercion." Chalmers Johnson, *Revolutionary Change* (Boston, 1966), 91.

41. Members of the Hutu counter-elite suspected that the Tuutsi had formulated plans to call up traditional units of the *umwami*'s army in an emergency. Aloys Munyangaju charged that one of the factors keeping Hutu in a servile condition was "the conception of the traditional socio-military armies which the feudal reactionaries are secretly trying to revive." (Munyangaju, *L'Actualité politique au Ruanda*, 41). But Kayibanda, at least, was not going to be caught off guard. Hutu in the northern regions were organizing themselves for action according to a cell-type model. Kayibanda had become acquainted with the organizational tactics while on a training program for journalists in Belgium.

42. Hubert, *La Toussaint rwandaise et sa répression* (Brussels, 1965), 63. For more detailed accounts of the events leading up to the November uprising see Hubert, passim; Lemarchand, *Rwanda and Burundi*, 145–169; Murego, *Révolution rwandaise*, 909–922; Linden, *Church and Revolution*, ch. 10; M. Catharine Atter-

bury, "Revolution in Rwanda," Occasional Paper No. 2, African Studies Program, University of Wisconsin-Madison (1970), 44–72; Reyntjens, *Pouvoir et droit*, 233–263.

43. Hubert, *Toussaint rwandaise*, 63.

44. U.N. Trusteeship Council, *Report of the Visiting Mission* T/1538 (1960), par. 202–203.

45. Reyntjens, *Pouvoir et droit*, 267–269.

46. A. del Castel, "Interlocuteurs valables au Ruanda: En marge d'un document du Conseil de Tutelle," *La Revue Nouvelle* 32.8/9 (1960): 199–203. This article is generally believed to have been written by Marcel d'Hertefelt.

47. Hubert, *Toussaint rwandaise*, 34–41. Hubert's information was based upon the finding of the *conseil de guerre* and the *Tribunal de première instance*. Hubert includes in his account the comment that there were several courageous Tuutsi chiefs who "refused to become assassins" and attempted to protect Hutu in their area.

48. The Belgian administration believed that if Tuutsi partisans of UNAR were to regain control, they would retaliate against the Hutu on a massive scale. Harroy even asserts that UNAR consciously provoked the Hutu uprising in November. They did this in order to stage a "crushing counterrevolution" in which the traditionalist Tuutsi planned to kill "all the Hutu leaders—according to a carefully prepared list—and to carry out in selected regions—Astrida—enough massacres of the peasant population to eliminate the possibility of a Hutu reaction before independence . . . or after" (Harroy, *Rwanda*, 291, 305). The total number of reported deaths resulting from the November conflicts was 50; 37 of these were allegedly caused by Tuutsi, and 13 caused by Hutu (Hubert, *Toussaint rwandaise*, 40). These official figures almost certainly underrepresent the actual numbers of deaths and injuries resulting from the "événements."

49. Harroy, *Rwanda*, 296–297. These measures increased the number of military personnel in Rwanda from 300 (or 550 for Ruanda-Urundi) to about 6,000.

50. Under the state of emergency (régime d'exception) the military were empowered to sentence persons to house arrest and to ban publications, meetings, and associations. This remained in effect until November 1960, but military rule (régime militaire) lasted only from 12 November 1959 to 15 January 1960. The major characteristic of military rule was that judicial power was placed in the hands of a military tribunal (conseil de guerre) whose decisions could not normally be appealed. Marcel d'Hertefelt, "Les élections communales et le consensus politique au Rwanda," *Zaïre* 14.5/6 (1960): Hubert, *Toussaint rwandaise*, 42.

51. B. E. M. Guy Logiest, "A propos de 'Le Rwanda, son effort de développement,'" *Chronique de Politique Etrangère* (1972), cited in Reyntjens, *Pouvoir et droit*, 272.

52. Reyntjens, *Pouvoir et droit*, 267–271; Harroy, *Rwanda*. See also Lemarchand, *Rwanda and Burundi*, 167–168; Linden, *Church and Revolution*, 270.

53. Some observers date the end of the Revolution to January 28, 1961, when Rwandan authorities assembled to declare a Republic and choose a legislative assembly (in a meeting of burgomasters and communal councilors assembled for the occasion). This government, although given de facto recognition by the Belgian administration, was not recognized externally and was in fact directly rejected by the United Nations. Cf. Reyntjens, *Pouvoir et droit*, 235.

54. Reyntjens, *Pouvoir et droit*, 281–284.

55. Nkundiye 25/10/70; Territoire de Shangugu, "Rapport en réponse au questionnaire sur les élections communales de 1960," 20 August 1960.

56. Nkundiye, 29/10/70, 8–9. Nkundiye, a resident of Nyamirundi (Impara) recounted that he and Sarukondo barely escaped being killed when they went to Abiiru region to organize among Hutu there.

57. Kanyamasovu 19/6/71, 1; Karamira 17/6/71, 3. Aside from such intimidation, UNAR did little campaigning in public. The party held only one popular meeting before the elections. Territoire de Shangugu, "Rapport sur les élections communales."

58. Interview with Aloys Munyangaju, 8 November 1971.

59. "Un Aprosoma virulent devient Parmehutu!" Territoire de Shangugu, "Rapport sur les élections communales." This report also described PARMEHUTU as having a "more intense racist orientation."

60. Sarukondo 14/10/72; Munda 16/6/71; Kanyabacuzi 8/7/71, 2–3; Nkundiye 29/10/70, 9; Seemirama 1/12/71, 13.

61. Nkundiye 29/10/70, 8–9; Rukeeratabaro 10/7/71; Karamira 17/6/71, 3.

62. Seemirama 1/12/70, 1.

63. The boycott had only a marginal effect in Kinyaga, however. Turnout was very low in Murehe Commune (in Abiiru), where only 35 percent of the total registered voters voted. But this was the only commune where turnout was less than 50 percent. In five communes the turnout ranged from 50 to 80 percent of the registered voters: Shangugu in Abiiru; Bugarama in Bukunzi; Mibirizi, Munyove, and Giheke in Impara. The remaining thirteen communes all had a turnout of more than 80 percent of registered voters: Mururu in Abiiru; Mwezi, Mwegera, and Nyamubembe in Bukunzi; Buhoro, Muramba, Nyakabingo, Nyamasheke in Cyesha; Nyamirundi, Shangi, Mwito, Nkombo, and Muhari in Impara. Statistics on election turnout are found in Territoire de Ruanda-Urundi, Service des Affaires Politiques et Administratives, "Elections communales, résultats pour l'ensemble du Ruanda." Consulted courtesy of Jan Vansina.

64. The PARMEHUTU-APROSOMA coalition received 82.89 percent of the votes in Cyangugu as a whole, while the Hutu parties won 80.42 percent of the seats on the commune councils. Territoire de Shangugu, "Elections communales, 1960," Annexe X, 1 August 1960.

65. Territoire de Shangugu, "Rapport sur les élections communales."

66. CINAM, Etude du développement, vol. 2, maps 11, 14, 18, 20. The statistics on which these maps are based are from 1969; they may be taken as more or less representative of regional differences in Kinyaga during the 1950s, with the caveat that intensity of coffee cultivation probably increased over the decade.

67. Coffee cultivation exacerbated land pressure in this densely populated area. Moreover, it appears that administrative regulations and chiefly exactions relating to the development of a coffee cooperative in the area of Mwito/Nyamirundi in the mid-1950s increased the burdens on the population. The socioeconomic and political impact of the abrupt drop in coffee prices in Rwanda during the 1950s is a subject that needs further study. Dorsey's study of colonial economic policy in Rwanda provides an excellent overview of the introduction and development of coffee cultivation up to 1939. Dorsey, "Rwandan Colonial Economy."

68. "In Biru, [where the population was] little politicized and under the influence of false rumor, RADER members feared they might lose votes because of the linkage between RADER and the anti-Kigeri cartel; so [in Abiiru] RADER ran under the

name Intérêts Communaux du Kinyaga." Territoire de Shangugu, "Rapport sur les élections communales."

69. INTERCOKI won 9 of its 12 seats in Murehe Commune, where turnout was very low (less than 50 percent of those registered). The seats going to UNAR were concentrated in Mururu Commune (4 seats), where MUR also received one seat. UNAR and MUR received one seat each in Shangugu Commune; RADER's one seat was also in Shangugu Commune. Territoire du Ruanda-Urundi, "Elections communales, résultats pour l'ensemble du Ruanda."

70. Lemarchand, *Rwanda and Burundi*, 202. Rukeba's family comes from Bushi where his clan is strongly represented along the western shore of Lake Kivu.

71. Hutu campaign statements in Kinyaga tended to stress the injustices of Tuutsi rule. In some of the meetings held before the 1960 elections (especially those led by PARMEHUTU adherents) demands for abolition of the monarchy were made. In others, however, especially those held in conjunction with RADER, the stand on the monarchy was more moderate. Campaign statements by RADER leaders attempted to explain to the population the distinction between the Hutu parties' opposition to the ultra-conservative Kigeri Ndahindurwa (the incumbent *umwami* who had been installed after Rudahigwa's death in July 1959), and the monarchy as an institution. "Compte Rendu des meetings en Territoire de Shangugu," in Territoire de Shangugu, "Rapport sur les élections communales."

72. CINAM, *Etude du développement*, vol. 2, map 13.

73. Kirsch and Verhelst to A.T. Shangugu, 3555/A.I., 19 October 1956.

CHAPTER 10

1. There are parallels here with Michael Hechter's internal colonial model of ethnic mobilization. Hechter attributes solidarity among Celtic peoples in the British Isles to the emergence of a particular type of stratification system involving a "cultural division of labor." This system of stratification, created in Hechter's view by an uneven process of industrialization and maintained by political domination, relegates certain groups, culturally defined, to a subordinate position in productive relations. The exploitation and domination inherent in such a system, viewed in historical perspective, appear as potent mobilizing factors in the growth of ethnic consciousness. My analysis recognizes the important impact of economic changes on political relations but stresses more the role of political domination as a major force shaping the stratification system.

2. Efforts of dominant classes to manipulate state power in order to maintain ethnic/racial inequality and ensure control over subordinate groups forms a central theme in Stanley Greenberg's study of racial divisions in South Africa and several other cases. See Stanley B. Greenberg, *Race and State in Capitalist Development* (New Haven, 1980).

3. The Esoteric Code specified the form and content of specific rituals to be carried out by the king and his ritual specialists. It also laid down rules for succession, naming of kings, prohibitions on royalty, etc. The text of the Esoteric Code in Ikinyarwanda, with an annotated translation into French, is most fully presented in d'Hertefelt and Coupez, *Royauté sacrée*.

4. An analysis of differences among regions of Rwanda in the manifestation of anti-Tuutsi sentiment (as reflected in voting returns for the 1960 commune elections)

is found in my "Colonialism Ethnicity, and Rural Political Protest: Rwanda and Zanzibar," 267–269.

5. In 1960, Tuutsi constituted only 2.9 percent of the population of Ruhengeri Prefecture and 6.06 percent of the population of Gisenyi Prefecture. This is significantly lower than the proportion of Tuutsi in Cyangugu Prefecture in the same year (19.79%). d'Hertefelt, *Clans*, Annexes, Tableau 2.

6. d'Hertefelt found that conflicts between land patrons and land clients influenced voting during the 1960 communal elections in Ruhengeri and Gisenyi Prefectures. d'Hertefelt, "Elections communales," 436. For a discussion of the question of land reform in the northwest, see Lemarchand, *Rwanda and Burundi*, 230–233.

7. The Tuutsi constituted 19.52 percent of the Kibungo Prefecture population in 1960 and 19.79 percent of the Cyangugu Prefecture population in the same year. This can be compared with a Rwandan average of 15.91 percent Tuutsi population. d'Hertefelt, *Clans*, Annexes, Tableau 2.

8. Gravel found in Remera (Gisaka) that 73 percent of the total adult male population had been abroad at least once, but this figure was 84 percent for Hutu and 34 percent for Tuutsi. Of the total voyages recorded by Gravel, 92 percent were Hutu voyages abroad. Finally, from the Remera survey of absences for labor migration on a given date (31/3/61), it was found that 77 percent were Hutu. This is only slightly greater than the population range, but it also was surveyed during the revolutionary period when Tuutsi emigration may have been inflated. In his survey, Gravel found a rough balance in marital status for Hutu emigrants (55% unmarried, 45% married); there were, nonetheless, almost twice as many Hutu men who had been away for more than one year relative to those who had been for "less than one year" or "approximately one year." While Gravel points out that these figures are low in comparison with other African countries, they would nevertheless seem high relative to most other areas of Rwanda, and particularly central Rwanda. Gravel, *Remera*, 111–117. See also Des Forges, "Musiinga," 335.

9. Almost four decades ago in a classic article, Lloyd Fallers analyzed the psychological conflicts inherent in the roles of African chiefs subject to older, particularistic pressures as well as the universalistic norms of European-introduced bureaucratizing measures. Later, Martin Kilson's study of colonialism placed more emphasis on the changing political and economic prerogatives of chiefs as colonial agents. See Lloyd Fallers, "The Predicament of the Modern African Chief," *American Anthropologist* 57.2 (1955): 290–305; and Martin Kilson, *Political Change in a West African State* (Cambridge, 1966), esp. chs. 4 & 11–13. More recent studies have highlighted processes of class formation that accompanied transformations in the powers of chiefs and the erosion of legitimacy that the chiefs' roles as colonial collaborators generated. For some examples, see Joan Vincent, "Colonial Chiefs and the Making of Class: A Case Study from Teso, Eastern Uganda," *Africa* 47.2 (1977): 240–259; David Newbury and Catharine Newbury, "King and Chief: Colonial Politics on Ijwi Island (Zaïre)," *The International Journal of African Historical Studies* 15.2 (1982): 221–246.

10. Study of such internal processes of change and struggle, whereby local conditions and the historical struggles of different classes within dependent states mold (and are molded by) the external forces acting upon them forms a central theme of much of the recent work by dependency theorists focusing on Latin America. For an influential example, see Fernando Henrique Cardoso and Enzo Faletto, *Dependency and Development in Latin America* (Berkeley, 1979).

11. Frederick Cooper's work has been pathbreaking in this regard. See his *From Slaves to Squatters* (New Haven, 1980); and "Africa and the World Economy," *The African Studies Review* 24.2/3 (1981): 1–86.

12. Oral data are of course crucial for studying, over time, the views and behavior of non-elites. A decade ago, Terence Ranger, in reviewing a study of agrarian poverty based largely on archival sources, issued a plea for more fieldwork and more collection of oral evidence as a means to understanding the variety of ways in which rural non-elites in Africa were affected by, and themselves shaped, the changes wrought by colonial capitalism. See Terence Ranger, "Growing from the Roots: Reflections on Peasant Research in Central and Southern Africa," *Journal of Southern African Studies* 5.1 (1978): 99–133.

13. See, for example, Joseph LaPalombara, "Penetration: A Crisis of Governmental Capacity," Leonard Binder et al., eds. *Crises and Sequences in Political Development* (Princeton, 1971), 208–209.

14. As Leys has pointed out:

> From the standpoint of the mass of ordinary people, . . . the 'leaders' appear, more often than not, as part of the problem, not part of the solution. . . . It is a consideration of the experience and interests of the ordinary people . . . that really forces one to explore systematically the economic and social structures, and the patterns of exploitation and manipulation, which are at least as much a part of political reality as the 'development' rhetoric of 'leaders,' aid officials, and academics.

Colin Leys, review of Michael Lofchie, ed., *The State of the Nations*, in *Journal of Modern African Studies* 11.2 (1973): 317.

15. When applied to the study of political clientelism, such analysis has helped to explain how and why colonial statebuilding and the expansion of capitalism serve to transform rural class relations. For examples of such work, see James C. Scott, and Benedict J. Kerkvliet, "How Traditional Rural Patrons Lose Legitimacy—A Theory With Special Reference to Southeast Asia," *Cultures et Développement* 5.3 (1973): 327–339; Laura Guasti, "Peru: Clientelism and Internal Control," Steffen W. Schmidt et al., *Friends, Followers, and Factions* (Berkeley, 1977), 422–438; René Lemarchand, "Comparative Political Clientelism: Structure, Process and Optic," S. N. Eisenstadt and René Lemarchand, eds., *Political Clientelism, Patronage and Development* (Beverly Hills, 1981), esp. 17–19; James C. Scott, "Everyday Forms of Class Struggle Between Ex-Patrons and Ex-Clients: The Green Revolution in Kedah, Malaysia," *International Political Science Review* 4.4 (1983): 537–556; idem, *Weapons of the Weak: Everyday Forms of Peasant Resistance* (New Haven, 1985); idem, "Everyday Forms of Peasant Resistance," *Journal of Peasant Studies* 13.2 (1986): 5–35.

APPENDIX I

1. Altitudes range from a low of 800–1000 m. in the Bugarama plain to 1460 m. at Lake Kivu, and 2000–2900 m. in the mountains of eastern Kinyaga. On the ecological and social background of the areas in which Bugarama is located, see H. Guillaume, "Monographie de la plaine de la Ruzizi,'" *Bulletin des juridictions indigenes et du droit coutumier congolais* (Elisabethville) No. 18 (1950): 33–66.

2. A 1938 report gave the total number of cattle in Kinyaga as 10,893; for some

of the areas included in the figures, however, statistics date from different years
varying from 1925–1931, and for others, from 1934–1937. (Territoire de Shangugu,
"Rapport sur le nombre des H.A.V. et gros bétail pour chaque sous-chefferie," 25 May
1938.) Kinyagans commented frequently that there were more cattle in the pre-
European period than later, and more cattle in the colonial period than in the period
since independence. Raids, epidemics, and taxes have contributed to the reduction
of herds. In 1970, Cyangugu Prefecture statistics estimated the number of cattle in
the region at 20,903. Préfecture de Cyangugu, "Rapport des Commissions Préfectorales de Planification," 1970, Part I, Agriculture et Elevage, 11.

3. The differences are most clearly apparent in such things as hut construction,
crops (banana plants are scarcer and not as healthy because of the greater altitude;
peas and maize are more common), linguistic variations, and the use of products
from the forest.

4. République Rwandaise, Ministère du Plan et des Ressources Naturelles, Direction de la Documentation et des Statistiques, *Enquête démographique du
Rwanda*, 1970, T.I., 16.

5. However, if account were taken of the lake and forest area of Cyangugu Prefecture, the population density would be somewhat higher. A land area of 1499.6 km^2
(i.e., excluding forest and lake) with a population of 251,310 would give a population
density of 174 per km^2. If the land area figure including forest, but excluding lake
were used (2044.8), the density would be 123 per km^2. Land area figures are given in
CINAM, *Etude du développement du Lac Kivu* (Rwanda) vol. 2 (Paris, 1973), Annexe, Tableau I.

6. The land area on which the figures in table 9 are based excludes forest and
lake regions of Cyangugu Prefecture. Note also that the population figures are based
on government population statistics for 1970 (284,038), which are higher than estimates of the demographic survey conducted in 1970 (251,310).

7. When subchiefdoms were abolished in 1960, 19 provisional communes were
created in Kinyaga, regrouping but on the whole following the former subchiefdom
boundaries. After independence, the number of communes was reduced to 11, with
the boundaries redrawn to cut through areas that had served as a focus for loyalties
in the past.

8. This description applies to the time at which the research was carried out in
1970–1971. After July 5, 1973, when the government of Major General Juvenal
Habyarimana took power in a coup, a number of modifications were introduced. For
example, burgomasters were appointed directly by the central government at Kigali,
and the former ruling MDR-PARMEHUTU party was abolished. The National Assembly was also abolished and legislative elections scheduled for September 1973
under the previous government were postponed. These changes do not enter into the
present discussion.

9. Data on the 1971 elections are drawn from material collected from each of
the communes during and after the campaign.

10. A burgomaster in at least one commune had been removed following petitions
made by the population to the central authorities in Kigali. In another commune, a
duly elected burgomaster was deposed by the Prefect at Cyangugu; after appeal to
Kigali, he was later reinstated.

11. In Cyangugu Prefecture, there are five Tribunaux de Canton—approximately
one for every two communes.

12. Préfecture de Cyangugu, "Rapport Commissions Préfectorales," Part V, Administration et Justice, 4–9.

13. On the nature of such differences in Butare Prefecture, see Saucier, "Patron-Client Relationship," 256–257.

14. Several would-be candidates for the 1971 communal elections, including at least two incumbent burgomasters, were unable to stand because their names had been barred from the list.

15. The reasons people gave for the barring of candidates from the communal slates in 1971 were frequently that the persons in question had been associated with a former minister from Cyangugu who had lost his position in 1969 during the Cabinet reshuffles prior to the legislative elections in that year. On a more general level, there appeared to be a systematic attempt to weed out of office individuals who had been linked to the APROSOMA party during the revolutionary activity of the late 1950s. Shortly after independence, APROSOMA was merged into the ruling PARMEHUTU party; I received the impression that former activists of APROSOMA were often regarded as somewhat "suspect."

16. Mibirizi (1903); Nyamasheke (1928); Shangi (1940); Mwezi (1944); Mururu (1956); Mushaka (1963); Hanika (1970). The Catholic missions are now called parishes ("paroisses") and are incorporated in the diocese of Nyundo.

17. Kibogora, a Free Methodist establishment, and Gihundwe, a Pentecostal mission. There are also several outposts of the Mission of Seventh Day Adventists, which is located in Kibuye Prefecture to the north.

18. Two secondary schools, one for girls and one for boys, are located at Nyamasheke, forming part of the Catholic mission complex there. In 1971 the girls' school offered a four-year course oriented primarily toward teaching. The boys' school had a full six-year cycle of humanities. At Kibogora Mission, the initial two years of secondary school had been launched by 1971, and there were plans to increase this to at least the three-year cycle (Tronc commun) in 1972. For girls, several missions had organized "Ecoles Ménagères" (consisting of one to three years beyond sixth grade), in which subjects such as cooking, sewing, health, and housekeeping were taught.

19. In 1965, of 910 pupils completing the sixth year of primary school, 101 (about 11%) were admitted to secondary school. In 1969–1970, 1,849 young Kinyagans completed sixth grade, but of these, only 144 (about 7.7%) went on to secondary school. Préfecture de Cyangugu, "Rapport Commissions Prefectorales," Commission Sociale et Culturelle, 18.

GLOSSARY

Abapari:	Belgian officers with African soldiers who occupied south-western Rwanda in the mid-1890s
Abagaragu:	Plural of *umugaragu*
Abakaraani:	Clerks; European-educated chiefs
Akazi:	Corvée
Amakoro y'ubutaka:	Prestations for land
Amatega:	Plural of *ubutega*
Guhakwa:	To pay court
Ibikingi:	Plural of *igikingi*
Ikoro:	Singular of *amakoro*; prestation
Igikingi:	Domain granted by a political authority, comprising pasture and agricultural land
Imbaata:	Personally owned cattle
Ingabo:	Regionally based unit of army organization
Intoore:	Close followers of a chief recruited as youths for social and military training
Shebuja:	Patron
Ubuhake:	Form of clientship; often, cattle clientship
Ubukonde:	Land held through right of occupation, not granted by a chief
Ubureetwa:	Form of clientship involving manual labor performed by Hutu for chiefs
Ubutaka:	Land
Ubutega:	Fiber bracelet
Ubwooko:	Clan
Umuheto:	Form of clientship; named group comprised of those who contribute prestations to a particular chief
Umugaragu:	Client
Umuryamo:	Rinderpest epidemic, early 1890s
Umuryango:	Lineage
Umutware:	Chief
Umwami:	King

BIBLIOGRAPHY

LIST OF ACRONYMS

AIMO	Affaires Indigènes et Main d'Oeuvre
IRCB	Institut Royal Colonial Belge
ARSC	Académie Royale des Sciences Coloniales
ARSOM	Académie Royale des Sciences d'Outre-Mer
CEDAF	Centre d'Etude et de Documentation Africaines
CRISP	Centre de Recherche et d'Information Socio-Politiques
INRS	Institut National de Recherche Scientifique
MOI	Main d'Oeuvre Indigène
MRAC	Musée Royal de l'Afrique Centrale
UNAZA	Université National du Zaïre
UNR	Université Nationale du Rwanda

"Admission au Groupe Scolaire." *Servir* 7.3 (1946): 146–148.

Amselle, Jean-Loup, and Elikia M'bokolo, eds. *Au coeur de l'ethnie: ethnies, tribalisme et état en Afrique.* Paris: Editions la Découverte, 1985.

Anstey, Roger. *King Leopold's Legacy.* Oxford: Clarendon, 1966.

Atterbury, M. Catharine. "Revolution in Rwanda." Occasional Paper 2. University of Wisconsin-Madison: African Studies Program, Spring 1970.

Bailey, F. G. *Stratagems and Spoils.* New York: Schocken Books, 1969.

Balandier, Georges. "The Colonial Situation: A Theoretical Approach." Immanuel Wallerstein, ed. *Social Change: The Colonial Situation.* 34–61. New York: Wiley, 1966. [Originally "La situation coloniale: approche théorique." *Cahiers Internationaux de Sociologie* 11 (1951): 44–79.]

Barnett, Marguerite R. *The Politics of Cultural Nationalism in South India.* Princeton: Princeton University Press, 1976.

Barns, T. Alexander. *Across the Great Craterland to the Congo.* London: Benn, 1923; New York: Knopf, 1924.

Bashizi, C. "Processus de domination socio-économique et marché du travail au Bushi (1920–1940)." *Enquêtes et Documents d'Histoire Africaine* 3 (1978): 1–29.

Belgium. Gouvernement Belge, Ministère des Colonies. *Plan décennal pour le développement économique et social du Ruanda-Urundi.* Brussels: n.p., 1951.

—— *Rapport sur l'administration Belge des Territoires occupés de l'Est-Africain Allemand.* Brussels: M. Hayes, 1921.

—— *Rapport présenté par le Gouvernement Belge au Conseil de la Société des Nations au sujet de l'administration du Ruanda-Urundi, 1924–1937.* Genève: Société des Nations, 1925–1938.

—— Ministère des Colonies/Ministère du Congo Belge et du Ruanda-Urundi. *Rapport présenté par le Gouvernement Belge au Conseil de Tutelle des Nations Unies sur l'administration du Ruanda-Urundi, 1948–1959.* Brussels: n.p., 1949–1960.

—— Office de l'Information et des Relations Publiques pour le Congo Belge et le Ruanda-Urundi. *Le Ruanda-Urundi.* Brussels: M. Weissenbruch, 1959.

Berger, Iris. *Religion and Resistance: East African Kingdoms in the Precolonial Period.* Tervuren: MRAC, 1981.

Berman, B. J., and J. M. Lonsdale. "Crises of Accumulation, Coercion and the Colonial State: The Development of the Labor Control System in Kenya, 1919–1929." *Canadian Journal of African Studies* 14.1 (1980): 37–54.

Bethe, Heinrich. "Bericht über einen Zug nach Ruanda." *Deutsches Kolonialblat* (1899): 6–12. [Also published as "Compte rendu d'un voyage au Ruanda." French translation edited by Bernard Lugan. *Etudes rwandaises* 14, numéro spécial (oct. 1980): 54–59.]

Bimanyu, D. K. "A propos des premiers mouvements de résistance: cas de la révolte de l'expédition Dhanis (14 fevrier–19 mars 1897)." Mémoire de Licence en Histoire, Université Louvanium, 1970.

Binder, Leonard, et al., eds. *Crises and Sequences in Political Development.* Princeton: Princeton University Press, 1971.

Birhakaheka Njiga, and Kirhero Nsibula. "Nyangezi dans ses relations commerciales avec le Rwanda, le Burundi, et le Bufulero (fin 19e siècle-début 20e siècle)." *Etudes rwandaises* 14.1 (mars 1981): 36–51.

Bisamunyu, E. N. "Baganda Agency, 1911–1924." Donald Denoon, ed. *A History of Kigezi.* Kampala: National Trust, [1971].

Bishikwabo Chubaka. "Un aspect du colonat belge: le sort des travailleurs du Kivu (1900–1940)." *Genève-Afrique* 16.2 (1977–1978): 25–44.

—— "Le Bushi au XIXe siècle: Un peuple, sept royaumes." *Revue Française d'Histoire d'Outre-Mer* 67.246/247 (1980): 88–98.

—— "Essai sur l'exercice du pouvoir politique au Bushi (1890–1940)." Mémoire de Licence, UNAZA, Lubumbashi, 1973.

—— "Histoire d'en état Shi en Afrique des Grands Lacs: Kaziba au Zaïre (ca. 1850–1940)." Diss. Louvain-la-Neuve, 1982.

Botte, Roger. "Rwanda and Burundi, 1889–1930: Chronology of a Slow Assassination." *International Journal of African Historical Studies* 18.1/2 (1985): 53–91, 289–314.

Bourgeois, R. *Banyarwanda et Barundi.* 3 vols. Brussels: IRCB, ARSC, 1954–1957.

—— *Banyarwanda et Barundi. L'évolution du contrat de bail à cheptel au Ruanda-Urundi.* Brussels: ARSC, 1958.

—— "Moeurs et coutumes des Banyarwanda en territoire de Shangugu en 1935." *Bulletin des juridictions indigènes et du droit coutumier congolais* 5 (1945): 133–158.

Bourgeois, R. *Témoignages.* Vol. 1. Tervuren: MRAC, 1982.

Bourgeois, R. Ch. "Le passage du premier Belge au Ruanda, le Lieutenant Sandrart (1896)." *Servir* 12.3 (1951): 140–145.

Brass, Paul R. "Class, Ethnic Group and Party in Indian Politics." *World Politics* 33.3 (1981): 449–467.

—— "Ethnicity and Nationality Formation." *Ethnicity* 3 (1976): 225–241.

Bucyalimwe Mararo. "Une rationalisation? Les migrations rwandaises au Kivu, Zaïre." Bogumil Jewsiewicki and Jean-Pierre Chrétien, eds. *Ambiguités de l'innovation. Sociétés rurales et technologies en Afrique centrale et occidentale au XXème siècle.* 39–54. Québec: Editions Safi, 1984.

Centre de Civilisation Burundaise, ed. *La civilisation ancienne des peuples des Grands Lacs: Colloque de Bujumbura, 1979, organisé par le Centre de Civilisation Burundaise.* Paris: Karthala; Bujumbura, Centre de Civilisation Burundaise, 1981.

Chrétien, Jean-Pierre. "Confronting the Unequal Exchange of the Oral and the Written." Bogumil Jewsiewicki and David Newbury, eds. *African Historiographies: What History for Which Africa?* 75–90. Beverly Hills: Sage, 1986.

—— "Echanges et hiérarchies dans les royaumes des Grands Lacs de l'Est africain." *Annales Economies, Sociétés, Civilisations* 29.6 (1974): 1327–1337.

—— *Histoire rurale de l'Afrique des Grands Lacs: Guide de recherches. Bibliographie et textes rassemblés.* Paris: Edition AFERA (diffusion Karthala) en collaboration avec l'Université du Burundi, 1983.

—— "Hutu et Tutsi au Rwanda et au Burundi." Jean-Loup Amselle and Elikia M'bokolo, eds. *Au Coeur de l'ethnie: Ethnies, tribalisme et état en Afrique.* 129–166. Paris: Editions la Découverte, 1985.

—— "La révolte de Ndungutse (1912). Forces traditionnelles et pression coloniale au Rwanda allemand." *Revue française d'histoire d'outre-mer* 59.4 (1972): 645–680.

—— "Une révolte au Burundi en 1934." *Annales Economies, Sociétés, Civilisations* 25.6 (1970): 1678–1717.

—— "Roi, religion, lignages en Afrique orientale précoloniale: royautés sans État et monarchies absolues." E. le Roy Ladurie, ed. *Les monarchies.* 115–133. Paris: Presses Universitaires Françaises, 1986.

—— "Des sédentaires devenus migrants: les motifs des départs des Barundi et des Banyarwanda vers l'Uganda (1920–1960)." *Cultures et Développement* 10.1 (1978): 71–101.

CINAM. *Etude du développement du Lac Kivu* (Rwanda). 3 vols. Paris: n.p., 1973.

Classe, Léon. "Le Rwanda et ses habitants." *Congo* 1.5 (May 1922): 677–693.

Codere, Helen. *The Biography of an African Society: Rwanda, 1900–1960.* Tervuren: MRAC, 1973.

—— "Power in Rwanda." *Anthropologica* ns 4.1 (1962): 45–85.

Colle, P. *Monographie des Bashi.* 1939. 2nd ed. Bukavu: n.p., 1971.

Colson, Elizabeth. "Contemporary Tribes and the Development of Nationalism." June Helm, ed. *Essays on the Problem of Tribe.* 201–206. Seattle: University of Washington Press, 1968.

Cooper, Frederick. "Africa and the World Economy." *The African Studies Review* 24.2/3 (1981): 1–86.

—— *From Slaves to Squatters.* New Haven: Yale University Press, 1980.

Coquery-Vidrovitch, Catherine, et al. *Rébellions/Révolutions au Zaïre.* 2 vols. Paris: l'Harmattan, 1987.

Coupez, A., and Th. Kamanzi. *Littérature de cour au Rwanda*. Oxford: Clarendon, 1970.

Cuypers, J. B. *L'alimentation chez les shi*. Tervuren: MRAC, 1970.

Czekanowski, J. *Forschungen im Nil-Kongo-Zwischengebiet*. Vol. 1: *Ethnographie*. Leipzig: Klinkhardt & Biermann, 1917.

"Décolonisation et indépendance du Rwanda et du Burundi." *Chronique de politique étrangère* 16.4/6 (1963): 439–718.

Delmas, Léon. *Généalogies de la noblesse du Ruanda*. Kabgayi, Rwanda: Vicariat Apostolique du Ruanda, 1950.

Denoon, Donald. "The Allocation of Official Posts in Kigezi, 1908–1930." Donald Denoon, ed. *A History of Kigezi*. 211–230. Kampala: The National Trust, [1971].

Des Forges, Alison L. "Court and Corporations in the Development of the Rwandan State." Unpublished essay.

—— "Defeat is the Only Bad News: Rwanda under Musiinga, 1896–1931." Diss. Yale University, 1972.

—— " 'The Drum is Greater than the Shout': The 1912 Rebellion in Northern Rwanda." Donald Crummey, ed. *Banditry, Rebellion and Social Protest in Africa*. 311–331. London: James Currey; Portsmouth N.H.: Heinemann, 1986.

—— "Kings without Crowns: The White Fathers in Ruanda." Daniel F. McCall, Norman R. Bennett and Jeffrey Butler, eds. *Eastern African History*. 176–207. Boston University Papers on Africa 3. New York: Praeger, 1969.

Deutsch, Karl. "The Growth of Nations: Some Recurrent Patterns of Political and Social Integration." *World Politics* 5 (1952): 158–195.

—— *Nationalism and Social Communication*. Cambridge: MIT Press, 1953.

Dorsey, Learthen. "The Rwandan Colonial Economy, 1916–1941." Diss. Michigan State University, 1983.

Dufays, Félix, and Vincent de Moor. *Au Kinyaga. Les enchaînés*. Brussels: Editions universelles, 1938.

Edelman, Murray. *The Symbolic Uses of Politics*. 1964. Urbana: University of Illinois Press, 1967.

Eisenstadt, S. N., and René Lemarchand, eds. *Political Clientelism, Patronage and Development*. Beverly Hills: Sage, 1981.

Enloe, Cynthia. *Police, Military and Ethnicity*. New Brunswick, NJ: Transaction Books, 1980.

—— "State-Building and Ethnic Structures: Dependence on International Capitalist Penetration." Terence K. Hopkins and Immanuel Wallerstein, eds. *Processes of the World System*. 266–288. Beverly Hills: Sage, 1980.

Erny, Pierre. "L'impact des missions chrétiennes sur le paysage au Rwanda." *Neue Zeitschrift für Missionswissenschaft* (Immensee) 37.4 (1981): 276–283.

Etzioni, Amitai. *Political Unification: A Comparative Study of Leaders and Forces*. New York: Holt, 1965.

Fallers, Lloyd. *Bantu Bureaucracy*. 1956. Chicago: Phoenix Books, 1965.

—— "The Predicament of the Modern African Chief: An Instance from Uganda." Immanuel Wallerstein, ed. *Social Change: The Colonial Situation*. 232–249. New York: Wiley, 1966. [Originally published in *American Anthropologist* 57.2 (1956): 290–305.]

Feltz, Gaëtan. "Evolution des structures foncières et histoire politique du Rwanda (XIXe et XXe siècles)." *Etudes d'Histoire Africaine* 7 (1975): 143–154.

Fetter, Bruce. "L'Union Minière du Haut-Katanga, 1920–1940: La naissance d'une sous-culture totalitaire." *Cahiers du CEDAF* 2.6 (1973).

Flament, F., et al. *La Force Publique de sa naissance à 1914.* Brussels: IRCB, 1952.

Freedman, Jim. "East African Peasants and Capitalist Development: The Kiga of Northern Ruanda." David H. Turner et al., eds. *Challenging Anthropology: A Critical Introduction to Social and Cultural Anthropology.* 245–260. Toronto: McGraw-Hill, 1979.

—— *Nyabingi: The Social History of an African Divinity.* Tervuren: MRAC, 1984.

Geertz, Clifford, ed. *Old Societies and New States.* New York: Free Press, 1968.

Gellner, Ernest, and John Waterbury, eds. *Patrons and Clients in Mediterranean Societies.* London: Gerald Duckworth & Co. in cooperation with the Center for Mediterranean Studies of the American Field Universities Staff, 1977.

Gluckman, Max, J. C. Mitchell, and J. A. Barnes. "The Village Headman in British Central Africa." Gluckman, ed. *Order and Rebellion in Tribal Africa.* 146–171. London: Cohen & West, 1963. [Originally published in *Africa* (1949).]

Gotanègre, Jean-François. "La banane au Rwanda." *Cahiers d'Outre-mer* 36.144 (1983): 311–342.

Gravel, Pierre B. *Remera: A Community in Eastern Ruanda.* The Hague: Mouton, 1968.

—— "The Transfer of Cows in Gisaka (Rwanda): A Mechanism for Recording Social Relationships." *American Anthropologist* 69.3/4 (1967): 322–331.

Graziano, Luigi. "A Conceptual Framework for the Study of Clientelistic Behavior." *European Journal of British Research* 4.2 (1976): 149–174.

Greenberg, Stanley B. *Race and State in Capitalist Development.* New Haven: Yale University Press, 1980.

Guasti, Laura. "Peru: Clientelism and Internal Control." Steffen W. Schmidt et al. *Friends, Followers, and Factions.* Berkeley: University of California Press, 1977.

Guillaume, H. "Monographie de la plaine de la Ruzizi." *Bulletin des Juridictions Indigènes et du Droit Coutumier Congolais* (Elisabethville) 18 (1950): 33–66.

Habimana, Bonaventure, and Jean-Paul Harroy. "Instauration et abrogation des cultures vivrières obligatoires au Rwanda." *Civilisations* 30.3/4 (1980): 176–213.

Hakiba, Buki O. "Contribution à l'étude historique de l'importation de la main-d'oeuvre du Ruanda-Urundi à l'UMHK 1925–1973." Mémoire de Licence en Histoire, UNAZA, Lubumbashi, 1974.

Harroy, Jean-Paul. *Rwanda: De la féodalité à la démocratie.* Brussels: Hayez, 1984.

d'Hertefelt, Marcel. *Les clans du Rwanda ancien: éléments d'ethnosociologie et d'ethnohistoire.* Tervuren: MRAC, 1971.

—— "Les élections communales et le consensus politique au Rwanda." *Zaïre* 14.5/6 (1960): 403–438.

—— "Le Rwanda." M. d'Hertefelt et al., eds. *Les anciens royaumes de la zone interlacustre méridionale, Rwanda, Burundi, Buha.* 9–112. Tervuren: MRAC, 1962.

—— "The Rwanda of Rwanda." James L. Gibbs, ed. *Peoples of Africa.* 405–440. New York: Holt, 1965.

d'Hertefelt, Marcel, and André Coupez. *La royauté sacrée de l'ancien Rwanda: texte, traduction et commentaire de son rituel.* Tervuren: MRAC, 1964.

d'Hertefelt, Marcel, and D. de Lame, *Societé, Culture et histoire du Rwanda. Encyclopédie bibliographique, 1863–1980/87.* Tervuren: MRAC, 1988.

Heusch, Luc de. "Nationalisme et lutte des classes au Rwanda." W. Frolich, ed. *Afrika im Wandel seiner Gesellschaftsformen.* 96–108. Leiden: E. J. Brill, 1964.

—— *Le Rwanda et la civilisation interlacustre.* Brussels: Université Libre de Bruxelles, Institut de Sociologie, 1966.

Historique et chronologie du Ruanda. Kabgayi: n.p., 1956.

Hostelet, G. *L'Oeuvre civilisatrice de la Belgique au Congo de 1885 à 1953.* Brussels: ARSC, 1954.

Hubert, Jean R. *La Toussaint rwandaise et sa répression.* Brussels: ARSOM, 1965.

Huntington, Samuel. *Political Order in Changing Societies.* New Haven: Yale University Press, 1968.

Isaacman, Allen, and Barbara Isaacman, "Resistance and Collaboration in Southern and Central Africa, c. 1850–1920." *International Journal of African Historical Studies* 10.1 (1977): 31–62.

Jewsiewicki, Bogumil. "African Peasants in the Totalitarian Colonial Society of the Belgian Congo." Martin A. Klein, ed. *Peasants in Africa.* 45–75. Beverly Hills: Sage, 1980.

—— "Unequal Development: Capitalism and the Katanga Economy." R. Palmer and N. Parson, eds. *The Roots of Rural Poverty in Central and Southern Africa.* 317–344. Berkeley: University of California Press, 1977.

—— "The Great Depression and the Making of the Colonial Economic System in the Belgian Congo." *African Economic History* 4 (1977): 153–176.

—— "Modernisation ou destruction du village africain: l'Economie politique de la 'modernisation agricole' au Congo Belge." *Cahiers du CEDAF* no. 4 (1983).

—— "Political Consciousness among African Peasants in the Belgian Congo." *Review of African Political Economy* 19 (1980): 23–32.

Johnson, Chalmers. *Revolutionary Change.* Boston: Little, Brown, 1966.

Joseph, Richard. "Class, State, and Prebendal Politics in Nigeria." *Journal of Commonwealth and Comparative Politics* 21.3 (1983): 21–38.

—— "Ethnicity and Prebendal Politics in Nigeria: A Theoretical Outline." Annual Meeting of the American Political Science Association, Denver, Colorado, 2–5 September 1982.

Kagame, Alexis. *Un abrégé de l'ethno-histoire du Rwanda précolonial.* Vol. 1. Butare: Editions Universitaires du Rwanda, 1972.

—— *Un abrégé de l'histoire du Rwanda.* Vol. 2. Butare: Editions Universitaires du Rwanda, 1975.

—— *Le code des institutions politiques du Rwanda précolonial.* Brussels: IRCB, 1952.

—— "La documentation du Rwanda sur l'Afrique interlacustre des temps anciens." Centre de Civilisation Burundaise, ed. *La civilisation ancienne des peuples de Grand Lacs: Colloque de Bujumbura, 1979, organisé par le Centre de Civilisation Burundaise.* 300–330. Paris: Editions Karthala; Bujumbura: Centre de Civilisation Burundaise, 1981.

—— "Les grands tournants dans l'histoire de la culture rwandaise." *Etudes rwandaises* 2 (mars 1978): 1–10.

—— *L'histoire du Rwanda.* Leverville: Bibliothèque de l'Etoile, 1958.

—— *L'histoire des Armées-Bovines dans l'ancien Rwanda.* Brussels: ARSOM, 1961.

—— *Les milices du Rwanda précolonial.* Brussels: ARSOM, 1963.

—— *Les organisations socio-familiales de l'ancien Rwanda.* Brussels: IRCB, 1954.

—— *La poésie dynastique au Rwanda.* Brussels: IRCB, 1951.

—— "La possession du sol et l'administration dans l'ancien Rwanda." *Compte rendu des travaux du séminaire d'anthropologie sociale tenu à Astrida en juillet 1952.* Astrida: IRSAC, 1952.

Kajiga, Gaspard. "Cette immigration séculaire des ruandais au Congo." *Bulletin Trimestriel du Centre d'Etude des Problèmes Sociaux Indigènes* (Elisabethville) 32 (1956): 5–65.

Kalemaza, Kavuha. "Le développement de l'agriculture au Kivu colonial, 1903–1940." Mémoire de Licence en Histoire, UNAZA, Lubumbashi, 1973.

Kandt, Richard. *Caput Nili.* 4th ed. 2 vols. Berlin: Dietrich Reimer, 1919 [first published 1905].

—— "Ein Marsch am Ostufer des Kiwu." *Globus* 86.13, 15 (1904): 245–249.

Karugire, Samwiri R. *A History of the Kingdom of Nkore in Western Uganda to 1896.* Oxford: Clarendon, 1971.

Kasfir, Nelson. *The Shrinking Political Arena: Participation and Ethnicity in African Politics, with a Case Study of Uganda.* Berkeley: University of California Press, 1976.

Kaufman, Robert R. "The Patron-Client Concept and Macropolitics: Prospects and Problems." *Comparative Studies in Society and History* 16.3 (1974): 284–308.

Kuper, Leo. *The Pity of It All.* Minneapolis: University of Minnesota Press, 1977.

—— "Plural Societies: Perspectives and Problems." Kuper and M. G. Smith, eds. *Pluralism in Africa.* 7–26. Los Angeles: University of California Press, 1971.

Kuper, Leo, and M. G. Smith, eds. *Pluralism in Africa.* Los Angeles: University of California Press, 1971.

de Lacger, Louis. *Le Ruanda.* 2nd ed. Kabgayi, Rwanda: 1961.

Landé, Carl. *Leaders, Factions and Parties: The Structure of Philippine Politics.* Yale Southeast Asia Monograph Series, No. 6. New Haven: Yale University Southeast Asia Studies, 1965.

LaPalombara, Joseph. "Penetration: A Crisis of Governmental Capacity." Leonard Binder et al., eds. *Crises and Sequences in Political Development.* 205–232. Princeton: Princeton University Press, 1971.

Leach, Edmund R. *Political Systems of Highland Burma.* Boston: Beacon, 1965.

Lemarchand, René. "Comparative Political Clientelism: Structure, Process and Optic." S. N. Eisenstadt and René Lemarchand, eds. *Political Clientelism, Patronage and Development.* Beverly Hills: Sage, 1981.

—— "The Coup in Rwanda." Robert Rotberg and Ali Mazrui, eds. *Protest and Power in Black Africa.* 877–923. New York: Oxford University Press, 1970.

—— "Political Clientelism and Ethnicity in Tropical Africa: Competing Solidarities in Nation-Building." *American Political Science Review* 66.1 (1972): 68–90.

—— "Rwanda." R. Lemarchand, ed. *African Kingships in Perspective.* 67–92. London: Cass, 1977.

—— *Rwanda and Burundi.* London: Pall Mall, 1970.

—— "The State and Society in Africa: Ethnic Stratification and Restratification in Historical and Comparative Perspective." Donald Rothchild and Victor A. Olorunsola, eds. *State Versus Ethnic Claims: African Policy Dilemmas.* 44–66. Boulder: Westview, 1983.

Lemarchand, René, and Keith Legg. "Political Clientelism and Development: A Preliminary Analysis." *Comparative Politics* 4.2 (1972): 149–178.

Leys, Colin. Rev. of *The State of the Nations: Constraints on Development in*

Independent Africa, Michael F. Lofchie, ed. *Journal of Modern African Studies* 11.2 (1973): 315–317.

Linden, Ian, and Jane Linden. *Church and Revolution in Rwanda.* Manchester: Manchester University Press; New York: Africana Publishing, 1977.

Lonsdale, J. M., and B. J. Berman. "Coping with the Contradictions: The Development of the Colonial State in Kenya 1895–1914." *Journal of African History* 20.4 (1979): 487–505.

Lonsdale, John. "States and Social Processes in Africa: A Historiographical Survey." *The African Studies Review* 24.2/3 (1981): 139–207.

Louis, William Roger. *Ruanda-Urundi, 1884–1919.* Oxford: Clarendon, 1963.

Louwers, O. *Le problème financier et le problème économique au Congo belge en 1932.* Brussels: IRCB, 1933.

Lugan, Bernard. "Causes et effets de la famine 'Rumanura" au Rwanda." *Canadian Journal of African Studies* 10.2 (1976): 347–356.

—— "Le commerce de traite au Rwanda sous le régime allemand (1896–1916)." *Canadian Journal of African Studies* 11.2 (1977): 235–268.

—— "L'église catholique au Rwanda 1900–1976." *Etudes Rwandaises* 2 (mars 1978): 69–75.

—— "Les pôles commerciaux du lac Kivu á la fin du XIXe siècle." *Revue Française d'Histoire d'Outre-Mer* 64.235 (1977): 176–202.

Lugan, Bernard, and Antoine Nyagahene. "Les activités commerciales du sud Kivu au XIXe siècle à travers l'exemple de Kinyaga (Rwanda)." *Cahiers d'Outre-Mer* 36.141 (1983): 19–48.

Maquet, Jacques J. "La participation de la classe paysanne au mouvement d'indépendance du Rwanda." *Cahiers d'Etudes Africaines* 4.4 (1964): 552–568.

—— "Les Pasteurs de l'Itombwe." *Science et Nature* 8 (1955): 3–12.

—— *The Premise of Inequality in Ruanda.* London: Oxford University Press, 1961.

—— "Rwanda Castes." Arthur Tuden and Leonard Plotnicov, eds. *Social Stratification in Africa.* New York: Free Press, 1970.

—— *Le système des relations sociales dans le Ruanda ancien.* Tervuren: MRCB, 1954.

Maquet, Jacques J., and Marcel d'Hertefelt. *Elections en société féodale: Une étude sur l'introduction du vote populaire au Ruanda-Urundi.* Brussels: ARSC, 1959.

Maquet, Jacques J., and Saverio Naigiziki. "Les droits fonciers dans le Ruanda ancien." *Zaïre* 11.4 (1957): 339–359.

Marzorati, A. "The Belgian Congo and the Ruanda-Urundi (Political and Legal Surveys)." *Civilisations* 1.3 (1951): 149–154.

Masson, Paul. *Trois siècles chez les Bashi.* 2nd ed. Bukavu: La Presse Congolaise, 1966.

Mbonimana, Gamaliel. "Christianisation indirecte et cristallisation des clivages ethniques au Rwanda (1925–1931)." *Enquêtes et Documents d'Histoire Africaine* 3 (1978): 125–163.

—— "L'instauration d'un royaume chrétien au Rwanda (1900–1931)." Diss. Louvain-la-Neuve, 1981.

Melson, Robert, and Howard Wolpe. *Modernization and the Politics of Communalism.* East Lansing: Michigan State University Press, 1971.

Merlier, Michel. *Le Congo de la colonisation belge à l'indépendance.* Paris: François Maspero, 1962.

Meschi, Lydia. "Evolution des structures foncières au Rwanda: Le cas d'un lignage hutu." *Cahiers d'Etudes Africaines* 14.1 (1974): 39–51.

Mitchell, J. Clyde. *The Kalela Dance*. Manchester: Manchester University Press, 1958.

Moore, Barrington. *Social Origins of Dictatorship and Democracy*. Boston: Beacon, 1966.

Munyangaju, Aloys. *L'actualité politique au Rwanda*. n.c.: n.p., 1959.

Murego, Donat. *La Révolution rwandaise, 1959–1962*. Louvain: Institut des Sciences Politiques et Sociales, [1975].

Mutombo, R. "Marchés et circuits commerciaux de la région de Masangana à la fin de l'époque précoloniale." *Etudes rwandaises* 2 (mars 1978): 35–45.

Nahimana, Ferdinand. "Les Bami ou roitelets Hutu du corridor Nyabarongo-Mukungwa avec ses régions limitrophes." *Etudes rwandaises* 12 (mars 1979): 1–25.

—— "Conversion du peuple rwandais au Catholicisme entre 1900 et 1916." *Etudes rwandaises*, 2, numéro spécial (mars 1978): 46–68.

—— "L'expansion du pouvoir central des rois Abanyiginya au Rwanda septentrional: mythes et réalités." *Education, Science et Culture/Uburezi, Ubuhanga n'Umucu* 3 (1982): 41–84.

—— "Les missions catholiques et l'enseignement au Rwanda, de 1917 à 1931." *Dialogue* 74 (1979): 30–44.

—— "Les principautés hutu du Rwanda septentrional." Centre de Civilisation Burundaise, ed. *La Civilisation ancienne des peuples des Grands Lacs: Colloque de Bujumbura, 1979, organisé par le Centre de Civilisation Burundaise*. 115–137. Paris: Editions Karthala; Bujumbura: Centre de Civilisation Burundaise, 1981.

Newbury, David. "'Bunyabungo': The Western Rwandan Frontier, c. 1750–1850." Igor Kopytoff, ed.*The African Frontier: The Reproduction of Traditional African Societies*. 162–192. Bloomington: Indiana University Press, 1987.

—— "Bushi and the Historians: Historiographical Themes in Eastern Kivu." *History in Africa* 5 (1978): 131–151.

—— "Les campagnes de Rwabugiri: Chronologie et bibliographie." *Cahiers d'Etudes Africaines* 14.1 (1974): 181–191.

—— "The Clans of Rwanda: An Historical Hypothesis." *Africa* 50.4 (1980): 389–403.

—— "Lake Kivu Regional Trade in the Nineteenth Century." *Journal des Africanistes* 50.2 (1980): 6–36.

—— "Kings and Clans: Ijwi Island (Zaïre) c. 1780–c. 1840." Diss. University of Wisconsin-Madison, 1979.

—— "Rwabugiri and Ijwi." *Etudes d'Histoire Africaine* 7 (1975): 151–175.

Newbury, David, and Bishikwabo Cubaka. "Recent Historical Research in the Area of Lake Kivu: Rwanda and Zaïre." *History in Africa* 7 (1980): 23–45.

Newbury, David S., and M. Catharine Newbury. "King and Chief: Colonial Politics on Ijwi Island (Zaïre)." *International Journal of African Historical Studies* 15.2 (1982): 221–246.

Newbury, M. Catharine. "Colonialism, Ethnicity, and Rural Political Protest: Rwanda and Zanzibar in Comparative Perspective." *Comparative Politics* 15.3 (1983): 253–280.

—— "Deux lignages au Kinyaga." *Cahiers d'Etudes Africaines* 14.1 (1974): 26–39.

—— "Ethnicity in Rwanda: The Case of Kinyaga." *Africa* 48.1 (1978): 17–29.

—— "Réflexions sur les racines rurales de la révolution: Rwanda et Congo oriental."

Catherine Coquery-Vidrovitch et al., eds. *Rébellions/Révolutions au Zaïre*, Vol. 2 95–105. Paris: l'Harmattan, 1987.

—— "Ubureetwa and Thangata: Catalysts to Peasant Political Consciousness in Rwanda and Malawi." *Canadian Journal of African Studies* 14.1 (1980): 97–112. Also published in Centre de Civilisation Burundaise, ed. *La Civilisation ancienne des peuples des Grands Lacs*. Paris: Editions Karthala, 1981.

Newbury, M. Catharine, and Joseph Rwabukumba. "Political Evolution in a Rwandan Frontier District: A Case Study of Kinyaga." Institut National de Recherche Scientifique, ed. *Rapport pour les années 1965–1970*. 93–119. Butare: INRS, 1971.

Njangu Canda-Ciri. "La résistance Shi à la pénétration européenne, 1900–1916." Mémoire de Licence, UNAZA, Lubumbashi, 1973.

Nkundabagenzi, F. *Rwanda politique, 1958–1960*. Brussels: CRISP, 1961.

"Note sur les traitements." *Servir* 5.7 (1944): 291–294.

Ntezimana, Emmanuel. "L'arrivée des Européens au Kinyaga et la fin des royaumes du Bukunzi et du Busozo." *Etudes rwandaises* (juin 1980): 1–29.

—— "Coutumes et traditions des royaumes du Bukunzi et du Busozo." *Etudes rwandaises* (avril 1980): 15–39.

—— "*Kinyamateka, Temps Nouveaux d'Afrique* et l'évolution socio-politique du Rwanda (1954–1959)." *Etudes rwandaises*, numéro spécial (mars 1978): 76–94.

Nyagahene, Antoine. "Les activités économiques et commerciales du Kinyaga dans la seconde partie du XIXe siècle." Thèse de Licence, Université Nationale du Rwanda, Butare, 1979.

Pagès, A. *Un royaume hamite au centre de l'Afrique*. Brussels: IRCB, 1935.

—— "Au Rwanda. Droits et pouvoirs des chefs sous la suzeraineté du roi hamite: Quelques abus du système." *Zaïre* 3.4 (1949): 359–377.

Paternostre de la Mairieu, Baudouin. *Le Rwanda: Son effort de développement*. Brussels: Editions A. de Boeck; Kigali: Editions Rwandaises, 1971.

Pauwels, Marcel. "La Bushiru et son Muhinza ou roitelet Hutu." *Annali Lateranensi* 31 (1967): 205–322.

Pilipili Kagabo. "Contribution à la connaissance des origines du centre de Bukavu (Kivu) de 1870 à 1935." Mémoire de Licence, UNAZA, Lubumbushi, 1973.

"Province de Costermansville, liste des colons installées à la date du 8 mai 1934." *Congo* 1.1 (1935): 118–127.

Ranger, Terence. "The People in African Resistance: A Review." *Journal of Southern African Studies* 4.1 (1977): 125–146.

Reisdorff, I. "Enquêtes foncières au Ruanda." Mimeo, 1952.

Reyntjens, Filip. *Pouvoir et droit au Rwanda*. Tervuren: MRAC, 1985.

Richards, Audrey. *Economic Development and Tribal Change: A Study of Immigrant Labour in Buganda*. Cambridge: W. Heffer & Sons, 1956.

Roberts, A. D. "The Sub-imperialism of the Baganda." *Journal of African History* 3.3 (1962): 435–450.

Rothchild, Donald, and Victor A. Olorunsola, eds. *State Versus Ethnic Claims: African Policy Dilemmas*. Boulder: Westview, 1983.

Rwabukumba, Joseph, and Vincent Mudandagizi. "Les formes historiques de la dépendance personnelle dans l'Etat rwandais." *Cahiers d'Etudes Africaines* 14.1 (1974): 6–25.

Rwanda. République Rwandaise, Ministère du Plan et des Ressources Naturelles, Direction de la Documentation et des Statistiques. *Enquête démographique du Rwanda*. 3 vols., 1970.

—— République Rwandaise. "Presentation du Rwanda: Situation actuelle et perspectives de développement pour la décennie 1981–1990." United Nations Conference on the least developed countries. Addis-Ababa, 4–15 May 1981.

Saucier, Jean-François. "The Patron-Client Relationship in Traditional and Contemporary Southern Rwanda." Diss. Columbia University, 1974.

Schatzberg, Michael G. *Politics and Class in Zaïre: Bureaucracy, Business and Beer in Lisala.* New York: Africana, 1980.

Schmidt, Steffen W. et al. *Friends, Followers, and Factions.* Berkeley: University of California Press, 1977.

Schumacher, Peter. "Les Bashakamba (ou l'Histoire de Corps de Guerriers au Pays du 'Royaume hamite')." *Die Wiener Schule* (1956): 237–252.

Scott, James C. "Everyday Forms of Class Struggle Between Ex-Patrons and Ex-Clients: The Green Revolution in Kedah, Malaysia." *International Political Science Review* 4.4 (1983): 537–556.

—— "Everyday Forms of Peasant Resistance." *Journal of Peasant Studies* 13.2 (1986): 5–35.

—— "Hegemony and the Peasantry." *Politics and Society* 7.3 (1977): 267–296.

—— *The Moral Economy of the Peasant.* New Haven: Yale University Press, 1976.

—— "Patronage or Exploitation?" Ernest Gellner and John Waterbury, eds. *Patrons and Clients in Mediterranean Societies.* 21–40. London: Duckworth, 1977.

—— *Weapons of the Weak. Everyday Forms of Peasant Resistance.* New Haven: Yale University Press, 1985.

Scott, James C., and Benedict J. Kerkvliet. "How Traditional Patrons Lose Legitimacy—A Theory with Special Reference to Southeast Asia." *Cultures et Développement* 5.3 (1973): 327–339.

Shaw, Bryant P. *"Force Publique, Force Unique:* The Military in the Belgian Congo, 1914–1939." Diss. University of Wisconsin-Madison, 1984.

Sigwalt, Richard D. "The Early History of Bushi. An Essay in the Historical Use of Genesis Traditions." Diss. University of Wisconsin-Madison, 1975.

Silverman, Sydel F. "Agricultural Organization, Social Structure, and Values in Italy: Amoral Familism Reconsidered." *American Anthropologist* 70 (1968): 1–19.

—— "Patronage as Myth." Ernest Gellner and John Waterbury, eds. *Patrons and Clients in Mediterranean Societies.* London: Duckworth, 1977.

Sklar, Richard L. "The Nature of Class Domination in Africa." *Journal of Modern African Studies* 17.4 (1979): 531–552.

Skocpol, Theda. "Bringing the State Back In: Strategies of Analysis in Current Research." Peter Evans et al., eds. *Bringing the State Back In.* 3–29. Cambridge: Cambridge University Press, 1985.

—— *States and Social Revolutions: A Comparative Analysis of France, Russia, and China.* Cambridge: Cambridge University Press, 1979.

—— "What Makes Peasants Revolutionary?" Robert P. Weller and Scott E. Guggenheim, eds. *Power and Protest in the Countryside.* 157–179. Durham: Duke University Press, 1982.

Smith, M. G. "Institutional and Political Conditions of Pluralism." Leo Kuper and M. G. Smith, eds. *Pluralism in Africa.* 27–65. Los Angeles: University of California Press, 1971.

Smith, Pierre, ed. *Le récit populaire au Rwanda.* Paris: Armand Colin, 1975.

Sosne, Elinor D. "Kinship and Contract in Bushi: A Study in Village Level Politics." Diss. University of Wisconsin-Madison, 1974.

Southall, Aidan. "The Illusion of Tribe." *Journal of Asian and African Studies* 5.1/2 (1970): 28–50.

Spitaels, R. "Transportation des Banyaruanda dans le Nord-Kivu." *Problèmes d'Afrique Centrale* 6.2 (1935): 110–116.

Ssebalijja, Yawana. "Memories of Rukiga and Other Places." Donald Denoon, ed. *A History of Kigezi*. 179–199. Kampala: National Trust, [1971].

Studdert-Kennedy, Gerald. *Evidence and Explanation in Social Science*. London: Routledge & Kegan Paul, 1975.

Thomas, H. B. "Capax Imperii: The Story of Semei Kakunguru." *Uganda Journal* (1939).

Tshilema Tshihiluka. "Ryamurari, capitale de l'ancien royaume de Ndorwa (Mutara, Rwanda): Une interprétation culturelle préliminaire." *Africa-Tervuren* 29.1/2 (1983): 19–26.

Twaddle, Michael. "Politics in Bukedi, 1900–1939." Diss. University of London, 1967.

Van den Berghe, Pierre L. "Pluralism and the Polity: A Theoretical Exploration." Leo Kuper and M. G. Smith, eds. *Pluralism in Africa*. 67–81. Los Angeles: University of California Press, 1971.

Vanhove, J. "Une réforme d'importance au Ruanda: La suppression du bail à cheptel." *Journal des Tribunaux d'Outre-Mer* 10 (1954): 97–98.

Van Overschelde, Antoine. *Un audacieux pacifique. Monseigneur Léon Paul Classe, apôtre du Ruanda*. Namur: Collection Lavigerie, Grands Lacs, 1948.

Vansina, Jan. *L'évolution du royaume rwanda des origines à 1900*. Brussels: ARSOM, 1962.

—— *La légende du passé: Traditions orales du Burundi*. Tervuren: MRAC, 1972.

—— *Oral Tradition: A Study in Historical Methodology*. Chicago: Aldine, 1965 (originally published 1961).

—— "Les régimes fonciers Ruanda et Kuba—une comparaison." Daniel Biebuyck, ed. *African Agrarian Systems*. 348–363. London: Oxford University Press, 1963.

—— *De la tradition orale: Essai de méthode historique*. Tervuren: MRAC, 1961.

Vanwalle, Rita. "Aspecten van staatsvorming in West-Rwanda." *Africa-Tervuren* 28.3 (1982): 64–78.

Vellut, Jean-Luc. "La misère rurale dans l'expérience coloniale du Zaïre, du Rwanda, et du Burundi." 26th Annual Meeting of the African Studies Association, Boston, December 1983.

Vellut, Jean-Luc, comp. "Enquêtes sur la main-d'oeuvre au Kivu (1930)." *Enquêtes et Documents d'Histoire Africaine* 3 (1978): 30–38.

Vidal, Claudine. "Economie de la société féodale rwandaise." *Cahiers d'Etudes Africaines* 14.1 (1974): 52–74.

—— "Enquêtes sur l'histoire et sur l'au-delà: Rwanda, 1800–1970." *L'homme* 24.3/4 (1984): 61–82.

—— "Le Rwanda des anthropologues ou le fétichisme de la vache." *Cahiers d'Etudes Africaines* 9.3 (1969): 384–401.

—— "Situations ethniques au Rwanda." Jean-Loup Amselle and Elikia M'bokolo, eds. *Au coeur de l'ethnie: ethnies, tribalisme et état en Afrique*. 11–48. Paris: Editions la Découverte, 1985.

Vincent, Joan. "Colonial Chiefs and the Making of Class: A Case Study from Teso, Eastern Uganda." *Africa* 47.2 (1977): 240–246.

von Parish, F. R. "Zwei Reisen durch Ruanda 1902 bis 1903. Aus Tagebüchern, Briefen und hinterlassen Papieren des Oberleutnants F. R. von Parish." *Globus* 85–86 (1904): 5–13, 73–79.

Wagoner, Fred E. "Nation Building in Africa: A Description and Analysis of the Development of Rwanda." Diss. American University, 1968.

Weber, Max. *The Theory of Social and Economic Organization.* 1947. Talcott Parsons, ed. New York: Free Press, 1964.

Weiner, Myron. *Sons of the Soil: Migration and Ethnic Conflict in India.* Princeton: Princeton University Press, 1978.

Weiss, Herbert F. *Political Protest in the Congo: The Parti Solidaire Africain During the Independence Struggle.* Princeton: Princeton University Press, 1967.

Wolf, Eric. *Peasant Wars of the Twentieth Century.* 1969. New York: Harper, 1973.

Young, Crawford. "Nationalism, Ethnicity, and Class in Africa: A Retrospective." *Cahiers d'Etudes Africaines* 26.3 (1986): 421–495.

—— "Patterns of Social Conflict: State, Class, and Ethnicity." *Daedalus* 3.2 (1982): 71–98.

—— *Politics in the Congo: Decolonization and Independence.* Princeton: Princeton University Press, 1965.

—— *The Politics of Cultural Pluralism.* Madison: University of Wisconsin Press, 1976.

—— "The Temple of Ethnicity." *World Politics* 35.4 (1983): 652–662.

ARCHIVAL AND DOCUMENTARY SOURCES

Bourgeois, R. "Notes sur l'administration du Territoire du Shangugu." Derscheid Collection.

—— "Rapport de sortie de charge." Derscheid Collection.

Classe, Léon. "Notes sur la famille de Musinga." Unpublished essay, n.d. [Consulted courtesy of R. P. Hoffscholte.]

Declerck, Major. "Rapport d'ensemble sur la situation de la Résidence du Ruanda et sur l'activité de l'Administration." Gouvernement Belge, Ministère des Colonies, Service des Territoires de Colonies, Dossier AE/II no. 1847, portefeuille 3288x. Archives Africaines, Brussels, 10 October 1918.

Delmas, Léon. "Histoire des provinces de l'Impara et du Biru (Kinyaga) sous le règne de Kigeri III Ndabarasa." Derscheid Collection.

—— "Station de Mibirizi-Nyamasheke." ts. 25 January 1929. Archives of the Société des Missionnaires d'Afrique, Rome.

Dryvers, P. "Politique et justice." Statement submitted on 25 November 1932 by the Territorial Administrator at Kamembe.

Mission de Mibirizi. "Diaire."

Mission de Nyamasheke. "Diaire."

"Notice sur le Ruanda." Typescript, with handwritten note: "rédigé en 1916 par un missionnaire du Ruanda pour servir aux troupes Belges." Gouvernement Belge, Ministère des Colonies, Service des Territoires des Colonies, Dossier AE/II no. 1847, portefeuille 3288x. Archives Africaines, Brussels.

Préfecture de Cyangugu. "Rapport des Commissions Préfectorales de Planification," 1970.

"Quelques notes pour le Mwami du Ruanda à l'occasion de son passage au Kinyaga le 26 avril 1942." ts., 1942. Archives of the Société des Missionnaires d'Afrique (Pères Blancs), Rome.

Territoire de Kamembe [Shangugu]. "Rapport établi en réponse au Questionnaire addressé en 1929 par M. le Gouverneur du Ruanda-Urundi à l'Administrateur du Territoire de Kamembe." Derscheid Collection.

Territoire du Ruanda-Urundi, Service des Affaires Politiques et Administratives. "Elections communales, résultats pour l'ensemble du Ruanda," 1960. [Consulted courtesy of Jan Vansina.]

Territoire de Shangugu. "Avis et considérations de l'Administrateur Territoriale de Shangugu quant à l'établissement de prévisions des ressources des indigènes de son Territoire pour l'année. . . ."

—— "Elections communales, 1960," 1 August 1960.

—— "Entreprises agricoles des non-indigènes, énumeration des entreprises et superficies." *Rapport annuel agricole,* 1946.

—— *Rapport annuel agricole.*

—— "Rapport annuel AIMO."

—— "Rapport en reponse au questionnaire sur les élections communales de 1960," 20 August 1960.

—— "Rapport sur le nombre des H.A.V. et gros bétail pour chaque souschefferie," 25 May 1938.

—— "Relève des concessions agricoles accordées au 31 décembre 1948." *Rapport annuel agricole,* 1948, annexe submitted on 3 March 1949.

United Nations Trusteeship Council. "Report of the U.N. Visiting Mission to East Africa." T/1168, 15th Session, Supp. no. 2, 1955.

—— "Report of the U.N. Visiting Mission to the Trust Territory of Ruanda-Urundi under Belgian Administration." T/217, 4th Session, Supp. no. 2, 31 October 1948.

—— "Visiting Mission to the Trust Territories in East Africa, 1960—Report on Ruanda-Urundi" (March 2–April 1, 1960). T/1538, 26th Session, Supp. no. 3.

INDEX

Bukavu racetrack, 167

Bukavu, 161, 163, 200. *See also* Labor: demands for

Bukunzi-Busoozo-Bugarama Province, 69, 183, 201

Bukunzi Kingdom, 35, 39, 201; incorporation of, 63–65; military occupation of, 65, 258–59*n*42

Bureaucracy: administrative units, 62–63; expansion of, 136–37; in Kinyaga, 222; and tax collection, 155. *See also* Chiefs; Political unification

Burgomasters, 198, 200, 222–23, 225, 292*nn*8, 10

Burundi emigrants, 35

Burundi famine. *See* Famine

Bushi, 269*n*9

Businesses, European, 279*n*46. *See also* Mining; Plantations; Protanag Company

Busoozo, 39, 65–66

Butera, Sixte, 263*n*34

Capitalism, 151, 291*n*12

Cash crops, 154, 157. *See also* Bananas; Coffee cultivation; Cotton; Manioc; Obligatory cultivation

Caste, 3–5, 11–13. *See also* Functionalist Model; Maquet, Jacques-Jean

Caste system, 243*n*3

Catholic Church: conversion to, 277–78*n*17; Hutu political organization within, 181, 190; political role of, 115, 155–56; role in elections, 185, 284–85*n*15; role in Hutu protest, 183, 211. *See also* Missionaries; Missions

Cattle clientship. *See Ubuhake* clientship, cattle

Cattle: economic role of, 220–21; in non-*ubuhake* relations, 231–32; in patron-client relations, 273*nn*54, 60; political function of, 270*n*21; population, 291–92*n*2; social function of, 118, 220–21, 273*n*59; in *ubuhake* clientship, 125–26, 136. See also *Ubuhake* clientship, cattle; Umuryamo cattle epidemic

Census, 155

Central chiefs, 46–47

Changuvu, 256*n*17

Chiefs: in Abiiru province, 205–206; as collaborators, 290*n*9; and collection of prestations, 40; and colonialism, 290*n*9; dismissal of, 197, 281*n*72; division of power, 45–46; education of, 155; exploitation of labor, 167–68; as labor recruiters, 158–59, 165–71, 280*n*62; powers of, 170–71; relations with Belgian administration, 132–33, 155, 170–71, 271*n*32, 290*n*9; relations with Rwabugiri, 40; religious affiliation, 155, 277–78*n*17; responsibilities, 42; salary, 275*n*84; succession of, 263*n*35; as tax collectors, 156. *See also* Hill chiefs; Land chiefs; Pasture chiefs; Patrons; Provincial chiefs; Subchiefs; *Umuheto* chiefs

Chrétien, Jean-Pierre, 247–48*n*13, 271*n*29

Clans, 96, 266*n*4; distribution of, 27–28. *See also* Kinship groups

Class: in Abiiru province, 206; conflict, 213; differentiation, 147, 208; and defining ethnic differences, 11–13; formation, 290*n*9. *See also* Caste; Hutu-Tuutsi relations

Classe, Father Léon, 12, 67, 115

Clients: exploitation of, 127–28; in *igikingi* relations, 80; in *ubuhake* clientship, 135, 136; in *ubukonde* relations, 79, 80; in *umuheto* relations, 125. *See also* Clientship: oppression in; Patron-client relations

Clientship, 17, 73–90, 135; of Abeere-kande lineage, 88–89; in Abiiru province, 205; effects of colonialism on, 117–47; to Europeans, 55–56, 144; expansion of, 136; influence of the state, 17, 59, 90; in Kinyaga, 70, 82, 90; and land pressure, 205; under Ntiizimira, 88; oppression in, 136–37; and population density, 205; precolonial, 74–79; reasons for entering, 137–39; role in political protest, 209; and social differentiation, 18; and the Umuryamo cattle epidemic, 119; and